THE
KLAN

THE
KLAN

Patsy Sims

DORSET PRESS
New York

Excerpts from Don Whitehead's book
*Attack on Terror: The FBI Against
the Klu Klux Klan in Mississippi*
reprinted by permission of Funk & Wagnalls,
division of Harper & Row, Publishers, Inc.

This edition published by Dorset Press,
a division of Marboro Books Corporation,
by arrangement with
Stein & Day/Publishers.
1988 Dorset Press

ISBN 0-88029-181-8
(formerly ISBN 0-8128-6096-9)

Printed in the United States of America
M 9 8 7 6 5 4 3 2 1

Acknowledgments

I have been told the first book is always the hardest. I hope so. For me, the endeavor has been as grueling as it has been rewarding. I never could have made it to the Epilogue alone, without the many people who called, wrote, offered advice, consoled, rejoiced, listened, encouraged, fed, and financed me.

My thanks go to my literary agent, Mel Berger, who is perhaps responsible for the book's beginning; to my editors, Michela Hamilton and Patricia Day, who guided it to an end, and to all those in between: Iris Day, for contributing her sensitivity for verbs, adjectives, commas, and style as well as sending bits of "sunshine" during my "confinement"; Ferrel Guillory and Dottie Vann for "talking Southern" and offering advice on the manuscript; the Anti-Defamation League (ADL) of B'nai B'rith, the National Association for the Advancement of Colored People (NAACP), the Federal Bureau of Investigation (FBI), Pulaski historian Margaret Butler, and numerous law enforcement people—especially Alabama Attorney General William J. Baxley and investigators Jack Shows and Tom Ward—for providing background information and answering questions; the Reverend Will D. Campbell, for sharing his very special insights into human beings; to Sue Gwinner, Barbara Richardson, and Cindie Vann for punctuating their typing with moral support, and to Barbara Rowell, Elizabeth Bennett, and David Walker for keeping me and my typewriter going.

For providing valuable background information, anecdotes, personal experiences, and sources, I am indebted to numerous journalists and the publications for which they work. The periodicals, writers, and editors are too many to list, but I am especially grateful to Jim Adams, the *Louisville Courier-Journal;* Wayne Greenhaw, author of *Look Out for George Wallace;* D. L. Hoover, publisher, the *Giles Free Press;* Ray Jenkins, editorial-page editor, the *Montgomery Journal;* Wayne King, *The New York Times;* Jack Nelson, Washington Bureau chief, *Los Angeles Times;* Gene Roberts, executive editor, the *Philadelphia Inquirer;* Claude Sitton, editor, the *Raleigh News and Observer;* Paul Valentine, the *Washington Post;* Nicholas von Hoffman, King Features

Syndicate columnist; Roger Williams, senior editor, *Saturday Review;* Jeff Woosnam, assistant news editor, *Ashland Times Gazette,* Ashland, Ohio; and the *Louisville Times'* investigative reporting team—J. Stephen Fagan, Patrick Howington, Richard Krantz, and Tom Van Howe.

My research was also made easier by competent librarians such as Tim Mulligan, the National Archives; Bernard Pasqualini, the Free Library of Philadelphia, Pennsylvania; Ernest Perez, *The Houston Chronicle,* and the staffs of the Library of Congress' news and periodicals room and the District of Columbia Public Library's telephone reference service.

But, perhaps most of all, I thank the klanspeople who allowed me into the Invisible Empire and without whose cooperation this book could never have been possible.

Contents

List of Illustrations

THE
KLAN

"Somehow, we cannot hate the racist, for most of us do not know how or when we left his ranks, if we have left them at all."

The Rev. Will D. Campbell, *director,*
the Committee of Southern Churchmen

1

Entering the Invisible Empire

It looked like an ordinary black box, the kind many families used to store "valuables" before safe-deposit boxes came into vogue. I was six, at the most, when I discovered it in a bedroom closet. Inside was a nostalgic kaleidoscope of fading photographs, telegrams, yellow clippings, and other memorabilia: a snapshot of Great-Grandpa Valentine Hans, prosperously vested, his white hair and mustache trim, his boots thirsty for polish; Grandma Sims' tortoiseshell comb and strands of her silvering hair; my father's pass to the 1928 Democratic National Convention; and a picture postcard of fifty or so robed and hooded men marching down Main Street in Beaumont, Texas, in the early twenties.

That was my introduction to the Ku Klux Klan. I was too young to know the name or what it stood for or did. Yet those masked men—led by two on robed horses, one rider carrying an American flag, the other, an imitation flaming cross—captured my imagination and held it. Again and again, I studied that browning photograph as though I might eventually discover a clue as to who they were, what they were like, and why they were marching with their faces masked.

Who? Why? Over the years, the questions grew with me and within me. Especially, in the sixties, when violence spread like kudzu across the Southern countryside, when Alabama and Mississippi became frightening to me in the same mysterious way that darkness frightens a child. Just as the postcard had seized my imagination, so did the news accounts and photographs of men accused of murdering three civil rights workers in Philadelphia, Mississippi; men accused of gunning down Viola Liuzzo on a lonely road outside Selma; men accused of slugging Freedom Riders with pipes and nightsticks and leaded bats; men accused of bombing and burning churches and synagogues and homes.

And, again, I wondered: Who *are* these men? What makes them tick? Do they ever fall in love and get spring fever? Do they laugh at jokes and, sometimes, at themselves? Do they cry at funerals and sad movies?

Or do they only hate? Is there good in them or only evil? What are they *really* like?

I am from the South. Born and raised and lived there most of my life. I remember when everything—water fountains, restrooms, depots, even churches—was labeled "Colored" and "White." Nobody asked "Why?" I remember the before, the during, the after, when the labels merged and the "dividers" on streetcars and buses disappeared. As a journalist in south Louisiana, I came to know many blacks, the traditional victims of the Klan: a bootblack, a woman who sells "soul food" along the Mississippi, a school-board member, an assistant to the mayor of New Orleans, judges, legislators, jazz musicians, debutantes, prostitutes, drug addicts, police officers, Black Panthers, cane-field workers, janitors who cleaned the newsroom floors.

But I never got to know a klansman. I never met one—that I was aware of—or knew anyone who had. I had no idea then that Beaumont—just west of the Louisiana border, where my family lived until I was ten—had made some of the biggest Klan headlines in the twenties, that Beaumont Klavern No. 7 had gone in for whipping and tar and feathering and worse and counted among its members the mayor and the district attorney. Even the state's first Grand Dragon—an Episcopal minister named Dr. A. D. Ellis—hailed from my home town.

It wasn't until I began research on this book that my father told me *he* had joined the Klan, once. Back in the twenties, back when *everyone* was joining. Harry Truman, Hugo Black, governors, senators, mayors. sheriffs, lawyers, businessmen, ordinary working folks, like my father. Four or five million, altogether. More up North, historians say, than down South. Ohio, with four hundred thousand, boasted the largest membership in the Invisible Empire, as the Klan still refers to its domain. Pennsylvania had an estimated one hundred thousand, a third of them in Philadelphia.

Indiana elected a klansman as governor and another to the U.S. Senate. At least eleven more governors were elected, and one was impeached, by power of the Klan, as were scores of congressmen, senators, and local officials. Those were the days when the Klan often determined a politician's fate, when it marched forty thousand strong down Pennsylvania Avenue, when it was rumored—and denied—to have held initiations on the Capitol steps and in the White House, and when an anti-Klan platform plank turned the 1924 Democratic National Convention and Madison Square Garden into fist-swinging pandemonium that couldn't be quelled even by a band blaring "While We Go Marching Through Georgia." The plank, which would have condemned the Klan and its activities, lost by one vote—541 3/20 to 542 3/20—and sports promoter Tex Rickard conceded: "Of all the fights I ever pulled off in the old Garden, that was the best draw I ever saw."

Before the Klan got hit by the Depression and a $685,000 federal back-tax bill, it built an Imperial Palace in Atlanta, sent a special "ambassador" to Washington, opened a small sales office in New York City, and considered buying Valparaiso University.

But my father was never a part of any of that. He never owned a robe or a hood or a membership card because he never went back after he and a hundred others were initiated at the East Texas State Fair Grounds in Beaumont. He—like other "aliens," the Klan term for outsiders—soon cringed as the Invisible Empire took law and order and morals into its own hands, and flogged and lynched and tarred and feathered and fed screaming victims through rock grinders. Live cremations were sometimes staged before spellbound audiences in town squares and ballparks.

The Klan's victims, white as often as black in those days, included anyone, anything, the Klan didn't like, and its dislikes were many: Negroes, Jews, Catholics, Orientals, Mormons, immigrants, drugs, liquor, marital "goings on," Franklin D. Roosevelt, and Louisiana's all-powerful Huey P. Long. But it was Catholics—from presidential hopeful Al Smith to Pope Pius XI—who probably bore the biggest brunt of their hatred.

A Klan lecturer once warned his audience in North Manchester, Indiana: "The pope may even be on the northbound train tomorrow! He may! He may! Be warned! Prepare! America is for Americans! Search everywhere for hidden enemies, vipers at the heart's blood of our sacred republic! Watch the trains!" The next day, more than a thousand people mobbed the station to meet the Chicago-bound train and its one passenger: a corset salesman who talked a frantic half hour before convincing the crowd he was not the pope in disguise.

The Klan literally overstepped its bounds in 1934 when then-ruling Imperial Wizard, Dr. Hiram W. Evans, a cut-rate dentist from Dallas, announced plans to go to Louisiana and campaign against Huey Long in his bid for the presidency. A U.S. senator at the time but still in full control of his home state, Long—after hearing the news—burst into a state legislative session and boomed to the press: "Quote me as saying that the Imperial bastard will *never* set foot in Louisiana, and that when I call him a sonofabitch, I am not using profanity but am referring to the circumstances of his birth." Furthermore, he warned, if "that tooth-puller" did come to the Pelican State, he would leave with "his toes turned up."

That was the end of the Klan versus Huey Long.

The Klan was not designed to hate, originally, when six young Confederate army veterans gathered on Christmas Eve 1865 in a Pulaski, Tennessee, law office and decided to form a club to relieve their postwar boredom. At a second meeting, they devised the name "Ku Klux" (a corruption of the Greek word for circle, *kuklos),* added "Klan" because they were all Scotch-Irish, and created a conglomeration of preposterous titles: the Grand Wizard and his Grand Dragons and Hydras and Furies and Cyclops. The members—the names kept absolutely secret—were called Ghouls. To celebrate, the men—educated and from "good" families—raided the linen closet, draped themselves and their horses in sheets, and paraded through town. The next morning, they were both delighted by the comments of their mystified friends and surprised by the reaction of the recently freed slaves who mistook them for ghosts of the Confederate dead. The nocturnal appearances soon evolved from innocent to violent, spreading across the Reconstruction-torn South. The violence and the Klan's growth were halted only after Congress conducted an investigation in 1871 and passed a series of civil rights laws, informally known as the Ku Klux Klan Acts and resurrected during the turbulent 1960s.

Even "Colonel" William Joseph Simmons, who coordinated his revival of the Klan in 1915 with the Atlanta opening of *Birth of a Nation,* initially saw it as another venture in his long career of fraternal organizing. An announcement next to the newspaper advertisement for the movie read: "The World's Greatest Secret, Social, Patriotic, Fraternal Beneficiary Order." When he teamed up with Edward Young Clarke and Bessie Tyler—the Southern Publicity Association, the pair called themselves—it was to build the renamed "Knights of the Ku Klux Klan" membership and to make money. They achieved both goals, in startling figures.

Since that Thanksgiving night in 1915 when Simmons held his first cross burning on Stone Mountain, within view of downtown Atlanta, the Klan's flame has flickered and flared and smoldered, only to be fanned from time to time into another brush fire by yet another "cause," as it was in the fifties and sixties when court-ordered integration came to schools and lunch counters and public transportation.

Until recently, most people probably thought klansmen and cross burnings were skeletons relegated to this country's closet. If asked, they probably would have said the five million members from the twenties, the estimated forty thousand from the sixties, had died or disappeared or had a change of heart. Then, in 1975, and especially the spring of 1976, the Klan began popping up like crabgrass: throwing its hood into the vice-presidential race; infiltrating the Marine Corps; protesting busing in Boston and Louisville; joining the textbook fight in Charleston, West Virginia; creating a scandal in the New York state prison system; prompting the Illinois legislature to conduct a major investigation; burning crosses from California to Maryland; going to court to sue and be sued, and appearing on national talk shows.

By 1977, the Klan had exploded on to the front page and prime-time television: plotting to blow-up communications facilities and a generating plant at the supersecret National Security Agency; threatening the life of Coretta King; evoking a stern warning from the archbishop of Washington, D.C., that Catholics were not to join; electing delegates—including the Mississippi Grand Dragon's wife—to the National Women's Conference; and organizing klaverns next door to New York City.

On July 4, 1977, the Klan found itself on the receiving end of violence: first when an anti-Klan protestor plowed his Jaguar into the midst of a rally in President Jimmy Carter's home town, and, two days later, when a mob of egg-throwing, club-wielding demonstrators routed klansmen from the steps of the Ohio state capitol. Then, in March 1978, the Klan crossed the Atlantic to expand its activities, with David Duke leading Scotland Yard on a merry chase after he slipped through British customs and avoided their attempts to nab and deport him.

Was the Klan staging a comeback? Was it again gaining control of emotions and reasoning as it did during the sixties? Was its strength, like the headlines, growing? What was happening in society to breathe new life—or at least new hope—into an organization thought dead? Was the Klan once more becoming a force to be reckoned with?

The FBI says no. Publicly, it has proclaimed the Klan all but dead, with a national membership of less than two thousand. Klan leaders, known to exaggerate, scoff at that estimate. They hide behind their secrecy oath but hint there are more, *many* more. Robert Shelton, Imperial Wizard of the United Klans of America (UKA), says: "We're big enough to put our boots on but not quite big enough to lace 'em up." David Duke—the Klan's answer to Robert Redford—brags that he has drawn more than two thousand to a single rally. When asked the size of his New Orleans-based Knights of the Ku Klux Klan, he hedges. "I'll just say three thousand is low." Then, in November 1977, the Anti-Defamation League of B'nai B'rith (ADL) conceded that membership in the three major Klan groups—UKA, Duke's Knights, and a new Confederation of Independent Klans—had risen twenty percent in two years, up to eight thousand from sixty-five hundred in 1975. But Klan leaders called even those figures low.

Which is accurate: the FBI estimate or the Klan boasts? It is impossible to say. I attended one rally that drew less than fifty and another that attracted twenty-five hundred. Although individuals may choose to identify themselves as klansmen, membership has been secret since Reconstruction days. Shelton and two of his Grand Dragons went to prison rather than divulge names and numbers during an investigation in the sixties by the House Un-American Activities Committee

(HUAC). They are no more willing to talk now than before. Equally close-mouthed is the FBI, embarrassed by Senate disclosure of its own harassment of the Klan during the Civil Rights Movement and hindered by the Privacy Act of 1974.

Former Georgia Grand Dragon Calvin Craig once boasted: "I can take five men in a city of twenty-five thousand, and that is just like having an army. That five can almost control the political atmosphere of that city." Maybe therein lies the answer to the Klan's true size. Maybe its growing visibility is an illusion. Maybe today's klansmen are more publicity oriented, more open, more willing—and eager—to be photographed and quoted. Or maybe there *are* more klansmen—and women—than the public is aware of or the FBI is willing to admit. I don't know. But whatever their numbers, are they to be any less feared? In the midsixties, Dore Schary, then chairman of the Anti-Defamation League of B'nai B'rith, agreed in essence with Calvin Craig, warning, "It doesn't take many men to bomb a church, to flog a Negro or a white, or to commit other acts of violence in the dark of night."

During my eighteen months of research, the Klan made headlines almost weekly, in newspapers from the *Medina County Gazette* in Ohio to the *Mobile Press Register* to *The New York Times*. I read about the Klan there and in the microfilm of the fifties and sixties, at the National Archives, and in assorted history books. I came away with names and dates and figures and countless horror stories. But I still hadn't answered the question I have pondered since childhood, the question people now ask me:

What are klansmen like?

Race relations are a special interest of mine, something I have written, read, and talked about. Yet, curiously, I realized I didn't know the white man who is not ashamed to call himself a racist, the one who proudly joins the Klan. What makes him hate so intensely? Why does he feel so threatened, so cheated? Who is he, deep inside, underneath his robe?

Reporters who worked in the South in the sixties described the rank and file members as "prisoners of their own jail" and "portraits of despair." In the Charlotte, N.C., *Observer,* James K. Batten and Dwayne Walls wrote of them as "the backwash of white society, the low-income, poorly educated laborer or farmer who sees in the Ku Klux Klan the only champion of his cause and the only hope of preserving his station in society's changing order." Most of the reporters portrayed the leaders as "con artists" and "charlatans" who were sometimes surprisingly charismatic and likeable.

I wanted to find out for myself both what they were like and what power they wielded. So I set out to meet the Klan, the leaders, the rank and file, their wives and children and mothers and fathers and neighbors.

I drove more than ten thousand miles over interstates and backwoods roads and traveled another thousand or so miles by Greyhound, commercial airlines, and in Robert Shelton's carpeted Executive camper and David Duke's aging Montego. For three months, I listened, rode, rallied, ate, and said grace with them, and for another eighteen months, I communicated by letter and telephone and over lunch when they passed through town.

I learned a new vocabulary. The chaplain was called "Kludd" and the vice president, "Klaliff." July was "Terrible" on their "kalendar," and their "heroes" were David Duke and Robert Shelton and James Venable and "Colonel" William Joseph Simmons and General Nathan Bedford Forrest. I learned that rallies are held to recruit members, not to plan violence; that small, secret action groups—like those that terrorized the South in the sixties—still exist; that the Klan is not confined to the South; that it is as much at home in big cities and on college campuses as it is in small towns and rural areas; that women are on an equal status with men in some groups; and that people join for more reasons than racial hate: a need to belong and to feel important, a need to brighten drab lives, a need for religious fulfillment, a need to be liked and accepted.

I learned, too, that there is no such thing as *the* Ku Klux Klan. There are many Klans, with many variations on the name: The United Klans of America, Knights of the Ku Klux Klan, Inc.; The Invisible Empire, Knights of the Ku Klux Klan; The Knights of the Ku Klux Klan, Invisible Empire; The National Knights of the Ku Klux Klan; The Knights of the Ku Klux Klan; The Original Knights of the Ku Klux Klan; The Dixie Klans. Ad infinitum. Some Klans claim to have members in every state; one admittedly exists in only one Louisiana congressional district.

The number of splinter groups—like the leaders—varies from day to day, depending on who is feuding with whom and breaking away to form yet another Ku Klux Klan. For klansmen get along no better with each other than they do with their enemies. The leaders profiled in this book may not be the leaders when you read it or may not be the leaders of the particular Klan they led when I interviewed them. The pattern changes constantly, as it has since the late forties when the splintering began. Dwayne Walls and James K. Batten aptly described the situation in the *Charlotte Observer:* "It is impossible to tell the grand dragons, wizards and kleagles apart without a program." David Duke refers to church demoninations: "A thousand years ago there was only one Christian church, but look at all the factions you have now." Since he made that statement, his group has split . . . at least twice.

I came to wonder also if perhaps society, in its attempt to right the many decades of wrong against the black man, had overlooked the possibility that these people also needed help and understanding and opportunity.

So what are klansmen like?

Before my travels, a minister, whose friends run the gamut from Black Muslims to Kluxers, cautioned me: "I hope you'll use a fine stroke instead of a broad brush." Later, a reporter, who wrote a series on the Klan in the sixties, made that same plea almost verbatim.

Two years and a book later, I know that all klansmen are not alike. I have met hundreds and become acquainted with many. I now know that they are not all crude, tobacco-chewing-and-spitting rednecks who wear white socks, cuss, and drive pickups with CB radios and gun racks in their rear windows. They are not all mean men who'd shoot as quick as look at you. Some *are* as easily inflamed as the fiery cross. But even men I *knew* I would hate turned out to have some redeeming qualities. In short, klansmen do not fit neatly into a single mold. And so this book is to introduce the reader not just to the Klan but also to its people, beginning with the first man I met, gradually adding new faces, new personalities, new lives, and finally populating the diverse community that *is* the Klan.

I hope I have used a fine stroke.

The night before I flew to Charleston, West Virginia, for my first rally, I telephoned Dale Reusch—the Klan's candidate for vice-president of the United States—to exchange descriptions before we met at the airport.

"I'm six-foot-four, two-hunderd-an'-eighty pounds, with light brown hair and brown eyes," he said, ". . . and gener'ly, I wear two forty-fives on my hips."

2
Dale Reusch: Tossing His Hood into the Ring

Charleston, West Virginia

"*Mister Roysssch!* Mister Dale *Roysssch,* please come to the Allegheny ticket counter!"

The voice spread through the air terminal, invading the coffee shop, the newsstand, and the waiting areas, but no one headed toward the Allegheny counter or turned except to look at a clock on the wall. There were no red carpets, no Secret Servicemen, no visible signs of the imminent arrival of a 1976 vice-presidential candidate *or* a national Klan leader. Just routine arrivals and departures of people and planes.

Ten past eleven. Fifteen. Twenty. Finally, a hefty man strode through the entrance. He was at least six foot four, two hundred eighty pounds, and his hair was a thinning light brown. His trouser cuffs and shoes were caked with gray mud, and he wore a green satin bowling jacket with a round emblem on the front. I squinted. It was the same emblem I'd seen again and again on the robes of the klansmen parading in the picture postcard: a white Maltese cross with, in its center, a large red "comma"— a tear? a drop of blood?

The people in his path stepped aside as he hurried toward me, until we were face to face. Opposite the emblem, white machine stitching spelled "Dale Reusch" and his now-outdated title, "Grand Dragon." One sleeve bore a "Realm of Ohio" patch; the other was ripped at the seam. Underneath, his stomach poked through a partially unbuttoned sports shirt. He reached out and gave me a sandpapery handshake, his fingernails outlined in grease from testing engines on a Ford Motor Company assembly line where he has worked, mostly, since he graduated from high school and abandoned his father's farm.

Reusch looked older than thirty-seven. Perhaps the facial mileage was from growing up on a farm as one of six children. Perhaps it was from commuting seventy-two miles a day to support a wife, two teenage sons, and a house mortgage, with the prospect of a divorce looming ahead. Or perhaps it was his nonstop crusade for Klan members and vice-presidential votes. His double chin needed a shave. And his eyes were etched in red from talking until four this morning with two Canadian klansmen and getting up at six to drive down with them from his home in Lodi, Ohio—just west of Akron—for tonight's rally.

"C'mon, we gotta meet the Grand Dragon of South Carolina," he said, heading toward the arrival area.

The back of the jacket was taken up by a white satin appliqué of the traditional robed knight on a rearing steed and, in large block letters: KNIGHTS—KU KLUX KLAN. Reusch wore it with the ease of a Friday night bowler, seemingly oblivious to the wake of raised eyebrows. But later, at the luggage carousel, he confessed to John Howard, the South Carolina Dragon, and to me that he was having fun with the airport crowd. "They're lookin', all right," he laughed. "I been at it so long, I'm used to it. But they're lookin'."

John Howard was a small man of thirty, with close-cut brown hair and the beginnings of a mustache, who looked young enough to be a Marine recruit home on leave in his leisure suit and coordinated print shirt. But instead of a military uniform, the garment bag slung over his shoulder concealed the green satin robe he wore as Grand Dragon of South Carolina. His mild manner seemed incongruous with his arrest on suspicion of murder in 1970 when a rival klansman was shot near a rally held by Robert Scoggin, the leader of another South Carolina Klan. Scoggin, Howard, and several other officers were indicted, and bail was set at five to seven thousand dollars.

John Howard, his foot resting on the carousel, shrugged. "All I knowed about it, a guy got killed up the road. A bullet went in up there." He pointed to his head. ". . . and come out here. Killed him instantly. But it was throwed outta court. They didn't have enough evidence." Howard insisted that his racial views always remained outside the school where he works in Laurens. And the only outward sign of his twelve years in the Klan was a ring with a red stone and gold-embossed "A," for "AKIA," a password meaning "A Klansman I Am."

"I been Grand Dragon four or five years," John Howard boasted, proudly handing me his "business" card. On one side was a fuzzy black-and-white photograph of him in the robe and a matching satin hood; on the other, a miniature application for membership with the heading: YOU ARE ELIGIBLE TO JOIN THE NATIONAL KNIGHTS OF THE KU KLUX KLAN.

"Cross out the 'National,'" he said. "That was when I was with Venable. I'm with Dale now, with the Invisible Empire, Knights of the Ku Klux Klan."

John Howard's switch in allegiance had come a year ago, in September 1975, when he, Reusch, and three other Grand Dragons broke away from the National Knights of The Ku Klux Klan to form their own Klan, naming Reusch the new Imperial Wizard. The split triggered an exchange in the press between the Grand Dragons and their former leader, James R. Venable. The five Dragons accused Venable of being senile, and the seventy-one-year-old lawyer, from his home in Stone Mountain, Georgia, shot back: "My mind is as brilliant as it was forty years ago." The Dragons said they had abandoned Venable; he insisted he had "banished them *forever*" and revoked their commissions as Grand Dragons. Tony LaRicci, the "ousted" Grand Dragon from Maryland, told the press Venable couldn't banish them without approval of the Imperial Board and, "We are *two-thirds* of the board." Venable countered that "LaRicci doesn't know any more about the constitution than a goat does. I appointed them and I can banish them." He accused the five men of conspiring against him and taking in unfit members. "Why," Venable fumed, "they been runnin' over states creatin' trouble and gettin' in undesirable members, takin' in anybody who had fifteen dollars." No one mentioned that in 1965, when a black Catholic janitor wrote for an application, Venable had named him Great Titan of Idaho.

John Howard lifted his suitcase from the carousel. "We got five or six Klans in South Car'liner right now," he said, adding that he had belonged to four of them, so far. "Our dream is to one day overcome all this jealousy an' bickerin' an' power struggles an' money-grabbin' an' u-nite into one. But fer thirty-five or forty years, throughout the whole U-nited States, throughout the whoole Empire of alll the Klans, it has always been an' it always will be, until that day comes that somethin' changes, a bickerin', a lust fer power, a lust fer money an' the domination over a human bein'."

His monologue had reached fire-and-brimstone fervor by the time we got to Reusch's battered 1970 Buick Skylark. Reusch opened the car door and suggested I push aside a crumpled grocery bag that was on the front seat. The contents were heavy and moved with the dull thud of metal.

The forty-fives? I wondered.

The Buick was dusty inside and out and cluttered with leaflets titled "Why You Should Become a Klansman," "Boycott Jew Stores" bumper stickers, copies of the news story published when Reusch filed for West Virginia's vice-presidential primary, and an anti-abortion ad headlined

"SLAUGHTER of all TIMES" with photographs of a fetus and a rare steak. A faded green satin robe hung over a back window, and the dashboard was lettered in gold plastic, K K K.

Reusch apologized for the littered Buick. "I put a hunderd and six thousand miles on this since I bought it secondhand two years ago. I'm on the road ever' weekend, for the Klan. I go to Pennsylvania, North Carolina, South Carolina, Missouri, Arkansas, Indiana, Canada." Lately, his travels had been confined to West Virginia to round up votes for the state's upcoming primary, one of the few open to vice-presidential hopefuls and one that ironically included in the Democratic column a presidential contender who had been a klansman in the forties, Senator Robert C. Byrd.

The primary was of historic importance to Reusch and the Klan. In the past, the Invisible Empire had helped elect presidents—Calvin Coolidge, for one—and had sent special delegations to the national conventions of both political parties in 1924 and 1928. Woodrow Wilson had been considered—at the very least—sympathetic, allowing a White House screening of *Birth of a Nation* with its flattering portrayal of the Reconstruction Klan. And Warren G. Harding was rumored to have been given a Klan burial in Marion, Ohio, less than a hundred miles from Dale Reusch's home. Several modern-day klansmen had campaigned, with some success, for local and state offices, and at least three were making current political bids in Georgia, Florida, and South Carolina. But Reusch was the first person to head what started out as a national Ku Klux Klan ticket.

Initially, he was to be the Klan's standard bearer, and a Houston gas-meter reader, Scott Monroe "White" Nelson, the vice-presidential candidate, their nominations made and confirmed at a meeting in Georgia at James Venable's house. When Reusch failed to muster enough support, he dropped down to the vice-presidential slot, and Nelson dropped from sight. Actually, Reusch was not a political novice. He had run, unsuccessfully, for governor of Ohio in 1974 and for sheriff of Medina County in 1968 and 1972, the last time losing 1,910 to 3,833. Venable and his Knights apparently considered that ample preparation for the national political arena.

The Buick pulled out of the airport parking lot on to a road that wove through the hills, along a river, to the motel. Reusch looked up and around and sucked in a chestful of crisp April air. "You're in Klan country now!" he boasted. "The textbook issue is what's causin' the Klan to grow in Kanawha Valley. These people have tried demonstratin' an' ever'thang else. They *know* the Klan is their only hope."

Reusch probably had turned to politics for the same reasons he, and many others, turned to the Klan: to become more than another cog in an assembly line. Without the purple robe, even without the green jacket, he would have been just a little man whose views went no farther than the supper table or lunch-box discussions at work, a man whose name made the birth and death notices but never headlines, a man who could gain power and esteem only among the other men and women who donned the satin robes for the same reasons he did.

In January 1975, Reusch and Venable—still a "father-son" team—had arrived in the midst of the Charleston textbook protests, promising to save irate parents and their children from the "Communism, Socialism and all other isms" being taught in the schools. On the State House steps, in the Civic Center Auditorium, at outdoor rallies, the two proclaimed themselves as saviors of the protestors. A number of people had been impressed by the elderly Imperial Wizard, in his purple satin robe, and Reusch, still in the presidential stage of his candidacy.

"The battle is a fight against government indoctrination and nationalized education," Reusch told one crowd of protestors, urging them to "go to your legislature with an ultimatum: Remove the textbooks or we'll remove you from office—*physically!*" He vowed to use boycotts, marches, and coal-mine strikes and promised to fight to the end.

Reusch's strike threat was ironic. In the twenties, the Klan in West Virginia had sided with mine owners *against* striking miners. Although some union men did join the Hooded Order, the United Mine Workers was then, as it is today, officially opposed to the Klan.

It was an influx of blacks and immigrants who came to work in the coal, gas, oil, and glass industries that first attracted klansmen to the state, most of them from neighboring Pennsylvania and Ohio. In communities surrounding the Kanawha and Monongahela rivers, the Klan met, marched, threatened, and voted, though never with the success it had had in other states, especially at the polls.

At the motel, Reusch promised to return in a half hour to drive me to the rally grounds. It was noon. At two o'clock, I called his room and was informed that Reusch had left but would return shortly.

The phone rang at five o'clock. A man named Hill said he was there to drive me to the rally. Hill was slight, in his twenties, with canary-yellow hair greased into ducktails and a mouth that, when he wasn't laughing or chewing gum, veered to the left in a smile. I found him near the elevator talking to John Howard and the klansmen from Canada. One was a tall sturdy blond in checkered sports jacket and slacks; the other, thin with sharp features and mustache, was quiet and gray in complexion and dress.

The larger Canadian gripped my hand. "I am Jack Prins, the Grand Dragon of Canada from Toronto," he said, his English still flavored by his native Holland. "And this is John Ross Taylor." The gray man, his hands loosely clasped in front of him, nodded. Both men had been in the Klan four or five years and were active, they told me, in the Western Guard, an extreme right-wing group that I later learned had made its own headlines in Canada. Taylor said he also headed the Social Credit Association, "a provincial and national party"; and Jack Prins, the White Confederacy of Understanding.

"We have now about twenty-thousand men in the white movement, in Klan-connected organizations," Prins estimated. "But we keep it a little bit underground. We don't say 'Klan' so much because the word had such a bad ... the same as Nazis are bad people, but they're *not* bad people!"

I looked up at the towering Prins, a truck mechanic, and he grinned. "Six, six-and-a-half, and it helps! I'm fifty-four, but I *still* fight in the street with a two-by-four in my hands."

"You have that kind of trouble in Canada?" I asked.

"Oh, yes! Oh, yes yes yes!" he exclaimed. He showed off a narrow leather holder attached to his belt. "A special knife," he explained. "They're not directly allowed, but I better to be dead than Red."

When I asked what issues most concerned him and his members, Prins proclaimed, *"The root of all evil is the Jew!* I was in forty-four in Germany when I worked as a so-called slave laborer on the V-one, V-two guided missile. I worked on the guiding mechanism in Germany. And then I started to realize that all the propaganda against Germany and against Hitler was a rotten Jew lie!"

"In Holland, did you ever fight against Hitler?"

Prins hung his head. "Yes, because I said, 'Why the hell these people come to my country?' But then later, I found it was totally fiction. I was in an underground movement in forty-two in Holland. And I even, I'm sorry to say, killed Germans and I cannot forgive myself."

Walking to the car, Prins continued to praise Hitler and lambast the Jews. *"Hitler never would have killed himself!* So *there* is another rotten Jew lie!" He looked down as he opened the car door for me. "Aren't you scared to ride weeth us? Vee eeet leetle babies for breakfast, you know." He laughed, like the villain in a horror movie, slammed the door, and slid into the front seat with Hill and John Ross Taylor.

The road followed the winding Kanawha River. Hills rose in every direction and, in the West, gently sliced the leftover sun. It was that tranquil time of late afternoon, and, for a time, the car's occupants also were quiet. Hill, his left elbow resting on the open window, loosely gripped the steering wheel with his right hand. Prins cleared his throat and turned to Hill. "What about the Jews? You have them here, the rotten Jews?" Hill ignored the question to point out a roadside monument. "See that there statue of Booker T. Washington? Well, somebody done smashed the face t'other day." His crooked grin widened, and he looked at Prins and Taylor for approval. "We took a shot at it with a machine gun one time, 'n the *po*leece never caught us or anythang. T'rowed paint on it, too."

Prins obliged with another horror-house laugh, then persisted, "But the Jews . . ." to no avail. John Howard, in the back seat, fidgeted while Hill continued to brag, anxious to impress the foreign visitors. "Yeah, we gettin' them niggers in line." He pulled the car up to a row of frame stores huddled against the hills and took a sandwich into the five-and-dime store to his wife Bonnie, who was cashiering the late shift. Prins' eyes shot down the line of businesses and focused on a dry-goods store. "Levin!" he exclaimed. "That is a Jew! Dirty, rotten Jews! They have taken over Germany lock, stock, and barrel! They have deevided the white man! Rotten Jews!"

He was still grumbling when Hill returned to the car. "Couple niggers 'er in there, so I tol' Bonnie, 'Got some Kluxers out there in the car. Don't know if I kin keep a'holt of 'em or not.' Bonnie jist laughed an' said, 'Aw, now you go on.' "

Prins and Taylor roared, and John Howard picked at his fingernails.

"Did they hear you?" I asked.

"Yeah," Hill answered, "they was *right* there."

He turned the ignition key, gunned the motor, and pulled back on to the highway, never letting up on the gas or his boasting. A stream rushed over rocks on one side of the narrow road; on the other side, small frame houses and trailers backed up to the hills. "We had to whup us a couple a niggers a while back," Hill continued. "We got 'em in line awright. One of 'em come after me 'n I near thought he was agonna beat me to death, but he didn't."

John Howard coughed. "You gonna give this lady the wrong idear with your jokes," he said.

Hill laughed. "Joke, hell! Wish it *had* been a joke!"

A small cardboard sign with four Ks and an arrow pointed to the left toward an open gate, where a man with a walkie-talkie clutched to his ear motioned us through. The car rumbled over the dirt road, kicking up a small dust storm that settled to where it belonged by the time we edged on to a large field, encased in hills and almost barren of people except for a dozen or so clustered around a makeshift speaker's platform and a brick-papered house converted into a concession stand. A rooster crowed from the far end of the hollow, from behind or under or near a small frame house, reduced even smaller by the distance. To the right, two house trailers squatted on concrete blocks, and a drying wardrobe of work shirts and khakis and cotton brassieres hung nearby.

Hill let the car idle a moment, its knocks mingling with the German marching music that blared from speakers mounted on a faded green Pontiac. Prins grinned approval as Hill parked parallel to a half-dozen cars and pickup trucks of assorted vintages, next to the brick-papered house that was an anthill of activity, of women setting out homemade cupcakes and filling a coffee urn and icing down Cokes and 7-Ups and grilling hot dogs. Over the doorway, a hand-printed sign listed the menu, and an illuminated clock kept unheeded tabs on the rally's starting time.

Reusch, his shirt tail out, his hands grimier than before, walked up and nodded toward his Buick. The hood was up, and two men were leaning over the motor. "Overheated again," he complained. It was the second time that day, and he grinned at the incongruity of an engine tester and a member of United Auto Workers not being able to keep his own car running. His expertise at diagnosing "knocks" on the Ford assembly line had won him cups of coffee in friendly wagers with his supervisor.

"Welllll," Reusch laughed, turning from the ailing Buick to the preparations for the rally. The speaker's stand was wrapped in red-white-and-blue-striped bed sheets and decked with flags. A revolving light was set up to alter the color, if not the mood, of the speakers and the audience. Next to the stand, under a budding tree, was a pile of worn automobile tires. And three rusty drums held torches, like giant Q-Tips, soaking in kerosene.

It was going to be a *big* rally, Reusch predicted, although not as big as the one when he joined the Klan and Venable's group in 1965 on an Ohio farm. "They figgered there was close to fifteen thousand. It would've been more, but the sheriff was against the Klan an' he took it at gun point an' turned the people back," he reminisced. "Yeah, we're gonna have a good crowd tonight."

Even after the sun gave way to dark, Reusch seemed undaunted by the crowd's stunted growth. Occasionally, a car or a pickup or a camper would rattle over the dirt road into the hollow. Still, the gathering of men and women leaning against fenders and talking in twos and threes and the children playing "tag" and rolling in the grass shifted positions but not size.

Except for the youth—still filled with "when-I-grow-up" hopes—there was about the people a weariness and boredom that came from too many years of drudgery and disappointments, of discount clothes and hand-me-downs, of lives as narrow as the hollows and valleys they dwelled in. They were a poor people, poor in material possessions, poor in learning, poor in hope. At the same time, they were a proud people, too proud to accept food stamps and welfare, too proud to take advantage of programs—like HeadStart—that might enrich their drab lives. Most of all, they seemed a people who desperately longed to be better than *somebody*. Much like Dale Reusch, they joined the Klan not just to protest textbooks but to bring excitement into their lonely Saturdays, to release into the night the pent-up frustrations, the hate, and the resentment they were unable to express in daylight, face to face.

Reusch looked from his watch to the clouds lowering into the valley, blending their promise of rain with the smells of frying hamburgers and brewing coffee and the kerosene and crude oil waiting for the thirty- to forty-foot cross being put together out in the field. A small cross, about five feet tall, had already been erected. Now a group of strapping men struggled with the big one, wrapping two tree trunks first with faded rags, then with strips of burlap. They wired the trunks together to form the cross, and paused to inspect it before dousing on the thirty-gallon mixture of oil and kerosene. The work was hard, not much easier than their construction or mining jobs, and they grunted and breathed heavily, and sweat darkened their shirts. But they didn't complain. They stood back, wiped their faces with their forearms, and accepted praise from Reusch and some admirers.

A slim man named Bob, with sunken chest and dull eyes, brightened briefly. "The night I come into this world, back in nineteen twenty-five, my mother looked out the hospital window down in Kentucky and on the hillside was a big cross burnin' an' my dad was helpin' on that cross. *He* was a member, in Kentucky." Bob had joined the Klan a year before, when Reusch and Venable first came to West Virginia to support the textbook protest. "But," he conceded, "the schoolbook deal's a lost cause. It's my country I'm worried about more than anythang else. It isn't ran by the people anymore. It's ran by the federal judges and the Supreme Court. Well, the people'll only take so much." He looked toward the speaker's stand at Reusch, and his prematurely withered face glowed. "I'll make a prediction," he grinned. "Dale's goin' to git more votes than George Wallace. People are afraid to go to parades and rallies, but in the privacy of the votin' booth, jes' watch. You jes' watch." Reusch had put up $625 to qualify for the West Virginia primary, Bob said, "and we ever' one of us give a dollar."

It was after eight o'clock, and the crowd had crested to maybe fifty. A few men and women had put on satin robes and high-peaked hats, color-matched to their offices: white for local klavern members and officers, red for provincial and state officers, green for Grand Dragons, and purple for the Imperial Wizard. Except for color and stripes edging the hems and sleeves, the robes were identical, with emblems—like the one on Reusch's bowling jacket—over each breast. Some people wore matching masks, but most made no effort to hide.

The loudspeakers blared an eclectic selection of Beethoven's Ninth,

John Denver's "Take Me Home, Country Roads," "The Old Rugged Cross," and "Stars and Stripes Forever." Then a sinister recorded voice began a history of the Klan, mingling but not competing with the conversations and concession-stand business. The Civil War was fought *not* over slavery, the voice insisted, but by European Jewish bankers to gain the manufacture and control of American money, which they have *to this day* under the Federal Reserve banking system. Slavery was only a political excuse. When Abraham Lincoln refused to pay the Jews the interest to finance the war, and when he planned to ship the freed slaves back to Africa, he was assassinated. "John Wilkes Booth," the record charged, "was a Jew!"

John Ross Taylor, the Canadian, joined me at the edge of the crowd to watch the accelerating activity. He wore a dark-gray topcoat and a red arm band with the Western Guard emblem that differed from the Nazis' only in that it bore a black cross instead of a swastika. Prins, snapping shut the front of the faded green robe I had seen in the Buick, huddled near the platform with Reusch and an equally sizable young man in a newer green robe. Occasionally, Reusch glanced away, toward the entrance in search of headlights.

In the background, the still-ignored recording continued spewing over the public address system the horrors of Reconstruction, of how white men were imprisoned and "fair white women" raped by their former slaves. "The braaavest Southern men went to see General Lee. He told these men he was on parole and whatever movement they adopted would have to be underground and operate in the greaaatest secrecy. It was General Lee who suggested the name 'The Invisible Empire.' Thus was born in Pulaski, Tennessee, 'The Invisible Empire of the Ku Klux Klan.' Within a year, the Nigra was completely disarmed. Trouble-makers both black and white were invited to leave the South *and they left*. The ravagers of white women—*both* white and black—were hanged without mercy. Or were flogged, for lesser offenses. The Klan restored law and order to the nation and, within two years, General Forrest ordered them disbanded. The Klan did more than save the virtue of Southern white womanhood. It saved the honor of the then-disgraced United States government!"

The ominous voice gave way to that of the Reverend H. G. Hill of Atlanta, Georgia, who droned on scratchily with a "spiritual explanation" of the fiery cross. As he spoke, the men in the field, their shirts stuck to their bodies, were digging a hole for the large cross. A small pickup truck backed up, and a rope was tied from it to the cross. The truck strained forward, slowly, pulling the cross upright with the help of the men pushing from behind. Now the cross was up but listing, and the men and the truck shoved and tugged without success and finally gave up.

Meanwhile, the Reverend Hill had relinquished the loudspeaker to the sinister voice, which progressed to a stand against Catholics, one that Reusch's Klan—among others—had abandoned. The Catholic church was the leader of mongrelization, the voice lashed out from the turntable before again aiming its wrath at blacks: "The poor ignorant Nigra doesn't know it yet, but he's already lost many of his freedoms. And when it's over, what will he have left if he escapes deportation?—*which we doubt.* Political freedom? Yes. Legal freedom? We doubt it. Social freedom? *Never!* This nation cannot exist half white and half black, and a mulatto citizenship is unthinkable even at the cost of annihilation of one or the other races. The tragedy will never be closed until the black man is returned to his home, Africa!" The voice paused for effect, then insisted: "The Klan is not a hate monger or anti-Catholic or anti-Jew. It is pro-white!"

The history over, the musical conglomeration resumed, creating an air of mini-carnival without prizes. Beyond the string of lights and the activity around the speaker's platform and the concession stand, the night was black, starless and bedtime still. The rally seemed as distant as when we first arrived. A German shepherd sniffed the barrels of soaking torches, the audience stared at their watches, and small children napped in their mothers' laps or on the grass.

W. B. Miller, II, the young man in the brighter green robe, joined John Ross Taylor and me. He was a massive man, with straggly brown hair and mustache, a tuft of hair below his bottom lip, and blue eyes that exuded more hate and belligerence than most people accumulate in twenty-two years. A jeweler by trade from nearby Huntington, Bill Miller had been a member little more than a year and Grand Dragon for even less time, but he had had a boyhood fascination with the Hooded Order. His grandfather had belonged in the thirties, and now the Klan consumed him: his thoughts, his feelings, his conversations, his friendships, his marriage. Linda, his wife of six months, was Kleagle, the organizer for West Virginia women. Their nights out were spent at rallies and meetings and with Klan acquaintances.

Miller glanced at the sprinkling of men and women and boasted that the Klan was already knocking on doors, already bringing about change in Kanawha Valley and in the state.

"Are you talking about nightriders?" I asked.

"Yeah, the nightriders, the Inner Circle," he answered without hesitation.

"You mean violence?" I pressed.

"I believe in vigilantes, and I believe in vengeance," he said forcefully. "I try to rationalize ever'thang an' I feel like if force is the only answer, then force must be used. As far as the Klan, marchin' days an' protestin' days are over."

The loudspeakers started a new verse of "America," and Miller went on. "The Klan in a sense is becomin' liberal. In my opinion, the Klan in the future will go completely underground, never to pass out literature, never to pass out applications again. Because a lot of people don't know how to weather the storm. They think it's a Klan rally, a game, an' because of the federal government, we're more restricted. If it was up to me, I wouldn't enjoy anythang better than gettin' on a horse an' bringin' about change."

He looked down at a small cloud of dust he had kicked up and then back at me. "I've had many situations travelin' in the night, an' I don't think anythang can give you more of a spiritual high than bringin' about this change. You don't really ask yourself the justification of *why* you do this. You feel that it is right."

I looked him in the eye. "And you *have* been on nightrides?"

"Yes."

"What kinds of things have you done?"

He hesitated for the first time. "*That,* I would rather keep to myself. I've never committed malicious murder, but . . ."

"Have you whipped or frightened people?"

Miller didn't look down or away. "I feel if you're gonna make a night-ride, then it's only *to* frighten, to bring about this change. An' I feel like when the Klan gets through, the country is goin' to have to take a bottle of Valium to settle their nerves because I have never approached anyone that didn't have it comin' to 'em."

Action groups, like the Inner Circle, had been credited with terrorizing the South in the sixties. In those days, the bands of five or six select men—their identities and missions concealed even from the general membership—hoarded arsenals of shotguns and carbines and were Klan trained not only in the use of firearms but also in judo and karate and how to make bombs and other explosive devices. One—the Secret Six— had plotted unsuccessfully to kill Martin Luther King, Jr., long before the civil rights leader died at the hands of another assassin.

A chain glimmered from underneath Miller's robe. "It's a cross," he said. "I've worn one for several years. I feel like anyone who believes in Christ should wear a cross."

While he was talking, Reusch strode on to the platform to get the program under way, a program that seemed more impromptu than planned, mental meanderings tied together by hate. Grasping the microphone in one hand and a Styrofoam cup in the other, Reusch looked like Jackie Gleason playing Ralph Cramden in a purple satin robe. Red, white, blue, and gold stripes encircled the sleeves of the still-shiny robe. And, underneath, he wore the mud-caked trousers and shoes.

The small audience greeted the Imperial Wizard with whistles and applause as he turned over the mike to the Kludd, who asked the Lord "to bless all Klan members and non-Klan members at this party," and then to Bill Miller.

At first, Miller's voice was even and low, almost a reading-aloud monotone that matched neither the passion of his subject nor his manner, a voice reasonably punctuated with commas and periods as he recited his Klan catechism about the suppression of the white minority and the takeover by the Negroes and the Jews. But the calm commas soon gave way to exclamation marks, the softness to shouting.

"Since I can ever count, Jews have corrupted, destroyed and defaced ever'thang that they've ever brought their hands on!" he shouted. "And anybody that tells you Jews are God's chosen people or Christ was a Jew, I wanta meet 'em." To prove his point, he quoted, by heart, from the Bible. "Saint John eight, forty-four: 'Ye are of your father, the devil, and a lust of your father ye will do for he was a murderer from the beginning and abode not with the truth, for there is no truth within him. For he is a liar and the father of it.' Now, Christ is speakin' directly to the Jews, and if you don't take my word for it, take the Bible's!"

A small circle of men and women hovered around the podium like moths attracted to a bare lightbulb. They listened intently at first, and one robed woman, leaning against the budding tree, interspersed a hearty *"Aaaaa-men, brother!"* Encouraged, Bill Miller shifted into high gear. "Now, let's go to the niggers!" He leaned over the railing, toward the increasingly restless audience. "Many of you people have daughters. Now what if your daughter'd come home one evenin' with a nice big black buck? Right now so many people scared of the niggers anyway, what diff'rence does it make? You'd accept it. You'd have mulatto children. And it comes back again to the greatest creation—the white man—and the bloodstream is polluted. Who gives anyone this right? No one! Not even God Himself!"

There were scattered claps and the lone *"Aaaaa-men!"* and Miller continued his racial hopscotch, finally bringing the Klan to the rescue. "Protest days are over," he warned. "They are a thang of the past. We get out an' march, what do we get? We get nuthin'! We are committed to do one thang, and that's *force* and *force* only!

"Aaaaaa-men, brother!"

Miller briefly aimed his wrath at the bickering and infighting among "brothers and sisters" of the Klan before returning to his appeal for members. "If you feel as we do, come forward an' let us teach you how we feel an' how the Klan is goin' to ride to save America!"

The crowd, reawakened, contributed cheers to the robed woman's *"Aaaaa-men!"* Miller acknowledged the ovation, then introduced John Howard.

After waving majestically to his listeners, Howard lunged into his own version of the Klan's history, about how, during Reconstruction, "the only way to take these black jiggaboos out of state offices was to form the first Klan." He was no longer the almost shy man at the airport. Basking in the red-to-green-to-blue spotlight, he gestured wildly, and his voice and temper rose:

"... An' when they got to South Car'liner, ladies an' gentlemen, they started hangin' niggers in York, South Car'liner, all the way down to Columbier," he recounted. "When they got to the state capital, they went into that capitol buildin' an' they swung those niggers an' carpetbaggers out by the seat of their britches, through the winders, an' they put men of their choice an' the choice of the majority in office!"

The veins in Howard's temples pulsed as he progressed from the Klan's revival in 1915 to present-day Boston and to "Kennedy and the rest of those jack legs." Leaning over the mike, he explained his usage: "Fine people, we use a lot of slang words in the state of South Car'liner. I'm nuthin' but an ol' redneck, ol' country boy, an' I tell it like it is. I take the rag off the bush!"

The woman by the tree yelled, *"Aaaa-men!"*

John Howard sounded like a Holy Roller preacher giving "the invitation" at a revival. "Ladies an' gentlemen, today is the day to join the Klan! When you have to remove a president of the U-nited States, Mister Nixon, when he was shaaakin' even the pews of our White House through crooked means, it's time fer the mass of people to open their eyes."

"Aaaa-men, brother!"

"Hey! Hey! Hey!"

"President Kennedy said one time on TV and it hit the hearts of *ever'* man an' woman throughout this nation. 'Ask not what you can do fer your,'" he hesitated, backed up and started again. " 'Ask not what your country can do fer you, but ask what you can do fer your country.' I'll go along with that. An' I'll add a little small phrase onto it. 'Ask not what the Klan can do fer you, but ask what you can do fer the Klan!' "

Again, the audience yelled, cheered, whistled, applauded, and John Howard, encouraged, moved on. "It's time to remove these money men that's takin' money off the table an' paddin' their pocketbooks while the poor people are sufferin' from it an' our children are bein' used by the federal government an' the Supreme Court in these public schools."

"Aaaaaa-men!"

"Yeah!"

John Howard toned down, smiling now. "I wanta say a small joke on the Imperial Wizard. I hope ever'one enjoys it. When I stepped off the plane an' got in the terminal over here at the airport, there was a nigger over there tryin' to git his ticket. He was goin' to Africer . . ."

A man shouted, "One way?"

"But he lacked a quarter. I seen him rush over to the Imperial Wizard. He says, 'Hey, uh, boss, how 'bout lettin' me have a quarter. I need it to git me a ticket, I'm goin' to Africer.' The Imperial Wizard pulled out a dollar. He said, 'Here, go grab ya three more an' take 'em with you.' " John Howard laughed with his audience. "We don't want anybody to think the Klan doesn't have a sense of humor."

Bill Miller returned to the podium to introduce his wife, Linda, a porcelain-skinned woman with red hair and a red robe, who apologized that this was her first time to speak in public. "We need more women," she started angelically. "We need the men, but we also need the women behind the men, to do little thangs like we've done this evenin'. Stand over there an' cook an' take your money."

Her blue-gray eyes made a timid sweep of the audience, then focused fiercely ahead. "So let's talk about another thang. What about the niggers? What about our little chil'ren that's goin' to school? The thangs they have to put up with?" Her saccharine voice turned sassy. "Niggers are *not* like us. We're goin' somewhere, where they're not. We've got the brains. They have nuthin'."

"Aaaaa-men, brother . . . I mean sister!"

"An' if we take 'em out a school because they're goin' to school with niggers, we're goin' to have some problems. So why not jist stand an' stare in their face. Say 'I was here first and I *am better* than you are!' "

Two robed women stood behind her erect and emotionless, arms crossed and eyes straight ahead, throughout Linda Miller's haphazard harangue that took issue with a proposed abortion law and with putting sex education in the schools and taking the Lord's Prayer out.

"We're goin' to have to start takin' our stand, women—and men— because if we don't, this world's goin' to be in a hell of a shape. It's already in one big one now. But it can become ten times worse. An' we don't want our kids bringin' home little nigger babies. *We want white!"*

This time, the applause and cheers surpassed the size of the crowd, and Linda Miller galloped down the steps, past two admiring young women. "Thank you, Linda," and, "That was reeeal nice," they complimented her. Linda Miller nodded a slight "thank you" and headed toward the concession stand, straightening her peaked hat. "I deserve a Coke!" she said.

When she came out of the brick-papered house minus the robe and hat, her T-shirt and hair were damp with sweat, and her flushed cheeks were glowing. She stood near me, drinking the Coke and half listening to Jack Prins, who had followed her on the program. I asked her about a man in a short, black robe.

"That's jist a Night-Hawk," she explained. "It's not really a Night-Hawk, it's *Night Run.* It's jist a short robe made for runnin', if you gotta run from some place, an' it's black as night an' you can't see it. It jist for whatever the guys do, which we women don't know."

"They don't tell you if they go nightriding?" I asked.

She swallowed some Coke. "No. They may. I don't know. Bill goes to the klavern meetin's, if they call or if they need him. But as far as that goes, I don't think there's much of that goes on."

Linda Miller had joined the Klan shortly before she and Bill Miller were married. She was like so many young women from low-income families whose horizons seldom stretch beyond high school and marriage and having babies and whose fairness soon turns to flab. But, unlike most, she had been rescued by a knight, of sorts, who offered her the adventures of the Klan. Like Bill Miller, she had gone to school in Huntington, where she was raised from the age of six by an outspoken grandmother who let Linda do what she wanted. That had included marrying young, having two children, and getting divorced. The grandmother was dead now, but Linda Miller speculated that the old woman wouldn't object to her Klan membership, either.

She talked about how she felt before her first rally, before her husband joined and told her about the Klan. "I really didn't understand. I thought back to the ol' history of the nigger hangin's, the rape, takin' 'em out an' tar 'n featherin' 'em and then hangin' 'em. Thangs that they did back then, which they were considered vigilantes. But the Klan is not that. They believe in God and country."

"But did it frighten you before you found out about the Klan?" I probed.

"No, because I figured they tried to do somethin' back then that should be done now. 'Let's straighten up the world,' " she answered.

"Do you think they ought to be doing tar and feathering and things like that now?"

"If they can get by with it, *fine,*" she said staunchly, adding—just as firmly—that she and most of the women would go along with it. "We're strong. We're dedicated. Somethin' has to be done, we'll do it."

I asked if she had a gun, and she shook her head. "No, don't want any. I've shot plenty of 'em. But I have no reason for 'em. If I can't do anythang with my fist, I don't need somethang else to back me up and he'p me feel big. God gave us fists before He gave us guns. That's what I use, if it comes to that."

It had started to sprinkle, scattering people into their cars and campers and the concession house. Although the applause was as light as the rain when Reusch mounted the platform, he seemed undaunted. He sized up the crowd as though it were ten times bigger and began verbally lynching big business, big government, Robert Byrd, the valley's ministers, taxes, gun control, and Jewish domination.

"This is one of the most vital elections in American history," he pronounced authoritatively. "History is bein' made in West Virginia! I filed as a vice-presidential candidate because the American people *has* to be heard at the Democratic National Convention! Only *through this,* will your voice *ever* be heard!"

The audience applauded.

"I don't wanta come to you and say I'm a politician," he said. "An' I've never used that phrase, that 'I'm a politician.' I consider myself a statesman. A politician'll sit there an' promise you nuthin' but lies! I promise you *ever'thang* an' give you action! Positive is action! Where it's action, it's bein' positive!"

"Aaaaaaa-men, brother!"

His eyes darting from side to side like a tommy gun, Reusch became almost incoherent as he ranted about "war drums beatin' in Israel an' Africa," about "the boob tube," about government interference in farming, about the betrayal of the people by the Democratic and Republican parties. Often he used and abused words, stringing them together into meaningless phrases and sentences to impress his audience.

"I'm tired of messin' with a bunch of cheap politicians that are squanderin' away your wealth, an' your heritage, for a lousy few gold coins!" he shouted. "Big government's like leeches, suckin' blood from your veins."

"That's right!"

"Hey! Hey! Hey!"

"Why is the Klan suppressed?" He answered his own question. "They say we're hate mongers. I don't hate. But the Bible says you can hate. One man, especially, *God* said, 'I hate.' Now, it's not a sin to hate. But I *dislike,* an' I will not follow anythang that is unrighteous an' unclean. An' *that* is what we have in politics."

Reusch's voice grew as heavy as the clouds. "The Klan is goin' to *stay* in this valley. Till it's the end of the valley. I spent one *haaard* year in this valley, one *treacherous* year. I was lookin' for soldiers of the cross. True soldiers. It took me a looong time to find those men an' those women. But they are comin'. They are takin' their stations. Like we would consider in the army: Take your battle stations! Man your guns! An' you *better* man your guns, because they're comin' to get your guns! That's people control! Without guns, the government controls the people! *With* the guns, *you* control the government!"

There was a vigorous outburst of agreement from the audience. Then, like a politician making his last pitch for votes, Reusch wound down, his voice softening, pleading, reaching out. "We got a primary an' I can see a vision," he said wistfully. "But that vision lies with the West Virginians. If I can win, I will go to the Democratic convention an' I will represent *you! And your issues!"* He spoke even more slowly now, for emphasis. "You've never seen a klansman in front of a bunch of liberal people in your life, but you'll see *one* klansman with his robe. An' I'll address allll the Jews. I'll address allll the blacks. I'll address allll the white blacks."

He rested his case and started down the steps to a round of applause cut short as the audience shifted its attention to voices clashing near the podium. A gray-haired woman in a white robe, flailing her arms, directed her fury at Bill Miller, who looked at her stonily. "He walked over an' he called me 'trash,' Bill Miller did!" she shouted to the accumulating crowd. "Walked right up to my face an' I never said a word to him! He sure did! I was standin' right there an' I never opened my mouth an' he called me 'trash'!"

Reusch had edged his way into the group and stood between her and Miller. The woman's face and voice reflected an anger and humiliation that few words—not even "bitch"—could evoke. And the people around her understood. "He won't call me 'trash' no more, Bill Miller won't, 'cause I'll take my fist an' knock him down!" she ranted. "Walked right up to my face an' called me 'trash,' as though I was the scum of the earth an' I never opened my mouth at him! *He's* the scum of the earth!"

Miller walked past her, uttering a calm but emphatic *"Burn in hell!"*

By now, the argument had grown to include the woman's daughter and Linda Miller. "I don't care if he *is* your husband! That's my mother! And you knock it off!" the daughter yelled at Linda Miller. "Tell him, mom! Go on, mom, Dale can take care of him!" The older woman grumbled, "I'm gonna tell Dale on you!"

Reusch tried to arbitrate, but the woman still fumed. "Anybody call me 'trash,' I'll knock all the hell out 'em!" Two young women led her to the concession house, and Reusch, shaking his head, returned to the platform and commanded: "Klansmen! Report to the cross!"

One man slipped a robe over his shirt and trousers, joining the twenty or so people who straggled across the field to gather with Reusch near the leaning cross. A few feet away, the small, already burning cross cast an eerie glow on the group, as the Imperial Wizard verbally rehearsed the ceremony. The loudspeakers came to life with a waltzed-up, organ-and-choral rendition of "The Old Rugged Cross," keyed more to revelry than reverence. At ten- to fifteen-foot intervals, the klanspeople filed past the small cross, igniting their torches in its flames. They encircled the still-dark cross, stopped, started, touched their firebrands to the ground, then raised them in salute—all at Reusch's stern commands. *"Maaaarch!"* *"Halt!"* *"Riiight face!"* *"Lower!"* *"Raise!"* The orders were repeated like the stanzas of an interminable song. Torchlight distorted the red, green, white, black colors of their robes, as the obedient figures circled the towering cross. Then, on command, they marched forward and laid their smoky flares at its base. Flames leaped skyward, up the kerosene-soaked burlap, and the air was filled with crackles and sparks. Sleepy grownups and children, some clinging to their mothers, closed in on the circle to watch. They stood silent and still, their eyes wide, reflecting and rising with the flames. Before them, the little group of robed klanspeople continued to march around and around as if mesmerized until Reusch, satisfied, barked, *"Halt! Return to the speaker's platform!"* In the background, the recording spun to a slow ending, *". . . I will cling to the old rugged cross and exchange it some day for a crown."*

The night smelled of burning burlap and kerosene, and the sparks sputtered and popped. Gradually, the flames tamed, licking gently at the cross, and the sparks floated away, into the dark. Men and women began dismantling the platform and the concession stand. They unwrapped the striped bed sheets, loosened the bolts, and folded the railings. Across the way, women packed hotdog buns and emptied coffee grounds. Cars and pickups raced their engines, and, shortly, we, too, were in the Buick, bumping over the dirt road to the exit. Behind us, the cross had dwindled to glowing coals, and the platform was a pile of pipes.

Back at the motel, Reusch and Jack Prins brought ice and a bottle of whiskey to my room. It was past midnight, yet Reusch's reddening eyes were the only indication of his around-the-clock Klan marathon. He was ready, eager to "kluck"—as he and other klansmen call it—another twenty-four hours. He poured drinks and sat back, rattling the ice in his glass as he contemplated the blacks and the Jews.

"It was never taught in my home. I learned this by experience an' thangs that I've seen in the past," Reusch reflected. "I went into the bigger cities an' I seen most of the problems. I seen non-Caucasians bein' flocked into the major cities. They were bringin' an environment to the Caucasian section where they had no environment. People couldn't walk the streets no longer without bein' attacked, raped, mugged, robbed. An' I talked to the people an' they were affected by it an' just one thang accumulated into another an' I was a man of action, a man of ideas, idealism, principles, basically this is what life is."

Prins wrinkled his brow as he listened, he and his tape recorder taking in every word as though Reusch were a great philosopher and Prins his disciple. The Canadian smiled and silently applauded at times and later joined the conversation, which soon dissolved into racial ramblings—almost a rerun of the rally without the cross.

"Every man seeks the truth for what he's lookin' for. Some men are seekin' money. Some are seekin' freedom. Ever'body has a goal in life. I imagine I picked my goal in the political field from my racial ancestry an' my Christian faith. So I took a positive stand. I seen an openin' an' that was the Klan. I didn't learn *all* my ideas from the Klan. I learned from other sources an' brought it back to the Klan an' taught it. From that point, it grew an' I got involved with the D.A.R.—Daughters of the American Revolution—differ'nt other right-wing groups."

"D.A.R.?" I asked.

"Yeah, D.A.R. That's where I consumed all my knowledge," he said, then shifted back to the Klan. "It was organized in Ohio and then it fell an' I picked it back up again. Reorganized it. In nineteen sixty-nine, when Venable appointed me, when I become Grand Dragon. We have one of the best unbreakable Klan organizations in the country. Better than three thousand members in Ohio. An' buildin' faaast."

In the twenties, Ohio was perhaps the largest state in the Invisible Empire, with an estimated membership of four hundred thousand. Columbus and Akron each had a reported fifty thousand members. Politically, the Klan won impressive victories: Its supported mayors were elected in Toledo, Akron, Columbus, Hamilton, Marion, Elyria, Newark, and at least five smaller cities. The mayor of Youngstown actually belonged to the Klan, as did his law director, Clyde W. Osborn, who became the state's first Grand Dragon. In spite of its success at the polls, the Klan did not always fare so well. The Knights of the Flaming Circle was organized to oppose the Klan in some of the smaller towns. Within the Klan's own ranks, bickering over money eventually led to rival factions. A later Ohio Grand Dragon, James A. Colescott, climbed to the Imperial Wizardship in the late thirties, but even he came to a bad end when word leaked of a tie between some klansmen and the German-American Bund and when the U.S. Internal Revenue Service filed a lien against the Klan for more than $685,000 in back taxes. "Maybe," Colescott grumbled when he hung up his hood, "the government can make something out of the Klan—I never could."

But, now, Reusch was optimistic about Ohio and the rest of his "empire."

"How many states are you in?" I asked.

Reusch mentally counted, then answered, "Roughly eighteen. Venable only had twelve or thirteen. I have expanded and expanded fast. I never thought I'd be in the position of bein' the leader myself. I really didn't want the job. Because if any man, from what I seen, faces the responsibility of that office, of Imperial Wizard, he has a job to do and it's a *hard* job, because you're dealin' with *hard* customers, *hard* problems, *hard* issues, an' you gotta deliver *hard* answers."

Reusch sat back and let the aura of bigness surround him and grow as we continued on to his nomination by the Klan, first for president, then vice president.

"We've had three presidents," he boasted. "Harding, Coolidge, McKinley."

His own presidency could have been the American people's salvation if he could have gathered the money and the votes to be elected, he said, dejected. But he admitted, "All it was, to be honest, was a smokescreen." Momentarily, his eyes and his voice grew sad, like those of a boy disqualified from the Soap Box Derby; then he jerked up in his chair and brightened. "But through that smokescreen came a spark! A spark in the night! That spark may roar into a very biiig fire," he ended dramatically, pausing long enough to ponder his chances in the West Virginia primary, the only one he would enter. "I'd say it's fifty-fifty."

I asked about the stories that Harry Truman had joined and then resigned, and Reusch sneered. "Truman submitted his application in Independence, Missouri, an' they rejected him."

"Why?"

"He was just a cheap politician," he answered.

"Somebody said Johnson was a member, but he triggered the House Un-American Activities Committee investigation of the Klan in the sixties, didn't he?" I asked, still not versed enough in Klan history to know that both LBJ and his father were antagonistic to the Invisible Empire, especially after a wealthy Texas klansman refused to allow the younger Johnson to marry his daughter.

"Yeah, he started the investigation," Reusch answered, and then leaned over to confide: "His wife is Jewish."

The word Jew excited Prins. "Lady Bird is translated 'Fogle' and 'Fogle' is a real Jewish name."

"I didn't know 'Fogle' was her name," I puzzled.

" 'Lady Bird,' " Prins corrected me.

"But 'Lady Bird' was only a nickname."

Prins was adamant, his Dutch accent growing heavier. " 'Lady Bird' was reeeally 'Fogle.' I don't know where we got the information she was Jewish . . ."

Reusch came to his rescue. "National States Rights Party. They exposed it. An' Eisenhower, they called him the *Swedish* Jew. Not a German Jew. Swedish Jew."

"That's worse," Prins moaned. "They gave me the name . . . the way he changed his name." He strained mentally but couldn't remember.

The two men became engrossed in a game of oneupmanship. "Roosevelt was a Jew," Reusch said. "It was *Rosenfelt!*" To which Prins added, "Yes, and his wife was a member of about thirty Communist front parties."

"They're the ones that allowed the Communists in the Pentagon," Reusch noted. "Dexter White, Alger Hiss . . ."

Prins interrupted, "Dexter White, his name is 'Weiss'. He's a Jew."

"All Jews!" Reusch exclaimed.

"All changed their names," Prins railed.

Slouched back in his chair, Reusch echoed the scratchy recording played at the rally. "We're not anti-Jew. We're pro-Christian." And then he unwound the Klan's version of racial evolution: "The Jews own the nigger. The nigger is the tool that destroys the society that we live in. So who owns the nigger but the Jew. He's destroyin' himself. Trotsky said, 'We'll drown the American Negro in his own blood!' "

Prins interrupted, "And what was Trotsky's name? 'Bronstein.' "

"Who formed Communism, the Manifesto?" Reusch resumed the quiz. "Who brought Social Security? Karl Marx."

"His name was Moses Mordecai Levy," Prins shot back.

Reusch swallowed some whiskey, leaned forward, and asked my religion. I was puzzled but answered "Protestant."

"Why do you say Protestant?" he pressed.

"The definition or the origin of Protestant is that it was a protest against the Catholic Church, against Catholicism," I answered.

Both men sighed, but Prins was the first to comment. "We all hate about Martin Luther. He found it was the Jews, and it was too late to rectify it. He walked out of the Catholic Church and started the Protestant movement and afterwards he regretted it, because, he said, 'Well, that's what the Jews wanted, the bastards!' He said, 'They wanted to deevide the Church and deevide and deevide and so control everything'."

In the midst of Prins' tirade, Reusch began opening and closing my dresser drawers. "Where's your Bible?" he finally asked. I pointed to the top of the television set. He thumbed through the Bible again and again, and Prins asked what he was trying to find.

"Revelations."

"Oh, yeah, the famous Revelations. It's very hard to look for," Prins consoled him.

Reusch cleared his throat and reminded me he was not a preacher. The Gideon resting in his right palm, his elbow on one knee, he read first, "Revelations second, nine," then flipped the pages. "O.K., heeere, we go. Saint John eight, verse forty-four: 'And the lust of your father, ye will do. He was a murderer from the beginnin' an' abominant not in the truth because there is no truth *in* him. When he speaketh a lie, he speaketh of his own, for he is a liar and the father of it'."

Prins asked, "That's what Jesus Christ said to the Jews, wasn't it?"

"That's right," Reusch said. "It's here in red."

"What about the man who was Grand Dragon in New York and killed himself after the story that he was a Jew ran in *The New York Times?* Did you know him?" I asked.

"Burros? No," Reusch shook his head. "All I knew was he committed suicide. Three bullet holes. Bad case of suicide. That's what they said, though."

"You think somebody else killed him?"

Reusch shrugged. "Don't know. But the state ruled suicide. He tried to kill himself once an' didn't succeed an' he pulled the trigger again. He was killed at Roy Frankhouser's house, the former Grand Dragon of Pennsylvania."

On the subject of blacks, Reusch was adamant that they were not equal to a white man and never would be. "The only way he'd become equal more so to a white man is interbreeding," he insisted.

"Some klansmen think that black people ought to go back to Africa or live apart," I started.

"It'd cost too much to send thirty, thirty-five million blacks back," Reusch interrupted.

Prins, on the edge of his chair, excitedly suggested, "What about they build their own boat?"

Reusch answered seriously, "I don't think they could engineer it. Ingenuity could not hold."

"That's what I mean!" Prins exclaimed, grinning. "It's very cruel to say, I guess, but that's what I like to see. Let 'em build their own boats!"

Sipping his whiskey, Reusch considered the suggestion before the subject changed. I asked about bickering, about fights like the one at the rally, if it happened often and how he handled it, and Reusch said, with an air of responsibility, "You seen me deal with it tonight. First of all, you've got to reason with people. An' through reasonin', you pacify it. You reach the nerve center of their true feelin'. Sometimes it plays out to be very successful. People make accusations that's under strain. The woman that was makin' all this is in very poor health. Lack of blood to the brain. Only expected maybe to live a couple of months or maybe three months."

"Sometimes," Prins interrupted admiringly, "I think, Mr. Roooosh, you should have some kind of psychiatric degree."

Reusch looked at my empty glass and encouraged me to "Drink up! You're lookin' good!" He poured another round and jokingly confessed that he had envisioned me, from our phone conversations, as looking like Jayne Mansfield. "Why, Mister Roooooosh," Prins exclaimed, "that's a side of you I never knew!" They laughed. Then there was a knock at the door, and the conversation grew to include Bill Miller, Bob, the security guard, and another man from the rally. Gray light was beginning to show though the curtains . . .

Later that morning, at checkout time in the motel lobby, I asked Reusch what kind of vice president he would make.

"Depends on how much power I'd have," he speculated. He gave me a photocopy of the news accounts of his filing for the West Virginia primary, with his platform printed on the back. "I'd probably clean the administration out. An' I would only keep an' appoint people that are basically of my philosophy, my Christian idealism, my racial brothers. But through this re-alter ever'thang: foreign policy, policies within the government itself an' establish Christian laws. White culture, stuff like that."

His staff wouldn't *have* to be klansmen, but they'd have to share the Klan philosophy, he said.

I asked about his future political plans. His eyes rolled up toward the acoustical tile and back to mine. "Welllll, if it's in the stars, there may be another political party. Perhaps, perhaps it'd be called the New Frontier. I've thought some about it, but I haven't given depth thought. But it'd be based on the white Caucasian culture."

Suddenly, Reusch bubbled as he envisioned himself in the purple robe and peaked hat, sharing the platform at Madison Square Garden with George Wallace and Teddy Kennedy and maybe even Robert Byrd, standing before the banner-toting delegates and expounding his views to the Democratic convention and the television public. It was as though he were envisioning his 103,861 to 61,594 victory over "Rolling Ray" Rollinson in the West Virginia primary, a victory that would earn him headlines but not a seat at the convention.

He and the Canadians were back in the dusty Buick now, ready to head home.

"There's a very strong undercurrent in America that the people are not aware of," he said softly, leaning out the car window. "And it's comin'! It's *strong!*"

"The Klan?" I asked.

And Reusch just whispered, "People."

3
Signs of the Times

Route 70, rural North Carolina

Only half the sign was left: a robed man on horseback and wordless letters against a blood-red background robbed of its boldness by the elements. Even now, wind and rain hovered to the west, darkening the sign and the sky and all beneath it. Until earlier high winds ripped it apart, the billboard had proclaimed: THIS IS KLAN COUNTRY.

The remnant was a faded reminder of a time, in the midsixties, when North Carolina was referred to as "Klansville, U.S.A." It was a time of sit-ins and soul-searching, when—at the hands of a former lightning-rod salesman—the Hooded Empire's state population exploded from seven to more than seven thousand; klansmen were elected to town and county offices; and klavern records were knowingly kept in at least one sheriff's safe. Similar billboards, encouraging motorists to JOIN & SUPPORT UNITED KLANS OF AMERICA INC., became as commonplace as Chamber of Commerce and Rotary Club greetings. Each year, the Klan paid five dollars per sign for a state permit to advertise like Coca-Cola and Philip Morris. Tourists gaped and pulled to the side of the road to take snapshots. Even newspapers, wire services, and television took notice of the signs' more controversial moments: When a disabled veteran countered with his own billboard defining KKK as KOOKS KROOKS AND KOWARDS, when one sign survived an attack by ax-swinging black protestors, and when the Goldsboro Klavern, in an effort to improve its image, staged a dismantling for *The New York Times* and then promptly put the sign back up.

Now most of the billboards had disappeared from the highways, along with the Klan's followers and their constantly moving Grand Dragon. There was a sign farther up Route 70, next to the Smithfield city limits; another, outside Goldsboro on 117 north, and this ravaged one, southeast of Raleigh, near Princeton. What was left of it stood next to a white frame house. At the right were crop planters, a tractor, a man guiding a power mower around grape trellises and cabbages, and a boy and girl pulling weeds. Beyond, young corn and tobacco plants were pushing through the soggy earth that the man's father and his father's father had plowed and planted and picked. A cottage for field hands was vacant. *Good help, reliable help, was hard to come by.* And the weather-frayed sign occupied a one-by-seventeen-foot strip of the land, leased by the Klan for a dollar a year with a written promise of immortality: the billboard would remain even if the man should die.

He looked like any other working man, in his late forties, with trim gray hair and sun-browned arms. But inside his house a white satin robe hung in a closet, for he attended klavern meetings with weekly regularity, just as he and his family went to the Baptist church. "People think klansmen are the lowest white people there are," he drawled. "But I'm as good as anyone else." He hadn't joined because of the race problem. Most people don't, he insisted. The Klan has changed. The Klan is a benevolent society. A good society. A neighborly group whose members help one another, even those who don't belong.

A family of blacks sat on a porch directly across the road. Several black families dwelled hereabouts now, their lives and their land touching and not touching the man and his. "We get along fine, but we don't socialize," he said softly. "That's where I draw the line." The black family kept to one side of the road, and the klansman and his wife and children and the sign stayed on the other. Sometimes, when the black children came home from college or from New York or Washington or Chicago or California, their friends came, too, and the friends crossed the road to look at the sign. But the man didn't run them off anymore.

"It's good publicity," he said.

And so, while the man mowed and his children weeded, the blacks sat on their porch across the highway, some in chairs, some on the steps, and looked at the sign—or what was left of it.

4

Bob Jones:
The Tattooed Dragon

Granite Quarry, North Carolina

The maze of roads led through the red dirt and corn and Queen Anne's lace to a green concrete-block house. Out front were a yard lamp with a weathered shingle lettered "The Dragon's Den" and a dying rosebush. The house, its cluster of neighbors, and the pine trees that shaded them stood out on the land, flat with only the summer's crop peeking through. The sign set the green house apart—the sign, three weather vanes, and lightning rods evenly spaced along the roof. Since my earlier visit, a pickup truck with JONES LIGHTNING ROD PROTECTION SERVICE and a telephone number on the doors had pulled into the carport.

J. Robertson Jones, who had been shielded behind a screen door, stepped into view, a miniature poodle and a Chinese pug playfully jumping at his ankles. Now nearly forty-seven and a grandfather, he was a shadow of the once blustery Klan leader who breathed verbal fire from flatbed trucks during the sixties. Gray hair was outgrowing the black, his stomach swelled over his belt, and he had, that same morning, been diagnosed as having high blood pressure. Bob Jones patted his stomach and chuckled, "That's middle-age spread. Jus' gettin' old."

Outwardly, he resembled neither the dynamic leader whom North Carolinians by the thousands looked upon as the godfather of white supremacy nor the charlatan the news media and congressional investigators accused of bilking his members through an assortment of levies and sales pitches. He seemed more "good ol' boy" than bad, this son of a poor railroad worker, who for ten years had lived beyond his means and dreams, perhaps off the scraped-together dues and fees of his own kind, his own people. He had collected their Green Stamps for an airplane, owned a brand-new Cadillac, built the green house, and drawn three hundred dollars a week—more than some of his followers earned in a month—in salaries for himself and his wife.

Now neither Grand Dragon nor a member of United Klans of America, Jones was back to selling lightning rods. But his life still revolved around the Klan, or his memories of it: meeting with the governor, being interviewed by national magazines and on television, even serving almost ten months in federal prison for refusing to give Klan records to the HUAC. A custom-made green robe, with blue piping and a dragon silk-embroidered across the front, hung in his master-bedroom closet, and the green house was as cluttered as his mind with Klan souvenirs.

Earlier that day in May 1976, Jones's mother-in-law had invited me in for iced tea. She had lived with her son-in-law and daughter nine years, since her husband died and the Joneses built the green house. Knotted and gnarled by arthritis, her left side paralyzed from brain surgery and a stroke, Muddy Bryan hobbled from room to room, pointing out mementos: a foot-high cross of glued-together matchsticks; a ceramic cuckoo clock with a red inscription: UNIT 4—KKKK—U.K.A.; expensively framed photographs of Jones and flaming crosses. An almost life-size color portrait of Jones in the elaborate robe dominated the master bedroom, and on Sybil Jones' makeup table, next to her cosmetics, were bronze praying hands and the photo of another cross. In the living room, card tables full of silver platters and goblets—from a party the night before celebrating the Jones' twenty-fifth wedding anniversary—temporarily overwhelmed random snapshots of the former Grand Dragon leading robed "walks" and motorcades and posing in the robe.

Muddy Bryan nodded toward an arrangement of red and white carnations. "Those are from Pete Young. You know him? Used to work on a TV station. Him an' Bob are close friends." She limped out of the room, returned with a manila envelope of photographs, which she spread on the kitchen table. The top eight-by-ten close-up pictured a corpse, laid out in a red satin Kleagle's robe, in a casket.

"That's Grady Mars. He shot himself," she explained, proceeding as casually as she would through a family album past a snapshot of Sybil Jones—in white robe, high heels, and pearl earrings—on a speaker's platform, some of Jones, and, finally, to a group of men in street clothes in front of the green house. She singled out Pete Young and lingered over another snapshot or two before returning them to the envelope.

As we talked, Muddy Bryan carved a turkey carcass left over from the party. She was a pleasant woman in spite of her stooped, shriveled appearance and occasional witchlike cackle. Neither she nor her husband had belonged to the Klan. "Most people think I did, because I was always at all the rallies, an' I never told 'em no diff'rent. Was none of their business." She leaned across the bowl of cut-up turkey. "You know, there are some of all kinds in the Klan, an' it's not for us to judge."

Neatly kept and furnished, the house had both a formal living room and pine-paneled den. But, as in many rural homes, life centered around the kitchen and its round table. A bottle of bourbon under the sink and a coffeepot on the stove stood ready for any occasion. Here decisions were made, crises dealt with, special occasions celebrated, friends and family entertained. Here, in the sixties, klansmen had wrestled with the rise of the black man, Bobby Shelton had held court, and Jones had been given a hero's send-off to the Federal Correctional Institute in Danbury, Connecticut.

Late one afternoon in March 1969 before Jones left for prison, neighbors and klanspeople gathered at the round table—some to offer moral support, others to share lessons learned from their own stay behind bars. As night approached, the Reverend Will Campbell brought out his guitar and sang and strummed and talk-sang about blacks and whites and ill-fated lovers. An earthy Baptist preacher, with degrees from Yale, Tulane, and Wake Forest, a far-flung congregation of klansmen, Muslims, and backwoods whites and blacks, and a somewhat unorthodox approach to ministering, he had flown in from Tennessee to see his friend off. The young and the old—even Muddy Bryan—sang and hummed and tapped their toes along with the reverend. His last song was, he told the group, "The whole New Testament boiled into one," adding seriously, "Now, we gotta take communion on this song, so ever'body get a drink in their hand." The adults scrambled for the bottle under the sink and stood with filled glasses as the reverend sang. Ending with a chord, he raised his eyes toward the ceiling. "Much obliged, Jesus, much obliged," he said. "Those who believe Jesus Christ is Lord, let them say *Hallelujah* and drink to His victory." The reverend laid down his guitar, shouted *Hallelujah!*, and emptied his water glass of bourbon. The sturdier klansfolk followed. And the kitchen and the house and the night echoed *Hallelujah!*

An automatic coffee maker had replaced the old percolator. Jones filled two cups and joined me at the table. He insisted he had nothing to say. Everything was public record. I could read the clips. I preferred that he reminisce, I explained, about his and the Klan's heydays in North Carolina. Even as he said no, I couldn't tape-record, he seemed to be sorting through his mental notes as though they were his most valuable possession.

"I still get ten calls a month, about 'When are you and the Klan goin' to do somethin' about this or that?' " he bragged, although finding him had led me in a frustrating series of circles and dead-ends, with little help from his one-time followers. "Jones?" they would hem and haw. "Naw, couldn't rightly say what become of 'im." But Jones seemed unaware of the collective case of amnesia.

"I don't regret a thing of the ten years I gave ·'em," he said, increasingly willing to talk. "When the organization's run the way it was meant to be, it's an excellent benevolent, fraternal order."

"So what's wrong?" I asked.

"Bobby Shelton. He's only in it to grab all the money. He wouldn't do *anything* if he had to do it without money. To my knowledge, he hasn't been a dues-payin' member of the Klan since nineteen seventy-one. An' he didn't even have a unit in his home town, in Tuscaloosa!"

"What about now?"

"I don't know, but I'd risk a hundred dollars on it!" he wagered.

The critical outburst contrasted with Jones' past attitude toward Shelton. When the Imperial Wizard left Birmingham with federal marshals February 14, 1969, for the drive to the Texarkana prison where he was to serve time for contempt of Congress, Jones had yelled, "Take care, son." Then, turning to the onlookers, he had grumbled, "This is a heck of a thing to do to a patriot like him." From time to time, there had been minor rumblings between the Imperial Wizard and his top Grand Dragon: once Shelton stepped on Jones's turf and allowed several North Carolina klaverns to forego sending rally collections to state headquarters; another time, Shelton launched a "purification program" to weed out informers and Jones told the UKA emissary to "take that lie box and go back to Alabama." But the final split produced neither headlines nor a public explanation.

Now, when I asked about their feud, Jones took a ballpoint pen from a kitchen drawer and read the inscription aloud: "U-K-A National Convention—Catawba County—Salisbury, North Carolina—June twenty-seventh and twenty-eighth, nineteen-seventy."

"What happened?" I pressed.

Jones hedged, "I could tell ya, but I ain't. But that's when it started." He plopped into his chair and shook his head. "I don't know what happened when he was in jail, but somethin' did because he wasn't the same cat came out that went in."

I expressed surprise that Jones had never become Imperial Wizard and asked if Shelton considered him a threat?

He brightened. "Definitely. A bunch a' delegates wanted me to run in sixty-five an' I stayed up all night, talkin' 'em out of it. And in nineteen seventy-one, he was *sure* I was gonna run *and he* stayed up all night an' all day politickin'. They allotted two hours for the Imperial Wizard election, and someone nominated *him* an' someone nominated *me,* and I immediately declined an' threw off the whole schedule."

Jones had been exposed to the Klan since boyhood. His father, a railroad worker with eight children, was a klansman in the twenties; his mother had belonged to the Ladies Auxiliary. "I can't help the way I think," Jones once told a reporter, "I was brought up that way." He himself had joined the U.S. Klans in 1954, rising to Grand Night-Hawk before he quit the organization put together in Atlanta by Eldon Edwards shortly after the Supreme Court's school desegregation decision. Edwards, a General Motors paint sprayer, had built his group around the remains of the late Dr. Samuel Green's Association of Georgia Klans. An Atlanta obstetrician, Doc Green had been a klansmen since the early twenties, eventually becoming Grand Dragon of Georgia and, finally, James Colescott's right-hand man. He formed his Association out of the pieces left by Colescott and the IRS in 1944, not limiting it to Georgia. During his reign, Doc Green, small, with a misleadingly mild appearance, rallied the support of young West Virginia politician Robert Byrd, helped elect Herman Talmadge governor of Georgia, spoke before an applauding South Carolina legislature, saw the Klan added to the attorney general's list of subversive organizations, and withstood attacks by Drew Pearson, Walter Winchell, and "Superman." When he died in 1949, his following—badly splintering along the way—passed first to Sam Roper, a former Atlanta policeman and head of the Georgia Bureau of Investigation, then to Eldon Edwards. The latter's death, in August 1960, set off a power scramble that eased—for a time—when several splinter groups merged into the still-dominant UKA with Robert Shelton at the helm.

From Reconstruction days to the present, the Klan's history in North Carolina was no less fragmented, its following rarely expanding beyond the Piedmont area northwest of Raleigh and the southeastern shore. In the twenties, State Superior Court Judge Henry A. Grady was "Colonel" Simmons' prized Grand Dragon. Many considered him heir to the Wizardry until Hiram Evans, a Texas dentist, and his backers maneuvered the "Colonel" into "retirement." The judge and Imperial headquarters then had their own fracas: first, over Grady's dismissal—against Evans' wishes—of the Grand Klaliff; next, over Klan-backed bills pending before the legislature. One forbade miscegenation, another punished derogatory remarks by Catholics, and a third banned the Knights of Columbus. Judge Grady refused to back the bills, pointing out that miscegenation was already against the law. The others, he said, were "silly, unseemly, and unconstitutional." Imperial Wizard Evans dispatched a flowery letter of dismissal. Grady replied, in essence, "You can't fire me, I quit," and released their correspondence to the press.

Although the Klan never evacuated the Tarheel State, its profile stayed low until the summer of 1950 when Tom Hamilton, a sporty wholesale grocer from Atlanta and a graduate of Doc Green's Association, arrived at the North-South Carolina border in a flurry of motorcades and cross burnings. He began hustling members, aided by William Morris, head of the Federated Ku Klux Klan of Alabama, and Bill Hendrix of the Original Southern Klans Inc. The three formed a loose alliance called the Northern and Southern Knights of the Ku Klux Klan and struck out to right the public's moral wrongs, with Hamilton working both sides of the Carolina border. Floggings and kidnappings thrived for almost two years in spite of efforts by sheriffs, the governors of both Carolinas, and two Pulitzer Prize-winning editorial campaigns. Hamilton's boast—"the Klan was too powerful to be stopped"—seemed to be accurate. Occasionally, the flamboyant Grand Dragon was arrested for carrying a battery-operated cross on his car—a violation, police charged, of the state's cross-burning law—and once he was fined a thousand dollars for mailing a defamatory postcard. But that was as close as law enforcement could get to him until 1952 when his klansmen dragged a man and a woman out of bed and took them across the state line, making the flogging a federal offense. That case and some equally gruesome beatings finally ended in the convictions of sixty-three klansmen, including Grand Dragon Hamilton, who drew four years at hard labor. After Hamilton, unimpressive Klan leaders paraded through the Carolinas almost unnoticed until a cold January night in 1958 when armed and whooping Lumbee Indians routed followers of James "Catfish" Cole—a former carnival pitchman, patent-medicine salesman, and Freewill Baptist minister—from a rally near Maxton, North Carolina. Then the Klan scene quieted until Bob Jones and the sixties came along.

Jones glowed as he unfolded for me the story of his own rise in the Hooded Empire. It had started the summer of 1963 as he and six of his morning-coffee regulars watched the courts eating away at rights once reserved for whites, *for them*. "We talked about it and talked about it," he remembered, "and we finally decided that to do anything at all, we were going to have to hook up with United Klans." So he contacted Shelton, the seven were initiated, and Jones was named temporary Grand Dragon that July.

"I was *elected* Grand Dragon August seventeenth, nineteen sixty-three," he said, as if it were his birth date. "Held my first rally that

August thirty-first, about three miles from here. There was about twelve thousand people. An' the papers played it big *and* kicked me around. Hell! they never said anythang nice about me," he digressed, then, smiling, returned to the rally. "That's about as scared as I been in my whole life, that night. Three-quarters of the people I knew by their first name an' they knew me, but none of 'em ever heard me make a speech, *because I'd never made one!*"

"How'd it go?"

Jones chuckled, "I guess okay. Once I got up there, I didn't have time to be scared." Tapping a cigarette from one of the three to four packs he smokes each day, he explained his later success on the podium. "I don't make speeches. I talk. If you got three years in grammar school or three years in college, you can understand."

A tenth-grade dropout, he quickly informed me that he had completed high school and two years of college correspondence courses in the navy. Furthermore, upon entering the Danbury Correctional Institute, he had made a perfect score on his prison math exam.

Getting up from the table, Jones disappeared into the master bedroom and returned with a green satin robe, a replica—except for gold instead of blue piping—of the one in the portrait. "I wore out a dozen of these things," he said, with boyish pride. "They're expensive, and hot!" This robe was neither faded nor worn from its tour of duty with the former Grand Dragon, who had shuttled from trouble spot to trouble spot, setting up klaverns. Jones admired the robe as he remembered those first days of organizing. "Unit one was in Salisbury. Unit two was in Monroe. Three, Gold Hill. Four, in Williamston." He recited his klaverns—from Salisbury through Winston-Salem—like a schoolchild reciting state capitals. "That was my first ten units. An' I had them *by* October nineteen sixty-three." He looked out the kitchen window, past a decal of a cross. "I knew ever' klansman by his first name and his dog's name. When we went to the hearings, in sixty-five, the House Committee said I had a hundred ninety-three men's units."

"Was that accurate?" I interrupted. "How many *did* you have?"

He glared. "I went to jail for not tellin' *them* that!"

Within his first year, the *Charlotte Observer* figured, Jones had two to three thousand hard-core members. By 1967, the HUAC conceded he had at least seventy-five hundred members and was still moving ahead. Some Klan watchers estimated the numbers grew to ten, maybe even fourteen, thousand. Jones would neither confirm nor deny the guesses, concentrating instead on his nonstop travels, more than a hundred thousand miles each year. "I run day and night, night and day. Went without sleepin' and eatin'."

I was reminded of a story told by an editor friend. In his version, Jones and his wife would drive up and down the highways in the Cadillac, hand-tooled gun holsters inside the doors, visiting truck stops. The couple would order coffee, and Jones would read the paper. "God awmighty, honey," he would bellow, "the niggers are takin' over ever'thang!" Then he would glance around the café, and someone usually would agree across the tables, "You're a hundred percent riiight about that!" or, "Man, you *know* what you're talkin' about!" Whereupon, Jones would introduce himself, collect the sympathizer's ten-dollar initiation fee, and head for the next truck stop.

Bob Jones grinned. "I was well-known in ever' truck stop in the state. One truck company gave out two applications to new employees: one to go to work and the other for the Klan. The company had three employes that weren't members of the Klan. One was black, and two were Catholics!"

Giving in to the restless energy that had kept him moving in the sixties, Jones motioned for me to follow him outside to a small green building attached to the carport. Its two rooms, like the house, were overtaken by Klan clutter: leaflets, stickers, color-postcard reproductions of the master-bedroom portrait of Jones in the fancy robe. He picked up a paperback volume from the HUAC's 1965 hearings on the Ku Klux Klan and spotted the name of an FBI agent. "He'd been to so damn many Klan meetin's, I thought he was a member," Jones chuckled, skipping through the book to his own testimony. Except for stating his name, it consisted of taking the Fifth, First, Fourth, and Fourteenth Amendments, even in response to Committee Chairman Edwin E. Willis's request to, please, speak into the mike.

For two days, chief HUAC investigator Donald T. Appell prodded Jones about Klan finances and suspected violence, about hefty deposits made to both the UKA account and his own, and about a list of suggested harassment that included "mad dogs," "itching powder," "sugar and molasses," and a reminder that "harassing should always have a humorous twist and be in the nature of Halloween pranks to obscure the deadly seriousness behind the work." Jones countered each question with the same answer, read from a prepared card, "I respectfully decline to answer," and an enumeration of the four amendments.

The investigation and hearings were not the first time Congress delved into the Klan. In 1871, Grand Wizard Nathan Bedford Forrest was questioned; and, in 1921, "Colonel" William Joseph Simmons took the stand. The 1965 probe was called for by President Lyndon B. Johnson and Georgia Congressman Charles L. Weltner after klansmen were accused of gunning down civil rights worker Viola Liuzzo near Selma,

Alabama, and riddling the previous summer and the Deep South with violence. The hearings ended with the House voting to cite Shelton, Jones, and five other leaders for contempt of Congress for their refusal to release Klan records. The seven were indicted by a federal grand jury, tried before U.S. District Judge John J. Sirica, and found guilty by a jury that included three blacks. The verdict was appealed all the way to the Supreme Court and rejected. Ironically, the appeal brief cited as a precedent for *not* releasing the records a case Justice Thurgood Marshall, as an NAACP attorney, had fought and won before the high court, a case that involved the refusal of NAACP officers to turn over membership lists to Alabama authorities. Along the way, charges were dropped against Marshall Kornegay, the Virginia Grand Dragon, and two North Carolinians, Robert Hudgins, the Imperial Kligrapp, and "the Reverend" George Dorsett, Imperial Kludd. Georgia Dragon Calvin Craig, who had since left the Klan, got off with a thousand-dollar fine, leaving only Shelton, Jones, and South Carolina Dragon Robert Scoggin to pay the fine and sit out a year in prison.

Still leafing through the book, Jones charged, "Craig sold us down the damn river's the reason he didn't go. He agreed to go to work for the Model Cities, which was a hundred-'n-eighty-degree turn from his stand before."

"Sold you down the river?"

"Yeah. Same guy came to see me. From the Justice Department. I ran him out. I told him *I* wasn't for sale in nineteen sixty-five, and I wasn't then, like Kornegay an' Hudgins an' Dorsett an' Craig."

Kornegay had died six months ago, Jones said, adding that *he* kicked out Hudgins and Dorsett in 1967, about the time Dorsett and "Catfish" Cole formed their own Confederate Knights of the Ku Klux Klan (with the help of the FBI, as it later developed). Jones, however, insisted that Dorsett wasn't an informer before the hearings. But I had read in early accounts that the two men were constantly at odds. In spite of his combined roles as Imperial Kludd, security guard, chaplain, Titan, and paid organizer, Dorsett craved more power, insiders said. They speculated that Jones tolerated the natty chaplain because of the following he had collected by moving, over the years, from Klan to Klan. At one point, Dorsett was sent to Florida to organize for United Klans—and to get him out of Jones's hair. But he soon returned, and the breach widened. Shortly after Dorsett's banishment, twenty of Jones's security guards, in gray storm-trooper uniforms and helmets, chased him from a rally site. "There are a hundred people here who would kill you!" one of the guards shouted as they rocked his Cadillac convertible. The sometimes housepainter, sometimes preacher, and occasional ambulance driver reached inside his jacket, and another guard yelled, "You put that up or I'll kill you right now!" Dorsett gunned the car's engine and roared away under a hail of rocks. When his role as a paid informer was made public in 1975 by the U.S. Senate Intelligence Committee, he was again "banished forever"—this time by the North Carolina Knights of the Ku Klux Klan, into which he had drifted.

At the time of the hearings, Jones had been as free with his brash comments to the press as he was with taking the Fifth. Now, however, he was almost nostalgic as he skimmed through his and Bobby Shelton's testimony and that of Grady Mars, who committed suicide a month after the committee questioned him about Klan finances.

Moving across the room to some dusty glasses and figurines, Jones picked up a lithograph of Abraham Lincoln and his family. "This is somethin' I'm proud of," he said. "It hung in the White House 'til about nineteen twenty-three. A friend gave it to me." Then, nodding toward two gilded busts of the Civil War president, he observed, "He was a good man. We wouldn't 've had any problems. I don't believe in slavery, but he an' I had the same idea, to ship 'em back to Africa."

On the podium, Jones had ranted about Jews and Communists and LBJ, but he had fueled the Klan fires with the black push for equality. He had been known to growl from flatbed trucks, "There ain't *no* nigger in this country good as me!" and to burst into restaurants, demanding loudly, "Do you serve niggers?" Sometimes his racial rampages were seasoned with tasteless humor, as when Martin Luther King, Jr., died. "Lord God," he told a rally crowd, "I didn't know you could assassinate a nigger. I always thought you just killed 'em." He quit ushering at the Lutheran church the day he was told to seat blacks.

"My feelin's haven't changed a bit," he said firmly. Yet he boasted that he had "a bunch" of black friends; even his prison caseworker was a Negro. "In my lifetime, I haven't—to my knowledge—done anythang to hurt anyone, black or white. I treat 'em like a human, but I don't socialize and I *don't* invite 'em to my home." He hesitated, then corrected himself. He *had* invited two blacks to the anniversary party, but they hadn't come—one, a Black Muslim who, he said, had saved his life in prison; the other, the first black FBI agent in North Carolina. "I'd known him since he was little, 'n *I* got him the job."

Jones picked up a brochure, showing me an article about his stay in prison. "James Mayberry, that was my black caseworker," he recalled. "First time I met Mayberry, he came in an' asked, 'What do you want to do?' I said, 'Be in charge of those twenty-two Jews and that nigger that burned their draft cards.' "

Jones laughed.

"You call them 'niggers'?" I asked.

"Sure, I say 'nigger.' You say 'pine tree,' don't you?" he said, nodding toward the trees outside.

Returning to the kitchen, we talked about Jones's unsuccessful run for a seat in the state House of Representatives in 1974, a defeat not nearly so crushing as when he came in last with sixty-six votes in his 1963 bid for the Granite Quarry Board of Aldermen. Sybil Jones had done somewhat better, placing third in a four-way race for Rowan County Clerk in 1966.

"You going to run again?" I asked Jones.

"Naw," he shrugged, "I offered my services. They didn't want them. So the hell with 'em!"

As Grand Dragon, Jones freely, and often triumphantly, swung his political weight. He was on the winning side in the 1964 gubernatorial elections, coming out publicly for former Superior Court Judge Dan K. Moore, who was slow to disavow the backing. In 1966, his home county, Rowan, elected two avowed klansmen: John Stirewalt, as sheriff, and Exalted Cyclops James Wayne Davis, as register of deeds. The new sheriff dutifully hung up his hood but later stirred up a political storm by naming Jones a special deputy and then, in the furor, rescinding the appointment. In New Hanover County, Marion W. Millis won re-election as sheriff after having admitted to the HUAC that he and six of his deputies had joined "to keep an eye" on the Klan and stored klavern records in his safe.

The afternoon was quiet except for the brief scrape of the match as Jones lit a fresh cigarette. I asked if he had a bodyguard. The question evoked a stream of mental reruns of intrigue and adventure, of guns and highway chases. "Most of the time," he said. "My board of directors said, 'Have one,' so I had one. I went through five or six. For ten years or better—with the exception of when I was in jail—I was never more than fifty feet from a gun. Most of the time *a lot* closer. Fifty feet on the outside."

"You ever been shot at?"

"On several occasions," he answered heroically. "There's been ten or a dozen threats on my life."

"By whom?"

"When folks shoot at me," he snapped, "I don't stop to get their names and addresses!"

Watching the cigarette smoke disappear into the sunlight, Jones reviewed the threats, the confrontations, the quarrels. "I was tough," he bragged. "T-U-F-F. Still am. Tough as nails. I been killed twice. Once in nineteen fifty-four and again in nineteen fifty-seven. Got hit in the face with three tons of steel in fifty-four and had a hundred and nineteen stitches *just* on my face." He leaned over to show me the scar that meandered down his forehead. "I was on a construction site, laid a brick, turned around, an' got hit! Then in fifty-seven, I was travelin'—sellin' lightnin' rods—and hit a bridge an' broke my neck in two places, fourth and fifth vertebrae." That accident temporarily paralyzed his left side, leaving him with a limp and a hand that wouldn't bend. But, he emphasized, he was still "T-U-F-F."

Klan violence? Jones scoffed. That ended with Reconstruction in his opinion. "You can't build an organization with the kinda people who would cause violence. Oh, some of 'em thought when they joined, they had license to go tear up somebody's head, an' I wouldn't put up with it." Or, as he bluntly put it to a newsman in the sixties, "I don't want to go to jail for killin' no damn sorry nigger."

Even the FBI and other law enforcement officers never considered the North Carolina Klan, in spite of its size, as violent as its Deep South counterparts. "Here," observed writer Dwayne Walls, "it was a money game. As long as Jones was in control, he deliberately held down the violence. He wouldn't tolerate it. It would have upset his nice little money game. And also the Klan was so heavily infested with informers, he knew he couldn't get by with it." In a special report in the sixties, Walls noted that almost any meeting of ten klansmen included one informer, either from a law enforcement agency or a private group such as the ADL of B'nai B'rith. At one meeting, at least three informers were present, none aware of the others' role.

Nevertheless, there *was* violence, some acts more serious than others: a cross burned in front of the governor's mansion; an attempt to set fire to a black church being painted in Elm City by out-of-state civil rights workers; three dynamitings near a civil rights rally in New Bern; the bombing of four black homes in Charlotte, and a two-county spree of burnings and bombings and shootings into black homes. In some cases, klansmen were arrested; in others, there was suspicion but not enough evidence. Then while Jones was incarcerated, came the Swan Quarter shoot-out between black and white demonstrators. It ended with the arrests of seventeen klansmen, including acting Grand Dragon Joe Bryant and the Reverend James Spears of Alabama, UKA's current Imperial Kludd.

Although the violence intimidated some members who viewed the Klan as a fraternal organization, almost a religion, something to *belong* to, others thirsted for more action, just as some of their leaders craved money.

The *Salisbury Post* estimated the North Carolina Klan took in $125,000 during 1966 from its share of dues and initiation fees, robe-making profits, raffles, rally collections, "special" funds, and insurance deals. With that report and disclosures during the HUAC hearings, the rank and file became increasingly curious as to where the money was going and equally reluctant to give. A memo from the eight-man "car committee," urging members to come forth with their share of the monthly notes on Jones's 1964 Cadillac, ended with this reprimand: "Gentlemen, we as brothers have no room in this tremendous fight for white survival for these petty quarrels. We know that some have not been pleased with the purchase, but they have been few in number, thank God."

The Widows Benevolent Fund, five dollars to join, guaranteed each member's beneficiary $999.95, the money to be raised at the time of death by collecting a dollar apiece from other fund members. When the "business" ran afoul of state insurance law, $5,824 was unaccounted for. Jones was rumored to have made $20,000 off the operation. Before it folded, however, two klansmen took the Klan for a $999.95 ride by enrolling a fictitious member and, after a respectable amount of time, "killing him off" and collecting their benefits. Other intra-Klan swindles were less ingenious. One treasurer simply walked off with the $4,000 in his klavern bank account.

"Yeah," Jones now admitted touchily, "there was a hassle over money. But if anybody can get rich on twenty-five cents a month (the state's slice of the dues), I'd like to see it. Not when you're payin' a thousand dollars a week in salaries."

Without bothering to knock, a beefy young man named Bobby, in a night watchman's uniform, strolled into the kitchen and tossed the afternoon paper on the table. It was opened to a photograph of Sybil and Bob Jones at the anniversary party.

"Made the society page," he ribbed the Dragon.

"Mr. and Mrs. J. Robertson Jones of Mehaffey Drive celebrated . . ." While Jones read, Bobby dropped a bundle of flower-seed packets on the table, and Jones reluctantly put aside the newspaper to sort through them. Flowers and gardening were a hobby, he explained, pointing outside to an iris bed, azaleas, and a hothouse out back.

"And the rosebush?" I ventured.

He and Bobby exchanged sheepish glances. "Wish you hadn't brought that up," Jones said. "That's a *sore* subject. It'd been doin' good, and then we decided to move it last week while Sybil was at work. Now it's dyin' an' she's all upset."

He looked at his watch. "It's about time for the War Department to be comin' home," he joked, signaling an end to the interview. "You know, she's the best female segregation speaker in the United States, bar none. Sounds just like Lurleen Wallace."

As we walked to my car, he invited me to visit the next time I was in the area. Suddenly, he stopped. "If you see Shelton," he snarled, "you ask him this, ask him how could he possibly put Craig back in the Klan in any capacity after what he did to us!"

I drove along the blacktop and gravel roads to Route 52 and pulled into a gas station. In the office, slumped in a straight chair, a bony black man was drinking an R.C. His graying head would tilt back for a long, leisurely guzzle, then droop forward again, his eyes aimlessly focused on the floor. Back and forth, slowly, rhythmically.

"You know Robert Jones?" I asked, entering while the old man's head was tilted, the bottle to his mouth. He raised his head and eyed me suspiciously.

"You mean *Bob* Jones?" he asked warily.

I nodded.

"Yeah, I know 'im." The old man drained the R.C. and sat, his body sagging with the heat, his eyes no longer meeting mine. A fly buzzed his head. He swatted, missed, and slumped forward again. His forearms rested on his knees, his hands—one clutching the empty bottle—dangled between them. The office was quiet except for the fly.

"What do you think of him?"

Like a turtle's venturing out of its shell, his head came upright. He looked me up and down.

"I'm writing a book about the Klan," I explained.

Again, the cautious look. "He's a very nice man."

The conversation seemed ended. But I tried again. "I just met Mister Jones. Spent the afternoon talking with him."

". . . very nice man. He's a very nice man." The old man gave me another cautious appraisal. Gradually, his hesitancy gave way. "First, I didn't know who *he was,* 'til somebody tol' me," he said. " 'N now I run into him quite often, down at the Dairy Bar, at breakfast. He calls me 'George,' an' I call him 'Mister Jones,' since I learned who he was. He never gave me no problems. I don't know nobody he give any personal problems to. He say he's a Ku Klux Klan, but I don't see much diff'rence. He jus' like any other person, to me. Or he seem that way. He never was violent that I knowed anythang about. But I know a lotta talk about 'im."

Sitting straight as the chair now, he continued. "They say, 'He's *head* of the klansmen,' stuff like that. There's a whole lot worse klansmen than *he* is."

The old man had lived in Rockwell almost forty years and had known Jones twelve of them. "He built hisself a house over there off Gold Knob Road, an' a lotta colored people he'ped him build it. So you *know* if he been violent like, an' if he been against colored people, they wouldn't 've did this.

"That's right, that's right," he muttered, his head bouncing slowly.

A lanky boy, the old man's teenage son, had entered the office and leaned against the Coke machine, listening.

"Tell 'er," the boy prompted his father, "tell 'er about the time you he'ped build that cross over there for a rally 'n you didn't know what it was."

The boy giggled, and the old man glared at him, then turned to me. "*I* didn't tell you that. Like I say, I seem to think Mister Jones is a very nice man."

From Granite Quarry to Salisbury—Jones's birthplace—to Charlotte is almost an hour's drive. At the motel, I found a message from the Reverend Will Campbell, who was passing through on a trip for the Committee of Southern Churchmen. We had met earlier in a long-distance conversation during which he had agreed to an interview when I got to Nashville. Now he invited me to join him and the Joneses for a belated anniversary dinner. Could I bring my tape recorder tonight? I asked. "Naw," he said, "you just come on. We're gonna relax an' have a good time."

A slight man in his fifties, with longish hair that drooped from a bald dome, Campbell looked as if he had stepped off a movie set. He wore a tan Western-cut suit and rococo-tooled cowboy boots. On the dresser in his motel room, next to a guitar case, was a wide-brimmed black hat that, as one writer had observed, gave him the appearance of "a fugitive from a Mormon wagon train." He was shopping at a nearby liquor store when I arrived but returned in time to greet the former Grand Dragon and his wife as if they were family. The three had been introduced in 1964 by a Raleigh TV newsman, who, like Campbell, had already befriended the Black Muslims and hoped to start a "storefront" ministry for klanspeople. The introduction had evolved into a friendship that endured the HUAC hearings, Jones's time in prison, the wedding of his only child, Sheila, and the funeral for the newsman's wife and child— with klansmen carrying one side of the casket, Black Muslims, the other.

The friendship with Jones was not Campbell's first encounter with the Hooded Order. As a small boy in Mississippi, he had watched a silent procession of robed men interrupt a Sunday-morning church service to place a large Bible and money at the pulpit. Then, as an adult, he had participated in the Civil Rights Movement and in 1957 escorted the first black children past the jeering mobs into Little Rock's desegregated schools. But over the years, he had come to regret that he and many liberals, in their efforts to help blacks, had replaced "niggers" with "rednecks."

Now as he mixed drinks, Campbell kidded Jones about scaring the priest who conducted the funeral. The Grand Dragon had pointed to the steeple and announced, "That's what I do," meaning he installed lightning rods.

"I don't know if the priest thought you burned churches or crosses or what," Campbell chuckled. "An' you know, a Baptist church *was* burned down a while after that."

Jones jokingly blurted, "I wasn't there!" and everyone laughed except Sybil Jones. A slender woman with sharp features and black hair, she sat stiffly through most of the bantering until the discussion turned to Mike, the Joneses' eight-month-old grandson. Then she opened her wallet and passed the latest snapshot around the group, which included two young couples invited by Campbell.

During the Klan decade, many considered Sybil Jones the brains behind the operation. She headed the Salisbury Ladies Auxiliary, handled the state books for a hundred dollars a week, kept the organization going while her husband was in prison, and was a willing, able speaker. But tonight, it wasn't until we were in the car, driving to the barbecue roadhouse on the outskirts of Charlotte, that she loosened up, talking in her Alabama drawl about the nursery school she operated and joining her husband in swapping news of Klan acquaintances with Will Campbell.

In the restaurant, no one took notice of the Grand Dragon. We ate our spareribs, paid the check, and left without a raised eyebrow.

Back at the motel, Campbell opened the case his guitar shared with a change of underwear, clean socks, and a tube of toothpaste and removed a hunk of cedar. He closed his eyes, sniffing the sweet wood, and with a pocket knife carved off a sliver, which he placed between his teeth. Then, drink in hand, he sat down to tune the guitar. The rest of us sat on the floor, in chairs, on the bed, waiting as he tightened and tuned.

"Play some Jim Reeves," Sybil Jones requested. "He's my favorite." She was relaxed now, in stocking feet, her back resting against the headboard, her legs stretched across the bed.

Sometimes Will Campbell gazed at the strings, but mostly his eyes moved from face to face around the room as though he were reading music. His fingers and the strings were seldom still as he mixed his own favorites with special requests, some he had composed, some by others, the heroes and victims of the songs both blacks and whites. Bob Jones sipped his Scotch and ginger ale, patted his toe, and smiled.

" 'Mississippi Magic'," someone requested. "Play 'Mississippi Magic,'

Will." Campbell slipped his fingers across the strings, and twanged a
ballad he had written.

> On that I-Central Railroad, riding way on up the track,
> Met a doll in Chicago;
> Said, "I ain't never going back."
> She say, "Where you from, Sport, Miss'sippi?"
> Say, "Yea, that's right. Miss'sippi."
> She say, "Why ain't you going back?" Say,
> "You like the blacks or the Kluxers?"
> I say, "I like the blacks and the Kluxers."
> She say, "What are you, some kind of va radical?"
> Say, "No, doll. I ain't no radical." Say,
> I just like everybody. And the blacks and the Kluxers is somebody."

Bodies swaying, feet pumping, the two couples joined Campbell on
the chorus.

> That Mississippi Magic, is Mississippi madness now.
> Whites don't like black people.
> Black don't like white nohow.*

Still strumming, Campbell explained he had written the next song on
his way back to Nashville after seeing Jones off to prison. "You never
heard this one," he told the Grand Dragon, winking at Sybil. "She an'
Sheila was all tore up. I don't know why." *Strum.*

"I was nervous as hell," Jones chuckled. "I'd never been inside no jail
before." Everyone laughed, and Will Campbell sang:

> . . . Bust Ole Rap for going armed,
> Just in case he meant us harm,
> We can't have this trouble on our streets.
> Lock 'em up—black or white—Beelzebub,
> Wrong is right, but it ain't flesh and blood,
> It's powers . . .
> Haul away the Ku Klux Klan,
> This time for sure we've got our man
> To put an end to all this hate for good.
> Lock him in big ol' jail
> Wife and baby weep and wail,

* Copyright 1969 United Artists Music Co., Inc.

But it ain't flesh and blood, it's powers.
And who'll be next to go?
It may be me, it may be you,
Draft resisters, Junior League,
Left-wing, Right-wing, picture man, or Jew
When they need someone to blame.
But it ain't flesh and blood,
It's powers.
And principalities, it's powers.
And who'll be next to go?

After a summer in the Deep South, I stopped by the green house again. The late-afternoon sun against the screen door hid the interior. Dialogue from a TV movie drifted into the carport.

"C'mon in," Jones's voice called.

In the dim paneled den, he was slouched in a rocker, barefoot and shirtless, his chest and arms a tattooed paisley. Sybil Jones lounged on a vinyl sofa, alternately watching the movie, reading the Sunday paper and napping.

"Forgot you were comin'," Jones apologized.

As we moved into the kitchen, to the round table, he was full of questions about my travels—where I had gone, the rallies I attended, the people I had met. "You seen Calvin Craig in Atlanta?" he asked. I said I had and that Craig was running for commissioner in his county.

"Wish I was down there."

"Why?"

"So I could vote against him! He sold us down the river's the reason *he* didn't go to prison. An' Shelton, you saw him?"

I nodded.

"Did he say 'confisicate' for you?" Jones chuckled, mimicking Shelton's four-syllable pronunciation. "Did Shelton say 'confisicate'?" The chuckle became a boisterous laugh that gradually mellowed into a smile of reminiscence—when he had laughed *with* Shelton, not *at* him; when they had shared the spotlight and the podium, ridiculing niggers and Jews and LBJ and, occasionally, the National Council of Churches. He became quiet as he inwardly relived those days of large crowds, towering crosses, fancy cars, big headlines, the glory of being *the J. Robertson Jones, Grand Dragon of North Carolina* rather than Bob Jones who sold lightning rods or awnings or laid bricks or worked as a security guard, which had become his occupation since my last visit.

When Jones returned from prison in January 1970, his "empire" had been reduced to no more than six hundred members. George Dorsett had formed the Confederate Knights of the Ku Klux Klan in the

Greensboro area; Woodrow Lynch, the Ancient Order, Invisible Knights of the Ku Klux Klan, in Shelby; and Joe Bryant and a group that burned their UKA membership cards while Jones was in Danbury made the split permanent by forming the North Carolina Knights of the Ku Klux Klan. Other members, intimidated by the increasing FBI infiltration and disgruntled about finances, had dropped out completely.

The revolt by Bryant, Grand Dragon in Jones's absence, had grown out of a feud between him and Shelton's prison replacement, Melvin Sexton of Alabama, over money and the hiring of an attorney for the Swan Quarter shoot-out. Initially, Bryant hoped Jones, too, would abandon UKA and head the dissidents. But Sybil Jones publicly sided with Sexton, and when Jones returned, he and Bryant exchanged insults and parted. In 1956, the stubby owner of "Dr. Bryant's Health Clinic" in Charlotte and his brother Arthur had attempted to form a Klan that folded with their arrests on mail charges. Although found not guilty on those charges the brothers already had police records: Arthur, for larceny and passing a bad check; Joe, for rape when he was fifteen and, as an adult, for soliciting for prostitution.

"His *own* members threw Bryant out," Jones sneered with obvious satisfaction. "Virgil Griffin, a fella in Mount Holly, heads the group now."

Sunlight from the kitchen window transformed Jones's tattooed torso into a fleshy comic strip, with renderings of "Maggie" and "Jiggs" circling his nipples. His chest, back, and arms were scrawled with an assortment of figures and proverbs and words collected, probably, during his naval tour of the China Sea.

Slowly, he ground a cigarette into an ashtray until the fire was out and the butt was twisted and bent, staring at it a while before reaching for another. "It got to lookin' like the more problems we had in this country—an' God knows we got a bunch!—the more complacent the people got. And Bobby an' I were at odds, an' it got tougher an' tougher." He looked up. "I *tried* to resign in February nineteen seventy-three, an' they wouldn't let me."

He hesitated, drawing circles on the tablecloth with the unburnt end of the match, as though telling the story was both satisfying and agonizing. "So I called a meetin' for the twenty-first of October in Wilson. Gaveled the meetin' to order, asked the chaplain to lead us in prayer, resigned, an' walked out. *And* I haven't been back since, an' I don't have any time set to *go back!*"

He ended abruptly, inhaled, and let the smoke float out peacefully. I pressed again, hoping that he was ready to talk about his falling out with Shelton. But he would repeat only the date—when the feud started, in 1970—and mutter vague hints.

"Shelton wasn't doin' the job right. He wasn't *always* right, but he was *always* boss. I couldn't get along with him, so I got out." He also complained that Shelton passed near the green house several times while he was still Grand Dragon but never called nor stopped by. Jones didn't miss the Klan, he assured me, yet he would probably rejoin if Shelton were out. "But not as long as Calvin Craig is in."

The sun was resting behind the distant trees now. And, like the day, Jones grew tranquil as he turned to better times, the days before many of his followers switched their allegiance to George Wallace. "I guess my favorite rally was the one in Municipal Auditorium, 'cause they couldn't tell no lies about it. We had more people *outside than inside.* I don't remember how many seats there were, but we had more than that outside. So we'd crawl out on the ledge an' talk outside when we finished speakin' inside. There was Bobby Shelton, Calvin Craig—the seven cited for contempt of Congress was who was there."

He paused. "That an' the one the *Raleigh News and Observer* gave me credit for having *three times* more people than Hubert Humphrey. That was probably the biggest rally ever held in the state of North Carolina. An' durin' the summer of nineteen sixty-five, I held rallies *ninety-three* days runnin'. That's the most consecutive rallies without gettin' rained out, to my knowledge, in the history of the country!"

When I asked the reason for so many rallies, he shrugged, "They just needed 'em," and began reciting his other "records."

"Yeah, I guess I 'bout set all the records in the Klan, an' they haven't been broken *yet.* Because I was Grand Dragon the *longest.* I held the *biggest* rally that's ever been held in the United States. Burnt the *biggest* cross that's ever been burnt in the United States. I didn't burn it," he corrected himself, "but it was burnt in North Carolina on *my* rally site—a hundred sixteen feet. Had the biggest clandestine organization in the United States in this century!"

He looked into the empty cigarette pack, crumpled it, and threw the wad onto the middle of the round kitchen table.

"Nope," he said brightly, "I don't know anythang I wouldn't do again."

5

At the Filling Station

Mount Holly, North Carolina

The man, well past retirement age, squirted the windshield of my MGB, alternately glancing through the glass at me and back at the numbers whirring on the gas pump.

"You know Virgil Griffin?" I called to him.

His brown-speckled hand interrupted its circular sweeps. He stood back and cocked his head. "How's that?"

"Virgil Griffin, you know him?"

Sliding off his billed cap, the old man scratched through his gray hair and rested his hand there a moment. He shook his head. "Naw. Don't think I do. You look 'im up in the telephone book?"

I nodded. "But I couldn't find him. He's Grand Dragon of the North Carolina Knights of the Ku Klux Klan, and I was told *anyone* in Mount Holly could tell me how to find him."

The old man gave the windshield a final rub before tossing the paper towel into a trash barrel. Not much taller than my car, he pulled himself to full height and stepped closer.

"Can't say as I ever heered of 'im, but *I* useta belong to that, years ago."

"You did?" I marveled.

His face crinkled into a grin. "Sure did!"

"Did you like belonging?"

"It was a good org'nization when it was run right. But, wellll, they were *niggers* back in them days, you know, an' the Klan durn near beat some of 'em to death."

The gas pump clicked off. The old man rested the nozzle in its cradle and hurried back to the car window. He had lived all his life in North Carolina, in and around Mount Holly, mostly. Just off Interstate 85, between Charlotte and the South Carolina line, it was a peaceful town of screened porches, St. Augustine lawns, sprawling oaks, and a sprinkling of hardware stores, pharmacies, and churches. Even at midday, the lights that dangled above Main Street seemed more like leftover Christmas decorations than traffic signals. But the old man's eyes blazed with memories of youthful nightriding and adventure in the twenties.

"I didn't go out with 'em too much. I worked for the railroad, an' didn't have time." He chuckled. "I could've gotten fired if they knewed!" His voice full of intrigue, he leaned close to the car. "An' you weren't supposed to know who the leaders was. Jus' the few men you was with. You'd hang your clothes in a locker and put on your hood an' mask, so nobody'd know who you was."

"Really?"

He nodded.

"Joined agin, four or five years ago, but I wasn't supposed to," he confessed like a mischievous child about to be scolded. "I was in law enforcement at the time, see."

But the Klan hadn't been the same then as in the twenties?

"No siree," the old man shook his head, grinning. "They pretty near beat them niggers to death. They was *rough* back in them days, the Klan was."

6

Robert Scoggin:
Inside the Klavern

Spartanburg, South Carolina

Bob Scoggin led the way as we climbed the cheaply carpeted steps. Glare slivered through cracks. Otherwise, the darkened garage was filled with shadows and hazy forms until a door at the top of the stairway opened, casting a rectangular light over dusty pipes and wrenches and a well-worn green robe.

"You ever been in a Klan den?" Scoggin called back.

"No," I answered.

At the doorway, he stepped aside and swept his arm in a dramatic introduction. *"This,"* he boomed, "is our meetin' place, *and* the state offices of South Carolina, riiight here!"

The room was large, covering the two-car garage below. But for all the Klan's boasts of Imperial Palaces and Empires, the "meetin' place" lived up to neither my fantasies nor the diagram and requirements in the ritualistic Kloran: a den must be furnished with an altar, a Bible opened to chapter 12 of Romans, an American flag, an unsheathed sword, a container of water, and a cross, in a layout similar to that of a Masonic lodge. I saw no altar, no Bible, nor most of the prerequisites for a klavern. A four-foot cross—studded with red light bulbs—and American and Confederate flags were all but hidden by a coffee maker, a printing press, reams of leaflets and flyers, odds-'n'-ends furniture, and a sales display of pocket knives and jewelry embellished with Klan insignias. The walls were taped and tacked with snapshots, official proclamations, letters, and pictures of George Wallace, Robert E. Lee, the blood-drop emblem and the night rider on the steed, rendered in charcoal, pencil, pastels, oils, water colors, even sequins. Over the coffee maker and powdered creamer, a large sign proclaimed:

> Black may be beautiful
> And tan may be grand

But white is still the color of
The BIG BOSS MAN

The overall effect was more messy than mysterious. It was difficult to envision klansmen here, in full regalia, following the "sacred"—and secret—Kloran instructions to face the Exalted Cyclops, or E.C., and give "Tsotf-c," then "Tsoc-1," then "raise Tsos," and then "Tsok-c," and, as the E.C. responded with "Tsok-c," "recover."

Behind the cross and flanked by the flags, a battered desk occupied the position designated in the Kloran as the E.C.'s station. And in the middle of the room, a kitchen table was surrounded by Scoggin's wife, another middle-aged woman, and a young couple, all drinking coffee. After the Grand Dragon introduced them, he turned to a lanky man comfortably molded into a vinyl chair. "An' this here's Mister McCorkle, the Grand Dragon of Missouri! Him an' these folks jus' drove in for *the Conference of Eastern Dragons* in Greenville tomorrow an' Sunday."

Tall and spare, Albert McCorkle slowly unfolded, until, with a boost from cowboy boots, he towered more than six feet, his long legs narrowed by jeans. He was bland looking, his face pale and plain, his head bald except for a ring of dust-colored hair. He spoke in a low, sliding drawl about his farm, north of Joplin, where he raised cattle, hogs, and a few crops. He and his companions had arrived by camper shortly before my visit. The women's eyes still roved about the room, but the young man, his face masked by a curly mustache and goatee, fixed his gaze on me like a double-barreled shotgun.

"This gal's writin' a book on me!" Scoggin bragged, moving toward the desk. Once South Carolina's unrivaled Dragon, he had changed little from the grim-faced man often overshadowed in the sixties by his then Imperial Wizard, Robert Shelton, and more gregarious counterpart, Bob Jones. Thin, with caved-in cheeks and chest, his wavy hair was slightly grayer, but his chin still jutted stubbornly, his eyes were untamed, and his mouth was a drooping slit. His hands, dirty as his crusted boots, had rings on most fingers: three from the Masonic Order, one with a gold blood-drop on a red stone, a sweetheart ring, and an elaborate two-headed dragon with jade eyes and teeth, fashioned, he said, for the Grand Dragon of South Carolina in 1899 and now fitted to size with adhesive tape.

Sitting in a chair of vintage equal to the desk's, Scoggin sifted through a chaotic archive of papers and magazines: *The American Rifleman,* one headlined "Martin Luther King: The Myth of the Century," another "Business Opportunities for Everyone." He picked up the May 1976 issue of the National States Rights Party's tabloid, *The Thunderbolt.*

"You read this, about Jimmy Carter an' Jack Kennedy?" he surveyed his audience.

No one had.

"Well, it says right here, they are *illegitimate brothers!*" Scoggin announced, showing off grinning head shots of the late and future presidents. "It *says,* 'Note physical similarities between the two men. They have the same nose, smile, teeth, heavy bags under the eyes and hair styles'."

Mrs. McCorkle looked smugly at her husband. "I was telling you that, about how much they looked alike!"

"They got the proof," Scoggin assured her, reading an excerpt. " 'It is well-known in the journalistic world that Joseph P. Kennedy was the biggest womanizer of 'em all. In nineteen twenty-three, Lillian Gord— Jimmy Carter's mother—went to work as secretary to Joe Kennedy. Sometime later, she moved back to Georgia, an' on October first, nineteen twenty-four, gave birth to a son—Jimmy Carter. Ever' time he flashes that toothy grin people remark how much he looks like a Kennedy.' That's what it says, riiight here in black an' white!"

Scoggin handed Mrs. McCorkle the paper, then eased back into his swivel chair. His wife tiptoed from the room as he launched into a synopsis of his Klan tenure, from his "naturalization" into U.S. Klans in the fifties, merging with it into UKA in 1961, and, under questionable circumstances, leaving UKA in 1970 and forming his present Invisible Empire, Knights of the Ku Klux Klan, Realm of South Carolina. In U.S. Klans, he had worked his way up from Exalted Cyclops of the "Twenty-One Club"—the cover, or "front," name of his klavern—to Grand Titan. With the formation of UKA, he became both Imperial Kladd and Grand Dragon of the Realm of South Carolina, alias the South Carolina Rescue Service.

His father had participated actively in the Klan, along with rearing ten children and working simultaneously as a farmer, builder, and music teacher in Polk County, North Carolina, just over the state line. The younger Scoggin had joined after returning from the navy.

"I went to the service, an' saw the handwritin' on the wall," he recalled, his voice a patriotic quiver. "Shrapnel hit me, an' I got the Purple Heart. I come back an' I could see my country goin' down hill. I *could see* the advancement of black nationalism an' the discrimination against the whites rather than the blacks. So I got in the fight!"

McCorkle beamed. "I'd have known you anywhere. Never saw you before today, but I'd have known you anywhere." Scoggin nodded "thank you" and continued his saga about being Grand Dragon from 1961 to 1969, part of that time leading both North and South Carolina Klans.

"Only man's ever been Grand Dragon of two states," he said, ignoring or unaware of his predecessors, Thomas Hamilton and James "Catfish" Cole, and their dual roles.

"Did you leave United Klans in sixty-nine?" I asked.

Scoggin bypassed the question. "I was called to Washington for the Klan investigation in sixty-five and sixty-six and was cited for contempt of Congress because we would not reveal the names of the membership. The Supreme Court had already ruled the Communist Party did not have to register its members nor neither did the Black Panthers. So common sense would say *they* shouldn't make a *twice*-recipient of the Purple Heart just because he believes another way."

He sighed like a martyr. "Served three months in LaTuna, Texas, and six more months in Safford, Arizona."

"So why didn't Calvin Craig go?" I pried.

Reluctant to share the spotlight, Scoggin shrugged, "I don't know. Anyway, *we* were the leaders of the three biggest states—North Carolina, South Carolina, Alabama—and accordin' to *inside* information, 'if we send the leaders, *the generals* off, the soldiers will quit.' And it didn't work. The boys an' the girls was all that got out; the men and women didn't. But it was just temporary. They knew they had people that would *die* before they would reveal the secrets of the Klan!"

"How many members did you have when you went to prison?" I asked.

"That," he bristled, "is not *classified* information. That's top secret! Only *I* know how many people are in South Carolina. No other living person does."

"What about units?"

He would not budge. "That would to a degree give you the minimum membership. The fact that we got ten units or a hundred. You've *got* to have twenty-five or more to have a unit, and that would give you an' idea. I wouldn't even tell Mister McCorkle here, close as I may be to him."

At the time of the hearings and his conviction, Scoggin was less than heroic in his comments to the press. "I'll go serve my damn year," he grumbled to one reporter who asked if he would turn over the records and answer subcommittee questions to avoid a contempt citation. "Nobody will get my records because they are in my head, an' I'm so confused I can't remember them!"

While in Washington for pre-sentencing interviews with federal probation officers, Scoggin scoured Capitol Hill seeking help from South Carolina's congressional delegation. After that failed, he asked that he, Shelton, and Jones at least be sent to a Florida prison because he preferred warm weather. As for the self-touted Purple Hearts, a congressional spokesman told the HUAC the Grand Dragon's injuries were suffered when a nearby ship exploded, throwing Scoggin against a bulkhead. The second injury occurred, the spokesman said, in friendly waters when he fell from a gangplank.

Nevertheless, when he returned from prison to a hero-of-sorts welcome Christmas Eve 1969, he limped from the plane in Charlotte, North Carolina, wearing a miniature Purple Heart in his lapel and carrying a red, white, and blue cane. He was met for the drive to Spartanburg by his wife, daughter, sister, and a cluster of klansmen toting a banner: DEDICATED AND LOYAL FRIEND AND LEADER, R. E. (BOB) SCOGGIN. Annoyed by the klansmen's presence, the sister fumed, "He isn't in it now, and with the grace of God, he never will be." But Scoggin, basking in the flash bulbs, told newsmen, "I have just begun to fight! Once a klansman, always a klansman!"

During the HUAC hearings, Chief Investigator Donald T. Appell hammered away at Scoggin's eligibility for full payment as a disabled war veteran, introducing evidence that the Grand Dragon didn't use a cane, was employable, and in 1964 had deposited $15,690 in three bank accounts while reporting income of $574 to the Veterans Administration. Appell also produced numerous checks the Grand Dragon had cashed at cafés and filling stations instead of depositing them in the Klan bank account and inferred that he had never filed an individual federal income tax return.

While McCorkle and the woman gazed admiringly at Scoggin, the young man kept me under surveillance. He crept across the room for a closer look at my tape recorder, my note pad, and me. Occasionally, we engaged in eye-to-eye combat as the Grand Dragon rambled on.

"But when you came back, *did* you remain with UKA?" I finally asked Scoggin.

He looked askance before answering. "No. When I came back, thangs had fallen apart. The Klaliff, which is the vice president, took over temporarily. And by his not knowin' or carin' enough, the Klan fell quite a bit. They'd fallen off, from *many, many* lodges down to not so many."

As he talked, I remembered newspaper versions: Scoggin had been banished by UKA *before* he went to prison, and upon his return, he and his self-picked successor and next-door neighbor, Harry Gilliam, had had a tug of war over the title—and the benefits. During the struggle, UKA obtained a court order restraining Scoggin from using the name "United Klans, South Carolina Realm, Knights of the Ku Klux Klan." The secretary of state refused to charter his newly formed "Invisible Empire, Knights of the Ku Klux Klan, South Carolina Realm" because "the proposed name is a colorable imitation of the name of an incorporated organization previously existing in the state." To retaliate,

Scoggin accused Shelton of trying to make UKA "a dictatorship" and Gilliam of putting "fifth-grade dropouts on the state board." He maintained that his resignation—the day before he was sentenced to prison—was temporary and swore, "If he [Gilliam] doesn't resign, the Klan is dead in South Carolina. I've had groups here since I returned wantin' me to take it back." On the other side of the fence, Gilliam countered, "This phone has been hot with klansmen and other people telling me they don't want Scoggin back. Besides, Scoggin has been ousted for 'unklansmanlike behavior,' and once you're banished, it's impossible to return." As for their friendship, the interim Dragon snickered, "He won't even come out an' say 'hello' to me. I hope he's not afraid of me."

What the two were fighting over was not much: five hundred members, at most, less than a third of Scoggin's pre-HUAC following. In the end, Gilliam won, and Scoggin formed his current Klan. Or, as he told us now, "I visited the ol' units, got 'em back, established new units, an' we went back to the original charter, 'Invisible Empire, Knights of the Ku Klux Klan.' An' that's what most states are today."

"Who's your Imperial Wizard?" I asked.

"There's *not* an Imperial Wizard of the Invisible Empire, Knights of the Ku Klux Klan," he answered.

"Do you have any overall national head?"

Scoggin shook his head. "Jus' the Grand Dragons work together, swappin' ideas, swappin' thangs that will make 'em grow, and what might be holding 'em back. Because until it grows, it could not support a prestigious Imperial office an' pay its bills and have its printin' presses an' all."

By the Klans in each state keeping all their own money, they had already prospered in size and finances. "Allll the literature we put out, we make right over there." Scoggin pointed to the offset press. When I asked how many states formed the loosely affiliated Empire, he boasted that there was a Grand Dragon in every state and two in Florida.

"*Two* in Florida?"

"Yeah. There were two groups, an' they're both good fellas. So they're workin' together to get thangs organized. We're not tied to each other financially," he re-emphasized quickly. "I have no command over Mister McCorkle nor he over me."

Leaning back in the swivel chair, Scoggin speculated that by or before 1980, the Invisible Empire would be able to afford an Imperial Wizard *and* a national staff. He himself was working full time, "driving over a hundred thousand miles a year" to achieve that goal. Although I had read a 1965 clipping that he was becoming a full-time paid employee of UKA, he insisted he wasn't now nor never had been on a Klan payroll.

"I've never drawn *a penny* from the Klan."

"How do you do it?" I puzzled.

Scoggin hesitated, explained he was in the process of setting up a distributorship for insect-fogging machines, but ignored the past.

"So your Klan's growing?" I asked.

"Ever'where," he answered automatically, then backtracked to modesty, "It's *not* mine. *I* don't have any Klan. I'm just Grand Dragon of South Carolina, but I guess a lot of people must say that because I've been in so long, an' aided and assisted all these other states. I've spoken in *thirty-four* states since I've been in the Klan."

"Do you sort of act as spokesman?"

"Welllll, I would say so because of my longevity in the Klan. I am the oldest in the Klan, klanwise, in the United States."

The Missouri delegation sat erect, their respect growing.

"You've been in longer than Mister Shelton?" I asked.

Scoggin smiled.

"And Mister Venable?"

"Mister Venable *says* he joined the Klan forty years ago, but he's not been active, I'd say, six or seven years out of the whole forty. *I've* been active *ever'* day. Twenty-three years and about fifty days!" He paused, then added, "I'm not fightin' him. I'm not fightin' anyone. I've slept in Mister Venable's home! An' in nineteen seventy-two, he wrote me a letter that I have here on file saying, 'Mister Scoggin, I believe you're the only livin' man who can pull this Klan together'."

As for Shelton, Scoggin vowed, "I have no bone to pick with him. We just don't need an Imperial Wizard because we cannot afford it! No, I'm not fightin' anyone!"

Since his "departure" from UKA, Scoggin *had* shown up around the country with his sales items at the rallies of rival leaders, leading some to speculate that he is either a hustler or a government agent. "Robert Scoggin is to the Klan what flies are to a picnic," ridiculed right-wing migrant Jerry Dutton. "They call him the Prophet for Profit, because he's *such* a commercial person." A veteran reporter speculated, "The only reason he's been able to hang on so long is that he's an informer." After the HUAC hearings, even Bob Jones told the press, "He seemed to be reaaal close to those government investigators."

Now Scoggin looked up from shuffling the papers on his desk. "We got a lot more thangs to fight than we did."

"In the sixties, the Klan was mostly against Negroes . . . ," I started.

"No," he reprimanded, "it was *for* whites. I'm *anti* one thang. I'm *anti* anti-American. I'm anti-against 'em. I'm not *anti*-Negro, I'm *pro*-white. An' I'll tell the truth about a Jew and what they're up to. I don't care *who* it is. I even tell them *that*. They can call me anti-Semitic, anti-anythang. They're anti-Christian, so why couldn't I be anti-Semitic, if I wanted to?"

I stopped taking notes. *"What* do you mean, 'What they're up to'?"

The effect of the question was like turning on a long-play recording of the Klan's stand on Jews. Scoggin accused them of owning the Federal Reserve system, monopolizing the media, raising the cost of food because of kosherization, running the NAACP, creating the Klan's violent image, even getting prayer and Bible reading removed from the schools. He harped on the latter so long I asked, "Are you active in church?"

"Absolutely," he said. "I'm Southern Baptist. Right there is my church, across the street. Grace Baptist Church. My oldest brother is professor of theology, Hebrew, and the Old Testament at the South-eastern Theological Seminary in Wake Forest. He taught at the Southern Theological Seminary in Louisville after he finished there. My baby brother is pastor of one of the biggest Baptist churches in Savannah, Georgia. So I'm Baptist *and* I'm active in church!"

"Have you ever taught Sunday school?"

"Yeah, I taught Sunday school, way, way, waaay back," he answered proudly, then returned to the Jews. "You've had thirteen *notorious* spies since World War Two. *Ever'one* but one has been a Jew!"

His brother, the theologian, had been a missionary in Israel and was married to a Jew, so I ventured, "Do you like *any* Jews at all?"

"Even if I did," he sniffed, "I wouldn't say I did. They're the teachers of integration, all of 'em, an' their purpose is to destroy me through miscegenation."

Although some of Scoggin's eight children had attended mixed schools, he said that he didn't like integration in *any* form, forced or voluntary.

"But you had to do it?" I asked.

"I didn't *have* to, I could afford to put 'em in private schools. I *pay for* the public schools, and so they went. I didn't like it at all. I never made a statement that my children would never go to schools with a nigger. You don't know what you'll do when there's a bayonet stickin' in your back. I choose death myself!"

Still, when I asked about violence, Scoggin assured me the Klan had "never, never done all those thangs." And the murders of the three civil rights workers in Mississippi? He scoffed. "The sad part about it is a lot of people think they went to prison for murder an' they were *freed* of murder and sent to prison for conspiring to deprive people of their civil rights!"

I interrupted his tirade. "What are some of the other things? You said the Klan had broadened the number of things it opposes."

"Capital punishment. When they outlawed capital punishment, they made a new law—license to murder," Scoggin complained, gradually working his way back to busing and integration and the Jews.

"What are some reasons *you* joined?" I turned to McCorkle.

"Well, now, we've got into . . . ," he crumpled his brow, then nodded toward the South Carolina Dragon. "He's said so much, there, but I agree with him a hundred percent just exactly the way he said it."

Scoggin eagerly resumed the role of spokesman, proud that women could join alongside their husbands now and hold *five* of the ten klavern offices, the five not including Exalted Cyclops. Catholics could belong to *all*-Catholic units, though no such units currently existed in South Carolina.

After taking a brief phone call, Scoggin announced, "That was Jerry Greene!" When neither the McCorkles nor the young couple showed any sign of recognition, Scoggin explained: "He's runnin' for political office, House of Representatives, in District Thirty-seven. He's lived in New Jersey since forty-eight and's the Grand Dragon. But he's back here now, an' he'll turn it back over to New Jersey Sunday."

Quiet a moment, Scoggin grinned. "This weekend, you'll see more Grand Dragons than's ever been assembled at a public meeting in the history of the Klan, far as I can find out!" His pride passed around the room. Only the young man was unfazed, continuing to peer at me.

"So this is going to be the East Coast Conference of Grand Dragons?" I asked.

"Eastern Dragons, *not* jus' East Coast," Scoggin corrected me. "From Missouri, Illinois, Texas, Louisiana. I expect ten to fifteen . . ."

There was a light knock, the door swung open, and a short, sporty-looking man darted into the room.

"Hey, Jerry Greene!" Scoggin greeted him.

"How ya doin'?" Greene responded, barely altering his pace as he headed for the sales display and began to rummage through the tie tacks.

Scoggin introduced him. "Meet another Dragon here, from Missouri, Mister McCorkle. Jerry Greene from New Jersey, there." Jerry Greene, in bold plaid suit, his hair tonicked in place, shook hands, then resumed sorting through the tie tacks. Deciding on one, he paid Scoggin five dollars, stuck the pin through his tie, and dashed toward the door, apologizing, "I'm runnin' late."

"He was goin' to a political rally," Scoggin explained.

"Have any of his opponents said anything about him being a member of the Klan?" I asked.

"No, not that I know of. Three nigger ministers come over to his house this mornin' and said they're supportin' him because, 'You is shootin' straight with us, them others ain't. You *said* you was in the Klan. We belong to black org'nizations,' and they said, 'We don't care if you belong to the Klan.' "

Scoggin slapped his desk to give validity to the story. "Now *he* didn't ask them niggers for it. No klansman ever has. But when a politician says he don't want the Klan vote or he don't want the nigger vote or he don't want the Chinese vote, he's an unmitigated liar!"

Scoggin was adamant about the Klan's political power in South Carolina. "We have members in the State House, right now!"

"Very many?"

"I'm not gonna say how many," he dodged.

"I said, *'Very many?'* "

He held firm. "Ain't gonna say, whether there's a few, a whole lot or what. *But* we got different klansmen right now representing some counties. When the right time comes, they're goin' to come out an' say they're in the Klan. Then I dare anybody to discharge any of 'em for that reason!"

A similar claim by Scoggin in the press, in sixty-seven, that one of Spartanburg's eleven-man legislative delegation was a klansman, triggered a unanimous chorus of "Me? You're kidding! Not me!" In 1970, when the Grand Dragon announced his support of Erle Morris for lieutenant governor and Henry Mills for comptroller, both were quick to denounce the endorsement. Morris labeled it a "theatrical play obviously to embarrass me." The Klan stayed out of the gubernatorial race. The Democratic candidate was John C. West, who, as a state senator, already had had a run-in with the Klan during the fifties.

Neither campaign was the first time Scoggin and the Klan had caused a political furor in South Carolina. State officials of both parties were aghast when the Grand Dragon showed up in a reserved seat for Barry Goldwater's campaign stop at the Greenville-Spartanburg Airport in 1964. The Klan's biggest political feat, however, was its role in defeating former Governor and Supreme Court Justice James F. Byrnes in his first bid for the U.S. Senate in 1924. Reared a Catholic, the then-veteran congressman was a professed Episcopalian when he ran for the Senate. The day before the election, the Klan distributed a circular praising his youthful Catholicism as an altar boy. He narrowly lost the run-off election.

During the sixties, Scoggin attended the state Republican conventions and was a daily visitor to Goldwater campaign headquarters, but now, he told me, klanspeople were neither Democrats nor Republicans. "They're independent citizens. They vote for who they think is the best for the country. We don't control the vote. Before ever' election, ever' klavern will have a meetin' an' they'll give 'em the facts of who'll be the best for our country, the platform an' this and that, and tell 'em to go vote your convictions." As for endorsement, he said, "We never do it much unless we know positively that he's goin' to win."

There was another knock, and a brawny young man in Levis and boots, with a ten-gallon hat pressed down on his reddish hair, sauntered into the room.

"There come that cowboy Night-Hawk," Scoggin greeted him. The cowboy returned a sparsely toothed smile and flopped into a nearby chair for the rest of the interview.

I began putting away my tape recorder and notebook. "I can't think of anything else . . ."

"Abortion!" Scoggin spoke up. "We haven't talked about abortion. We're absolutely, bitterly opposed to abortion in any form but to save the life of the mother. It's legalized murder an' nuthin' else." He quoted what was, he said, a passage from the Hebrew Talmud prohibiting a Jewish doctor from delivering Gentile and Negro babies, then sneered: "And they're the ones that run the abortion clinics! They won't he'p one *into* the world, but they'll he'p it *out!*"

Turning to McCorkle, still coiled in the chair, I asked how long he had belonged to the Klan.

"Just nearly a year an' a half. We just nearly started in Missouri . . . ," he began, but again Scoggin bulldozed into the conversation.

"There's been a legitimate Klan in Missouri a long, long time, but it come an' go for lack of good leadership. Back in the sixties, we had a Klan in Missouri, but we couldn't git anybody to head it up or we couldn't git the backin' we needed because there wasn't enough of us to scatter around."

His face absent of expression, McCorkle waited out the interruption that grew into another rampage, curtailed only when I turned back to McCorkle and tried again. "You said one of the main reasons you joined was because of your interest in drug addiction?"

"Right, yeah. It's a problem . . ."

"I *think,*" Scoggin put in firmly, "he said it was one of the *main* reasons. It could have been dozens of reasons."

McCorkle looked as helpless as a lost hound dog at a busy intersection. ". . . At the start of it, but then after we got started there was other thangs sprang up too that I didn't realize we was really against."

John Howard, the South Carolina Dragon I first met in West Virginia, craned his neck to look past the second-story roof at the cloud-curtained sky, silently guessing the odds that Bob Scoggin's Conference of Eastern Dragons would be rained out tonight. He and another klansman had driven from nearby Laurens to my Greenville motel for an interview.

Except for occasional outbursts, John Howard treated it like a neighborly visit.

"I say a rally oncet a month, an' the people are satisfied," he said conclusively. "We had a good many rallies last year, but we found out it's too expensive, an' so many riffraff entered the Klan for self-gain.

"Now *Scoggin,*" he emphasized his former leader's name, "believes in rallies *ever'* Saturday and Sunday. An' ever' month, he cleans house. People jis' quit him, 'cause they find him out. An' he jis' *turns* over agin. Somehow or 'nother, the Lord's blessed the man with a gold or silver tongue—either which way you wanta call it—and he can handle people." He stopped temporarily but couldn't resist adding, "He can sit here, an' convince you that he's got a million people in South Car'liner ready to overthrow the U-nited States gover'ment, an' you'd believe him. He's jis' that kind of man."

Rubbing the tips of his cowboy boots, John Howard had second thoughts. "You better not print that. I talked to Dale last night, an' I was tol' not to say anythang detrimental about any Grand Dragon or org'nization." He glanced from James Eddlman, Jr., his bulky companion, to me and chuckled. "I had that klansman over there starin' at me when I was sayin' good thangs about Mister Scoggin." He laughed again nervously.

"I don't like Scoggin, period," Eddlman grunted.

A former Greenville city bus driver, he had introduced himself as a "grand officer." I assumed from his size that meant Grand Night-Hawk, or bodyguard, to the somewhat fragile John Howard, whose mouth probably packed more wallop than his muscles. Eddlman was quiet and humorless, in an out-of-character peach-colored leisure suit and print shirt. He puffed passively on a pipe throughout the Grand Dragon's nonstop march of words. Occasionally, the pipe wheezed, or an opinion rumbled its way up from his guts; otherwise, he settled into the chair like a sack of cement.

At the outset, John Howard was low-key, complimenting this Klan and that leader until he inadvertently let slip his night-before orders from Imperial Wizard Dale Reusch. Thereafter, he freely proceeded from insult to insult, following each with "Don't print that" and a chuckle.

"I've had the opportunity to be in at least four Klans, an' it's been a great honor," he began. But when I asked why he had left each one, he compiled his own Klan blacklist, with charges ranging from "thievery" to "age".

"U-nited Klans wasn't doin' anythang. They were interested in one thang, money. So I entered in with Mister Scoggin, an' we built it up into a good org'nization. One, er, was one of the best."

"Why did you leave Scoggin?"

His voice filled with self-righteousness. "I seen so much mismanagement, mistreatment of klanspeople—and too much drinkin'. You jis' can't have a man up on the platform that can't speak plainly, an' he's havin' to hold onto the microphone to speak."

On the edge of his chair, John Howard confided, "Robert Scoggin is a deadly enemy to the U-nited Klans. I don't know if you'll get Shelton to say somethin' against him, but I'm satisfied you'll git Dean Williams to say a lot!" He laughed raucously, then became serious again, "He was *banished* out of the U-nited Klans, Robert Scoggin was!"

"Why?"

"Drunkenness. Mismanagement of money." He recited what now sounded like Klan ritual, repeated almost verbatim about one klansman or another in many of my interviews.

"Is drinking a problem with a lot of klanspeople?"

"Absolutely. I didn't realize there *were* so many people that drank until I entered the Klan!"

Eddlman came to their group's defense with, "We don't allow that on our rally grounds, whatsoever," before John Howard continued his rundown of Klan leaders. He glossed over Harry Gilliam, Scoggin's prison replacement, and Dean Williams, the current UKA Dragon, and charged Venable with "mismanagement" and "age" before moving on to the one Klan he had yet to be affiliated with, the Association of South Carolina.

"Who's Grand Dragon of that?" I asked.

"That is a secret org'nization. *Their* members don't even know who their Grand Dragon is."

"Isn't that unusual?"

John Howard scrunched his shoulders. "No, that's the way the old Klan originated. They have a Grand Council that rules an' makes decisions for the org'nization."

I had read clips from the sixties about the Association, loosely affiliated at that time with James Venable and described as a descendant of Tom Hamilton's old group. Even then it was more secretive than Scoggin's Klan. The reputed head, Robert E. Hodges, a Columbia postal employee, claimed to be only the secretary and spokesman for the real leader. At rallies, all members wore masks.

Born in Spartanburg and raised in Laurens, John Howard had joined the Klan in the midsixties after watching racial demonstrations on television and had encouraged his wife and mother to become members of the Ladies Auxiliary. "I reached out an' started searchin' fer an org'nization that could do somethin' about the situation, an' I found the Klan," he explained.

As John Howard saw it, the Klan was still the only answer. "Not in a mob violent way," he assured me. "I'm talkin' about through due process of the org'nization, good leadership, notifying the people of the problems, where they can make the changes. The Klan's *not* a handful of vigilantes, or lawbreakers."

"So you're opposed to nightriding?"

"Totally," he said emphatically. "There's nothing accomplished in takin' the law in your own hands, goin' down an' shakin' Ol' Joe up a little bit. It's very childish. I cannot see a grown man participatin' in such as that when we have *such* good laws in our nation, an' good opportunity to put men in office to change these problems that we're havin' with our politicans."

Eddlman's pipe wheezed as Howard launched into a tirade about today's problems: how our freedoms are being taken away by the Supreme Court—"a bunch of outlaws an' ol' buzzards that should be impeached"; how "Hoover's burnin' in hell an' the FBI hasn't killed the Klan yet"; and how, "if Kennedy and Humphrey gits into office, you're goin' to see one of the damnedest messed up nations."

"What about Carter?"

"Carter is a good man. I don't like him. He's a Southerner. I do like that. Far as doin' somethin' good for this nation, he couldn't hurt it."

Sitting back in his chair, John Howard insisted blacks aren't this country's problem. "A lot of our politicians an' a lot of our American people blame it on a race of people, but it's not. It's *all* our faults. It's not a racial problem. It's a problem of the people, an' its goin' to take the people to solve the problems that we're havin' today." He drained a canned soft drink, analyzed the situation, and continued. "Now in my mind, the biggest problem we have is this integration. This busin'. To me, ever' individual should have the freedom to decide."

"Are you saying that if a person wants to go to an integrated school, he should, but if he doesn't, he shouldn't have to and he shouldn't have to be bussed?" I asked, trying to follow his logic.

"Right. Busin's achieving more racial hatred in the minds an' hearts of the white an' black children. The white children resent havin' to set in a school an' listen to the black culture when the majority of it was created out of the fantasy of a lot of white liberal politicians!"

"I'm just totally against blacks, myself," Eddlman grumbled.

Before the two left, I asked John Howard about Klan size. He explained with the frankness of a used-car dealer. "If any man or woman gives you an estimate of the membership in any state or in the nation, they're givin' you a lie. So you might as well be prepared for a lie."

"How does membership now compare with the sixties?"

The pipe wheezed, and John Howard cleared his throat diplomatically. "The Klan is waaaay down. If we had a racial riot here in South Car'liner or in Boston agin or in Louisville, Kentucky, the Klan would grow. Because that's what makes the Klan grow, racial problems. An' it's an insult to me! It's an insult to the Klan!"

His face reddened with indignation. "But klanspeople, that's what they join fer, because of racial problems. An' I say if this is what it's goin' to take to wake up the people an' say, 'Well, dammit, I've got to join somethin,' an' this is what turns 'em to the Klan, where I can git hold of 'em to convert 'em on the belief an' the knowledge of what this Klan really is, I say more power to it! Let 'em riot!"

On the flatbed truck, turned into a speaker's platform for the evening, Bob Scoggin gripped the mike with one hand and with the other grandly waved a small glass orb through the air.

"*And now,* we're gonna auction off the glass eye of the former Grand Dragon of Pennsylvania!" The announcement blared through the crowd, but no one seemed shocked by the latest item up for grabs or that its original owner had turned paid government informer and spy. A few eased forward, but most merely raised their voices or moved to the concession stand as the bidding got under way.

Wearing the faded green robe from the garage, Scoggin started the auction. "Awwwright, somebody said a two-dollar bill! Two dollars! This is the *actual* eye of the past Grand Dragon of Pennsylvania!"

"Three dollars!" someone yelled.

"Three dollars, riiight here!" Scoggin barked. "Cost ol' Roy *three or four hundred,* but you'll git it. . . . Five?" Leaning forward, he cupped his ear and held on to the mike.

"Five dollars!"

"An' the man says five! The man says five!" Scoggin picked up the pace. "He *must've* shook ol' Roy's hand an' *heard* him speak a time or two, 'cause *he was a speaker and a half!* O.K. Here it is, a five-dollar bill *one time!* Five-dollar bill *two times!* Five-dollar bill *three times!*"

Scoggin exchanged the eye for a five-dollar bill, chastising the audience. "An' you Southerners let this glass eye go back to Yankee country! Greaaaat day!"

Walking away from the podium, Earl Schoonmaker, Grand Dragon of New York, showed the brown eye to a few bystanders, then pocketed it.

Roy Frankhouser originally bought the glass eye to replace his own that had been kicked out in 1965 during a Reading, Pennsylvania barroom brawl, reportedly over the Klan. Arrested more than sixty times—on charges ranging from inciting a riot to conducting disorderly Klan rallies—Frankhouser was the product of a bitter custody struggle and three years in a children's home before he began his migration from the American Nazi Party, to the Minutemen, to the National States Rights Party, to the Klan, finally becoming a federal informer. The latter "career" ended when the government arrested him for dealing in stolen dynamite. The charges included selling explosives to the one-time bodyguard of Robert E. Miles, the former UKA Grand Dragon of Michigan, currently imprisoned for conspiracy in the 1971 school-bus bombings in Pontiac. Frankhouser contended he took part in the scheme thinking he was acting as an informant for the U.S. Bureau of Alcohol, Tobacco and Firearms (ATF); the government claimed he acted on his own. In February 1974, he was given five years' probation and a suspended sentence. His somewhat mysterious spy assignment, which hinted of CIA ties, was to infiltrate an alleged Canadian-based Black September plot to kidnap and/or kill some American Zionist leaders. According to the *Philadelphia Inquirer,* that mission was approved by the National Security Council, the White House, and ATF's John Caulfield, who later figured in the Watergate scandal when he tried to persuade burglar James P. McCord to remain silent in return for White House clemency. Frankhouser's turbulent life also has included testifying—or taking the Fifth—before the HUAC and witnessing the suicide, in his Reading apartment, of New York Dragon Daniel Burros.

The winner of the eye, Earl Schoonmaker, was a tall man, anemic in complexion, build, and voice. We had met earlier in the spring when I drove to Pine Bush, New York, to interview him and his outspoken wife. More than a year before, he had been dismissed as a teacher at the Eastern Correctional Facility in Napanoch, New York, because of his position as Grand Dragon in the Independent Northern Klans. The firing had triggered a rash of lawsuits and allegations that New York's prison guards were heavily infiltrated by the Klan. The publicity also had led to an unsuccessful attempt to remove Jan Schoonmaker from her elected position on the local school board. Schoonmaker was still unemployed, and the cases were working their way up in New York's courts.

Wedged between trees and an auto repair shop at the outskirts of Greenville, this rally—like the one in West Virginia—resembled a community fair. Outdated recordings, viciously mimicking "Amos n' Andy" and Lyndon Johnson's "Great Society," barged through the crowd and across the road where onlookers watched from their car hoods. At the highway's edge, robed men with signs and flashlights motioned motorists on to the field, while two patrolmen observed from the nearby repair shop. The cars and campers—many dusty and bug spattered from long drives—pulled onto the rally grounds in parking-lot rows, some within a few feet of the red flatbed truck.

A handmade sign, with a sketch of the night rider and the slogan THE KLAN IN ACTION, stretched across the back of the truck. On its bed were two rows of scarred movie-house chairs, double speakers, a rostrum, and the klavern's small cross. Close by, in a clearing, the unlit oil-blackened cross faded into the gathering darkness. In the glare of lights strung over the truck and a concession stand, a man and a woman were doing a brisk business in Klan-embellished T-shirts, tie clasps, necklaces, and bumper stickers.

The cowboy Night-Hawk, in freshly ironed white shirt, black trousers and a helmet lettered KKKK, strutted through the crowd, issuing orders to other security guards, some of whom wore storm-trooper uniforms with ascots. The lone female guard, young, with a waist-length ponytail, was dressed in all black. Like the cowboy, the guards paraded back and forth, directing traffic and attracting admiring glances.

As I wandered through the crowd, a thin, taut-faced woman with shoulder-length hair invited me to share her car hood. She introduced herself as Patricia Smithers, Queen Kleagle of Texas. "That means I'm in charge of the organization of women in the state of Texas." She dragged on a king-size cigarette. "My husband's the Grand Dragon."

Pat Smithers guessed that two hundred fifty women belonged to the Klan in Vidor, a small community just minutes away from my home town, Beaumont. "We take care of all the fund raisin' for the state of Texas," she boasted. "And we do the snoopin'."

"Snooping?"

"Yeah, we act as detectives. We can find out more than the men can, like when a man is mistreatin' his wife. Thangs like that. Then we pass it on to the men." I asked what the men did with the information, and she shrugged. "They don't tell us."

As we talked, white robes and a scattering of variously faded red and green ones gradually appeared from car trunks and laundry bags. Several men in white cotton robes grouped around Bill Wilkinson, Grand Dragon of Louisiana for his own Invisible Empire since he split with David Duke and the New Orleans-based Knights of the Ku Klux Klan in August 1975.

Eventually, I joined a cluster of green-robed men and introduced myself to Tony LaRicci of Maryland, Wilburn Forman of Illinois, and a tough-looking man who reached out to shake hands.

"Virgil Griffin," he said.

Small but muscular, Griffin had a beakish face and a missing front tooth. He spoke softly, liberally sprinkling his conversation with "ma'am" as he vowed without hesitation to be violent—even to kill—to halt integration. Age thirty-two and a textile worker, he said he belonged to the Klan because of his five children. "I don't want 'em goin' to school with niggers. I don't want 'em gettin' raped or beat by a nigger. That's why I'm in the Klan, to try to stop integration of the schools. Git the white people organized, an' take our schools back from 'em!"

"How would you take them back?" I asked.

"We can do it peacefully if we can git the people organized, an' if not, we can do it violent."

"To what length would you go?"

"Any length."

"Would you kill?"

"If that is necessary. I'd rather kill them than have them kill me!"

"But would you initiate it?"

"No comment."

"But you *would* be violent if you had to?"

His voice was low but positive. "Sure, the niggers are violent. Why not?"

LaRicci, a short wiry man, walked away to join Frances Reed, his combination girl friend and state Klan secretary, but Wilburn Forman stood by like a mummy as Virgil Griffin told me he carried a shotgun and a pistol most of the time. "Ever'body in North Carolina knows who I am. So I carry it for protection."

Starting time was long overdue, but the pre-rally antics stretched into the night in an open-end conglomeration of sales pitches, announcements, jokes, and racial slurs, with Scoggin assuming the role of standup comedian and carnival pitchman. His hand constantly in the audience's pockets, he auctioned off two photographs of Robert E. Lee, autographed by the eleven Dragons, and enticed the crowd to visit the sales table to pick up a T-shirt or Confederate pillowcases or a bumper sticker. Next, sending twenty or so robed klanspeople through the crowd with upturned helmets "for a little donation," he pleaded, "We don't git any Rockyfeller grants. We don't git any Carnegie Foundation grants. There's very few people here that couldn't afford a dollar or two. A dime, even a penny, will buy you an application card. So dig in your pockets. Twenty dollars won't hurt you."

The Missouri delegation leaned against a dusty car, bored and seemingly less taken tonight with the South Carolina Dragon. "He said *eight o'clock,* and it's twenty 'til nine," the young woman complained to Mrs. McCorkle. When the speakers blared another rerun of an "Amos n' Andy" recording, she grimaced. "They played that already!" Mrs. McCorkle seemed equally drained of enthusiasm until a young man, in black trousers and white shirt with epaulets and a leather strap across his chest, swaggered through the cars toward the flatbed truck.

"You know who that is?" she asked me.

"No," I answered, looking from the man's knee-high boots to his black leather Bible.

"That's Buddy Tucker, from Knoxville!" She hurried to the literature table and returned with a tabloid titled *The Battle Ax News*. "You won't like it all. But there's some good stuff too." The masthead identified the tabloid as the official publication of the National Emancipation of Our White Seed and included among its editorial staff—all "pastors"—Tucker and Neuman, Britton of Arkansas, a name I recognized from right-wing skirmishes in the sixties.

The rally's only semblence of an "official" beginning was the invocation by the Reverend Raymond Doerfler, Grand Dragon of Pennsylvania, who thanked God for "returning Sam Bowers," the head of the White Knights of Mississippi, who had just been released after serving six years in prison for "conspiring to injure, threaten, oppress and initimidate" three civil rights workers in Philadelphia, Mississippi. Still with bowed head, Doerfler lashed out at the informer who "ratted" on Bowers and ended with a reminder to the Lord to watch out for the "unjustly imprisoned" Reverend Robert Miles.

The featured speaker was Bill Wilkinson of Louisiana, but his talk about the mayor of Bogalusa cutting the ribbon to his Klan's new headquarters paled when Buddy Tucker took the mike. The Reverend Tucker surveyed the audience of a hundred twenty-five or so, many with minds by then as far away as home. *"Hey, man, we're glad to be here!"* His shouts, magnified by the speakers, drew the audience to attention. "We are expectin' ten thousand people out on the streets of Louisville, Kentucky, in a great whiiite march on the Fourth of Juuuly. We're goin' to spend about four or five hours that afternoon sendin' a message to Washington through this Jew-controlled media!"

"Wooooooooooo wheeeeee!" one man whooped.

"Aaaaaa-men!" another yelled, backed by a chorus of hand-hurting applause. Blasting the Jews, the Communists, and the news media at deafening decibels, Tucker quickly whipped the lethargic crowd into a frenzy. Their choruses of *"Amen!"* and *"Tell it to 'em, brother!"* and *"That's right, you betcha!"* sometimes overwhelmed his own railing. The crowd sounded ready to march on Greenville by the time Tucker, flapping his Bible in the air, stormed from the podium. Scoggin hurried past him and simmered the thunderous applause with a rerun joke before launching into his own "official" speech, a salute to law enforcement officers.

"Our policemen are being called 'pigs.' They are bein' slain on the highways, up an' down the United States of America," he started. "They're the most unsung heroes that I know of. All over America P-I-

G-S is not *po*leece. That means Pride, Integrity, Guts, and Service!"

The audience applauded as Scoggin reviewed his own patriotic record, "I've been in the Klan twenty-three years, *one* month an' about a week, an' I've got the first law to break. I've got the first policeman to shoot. I've got the first policeman to call PIG!"

Scoggin's self-proclaimed loyalty to law enforcement contradicted his own arrest record. In 1965, when arrested for drunken driving, he was fined an additional twenty-five dollars for cursing and spitting at the patrolmen in the booking room. Charges of conspiracy to commit robbery and accessory after the fact of murder—when a rival klansman was killed following one of his 1970 rallies—were dropped against Scoggin, John Howard, and several other leaders because of insufficient evidence. Yet the Grand Dragon raved on. "We have highway patrolmen in this organization in South Carolina, an' I happen to be the *only* man that naturalized 'em, an' I'm the only man that knows their names, until the proper time comes. And *then* they an' some of your Greenville police, Spartanburg police an' all over the United States are goin' to come up an' say, 'Yes, I'm in the Klan an' I have been and there's not a darn thang you can do about it!' "

The audience cheered as Scoggin bounced down the steps, then returned with a job request for a fellow klansman. "He's a good sober worker, an' you won't have to go lookin' for him in any beer hall!" When no employers came forward, the Grand Dragon announced the cross lighting, giving a brief history of similar burnings by Scottish clans in 1320. As he spoke, forty klanspeople drifted toward the clearing, toward the towering cross. Sluggishly, they encircled it, stopping and starting and saluting with fiery torches. A funeral-parlor version of "The Old Rugged Cross" quivered over the public address system as the Klaliff shouted, "Stop," "start," "salute." On cue, the robed figures hurled the torches toward the cross and walked away.

The sky brightened behind the flatbed truck, where a blue-grass band had begun setting up amplifiers. Soon the night was filled with the twang of guitars and the odor of exhaust fumes, and the lot thinned as the old headed home and the young stayed to dance.

7
Ed Dawson:
A Few Regrets

Greenville, South Carolina

"I got a reputation that I'd just as soon shoot as look at you," Ed Dawson said calmly. "When something happens, I don't back up. I stand and brazen it out. You build up a reputation with that, you see."

I knew his reputation. We had met during Scoggin's rally when Dawson, in full security guard dress, questioned my use of a tape recorder. Was I an agent or a spy from a rival Klan? As I explained, his brusqueness gave way to an eagerness to talk. The rally finished, and we stayed in his white Cadillac watching the leftover young people dance to the music of a blue-grass band. Light from the flatbed truck silhouetted the man beside me as he began to reconstruct the Swan Quarter shoot-out. It was quiet inside the car except for the eerie exchange of our bodiless voices, his sometimes thoughtful and searching, at other times, full of bravado.

"This was a hotbed down there, and I didn't know it," he said. "I mean, the niggers controlled this place."

That Fourth of July afternoon in 1969, Dawson and a group of klansmen and women arrived at the North Carolina coastal town for what he described as "a picnic and rally," and the news media as "a counterdemonstration to blacks protesting school desegregation policies in the community."

"About three o'clock these niggers started ridin' up and down," Dawson recalled. "They made some kinda gesture, a carload of niggers does, and the security guard stopped 'em, say, about a quarter of a block from this hall that we were gonna hold the rally in. A fight broke out and some shots were fired and the niggers' windows were broke out of the car.

"We started the rally, about six or seven o'clock at night. And the niggers were gathering something fierce. There were about two hundred and fifty niggers against fifty white people. They wouldn't come on the grounds. They just stood alongside the road, jumping up and down and screaming and carrying on.

"The highway patrol was there, and they kept saying, 'Hold the rally off, reinforcements are comin'.' It's a little hick place, and the sheriffs, a couple-a sheriffs come down. They had damn guns hanging down to their knees, you know. Big ol' things. They wouldn't know what to do with 'em if they *had* to use 'em. And *that* was our protection! We couldn't hold the rally because of the carrying on, so we had a band there. And this Reverend Spears and myself was standing on the platform and a shot was fired and hit a switchbox in the hall and all hell broke loose! I mean, it was just like a little Vietnam!"

When the shooting stopped, a young black girl had been hit, a patrol car had been shot up, and seventeen klansmen were arrested: thirteen for engaging in a riot, three for inciting to riot, and one for resisting arrest and assaulting an officer. Fifteen weapons were confiscated from the klansmen: pistols, shotguns, an automatic rifle, and an M1 carbine.

"Did you go to prison because of the Swan Quarter shoot-out?"

"No. Previous to the shoot-out, I was involved in a terrorizing act. They charged me with terrorizing the citizens of Alamance County, breaking and entering and destroying property, and they upheld terrorizing."

"What were you accused of doing?"

The voice beside me sighed. "Goin' about the highways and shooting, shooting people's homes up."

Had he done this? After a hesitant denial, Dawson unfolded his version of the story, his voice distant, coming from the past. "We were coming from a little gathering. There were four of us in the cab of my truck. And the fella sitting next to me, as we were approaching this particular store, he made a remark that he was in this nigger store and the fella wouldn't sell him no beer. He said, 'I oughta blow his G-D windows out.' I said, 'You had no damn business goin' in there to buy beer, in a nigger store. Forget it.' So we're still riding—I was going about forty-five, fifty—down the highway and we approached this store. We had four guns in the truck, and he just grabbed a gun and shot out the windows. Simple as that." Dawson's silhouette shrugged. "When we got to the main route, the sheriff was waiting."

For that, he got three concurrent eighteen-month sentences, reduced to nine months in return for his carpentry work at the prison. He and his codefendant appealed and lost. Next came the Swan Quarter shoot-out, when Dawson and Melvin Sexton—Shelton's prison replacement—clashed over the hefty legal fee paid to Arthur Hanes, mayor of Birmingham during the time of the Freedom Rides and at one point attorney for James Earl Ray.

"Arthur Hanes represented the seventeen of us for fifteen thousand dollars, which I definitely do not believe! But that's what us klanspeople hadda get together. I had a very good feeling that Arthur Hanes handled that case for, say eight or nine thousand dollars, and somebody pocketed the rest. This is something I accused Sexton of, which is one of the main reasons I got banished."

After his banishment, he and Joe Bryant, who also argued with Sexton over the money, formed the North Carolina Knights of the Ku Klux Klan.

In the dark, Dawson seemed like an actor describing his roles rather than a man recalling actual events. In reality, he was tall, slender, attractive, even somewhat distinguished looking, with gray hair and freshly creased uniform, an ascot tucked into the neck. Except for the KKKK stenciled across his white helmet, he could have passed for a legitimate military man instead of the colonel in charge of the North Carolina Knights' security guard. Fifty-eight and a self-employed contractor in Greensboro, North Carolina, he had come from a family of New Jersey builders—middle class, maybe even *upper* middle income until the Wall Street crash, he guessed. His father had left home when Dawson was nine, a brother and sister staying with their mother, Dawson going to live with his father. He had been on his own since age sixteen, when he joined Roosevelt's Civilian Conservation Corps and went to California. He moved to Greensboro, his late wife's home, in 1963 and joined the Klan the next year.

The voice beside me laughed, a nervous searching laugh. "Why did I join? I don't know. I can't answer that. We were *very, very* strong. North Carolina was number one, back at that time—about sixty-seven, sixty-eight. So this meeting was in the back of a garage and the fellas were there in overalls and work clothes, and I went neat, cleaned up. I had a convertible at that time—Cadillac—so I pulled up in that, walked over, and started talkin'. Well, soon as I opened my mouth—*'Yankee!'* Everybody run away from me!"

"They didn't like you?"

"Hell, no! They were afraid of me! 'FBI'!" the voice laughed heartily. "So I got teed off at 'em and I went on into the meetin', and it wasn't too long—maybe a month—*I* made officer. What they call Kladd, which picks up the password of the unit. I worked in Charlotte at that time, and they asked me to stop in at Bob Jones'. So I got more or less buddy-buddy with him, and when I was only in about six months, I got in with the security guard. I drove with Bob Jones, with Shelton and Sexton, with the echelon. I was put on the state board, and this is how I kept on gettin' deeper and deeper and deeper."

The voice continued, somewhat less enthusiastically. The arrests had come—and prison. His wife had been angry. "She wasn't workin'. All the money going out. None in. My sister wouldn't talk to me. My brother, in

New Jersey, was the same way. Just didn't understand—'Ku Klux Klan . . . some kinda nut? a freak or somethin'?' "

Still, Dawson had stayed in, building his reputation over the years. "Now I never *did* say anything, but people were there and they'd say, 'That goddamn Yankee ain't afraid of the devil!' In the meantime, I are!" He laughed. "I are!"

After a quiet pause, Dawson's voice repeated, "I just don't back off. Here about six months ago, we were up to Morganton up in North Carolina near Asheville. We had a street walk planned and a speech. But before you know it, there was six of us and two hundred niggers. Virgil Griffin was there. Okay? And Scoggin and Jerry Greene. They wanted to call it off. But when you start something, you gotta finish it. So they said to me, 'Whadda ya wanta do?' I says, *'Go!'* They say, 'How we gonna go? The niggers are lined up in the street.' So I put one of the security guards in front. I says, 'You take the front, I'll take the back.' So we get down to walkin'. It's all you could do."

The silhouette beside me shrugged. "Four blocks down, one across, four back. *All* through niggers. All through 'em. And the niggers would grab you, pull on you. I just kept looking straight. They were right in back of me, and I said, 'Keep your damn nigger hands off me'—loud and clear. You could hear it clean up front. Well, we got crossin' the street, and a little nigger gal come up and grabbed me, and I told her to take her nigger hands off me and she pinched me real good. So I hit her, and she's sprawlin' out in the street. And, of course, this builds your reputation up."

Pondering the incidents in Alamance and Swan Quarter, Dawson said, "It seems all my problems end up with niggers. I believe in segregation, definitely. But I'm not death against the colored people. There's colored people, and there's niggers. But I'm very high-strung, so I try to stay away from them."

"Do you regret anything you've done?"

Again the hesitation. "When you hurt yourself, that's one thing, but when you get your family involved . . . My wife went along with this bit, but I deprived her, while she was alive, of a lotta things. Like companionship. I was tied up in this thing—rally Saturday, Sunday, and during the week sometimes. And it takes money. I wasn't paid nothin', and it's money you take away from your home. Yeah, I can say I regret a few things.

"And as far as these rallies—runnin' up and down the road—I'll be travelin' over five hundred miles this weekend, putting mileage on my car, burning my tires up, gas. I work hard for what I get, and it's really silly. It really is."

He turned his head toward the almost vacant lot. "This rally tonight would have been a flop if it wasn't for all those from Pennsylvania, New York, New Jersey. They bought a lot of people with them. We had a rally this afternoon about forty miles from here. You know how many people showed up? None. *None!"*

"Is this happening at most rallies?"

"Yes. This Christmas just past, we put on a rally in Greensboro. And these things cost money. There was approximately a hundred and twenty people there—one hundred niggers and twenty white people." The laugh came again, as though at both the speaker and the Klan. "So we wait three months, and we put another one on. You know how many people were *there?* Virgil and I and his wife and the police department. That's who showed up."

Again the laughter, but with no hint of disenchantment, of wanting out. "I was nine months in prison, and my wife had to sacrifice something fierce. We had to borrow money, had to sell all my insurance, all my policies. We sold *this* and we sold *that* and put the debts off until I got out and was able to go back to work. When I got out, she asked me to promise her faithfully I would not go to a Klan meeting. But I got a call from Bob Jones and he said he wanted me to come down to a board meeting, which I did. They took up three hundred and fifty dollars. It's the only thing the Klan ever gave me."

"Did your wife find out?"

"Sure."

"Why did you risk putting the Klan before your wife?"

The voice was thoughtful now, its brashness gone. "We would have been married twenty-eight years, May eighth of this year. Her life with me was no big deal. Up in New Jersey, I was in it for myself and I drank heavy. So it was decided to move to Florida—Miami—and I just went from bad to worse down there. This went on for maybe six, seven years of my marriage. Then I became a compulsive gambler. Fell in love with the horses for the next seven years, and the next seven years it was the Klan. Even today, I have a nice woman I'm going with, and she's against the organization one hundred percent. We could get married today, but no Ku Klux Klan!"

"Do you think you'll ever give up the Klan for her?"

"Yes." It was a remote, uncertain answer.

"Does the Klan make you feel needed? Does it fill whatever need you had to gamble and drink?"

"Maybe so," he reflected. "I like people. I like to be around them. I emcee all our rallies. I introduce the speakers."

The voice stopped, and the faceless man shrugged.

"Why do I belong? I don't know. I guess I'll have to go to a psychiatrist."

8

The Day the Klan
Returned to Pulaski

Pulaski, Tennessee

Just north of the Alabama border and east of the country meeting house known as Shiloh Church, the town rested in the hills, passing its days like a grand old lady: partly in the present, mostly in the past; aging, but not changing with the times. The population had been a stable eight thousand as far back as most people could remember. The same families. The same names. The Reeds. The Joneses. The McCords. One generation died, and another was born, just as one cotton crop replaced another. As I entered the town that day in May, the aura of garden parties and swishing silk, of graciousness and pride, of parlors and piano lessons, of jasmine and wisteria, even of war wounds and Reconstruction, lingered just beyond reach, yet vividly within memory. The façades of once-stately mansions, converted into boarding houses and apartments, had crumbled but were otherwise unaltered. Others, freshly white, retained a musty elegance, a smell of furniture polish, of aging velvet and wood.

The courthouse sat in the center of town in the public square, surrounded by dogwoods and maples. Beyond them were the usual pharmacies, hardwares, dry-goods stores, and an occasional neon sign. Nearby, marble monuments rose above Confederate dead, a one-room museum was dedicated to a spy hanged by Union soldiers, and a bronze plaque was bolted to a one-story brick building:

> KU KLUX KLAN
> ORGANIZED IN THIS
> THE LAW OFFICE
> OF
> JUDGE THOMAS M. JONES
> DECEMBER 24th, 1865

NAMES OF ORIGINAL ORGANIZERS
CALVIN E. JONES · JOHN B. KENNEDY
FRANK O. McCORD · JOHN C. LESTER
RICHARD R. REEVES · JAMES R. CROWE

The plaque had not caused much stir since it was unveiled in 1917 by the United Daughters of the Confederacy. Most people paid no more attention to it than they did to the swiveling red, white, and blue pole on the other side of the doorway of what was now Banks' Barber Shop.

Even on May 28, 1976, the eve of United Klans' bicentennial rally, Forrest Eubanks clipped hair and gave shaves as he did every other day. He and the plaque had shared the building for four years, since he converted it from an egg-pickling factory. Like most residents, Eubanks, a frail, gray-haired man, viewed Pulaski's Klan heritage with mixed emotions: proud of the original organization and its rescue of the Reconstruction-ravaged South; embarrassed by its modern-day namesake.

Around the corner, D. L. Hoover was putting together *The Giles Free Press,* leaving front-page space for the rally on sixty-six acres of leased land north of town. The Giles County Historical Society had passed a resolution opposing the event and the present Klan's right to claim Pulaski as its birthplace, insisting the original Klan had been "irrevocably dissolved in 1869." Otherwise, the town had reacted with good manners and polite indifference.

"There's no welcome for them, no sense of pride attached to this happening, nor is there any organized animosity or any organized effort to block them," Hoover said. "Most people just hope they will come in, do whatever it is they've got to do, and get on out." He knew of no Klan activity in the thirty years he had lived in Pulaski, not even when the schools were integrated. A local black politician had issued statements about his past harassment by the Klan, but Hoover doubted the validity of his claim. "He may have been harassed by pranksters, but *not* the Klan."

So far, there had been no real curiosity, no talk in the cafés and banks or at the courthouse, and Hoover wasn't sure he was going to trouble himself to attend the rally, not even if the Klan's anticipated fifty thousand *did* show up. "I have no interest in publicizing what I expect to be the general line. We've heard all that." But before the day was over, Hoover had offered to lead the way to the rally site, bringing with him a reporter. We drove toward the thinning edges of town, where the buildings gave way to open fields and idle land, then followed a dirt-and-gravel road until it became clogged with cars and trucks and people. One man, hoisted overhead in a yellow lifter, was installing temporary power lines; another, inside a mobile concession stand, dipped apples and swirled sticks into pastel cotton candy.

At the far side of the large field, two mules hitched to a covered wagon emblazoned with BICENTENNIAL—UNITED KLANS OF AMERICA—KNIGHTS OF KU KLUX KLAN grazed next to a backdrop of trees. Nearby were two portable toilets, a tent, a sleek Executive van, and five or six men—arms crossed, hands to their chins—overseeing the proceedings. One man stood out, not because of size or appearance, but because the others deferred to him and because, unlike them, he wore a white dress shirt. Hoover and the reporter watched from the road as I approached the group for a closer look at the man who seemed vaguely familiar.

"Mister Shelton?" I asked.

The man turned and calmly surveyed my face, his lips barely moving when he answered, "Yes, ma'am?" His voice was bland and Alabama in more than accent. Soft, polite, it was schooled in the niceties and not-so-niceties of the South he grew up in: to call grownups "mister" and "miz"; to say "sir" and "ma'am"; to refer to blacks as "colored" or "Nigra" but *never* "Negro"; to believe that white people have their place and black people theirs.

He was an average-looking man, five foot nine, neither fat nor thin, his clothes neither expensive nor cheap. His sandy-red hair was receding at the part; his once-lean, hawkish face was rounded and lined like the maps he no longer needed to find his way around the backroads and interstates of the South. The media label of the sixties—"the shrewdest of the hate peddlers"—seemed no longer to fit, for he appeared incapable of any emotion, whether love or hate. Behind his purple-tinted glasses, he looked as bored and tired as a traveling salesman who, after twenty-six years of pushing a product, had lost his enthusiasm. Even as the preparations mounted around him, he showed no excitement.

Red clay oozed through the tall grass, leaving ruts where cars and trucks had bogged down. For days, rain had pounded the countryside. The sun was forcing its way through a shield of clouds, but Shelton looked up from his muddy boots at a black cloud directly overhead.

"This weather's going to cost us twenty-five thousand people," he said flatly.

Hoover and Bernice Kressenberg, the reporter, had inched on to the field, listening cautiously until their curiosity prompted questions about the rally and the Klan, about this middle-aged man who had been Imperial Wizard since 1961 when UKA was formed. It was a particularly polite interview, with the Southern upbringings of both sides showing through.

"This is your job? You're *paid* for this?" asked Bernice Kressenberg, who, though in her forties, was as bewildered by her subject as a cub reporter.

Shelton nodded. "Yes, ma'am, full-time job."

"What did you do before?"

"I was a salesman, sales representative for a corporation," he stated, skipping over the nondescript jobs—rubber worker, gas station attendant, air-conditioner salesman—he had held before his brief stint as sales representative for B. F. Goodrich and his rise to Klan chieftain.

"Are there Klan organizations in competition with yours?" Hoover asked.

"All in all, I'd say approximately twelve," Shelton estimated. "But really, we're the *only* Klan, far as that goes. The others are more or less splinter groups or individuals that have been dismissed or banished from this organization."

Hoover hesitated before asking delicately, "I'm sure you'll forgive us if we, through our ignorance, get into areas you don't want to cover, but could you talk in terms of national membership?"

"We don't give numerical strength. I went to prison a year for refusing to give the membership list to the government," Shelton answered, a tinge of heroism in his voice.

"How do you compare it now to the sixties?" I asked.

"Let's just say we're big enough to put our shoes on, but not *quite* big enough to lace our boots," he said, repeating the answer he has used since 1969 when he returned from the Texarkana prison and began trying to regroup what was left of his forces after the HUAC hearings. "But we're continually growing. People *now* are coming from all walks of life, where in the late fifties, early sixties, you might say it was the individual worker, or as they would refer to them, 'rednecks.'" He grinned slightly, unable to resist another favorite line. "There's nothing wrong with being a 'redneck,'" he drawled. "That's just a person that bends over to get an honest day's work and gets sun baked on the back of his neck. But today, doctors, lawyers, people from *all* walks of life, have recognized the fact we're not *quite* as ignorant or malicious as they had us pegged to be in the early sixties."

A light rain fell from the black cloud, and we four retreated to the concession van, continuing the interview amid whiffs of melting sugar and popcorn. Shelton speculated the rally would draw leaders from as far away as Indiana, maybe even Washington, D.C., Florida, and the Carolinas, but the rank and file members would come mainly from Tennessee, Georgia, and Alabama. As for that advance attendance figure of fifty thousand, he claimed he didn't know *where* that had come from.

"If the weather hadn't turned bad, how many were you expecting—twenty thousand?" Bernice Kressenberg asked.

"I'd say *no less* than twenty-five thousand." He looked out of the concession van at the people watching the rally preparations. Twenty-five or thirty, at most—some from the Klan, some from Pulaski.

When Hoover asked the qualifications for membership, Shelton replied that applicants had to be Christians and reputably employed. "You're screened by the membership itself. A person, just because he has the money to sign an application, doesn't mean he's going to be accepted."

"What could cause a man to be kicked out of the Klan?" Hoover probed.

"Total disregard for the virtues of womanhood; disregarding or disobeying laws—civil laws or Klan laws; any conduct that would be unbecoming for a klansman; going out and doing something in the name of the organization. This kind of thing."

Bernice Kressenberg had begun putting away her notebook when Hoover brought up the yard-type cross burnings and Klan warning cards.

"Eighty percent of this type activity is more or less a neighborhood dispute," Shelton assured him, "where one neighbor gets in an argument with another neighbor."

The next day, Forrest Eubanks graciously converted the back room of his barber shop into a dressing room for the men who asked to pose for snapshots in their robes next to the plaque. Cars double-parked around the square as drivers and pedestrians yelled to one another. "You gone out yet? What's it look like? Not much, huh?" Over the sale of hand lotion and nails and coffee, the town talked about the rally. Pulaski's curiosity had been aroused, and a sporadic caravan of cars began a slow procession to the field.

The sun had pushed aside most of the clouds, but cars and campers spun and slipped and struggled over the muddy grass. By early afternoon, vehicles with license plates from as far away as Ohio and Texas gradually filled the field except for the roped-off speaker's area. Shelton's Executive camper had been moved to the far side, next to the trees, and lined up wagon-train fashion with others of varying sizes and prices. Next to his van, husky men opened the sides of a portable speaker's platform, its paneled walls lined with antique robes. The speaker's stand bore a presidential-like crest, inscribed IMPERIAL WIZARD—UNITED KLANS OF AMERICA.

In between the cars, people greeted old friends and made new ones and picnicked on food from home or the concession stand. Men and women sold watermelon, fifty cents a slice, from the back of a truck; others hawked T-shirts and Klan paraphernalia. Children squealed as a mule-drawn wagon wheeled through the crowd.

Shelton was nowhere in sight. When I inquired about him, a young man asked, "You mean the boss?", and nodded toward the executive van. Occasionally, the Imperial Wizard stepped out of it, squinted toward the leftover clouds, and repeated, "This weather's gonna cost us twenty thousand people," as it became apparent the crowd would never grow to even his altered estimate. But the people didn't seem to mind that he remained apart from them.

Although some had driven for days, their fatigue—even the ingrained fatigue—gave way to frivolity, heightened by patriotic marches blaring over the public address system. Most of the women swapped gossip and recipes until I approached. Then their conversations usually turned into a defense of the Klan and how they really didn't *hate* blacks. They just didn't want to associate with them. Some had enrolled their children in the private "Christian" schools or academies hurriedly thrown together in trailers and Sunday school buildings when integration came to the South in the sixties. Others, unable to afford the tuition, had taken their youngsters out of school, deciding no education was better than sitting next to a black. Besides, they argued, blacks had lowered the educational system to such an extent that the children weren't learning much anyway.

Bobbie Rockhold was talking to another woman when I neared. Both looked like typical housewives and mothers who belonged to garden clubs and the PTA, but their outside interest proved to be the Klan's Ladies Auxiliary. Bobbie Rockhold was the wife of the new Grand Dragon of Alabama; Shirley Willis's husband held the same rank in Georgia.

"Do you become Klan widows?" I asked.

"No, ma'am," Bobbie Rockhold vehemently assured me. "I admire the Klan. I'm Klan from my toes to my head. Matter of fact, I don't think I ever really lived 'til I joined the Klan. I'm behind my husband one hundred percent." Petite, soft-spoken Shirley Willis agreed. "We joined as a couple, and that's the way it's remained. And when the children get old enough, they'll follow right in our footsteps."

Like the women in West Virginia, she and Bobbie Rockhold said they preferred to meet apart from the men. "I hate to admit it, but ladies gossip more than men," Shirley Willis confessed. "An' there are some thangs that I'd rather not know about. What I don't know, I cannot be questioned about."

While we talked, people began hurrying past us, heading down a knoll toward the caravan of campers. I strained to see the source of the commotion, but my view was blocked by the thickening crowd and by security guards, armed and uniformed.

"Would you excuse me while I see what's going on?" I asked.

"He's not with us. You don't want to talk to him," Bobbie Rockhold insisted. I broke past her verbal barricade and joined the crowd converging on a red, white, and blue bus. Through the heads, I glimpsed the Reverend Buddy Tucker on a makeshift platform, frantically flapping the black Bible.

His face was red and angry, but his shouting evaporated without a microphone. By the time I neared the platform, Tucker was gone, and the security guards had closed in on a male, also wearing a white shirt with epaulets, black pants, and knee boots. A man from UKA gestured angrily. "We don't try and break up or interrupt your rallies. Why are you tryin' to do it to us!" Tucker's partner, cowering, insisted he didn't know that Shelton and UKA would mind. I was about to turn on my tape recorder when someone grabbed my arm from behind.

"What are you doing?"

I slowly turned to face a security guard, his thin, loser's look bolstered by the storm-trooper uniform. We stared eye to eye before I hurriedly explained.

"Oh, yeah," he eased up, "you're the one doin' the book. I know *allll* about you. Is that turned on?" He brushed aside a note pad that covered my recorder. Satisfied it was off, he escorted me part way toward the cars. Eventually, I dared to look back. The crowd had scattered, and the flag-covered bus and the podium, along with the Reverend Tucker and his cohort, were gone.

By now, the field was sprinkled with women in red, white, and blue uniforms—members of the Ladies Auxiliary. When I asked one from South Carolina about Dean Williams, the Grand Dragon from her state, she hurried off and returned with a middle-aged man.

In a bright-green suit and tie, Williams had a look and manner tailored to his line of work: operating a combination grocery-gas station, with a used-car lot on the side. He was squat and energetic, with an accent as thick as his waistline and a penchant for talking. He led me to a van down the line from Shelton's, where Steve Broadway, a South Carolina state board member, joined us at the kitchen table. Williams sketched his background, of being raised by his grandmother after his parents separated, then quitting school in tenth grade to help support the family. Unaware that his own father had been a klansman, he joined in the early sixties, as he—like many white Southerners—anxiously watched the federal government eat away at what he considered his rights. Now, with four children of his own, Williams proudly listed his community activities: he was a member of the Loyal Order of Moose and the local board of the Veterans of Foreign Wars, and he regularly attended meetings of the Gaffney city council and school board. He had also served on Nixon's Foreign Affairs Committee, each month answering a mail questionnaire on foreign policy.

In the Klan, Williams had worked his way up from Kleagle to Titan to

Grand Klabe to, finally, Grand Dragon. "Just climbed the ladder," he boasted, a small-town boy who had made good.

"Did you succeed Robert Scoggin?" I asked.

"No, Harry Gilliam in Spartanburg succeeded Mister Scoggin," he answered, adding smugly, "*when* Mister Scoggin was banished from the organization."

"Was he banished while he was in prison or when he came back?"

Williams glanced across the table at Steve Broadway, who volunteered, "He was *on* his way to prison."

When I asked why Scoggin was banished, Williams at first offered "for several reasons," then, prompted by Steve Broadway, elaborated: "Mishandling of funds, which we have in black and white. Conduct unbecomin' a klansman. I can show you the charges. I probably got a copy of 'em right here now . . ."

"I'd be interested in seeing them," I said.

Williams brought a briefcase full of papers from the back of the camper. He handed me a photocopied sheet dated April 20, 1969, but before I could read it, he spread out a half-dozen or so canceled checks, similar to those introduced by HUAC investigator Donald Appell to prove Scoggin's misuse of Klan money.

As Williams began reading aloud, I wondered why he had the canceled checks—some more than ten years old—and the banishment papers with him in Tennessee. Did he always carry them in his briefcase, or had someone instructed him to bring them? Only a few people besides Williams knew I would be in Pulaski: Shelton, a South Carolina law official, and, I surmised, the FBI, who knew I was doing research in the South. Was Williams an informer, as some reporters had speculated? John Howard, the South Carolina Dragon I first met in West Virginia, had hinted at his own suspicions and predicted Williams would talk, *a lot*. A law enforcement officer had assured me, "Williams will spill his guts!"

"Now," Williams started, "this is a check made out to United Klans of America Incorporated for one hundred dollars from Florence, South Carolina—from the lodge—an' sent to Spartanburg, to Mister Scoggin." The check was labeled "For Defense Fund," but Williams noted it was not deposited in that account. "It was took to Kelly Jewelry Store and paid for the rings—that's where the Klan rings was bought."

He handed me the check, dated August 1, 1966, and another, made out to Scoggin on October 24, 1968. "See, he paid for the rings with a check that's s'posed to be deposited in the defense fund, which you see *very clear*. Then he comes back and writes his own self a check for five hundred twenty-two dollars and eighty-nine cents an' said he had paid for 'em hisself, which the Klan had already paid for."

Williams sat back, pleased with his detective work.

"But that's two years' difference between the checks," I pointed out.

"This is the kind of thangs he would do," Williams said. "It took awhile to find out about it."

Steve Broadway shook his head sympathetically. "It took a *lot* of investigation."

Picking up the banishment papers, Williams continued his case against Scoggin. "You see, some of the lies that's been tol'? I mean, I'm showin' it to you in black and white, an' this is the article that shows these charges, what he done." The charges ranged from "violation of allegiance to this order" to writing letters to members and nonmembers "saying their Supreme officer and some of the state board members and Imperial officers could not be trusted" to "commission of an act unworthy of a klansman, excessive lies, trying to hurt klansmen and klansladies, repeated commission of minor offenses." The paper was signed by the seventeen-member state board.

"Before this, was there anything constructive Mister Scoggin did?" I asked.

"Well, Mister Shelton, time after time, asked Mister Scoggin to quit his drankin' and lyin' an' this stuff," Williams said, "an' that he would make a good klansman. I *personally* have set at the table when the discussion would go on, and Mister Scoggin would tell him, '*No! No! No!*'" He pounded the table for emphasis. "An' he never did, which Mister Broadway will verify. He would of made a good klansman if he would not of done these thangs."

Steve Broadway agreed. "He was as good a organizer as this organization has ever had, if you could have kept him straight. And he's a good storyteller, an' he knows what's happenin', but he'll add a lie here an' there."

A power operator with DuPont Chemical Company for twenty-seven years, Steve Broadway was soft-spoken even when he leveled charges against Scoggin. Unlike many klansmen, he seemed content with his lot and hardly the type to wear a hood and robe, though he had belonged since 1955.

"Bob Scoggin is the man that come by and talked to me," he recalled.

"He recruited me, too," Williams added. "I followed on the road with him four or five years, different states, me an' him. At one time, I was close to him as any man."

After I returned home from my travels, I wrote Dean Williams for copies of the checks and the banishment papers. A few days later, I received a scathing letter from Scoggin. "Just today A [sic] most top official and associate of Mr. Dean Williams INFORMED [sic] me that Mr. Traitor Williams was again trying to stab me in the back," Scoggin wrote on elaborate photocopied letterhead. "He told me that Mr.

Williams had secured you to write a book dispicting [sic] me as some sort of rascal. He informed me that Mr. Williams was sending you some old canseled [sic] checks which I had endorsed on back plus some phoney [sic] banishment papers which he drew up while I was in Federal prison . . .

"I took Dean Williams into the Klan in 1964. He ran in early 65 when it was announced the Klan was to be investigated by the House Committee on Un-American Activities. He reinstated in later yrs [sic]. He was then and is today believed to be an informer. You Could [sic] write a good book on him. Ask the woman he lived with who bore 3 illigitimate [sic] for him who later married another man. He gave them a home only after he married a Girl [sic] about half his age. The officials around him donot [sic] trust him. . . . It is believed by old and new Klan members that Mr. Williams is in the Drug [sic] traffic . . .

"Be sure you print the truth also that Mr. Scoggin is a 32 Degree Mason. A Shriner and the recipient of the Purple Heart not once but twice." The letter was signed "R. E. Scoggin. Coordinator of KKKK, NORTH AMERICA."

I telephoned Dean Williams, who insisted he had never received my letter. It had been addressed to him—with no mention of "Klan" on the envelope—in care of a post office box he now said UKA no longer held. Mail to the box routinely was forwarded to him, yet this letter had been intercepted. At the post office? By the current box holder?

"You wrote me a letter, an' he got it an' wrote you back?" Williams repeated the incident I had related.

"Yeah."

"Heh, heh, heh. That's pretty good. Pretty sneaky, wasn't he?"

"Will that hurt anything?"

"Noooo! *I* don't care," he assured me. "So he got a letter addressed to me an' opened it up?"

"Unh huh."

He chuckled again, then grew serious. "I'll look into this. Ain't no tellin' how much mail I've gotten that they're turnin' over to him."

"He also made some accusations about you," I warned.

"Oh, yeah," Williams verbally shrugged. "This has been goin' on ever since he was banished from the Klan."

Later, while I was still trying to solve the letter mystery, I discovered an item in the final report of the HUAC investigation:

In the South Carolina Realm of the United Klans of America, members of an action group known as the Underground met in secret (outside of regular klavern meetings) to discuss and plan specific acts of violence. Members of the Underground were extremely militant and prone in violence. Committee investigation revealed the members took training in marksmanship and accumulated a large number of weapons. It is understood that the existence of this organization, whose first leader was Furman Dean Williams, was known to the UKA's grand dragon for South Carolina, Robert Scoggin.

I also discovered an old newspaper article outlining the Underground's rules: "Any member who gives out information to the enemy causing any other member prison and hardship shall suffer death." "Each member must own a gun and no less than 100 rounds of ammunition," and he must "practice self-defense, the use of his gun and guerilla warfare."

As the sun slipped behind the hills, a large bearded man began the rigorous ritual of erecting the tall cross, and gradually the people covered their shorts and jeans with the all-white satin robes. The crowd of the faithful and the curious grew to twenty-five hundred, as the evening turned into an outing for Pulaski residents and Klan members alike. A steady stream of people—new recruits, someone explained—moved in and out of Shelton's van, but the Imperial Wizard himself did not appear. At seven o'clock, the robed Grand Dragons and Imperial officers lined up outside the darkened van, shifting from foot to foot as the designated starting time passed. Finally, they dispersed. Another hour and a half went by before the rally got under way.

A festive atmosphere had settled over the field, with yellow lights flashing around the top of the concession van and "The Halls of Montezuma" marching through the air. Small Confederate and American flags fluttered here and there, and one man wielded a "UKA—Stop Forced Busing" sign. In spite of its late start and unlike those in West Virginia and South Carolina, the rally was orderly, planned, and low-keyed, devoid of shouting and the usual racial jokes, even of the word "nigger," as speakers vacillated between "Negro" and "Nigra" and, now and then, "black." Except for the thunderous applause before and after Shelton's speech and when a popular Grand Dragon was introduced, the crowd listened quietly.

The Grand Dragons and Imperial officers grammatically fumbled as they lashed out at the Federal Reserve System, the Supreme Court, and the United Nations in a series of resolutions adopted during the day in private huddles, but almost none raised his voice or showed signs of losing his temper. In robes—many with suit collars showing—most looked like small-town businessmen and civic leaders, seemingly more prosperous than their rough-hewn counterparts in some other Klans.

Shelton, in turn, was flat and subdued, his face and voice barren of emotion. Never a fiery speaker, he had been described in the sixties as "dreary" even when saying the most outrageous things. "He just drones on and on," one Southern editor remembered. Shelton now spoke no more than twenty or thirty minutes, avoiding both the racial slurs and jokes he had once delivered in his familiar one-note fashion. "You know how they found those three boys buried in that dam near Philadelphia, Mississippi?" he had asked a South Carolina audience shortly after the lynchings. "The FBI didn't find them. The mailman found them. He walked by there deliverin' welfare checks, and the nigger reached up to get his." Tonight he concentrated on his version of the Klan's history and patriotic jabs at Communism, appealing more to white pride than to black hate, and soft-pedalling the Jewish conspiracy theory.

Had he mellowed with age? Had he changed with the times? Or were he and his klansmen on their good behavior for the reporters and cameramen who flocked around the podium and for the Hooded Order's Pulaski kin?

By Monday, the field was empty. The two portable toilets and the blackened cross stood as stark memorials to the bicentennial rally. Buzzards soared and circled overhead, swooping down to pick at scraps of food.

The klanspeople had come and gone, their lives and Pulaski's scarcely altered by their brief encounter. The klanspeople would look back on the rally nostalgically, almost as a pilgrimage to sacred ground; the local residents, indignantly, as a blemish on the town's good name. Yet the two groups had much in common. Both had been reared with much the same racial traditions. Both had been taught the same Southern manners. Both revered many of the same heroes. And each was proud of its own Klan, staunchly justifying its deeds and its need to exist: to put the white and black man back in their proper places, to restore the old, stable social order they had grown up with, to retrieve rights they saw as inherently the white man's. And just as the excitement, adventure, and mystery of the first Klan made it legendary and heroic to Pulaski and much of the South, so was its modern-day namesake to *its* people.

But in spite of the likenesses, there was a gulf between the two groups. For even though crisscrossing interstates had left Pulaski stranded in the hills, the town was isolated geographically, while the klanspeople were isolated socially and economically. In a way, Pulaski residents looked down on the klanspeople, but differently than they had regarded the blacks in the days before segregation became unacceptable. With blacks, it had been color; with the klanspeople, a matter of class. Pulaski schools were integrated long before most in the area, but not, as one resident conceded, "out of any outpouring of brotherly love." For the feelings the klanspeople openly, and sometimes crudely, expressed lay subtly some-where below the surface in Pulaski.

"We do not appreciate their publicizing the fact their Klan was organized here," Margaret Butler complained. "It was organized in Atlanta, Georgia. General Nathan Bedford Forrest dissolved the Ku Klux Klan, and in his proclamation he said it could *never* be recalled into existence unless by the Grand Titan or an officer above that. And *those* officers died before this Klan was organized. It has *no* right whatsoever to the name!"

She spoke in a firm yet cultured Southern accent. A retired librarian and a director for the Giles County Historical Society, she—like most natives—had grown up with the original klansmen as her folk heroes. The war and Reconstruction were more than something she studied in school and the topic of her master's thesis. They were part of her heritage, events that molded her thinking, much as being poor and white had molded the klanspeople's. The original klansmen were not mere names on a plaque: the owner of the law office where the Klan was conceived was a distant relative; the six founders were kin to people she had known all her life. For her, the original Ku Klux Klan was a family heirloom she didn't want tarnished by the infamous acts of the sixties.

Just as most youngsters grow up hearing fairy tales, Margaret Butler remembered the old-timers' talk about the Klan. She remembered hearing two elderly neighborhood women tell about making Klan robes, how a bundle would be tossed through the window with instructions for making the uniforms and placing them for the anonymous klansmen to pick up.

Driving through town, Margaret Butler pointed out the former law offices, the once-handsome home where the founders first draped themselves and their horses in sheets, and the spot where they had held their regular meetings, in the basement of a house destroyed earlier by a cyclone.

"It started out as a prank, just as fun," she said, earnestly relating more of the stories she had heard since childhood. Stories about the white-robed sentinel stationed outside the basement to keep guard, telling Negroes who passed, "I am a spirit from the other world; I was killed at Chickamauga," and about the klansman—equipped with a concealed rubber bag—who visited the house of some troublesome blacks and, after downing several buckets of water, commented, "That's the first drink of water I've had since the Battle of Shiloh," then warned them to behave.

"The Negroes were very superstitious, and they thought these men were ghosts," Margaret Butler continued. "That just grew bigger and bigger as the Klan found out they could control these superstitious people in this way. And so they began to threaten them about going to the polls."

As word of the unexpected effect of Klan antics traveled across the South, the organization turned its attention from innocent merrymaking to overturning the State Reconstruction governments set up in 1867. The Klan operated with increasing violence as its lack of central control fostered out-of-hand lawlessness.

"Not much is written about the original Klan," Margaret Butler observed, "because these men were afraid for their lives. General Brownlow got the legislature to pass a law that anybody could be executed just for membership. So nobody dared to tell anything about it before it was dissolved."

She bristled genteelly. "He was a Reconstruction governor and the *most* radical man that ever lived!" Once, she related, Brownlow sent a man to Pulaski to infiltrate the Klan and learn the identities of its members. On his way back to Nashville, the informer got off the train in nearby Columbia. His body was found later in a river. That was one of the more violent things the Klan did, she said, but it was necessary to spare the lives of many men.

The Prescript—the original Klan's bylaws—was published secretly by the *Pulaski Citizen,* a weekly still in existence, she went on. "The Klan would take a brick out of the wall, place what they wanted printed in the hole, and the publisher would set it. The klansmen would return and remove the brick to get the printed copy."

On March 29, 1867, the first of many mysterious notices ran in the *Citizen:*

> The following mysterious "Take Notice" was found under our door early yesterday morning, having doubtless been slipped there in the previous night. Will anyone venture to tell us what it means? What is a Ku Klux Klan and who is this Grand Cyclops who issues his mysterious and imperative orders? The order follows:
>
> "TAKE NOTICE: The Ku Klux Klan will assemble at their usual place of rendezvous The Den on Tuesday night next, exactly at the hour of midnight, in costumes and bearing the arms of the Klan—by Order of the Grand Cyclops."

What few readers knew was that editor L. W. McCord was Grand Genii of the local lodge and related to founder Frank McCord.

"Our town was occupied by the federal forces. The citizens did not have any rights to vote. They couldn't hold office. They couldn't take part in government. They couldn't gather. *This* organization did a great deal to get the vote back for the people," Margaret Butler explained. "It was dissolved because the officers felt too many people were claiming to be members and doing things that would keep the federal army here longer."

In defense of the original six founders, she added, "These men were all well educated, well versed in Greek, and from the best families. The original Klan was not a blight! It was something we were proud of!"

Many historians would agree that, initially, the Klan was made up of the best citizens—many former Confederate officers, even generals—and that Robert E. Lee probably was offered the title of Grand Wizard. He supposedly refused because of the conditions of his surrender, saying his approval must be "invisible," giving the Klan its nickname, the Invisible Empire. Other historians have noted that the klansmen themselves boasted they were "a rough bunch of boys" and that membership eventually crossed class barriers, becoming most active where the economic distinction between blacks and whites was less pronounced. As it cut across the population, the violence became more brutal. The Klan flogged, stabbed, mutilated, shot, and hanged blacks who were "disrespectful" or who belonged to the Union and Loyal Leagues, as well as Yankee school teachers, Northern politicians, and carpetbaggers and scalawags.

The situation was soon out of hand, with the Klan's secrecy compounding the problem. "Secrecy was at first its strength. It afterwards became its greatest weakness," founder J.C. Lester wrote in 1884 in *Ku Klux Klan: Its Origin, Growth and Disbandment,* still concealing his own role. "The devices and disguises by which the Klan deceived outsiders enabled all who were so disposed, even its own members, to practice deception on the Klan itself. It placed in the hands of its own members the facility to do deeds of violence for the gratification of personal feelings, and have them credited to the Klan."

Even the name—Ku Klux Klan—encouraged violence, Lester wrote. "The order would never have grown to the proportions which it afterwards assumed, or wielded the power it did, had it not borne this name or some other equally as meaningless and mysterious. There was a weird potency in the very name Ku Klux Klan. The sound of it is suggestive of bones rattling together. The potency of the name was not wholly in the impression made by it on the general public. The members of the Klan were themselves the first to feel its weird influence."

And yet having been there that night in 1865 when the name was conceived, when its weirdness first shivered down its inventors' spines, Lester nevertheless insisted in his book, "The object was amusement—only this and nothing more." He, like Margaret Butler, related the Klan's disbanding in 1869 by order of Grand Wizard Forrest and the mass burning of rituals and robes. But modern historians have argued that that was only window dressing to provide greater invisibility. Most violence occurred after Forrest's orders were given, they have noted, and it was not curbed until passage of the Ku Klux Klan Acts of 1871.

Across town, some blacks sat outside a run-down house enjoying the late-afternoon breeze, their worries seemingly as far away as most of the klanspeople were by now. They, like their neighbors on porches up and down the street, watched as I approached. When I asked their reaction to the rally, they at first stared. Finally, a man in his thirties looked intensely at me and answered with his own questions: "Why did they have to come here? Why didn't they go to Mississippi or Alabama, somewheres else?"

9
The Poet

The voice on the other end of the phone was stern. I was to come alone to the interview. Otherwise, the deal was off. *Understand?* He would wait outside, on the porch, and give me a signal. I agreed, but before I could hang up, he explained, "I've gone underground, see. They're after me. This is a black man's town now."

The street was lined with trees and mansions, most of them converted into apartments. After I parked, I glanced across the street at a well-groomed man seated on the top step of a raised porch. He looked back and, without altering his solemn expression, passed his hand before his face in a semicircular sign. As I approached, he stood, shook hands, and guided me toward the front door. He knocked in code and exchanged passwords with a pimply-faced youth who opened the door. We headed toward a stairway, the man instructing me to lead the way to the basement. I proceeded apprehensively, aware both that no one knew where I was and that the man could have a gun in my back.

Downstairs, we walked past a half-dozen numbered doors, stopping at one marked "Exit." The man stepped ahead, the two of us entered, and the youth locked the door behind us.

I looked around the meagerly furnished room: a single bed was pushed to one side; in the opposite corner, a couch and chair bordered a card table, with a typewriter and scattered papers on top. The man gestured toward the couch, but as I began to sit down, I was startled by a thud. I jerked my head toward the sound, and there, on the table, was a pistol.

"What's that?"

"A thirty-eight," he answered calmly, reiterating he had gone underground because *they* were after him. Ten people, he warned, were watching us. Outside the high basement window, footsteps sounded. Were those neighbors, I wondered, or were we *really* being watched?

"Have you ever killed anybody?" I asked, still eyeing the gun.

"Yeah."

"Under what circumstances?"

"I would rather not talk about that," he hedged, "but I have killed *many* men."

"In the war, or what about here?"

"I don't know whether I have killed them or not, but I have shot at 'em and they left in a damn big hurry. I'm an excellent shot," he bragged. "We keep plenty of bullets. There is one thing we've got, and that is plenty of bullets. Plenty of damn guns."

Slender, with close-cropped gray hair, he had served seven years in the navy during World War II, he said, traveling through Europe when he completed his tour of duty. He was also a freelance writer, he emphasized, and had attended college.

I sat very still as our conversation turned to the protest marches and the Klans that rolled into Louisville along with school busing. He was a member of UKA, he boasted, and had led some of the marches.

For almost two hours, we talked about the Klan and busing and race relations, his views not too different from many I had interviewed. Then he squatted beside the bed, dragged out a cardboard suitcase, and opened it. Inside were yellowing manuscripts and clippings. *His* writing, the man announced with pride as he pulled out a tattered manuscript.

". . . the rocking stoplights twinkling their decision," he read, glancing up for approval.

"That's nice," I complimented.

The praise spurred him on, and he continued to read and to seek compliments until he accompanied me to the front door.

"I've enjoyed this," he said. "I get so tired of talking about the Klan and killing people."

10
Robert Shelton:
The Salesman

Tuscaloosa, Alabama

The Ramada Inn lobby, like the rest of downtown, was dreary and almost deserted. When George Wallace made his schoolhouse-door stand at the University of Alabama in June 1963, the place had been mobbed: first, when the Governor and his staff set up headquarters at what was then the Hotel Stafford; a week later, when Bobby Shelton and a battery of klansmen moved in. Every seat had been occupied, with scarcely room to stand as the Imperial Wizard handed out sandwiches and statements to the press with his own rough-hewn Madison Avenue flair. "Here goes another interview, boys," one of his Dragons would bark. "Let's give the Wiz a hand!" The flash bulbs popped, and the reporters clamored for interviews. The nights before and after Wallace's confrontation with the federal government, hundreds of klansmen—some armed with guns, knives, and clubs—had burned a sixty-foot cross in a bold show of force, and when the governor finally stepped aside, a cool Shelton staunchly maintained, "All is not lost. This is only one strike against us. There are lots more innings to play."

The innings were over—and lost—as far as the Klan was concerned. Legally, blacks could come and go anywhere they pleased, and the white mobs that openly jeered them and the Freedom Riders in the streets now did so only in private or at Klan rallies or in their hearts, if at all. But Shelton was still playing on the less fortunate whites' emotions and their fear of blacks, much as segregationist politicians—seeking their votes—did in the sixties before they had an expedient change of heart. For Shelton, the crusade was half-hearted, approached with weariness. His enthusiasm, low-keyed during the most turbulent sixties, had waned. The "cause" had become a job, a means of supporting a wife and three children, of holding on to a life-style. He held court at the hotel, but mostly with the afternoon coffee regulars. The public cross burnings, the flamboyant press conferences, his free access to the executive office at the state capitol in Montgomery, and his ability to intimidate law enforcement officers and judges were over. Public sentiment had soured toward the Klan and its tactics.

Now, on a hot afternoon in July 1976, Shelton sat quietly beside me in the lobby with its garish carpeting and plastic philodendron, awaiting the arrival of my rented car. At forty-seven, he looked like just another middle-aged man, but the people in the coffee shop and the teenaged boy behind the desk knew he wasn't. They knew he was *the* Robert Shelton—or the "Ku Klux man"—as youngsters had snickered behind his back for the last two decades.

A yellow compact pulled in front of the hotel. Its driver, a large black man, got out and hurried toward the entrance, hesitating when he spotted Shelton and me. Shelton's face remained devoid of expression even when I suggested I ride to the rent-a-car office with the black man and that he follow.

In the car, the driver, his face fatly wrinkled, his hair threaded with gray, was quiet. Only the widened whites of his eyes betrayed his feelings. His side of the conversation was polite and sparse.

"Weather sure is hot," I commented.

"Yessum."

"You know Mister Shelton?"

"I know who he *is*, that's all!"

At the rent-a-car office, he grabbed the keys for his next delivery and disappeared. The white man behind the counter was no less nervous as he watched Shelton pace back and forth while I filled in the forms.

"Be with you in a moment, sir," he called out when Shelton walked away.

"He's with me," I explained.

"Oh!" The man quickly looked down at the papers. "Now, if you'll sign here, and put your initials here . . ."

This time, I drove behind Shelton, first on a highway lined by discount stores and car dealerships, then on to a two-lane road, and finally a private lane that wound through pines to a rambling one-story brick house on a lake front shared by his mother's home and several others.

Between Shelton's house and the water, a small matching brick building served as his office. "We have two more offices over in town," he explained. "They used to be open to the public, but it got to the point where we had so much curiosity seekers and disturbances of the people just walking in, wanting to know what was going on, until you couldn't do anything. So we closed them as far as the public is concerned." In addition to himself, there were three salaried staff members and varying volunteers.

The house and its furnishings were neither pretentious nor poor. The paneled walls in the den were lined with photographs: of Shelton's late father holding up a thirteen-pound fish caught out back in the lake, George and Lurleen Wallace, former Governor John Patterson, and the late U.S. Senator James Allen, whose photo was signed "With sincerest best wishes to my good friend Robert M. Shelton, 8/19/68."

A television console was topped by an assortment of personalized mugs and trophies presented to Shelton and his wife for "patriotism and service." They were only the smaller tokens his members had showered upon him over the years. They had provided him with a WATS line, a half-dozen or so Cadillacs and Imperials, a twin-engine plane, and fifteen-thousand-dollar annual salary, plus expenses—money and luxuries most of them could never hope for. Yet, somewhat as poor blacks traditionally wanted the best for their ministers, the klanspeople—many making do with discount specials and battered cars—wanted their leader to make a good impression and to lead the life they coveted for themselves.

"Your members take a great deal of pride in you," I observed. "They seem to consider you more than just a paid employee."

"After all," Shelton shrugged, "I've been around twenty-six years. And if I wasn't being paid, I'd still be doing it. It's my belief and my philosophy. Has been. Hasn't changed. I've always been honest and straightforward with the membership. There's been no racket, no con-artist promoting deals."

During my travels, several former leaders who had split or been banished from UKA had questioned Shelton's real motives, accusing him of "being in it for the money," of "making a nice fat living off the Klan." During the HUAC hearings, prosecutors charged that he paid for cars and a diamond ring with Klan funds and disclosed that his wife Betty, using the alias "James J. Hendrix," had cosigned Klan checks instead of the authorized Imperial Klabee, or treasurer. "This disbursement procedure," the HUAC's final report read, "meant that Shelton exercised sole control over funds in the Imperial account. It is apparent to the committee that Shelton not only disbursed funds as he saw fit, but also disbursed most of them to his personal advantage."

Yet Shelton now was both convinced and convincing as to his integrity as he sat back in a black vinyl chair, not really relaxed, for in spite of his casual manner, his soft drawl, he never seemed completely at ease, not even in his own home.

"I'm not a greedy individual," he said, "long as I've got something to eat and some clothes to wear. I think the most I've ever drawn is about twelve thousand even though I'm authorized to get fifteen. If I were to put as much time working for some firm as I do for the Klan, I'd probably be making a *minimum* of fifty thousand dollars a year. Still, my wife supports me. She works free, gratis, herself, for the organization. She does secretarial work. But she is a little bit concerned about the children's education. One's already graduated from nursing school, and we've got another one that'll be in college next year, and a boy, in three, four years."

On the road most of the year from Wednesday through the next Monday, rallying in Florida and Texas during the winter, Shelton admitted, "It puts an extra burden on my family, me not being home all the time. And the fact of *who* I am, *what* I am, and *what* I'm doing—even my friends sometimes in a joking manner say a lot of things that make my family wonder. It's just the price you have to pay."

While we were talking, Nancy, the Shelton's seventeen-year-old daughter, entered the room and sat on the far end of the sofa with the family's miniature poodle. A senior at West End Christian School with plans to attend nursing school, earn a master's degree, and teach, she was working this summer as a part-time receptionist at a nearby hospital where her older sister, Cindy, was a nurse, and her mother, a full-time receptionist. Nancy was slightly chubby, yet pretty, with brown curly hair, fair skin, and her father's easygoing manner. She listened to the Klan stories and beliefs she had been weaned on, entering the conversation only when asked and then, softly and sparingly.

"I'd rather he stayed home," she confessed, adding supportively, "but we all believe in what he does. We're right behind him. They kid me a lot at school, but they're all friends. So it's no big problem."

I looked at her father. "Do you ever feel guilty about what you may be causing your family?"

"It doesn't bother me," he said. "If I'm going to assume the role as leader of the Klan and take the responsibility, there's bound to be some sacrifices. But I feel what I'm doing in the Klan, over a period of years, enables them to enjoy the heritage that they have. I think it's given my family the opportunity to actually participate in the rewriting of history, the making of history."

Even today, Shelton's face flashed across newspapers, magazines, and television screens; his name appeared in books on the Klan and on race relations and civil rights. The exposure was never favorable, yet it was, in its own way, an immortality that the son of a small-town grocer scarcely could have dreamed, especially when his early life unfolded into a series of drab, low-paying jobs. To be in the same books with Abraham Lincoln, Robert E. Lee, and Nathan Bedford Forrest, the heroes of the Civil War and Reconstruction—for his grandchildren and great-grand-children to read—was a bonus he hadn't expected when he paid his initiation fee and donned a robe and the blood-drop emblem.

Shelton's upbringing had differed little from that of most youngsters growing up in the South in the days before integration, in an "average" hard-working family whose income provided enough food but few extras, a family that attended the Methodist church every Sunday and believed that white folks and black folks had their own place. He wasn't taught to hate. That was just the way things were. It was a way of life that most whites and even many blacks never questioned. Until he served in the air force during the last half of the forties, his contact with blacks had been limited to Aunt Jane, the community's elderly midwife, a man who did yard work for his father, and a few others who worked in the grocery and around the farm.

"When Harry Truman first ordered integration in the armed services," he recalled, "we had a race riot over in Germany. The blacks broke into the supply room, they got carbines, and they tried to stand all the whites off. They forced themselves in with the white German girls—this was very irritating not only to myself but to the majority of the American white soldiers. And I began to realize that we were going to have the same problems in this country."

"Did you think of yourself as a racist?" I asked.

"No one was using that term then, 'racist.' Of course, I *do* think of myself as a racist. That's nothing to be ashamed of. I'm proud I'm white. Being a racist is an individual that is proud of his heritage, his integrity, and his own culture and ethnic background. But they have smeared the word 'racist' to associate it with something like the Gestapo or Hitlerism or Nazism," he protested.

When Shelton returned from the air force, he began looking for a way to fight integration and decided on the Ku Klux Klan. "Its background, its history, its principles and objectives were kindy in line with my thinking and my philosophy," he explained. But more than that, he had been raised among relatives and friends and neighbors who belonged to or sympathized with the Klan.

"I had always heard stories about the Klan from uncles and aunts and grandparents," he recalled.

"Had they been members?" I asked.

"Welll, they talked about activities of the Klan, and some had been in it. 'Course, I can remember the Klan itself when I was a young child—its activities an' knowing of it and hearing of it. It was just something that was attractive from the beginning." Over the years, various news articles had identified Shelton's father and grandfather as klansmen, but he now denied they had ever belonged.

He thought back to his boyhood, getting up at four every morning and firing the potbellied stove at the store, delivering groceries before and after school, playing baseball and basketball in what free time was left, the excitement of watching Klan parades.

"I can remember when there would be hundreds and hundreds of white robes that would parade in cars. Downtown here in Tuscaloosa, in the Bessemer area, or out in Holt. I'd say I was seven or eight years old, and I can remember recognizing some of the vehicles and knowing who they were, some of the neighbors."

"As a kid, did you feel in awe of all those men in white robes?"

"It give you kind of a funny feeling, but yet it give you a feeling of satisfaction, a feeling of desire, desiring to have one on yourself and become a part of it. I think *actually* a person is really born a klansman, and it just works out of him as he develops."

Shelton joined Eldon Edwards' U.S. Klans in the early fifties, in time for the federal court orders and the civil rights sit-ins and marches that were to swell Klan membership and propel him from the ranks of the unknown to a position of leadership. His rise also was helped along by his ill-fated predecessor, the Reverend Alvin Horn, who resigned as Alabama's Grand Dragon amid the furor over his runaway marriage to a fourteen-year-old girl, more than thirty years younger than the self-styled Baptist preacher. It was not the first time the Reverend Horn had made unfavorable headlines: he was indicted, though eventually acquitted, in the 1950 shooting of a Pell City, Alabama, storekeeper; his first wife, depressed over an operation, committed suicide, and after his second marriage, he was arrested for contributing to the delinquency of a minor. His wife's parents attempted to have the marriage annulled on grounds of nonconsummation but dropped the matter when it became apparent those grounds would not stand up.

Shortly before the murder indictment, Horn had been thrown out of the Klan for "treason." Nevertheless, he had the reputation of being Alabama's most potent organizer, credited with bringing fourteen thousand members into the U.S. Klans during the resurgence of the fifties. Thus, in the spring of 1960, when Edwards dismissed Shelton for what he called "incompetence, untruthfulness, and lack of cooperation" and what Shelton described as "a disagreement over the way he handled finances," Horn was named his replacement. It was Shelton's second ouster in less than six months. The first time, in November 1959, Edwards reinstated him three weeks later; the second time, however, Shelton pulled away most of his state's membership and formed the Knights of Alabama.

The frail rubber worker—once viewed as a "ne'er-do-well" by less sympathetic Alabamians—no longer needed Edwards or the U.S. Klans. He already had amassed enough strength to help put John Patterson in the governor's mansion in 1958, a feat he repeated four years later with George C. Wallace. When violence erupted in Montgomery with the arrival of the Freedom Riders in May 1961, Shelton was one of four men singled out by the federal district court in a restraining order aimed at curbing the rioting.

After Edwards's death in August 1960, the remnants of the U.S. Klans became disenchanted with his successor, Robert Lee "Wild Bill" Davidson, a young insurance salesman who came by his name because of his buckskin jacket. By the next spring, Calvin Craig, the second in command, broke away and began talks with Shelton about joining forces. On July 8, 1961, five hundred klansmen from several splinter groups gathered in Indian Springs, Georgia, to discuss a merger. Shelton arrived with an eight-man security guard, attired in black boots and blood-red ties—the latter designating guards instructed to shoot anyone who interferred with them. The show of force had its effect. Shelton walked away as Imperial Wizard of the new UKA.

Fired by Goodrich almost two years before—allegedly for his Klan activities—Shelton began working full time to build a self-styled Klan that was to become the most dominant and durable in modern history. It was the organization from which many of today's splinter groups emerged—including the National Knights formed by James Venable, who, in the beginning, was UKA's legal Klonsul. Yet neither UKA nor Shelton was seriously rivaled until articulate young David Duke began appearing on national talk shows in the early seventies.

"What went into building United Klans?" I asked.

Looking down at his boots, Shelton repeated with fatigued pride, "A lot of work, a lot of work. There was a lot of sacrifice on the part of my family because I was maintaining a job, and on Friday afternoon, my wife would fix a bag of peanut-butter sandwiches, and I would head out on the road. It wouldn't be anything to go from here to North Carolina and be back on the job Monday morning. You was just continuously moving."

"What were you doing?"

"Recruiting and laying the groundwork. I had a lot of good dedicated men in various areas, in the states, that worked and built it up." Up until the sixties, the Klan had had a reputation for changeover, he went on, quickly listing the turbulent shifts in command: Hiram Wesley Evans' maneuvering of William Joseph Simmons into early "retirement"; James Colescott's demise due to the federal back-tax bill and the Klan's tie to the German-American Bund; Dr. Sam Green's untimely death; Sam Roper's inability to curb the growing factionalism, and finally Eldon Edwards.

"There's never been any major change since sixty-one in our organization," Shelton boasted. "There hasn't been any scandals, and there hasn't been any charges of thievery and things of that nature."

Starting with Alabama, Georgia, Tennessee, Florida, and South Carolina, he had expanded to his present "thirty-something" states, he noted, describing the present Klan as being more determined than in the sixties, its members more sincere and dedicated. Even the tone of the rallies had altered.

"Twenty years ago—ten years, even—it was more an emotional appeal. I've heard a lot of speeches about the burr-head, liver-lipped Negro, which would excite some of the people, get some emotional feeling. But you can't depend on the emotional instability of an individual to build an organization because they're only geared to this one phase of hatred. And when you don't have this phase or this hate, they lose interest and fall by the wayside."

In the sixties, particularly fiery speakers sometimes did move audiences to violence, including the beating of victims before cheering crowds of men and women. Some of the incidents occurred after rallies staged by other Klans, some by UKA. Still, Shelton reiterated, "I wouldn't want to build an organization that you had to depend on a membership of people you had to stir up emotionally to get them in action to do something."

"But weren't your own speeches more fiery in the sixties?" I countered.

"Welll," he hesitated, "if they were, it was because blacks were out in the streets. They were robbing. They were stealing. They were assaulting. A lot of times, you could describe the action that transpired in a community, and it'd make you become more personally involved. And naturally, you're going to strike out verbally or in some instances with physical force because you could see the very thing that you detest the most, the thing that's destroying your community, involved."

If his own speeches seemed toned down, he reasoned, it was because there was less of that kind of activity, because blacks had been brought out of the streets by bureaucracy and were holding key government positions. "In essence, they've been bought off," he concluded.

Between 1954 and 1965, the Justice Department and local police officials, with the help of informers, had blamed the Ku Klux Klan for almost seventy bombings in Georgia and Alabama, thirty Negro church burnings in Mississippi, the sadistic castration of a black man in Birmingham, ten racial killings in Alabama, plus the more publicized murders of three civil rights workers in Mississippi and of the Reverend James Reeb and Viola Liuzzo during the Selma march and the sniper shooting of Colonel Lemuel Penn on a highway outside Athens, Georgia.

"There was a certain amount of hostility and violence involved," Shelton conceded. "After all, you were doing a complete one eighty turn in your society. It's unfortunate, really, that there wasn't more violence than what it was. I feel like had there been enough violence, it would have stopped all of this, and we wouldn't be in the position we're in today."

He looked up while Robert Jr. made an excursion to the refrigerator, then continued his argument. "There's still going to be a revolution. There's got to. There's no way to prevent it. We're witnessing job discrimination in reverse. The majority is paying the majority of the taxes but we're not having the representation."

Returning to the sixties, I asked, "But what about the cases in which people who were alleged to be members of the United Klans were arrested, as in the Liuzzo and the Penn murders?"

"The Penn case *wasn't* members of United Klans," he corrected me even though testimony during the HUAC hearings had shown otherwise. "They had been in, but they'd been dismissed from this organization. They formed their own group called the Black Shirts."

In Mississippi, one of eleven men convicted of a series of bombings in 1964 carried a card signed by Shelton; another man arrested for hauling an arsenal of weapons carried a black leatherette apron and hood—described as the Klan executioner's garb—and a UKA membership card that Shelton, at the time, identified as "just a business card." After Viola Liuzzo was gunned down while shuttling marchers between Montgomery and Selma after the Alabama Freedom March, United Klans honored the three defendants at rallies and parades and provided for their legal expenses. Shelton even sat at the defense counsel's table next to Collie Leroy Wilkins, the first to stand trial.

"What about, say, the Liuzzo shooting and the things the White Knights of Mississippi were accused of?" I asked. "If they *did* happen, do you condone that?"

"I'm opposed to taking the life of anybody," he drawled. *"However,* under the circumstances of Viola Liuzzo, they portrayed her as being the mother of five lovely children and a community worker. They *didn't* point out the fact that those five lovely children she had was by four different husbands. They didn't point out the fact that her husband hadn't seen her in two, three months. They didn't point out the fact she was living with two nigger men in Selma that was on this march. They showed a beautiful picture of her on the front pages of the papers. The picture was an *eighteen-year-old* picture. The fact is, she was a *fat* slob with crud that looked like rust all over her body. She was bra-less. There were traces of barbiturates in her blood. And you have to take under consideration the involvement. People come into an area where there's already a tense situation, come into an opposite philosophy that's a complete turn around, they can expect a certain amount of violence."

The room was quiet as Shelton concluded his logical maze, a reasoning that wound in circles, ending where it began, but a reasoning that satisfied him and his followers. It was the same kind of argument he had used when the Reverend James J. Reeb, a Unitarian minister from Boston, was clubbed to death in Selma less than two weeks before Viola Luizzo's murder: "He had been dying of cancer before he ever came to Alabama."

For the past thirteen years, Shelton had defended the Liuzzo killing with similar claims—most of them, like those he made now, unsubstantiated. In 1965, he told *Playboy* interviewers that Viola Liuzzo had been "an in-and-out patient" in a Detroit mental hospital, that there were "doubts" whether she and her husband had been living together for the three months prior to her death, and that she had been on court probation. At the time, her husband's attorney denied the allegations except for the probation, which, the lawyer said, had resulted from her refusal to send her children to school in order to call attention to the Michigan legislature's refusal to raise the compulsory school age from sixteen to eighteen. As for Shelton's added accusations now, records show that Liuzzo was the dead woman's third husband. Autopsy and toxicology reports did not mention any findings of "crud" or drugs, just as there was no evidence of sexual intercourse.

"But do you condone going as far as killing her?" I asked.

Unruffled, Shelton evaded the question. "I'm not satisfied, with the knowledge that's been brought forth, about who really killed her. And I've always had my doubts as to whether *any* of the men that were tried was guilty of shooting the woman because of the fact that Tommy Rowe was a paid pimp for the FBI. He's nothing but a fat slob. We *knew* he was an informer. A friend of ours on the *po*leece department in Birmingham informed me in the very beginning he was informing for the *po*leece department."

As he spoke, I remembered a scene from Gary Thomas Rowe's recent book, *My Undercover Years With the Ku Klux Klan,* in which Shelton allegedly confronted Rowe in a tense meeting, during which the Imperial Wizard's bodyguard warned the accused, "Watch your mouth or we'll put a bullet through it!" But Rowe had managed to convince Shelton he was not an informer and, he wrote, had served as one of Shelton's personal bodyguards for two years. Before his role as FBI informer surfaced, soon after he and three others were arrested for the Liuzzo killing, Rowe, in his book, quoted Klan Klonsul Matt Murphy as telling a group of klansmen, "I'll stake my life and reputation that he's not a Fed." The charges Shelton made to me took on credibility in July 1978 with controversial disclosures by Alabama investigators which linked Rowe to major Klan terrorism. Lie-detector tests made during the fall of 1977 were said to indicate that Rowe gave deceptive answers when he denied his true role in the Liuzzo killing and the Sixteenth Street Baptist Church bombing.

Again, I tried to get Shelton to explain why, if his organization was innocent and opposed violence, had it over the years paid for the defense of numerous men arrested and—sometimes—convicted? Why, after the murders of the three civil rights workers in Mississippi, were two of the defendents—Sheriff Lawrence Rainey and Deputy Cecil Price—honored at parades and rallies?

Shelton shrugged. "We were helping them based on the fact they were duly elected law enforcement officers and they were performing their duties. The federal government was involving itself in local affairs. We felt kindy obligated to help them."

"Would you say that when there were acts of violence by members of your organization, they were done without your knowledge?"

"It's possible," he answered. "I don't imagine a Methodist preacher knows about all the drinking his brothers and sisters do on Saturday night. I'm not going to advocate any acts of violence to the extent of looking for trouble, but I'm like any average citizen. If anybody walks up, gets on my toe, I'm gonna ask him nicely to get off. If he don't get off, I'm gonna do whatever's necessary to get him off."

Despite his bold words, Shelton remained placid. I wondered, was he really capable of rage? Was he rough and did he cuss when women and reporters weren't around? Had scenes described by Tommy Rowe actually occurred? Scenes like the one in an Alabama jail where a carload of Shelton's men—stopped on their way to Tuscaloosa for Wallace's schoolhouse-door stand—were being held for possessing an arsenal of carbines, twelve-gauge pump shotguns, bayonets, hand grenades, machine guns, dynamite, and a bazooka with six rounds of ammunition. As Rowe wrote:

Bobby strutted up as if he were little god. "What are you doing with my men?" he demanded.

The crew-cut deputy said, "We're trying to fingerprint them and take their pictures. You sit down over there; you can talk to them when we're through."

Bobby walked up to the officer and put his forefinger on the man's chest. "*You* go sit down till I get through talking to them, if you want to be around here tomorrow," he said.

The deputy's face reddened and he opened his mouth to reply, but Bobby cut him off.

"I'll tell you one better than that," Bobby went on. "If you don't go sit down right now, I'm going to let these two men beat hell out of you," and he nodded toward Brown and me.

According to Rowe, Shelton warned that every man better be out of that jail by three o'clock or "we're coming after them." When another deputy argued back, Shelton repeated the ultimatum: "Every man in here out by three o'clock or we'll tear the damned jail down a bar at a time." Before the day was over, the men were released and in possession of their weapons, with the help of a circuit judge, who commented, "If Tuscaloosa had a thousand more men like Bobby Shelton, it would be a better place to live."

Was *that* the real Shelton? Was he the bold man who lobbied against a state antiflogging bill, who threatened "bloodshed" if civil rights workers came to Alabama, who attended a course in the manufacture and use of explosives, who only six months ago told the press: "We are keeping a computerized list of people who have violated certain sanctions, such as interracial marriage, and committed other racial crimes; the day will come when they'll be punished." Or was he the quiet model husband, model father who didn't drink, smoke, or cuss? Or was he all of these?

In the late fifties, when Shelton was still Grand Dragon for U.S. Klans, a Montgomery columnist described him as "in appearance, at least, as harmless and friendly as a homeless kitten." But a more recent observation by another Alabama writer, who grew up in the same community with Shelton and watched him rise from service-station attendant to the powerful Klan leader who called the shots that riveted the South in the sixties, seemed more conceivable: "He's like a dog that looks so cute and nice, but you just know that dog will eat your ass. He's a mean son of a bitch!"

Even when Shelton was just starting out in his early twenties, and the writer—Wayne Greenhaw—was half that age, the latter remembered riding his horse past the Shelton grocery store in hopes of seeing "the Ku Klux man." The day before my trip to Tuscaloosa, Greenhaw recalled: "We just associated that store with being a Ku Klux place. Everybody around there knew of him in a sort of mysterious way, as being a Ku Kluxer."

Greenhaw's next recollection was after Shelton was employed as a rubber worker at B. F. Goodrich, where several of the writer's cousins—also Klan members—worked. "Bobby and others around him—but especially Bobby—really scared the living be-Jesus out of the common workers, mainly at the rubber mill but also the paper mill, around fifty-four, fifty-five. All of a sudden these people thought the blacks were going to get everything. Not only that these folks were going to be going to school with their children, but they were going to get their jobs. Just like that. Overnight.

"They had rallies all around. These cousins of mine, most of them lived around Holt—it's still a very poor section of town. And every Saturday night, I recall, there'd always be a cross burning when I was twelve, thirteen, fourteen, fifteen years old. Through the midfifties. Talking and screaming. It sounded almost like somebody talking in tongues, or that's my recollection. And they would say, 'Well, ol' Bobby's acting up again.'

"Bobby's always been lazy," Greenhaw reflected. "He worked in service stations at two different times, once in fifty-seven. He just put gas in the cars, but he was known then, even, as the Klan leader."

One of the stations had been across from the University of Alabama. In a 1964 magazine article, Shelton claimed he worked there because "it's the best position in town. That's where there's gonna be trouble next year or the year after. We have a Klan unit on campus, we can keep a check on what they're teaching, and who comes and who goes."

Then came the 1958 gubernatorial primary with State Attorney General John Patterson and a little-known circuit court judge named George Wallace outdistancing a dozen other candidates—including retired Admiral John G. Crommelin of Wetumpka, the States Rights Party's vice-presidential candidate in 1960 and the current associate editor of Klan leader David Duke's monthly tabloid.

In the third week of the run-off, the United Klans publicly endorsed Patterson, whose father had been killed gangland style while attempting to clean up corruption in Phenix City. Wallace, viewed as the more liberal candidate, decided to capitalize on the backing. On television, he warned statewide audiences: "If the Klan should now succeed in electing Patterson governor, the triumph might well lead to a revival of the Klan as the controlling political force in Alabama. Patterson chatters about the gangster ghosts in Phenix City, while he himself is rolling with the new wave of the Klan and its terrible tradition of lawlessness." When Wallace stumped, he took along a quilt-covered bed in the back of a pickup truck and after each speech asked the audience, "Where is John Patterson?" and then peeked under the covers. "Who's down there between the sheets with you, John? Are you in bed with the Ku Klux Klan?" And, as Greenhaw wrote in his recent book, *Watch Out for George Wallace,* the crowd howled.

Patterson, meanwhile, remained silent, and eventually, Wallace—at the urging of his advisers—dropped the issue. But it was too late. Patterson was elected. The Klan issue had backfired, and, according to Greenhaw's book, the defeated Wallace privately swore, "I'll never be outniggered again."

Patterson returned the Klan's political favor by awarding a $1.6 million government tire contract to B. F. Goodrich with the understanding that Shelton would be promoted from rubber worker to state sales manager. The then Grand Dragon was also given free access to the executive office. That relationship cooled after Governor Patterson's endorsement of John F. Kennedy for president. George Wallace began courting Shelton and the Klan in preparation for the 1962 elections.

After that victory, wrote Greenhaw, Wallace ensured Klan endorsement for future gubernatorial and presidential campaigns by pressuring a Mobile construction company doing business with the state docks to hire Shelton's father. Shelton himself was placed on the payroll of an engineering firm looking for upcoming interstate highway contracts. That move, together with other "irregularities" in the hiring of state consulting engineers, caused the U.S. Bureau of Public Roads to threaten to withhold forty thousand dollars in matching federal highway funds until Shelton and others were dropped from the bidders' payrolls. In the meantime, the Imperial Wizard had earned at least four thousand dollars. On another occasion, a member of the Klan Bureau of Investigation was placed on the state payroll to investigate Klan activities in Alabama. When word leaked to the press, Wallace removed him.

The rewards paid off for Wallace. Over the years, Shelton and the Klan openly and enthusiastically backed his numerous bids for governor and president and in 1963 pressured members of the Alabama state senate to pass a bill allowing Wallace to succeed himself as governor. In 1964, during Wallace's first try for the presidency, Shelton traveled to Indiana as part of an advance campaign team with Asa "Ace" Carter, the author of Wallace's now-famous "Segregation now! Segregation forever!" speech. Carter had headed his own Klan in Birmingham in 1957 when six of his members castrated a black handyman in what has been described as "one of the most shocking atrocities in Klan history." The accused mutilators, sentenced to twenty-year prison terms, were paroled after Wallace became governor. Meanwhile, Wallace steadfastly refused—even publicly—to disavow Klan support, appearing at rallies and telling Tom Wicker for an April 1967 article in *Harper's:* "At least a klansman will fight for his country. He don't tear up his draft card. But the Klan, it's just innocuous in size and they're just concerned with segregation, not subversiveness."

Now, sitting in his living room, the Imperial Wizard boasted that the Klan—*his* Klan—was responsible for George Wallace running for president. "We started back in nineteen hundred and sixty-three, and we put out over two and a half million cartons of paperback-type matches with his picture and 'Draft Wallace for President' on the cover and a Klan application on the inside. We put 'em out all over the United States."

"What has been his response to Klan backing?" I asked.

"Well, when he was running for governor, it was an accepted thing. But his attitude kinda changed when he started getting prominent. He had aspirations of going to Washington, and naturally he kinda drifted over toward the center, or to the left, a little bit. This is the cause of him not being where Jimmy Carter is today. 'Cause the attitude of the people is 'Well, if he's changing now, ain't no telling which way he'll change, so we can't trust him.' "

During the 1976 presidential primaries, klanspeople had supported Wallace halfheartedly, investing less time and energy than before, Shelton said.

I looked at the photograph of Lurleen and George Wallace on the wall behind me. "Are you still close to him?"

"I'm not too close to *any* politician anymore, because I found politicians are not dependable," he said. "I consider him a friend. I've known him a number of years. I've been very close to him. But since the assassination attempt, I haven't been too close to him, no."

Shelton had not limited his politicking to the state level. Greenhaw described him as being, in Tuscaloosa, "sort of the sideline conscience when people got too pushy. And he never worried about legalities." Nor did he have to.

Tuscaloosa's police force had been one of the worst in the state, Greenhaw remembered. "At least three-fourths of the police were klansmen in the fifties when I was growing up. There was just no doubt about it. They were open about it." In the fifties and sixties, it was not unusual in Southern towns and cities for the police and klansmen to be on friendly terms. Gary Thomas Rowe wrote about cooperation between the law and the Klan in Alabama, especially when the Birmingham police gave klansmen a prearranged fifteen minutes to roughen up Freedom Riders. At times, federal court orders were the only means to compel state and local police to protect civil rights workers and demonstrators from brutal beatings.

The liaisons were not confined to small towns or even to the South. Big-city departments—including those in Chicago and Houston—have uncovered klansmen in their ranks, even recently. On several occasions during my travels, I saw both uniformed and plainclothes officers fraternizing with Klan leaders. "They're our friends," one Grand Dragon said of three state police intelligence officers assigned to cover a Shelton rally. The Dragon from the neighboring state said he didn't know this trio, but the police who usually attended his rallies never presented a problem. "Actually," he confided, "I think they're on our side."

When I told Shelton he had been described as being both influential and knowledgeable in Tuscaloosa politics, he chuckled proudly. "That's my job. I'm supposed to kinda know what's going on, whether it's in Tuscaloosa, Birmin'ham, Mobile, Montgomery, wherever it is."

"Would you say, then, you're influential throughout the state?"

"Not just in the state," he corrected. "Pretty well all over the country, wherever we have the organization. I wouldn't say *I'm* all that influential as much as the organization and the structure itself is. Naturally, we're interested in who's going to be elected where we have the organization, whether it's in Louisiana, Texas, Florida."

Today the Klan seldom made public endorsements, Shelton said, "because we know where we can do good and we can do harm." What he didn't add was that the Klan sometimes endorsed candidates solely to discredit them. A classic example concerned Georgia's controversial Lester Maddox. In the 1962 lieutenant governor's race, Maddox—with the help of Klan leader James Venable—decided that the "kiss of death" for his opponent, Peter Zack Geer, would be a flyer containing the Invisible Empire's endorsement and an account of a Klan meeting Geer allegedly addressed. But, in 1974, when the same Klan publicly endorsed Maddox for governor, he knowingly called the move "a dirty trick" and disavowed the group's existence: "I don't even believe we have such an organization as the Ku Klux Klan in Georgia."

According to Shelton, legitimate endorsements were made after the membership investigated and voted on the candidates.

Currently, he said, UKA was testing the political strength of several known klansmen: Florida Grand Dragon John Paul Rogers was running for the state House of Representatives; former Georgia Dragon Calvin Craig, a veteran of several political campaigns, was making a bid for commissioner in the community where he now lived. They were not openly running as klansmen, but their affiliation was "common knowledge."

"In other words, they don't have posters saying 'Klan'?"

"No, we're not a political party or a political organization."

"Bill Wilkinson, over in Louisiana, ran for the legislature and he had the blood-drop emblem on his billboards," I related.

"That's a violation of the constitution of an organization," Shelton sniffed indignantly. "I don't even consider Bill Wilkinson a klansman *or* David Duke. They have no knowledge of klankraft. They don't even have any bylaws or constitution, any disciplinary procedure, organizational structure."

Would Shelton verify a statement he had made in Tennessee that David Duke had attempted to join UKA on two occasions, the most recent being last spring when he telephoned Shelton and asked to do television and newspaper interviews? Shelton nodded righteously. "He was rejected by the membership of Louisiana two or three years ago. David Duke first started out in the American Nazi Party. *That's* where my differences are with him. His entire movement is nothing in the world but the National Socialist White People's Party, or the Nazi Party."

Like most Klan leaders, Shelton had boasted of members in high places, members whose identities had to be kept secret to protect their positions and jobs.

"Do you have any in Congress?"

"Yes, uh, it's possible." He gave a low, secretive laugh.

"Would Congress be your highest office?" I pushed.

Again, he chuckled. "Wellll, at one time a president was a klansman and to get things straightened out, we might have to have another one." The answer to *which* president—Harding? Coolidge?—was glossed over with another private laugh.

Regarding the Klan's interests—other than politics—and its beliefs, Shelton loftily repeated the organization's stock line: "The Klan stands for ever'thing that's American. We're not anti-anything. We're simply *pro*-American." During the sixties, he had advocated sending the blacks back to Africa and at one point announced plans for special Klan communities, where his members could avoid racial mixing. As recently as August 1975, he told a Georgia rally crowd, "I am convinced that we can no longer live in an integrated society." But now, he conceded, removing blacks from society would be impossible. "I want the Negro to have his own way, his own opportunity, his own responsibility. Let me have mine. I'm gonna stay out of his hair, and I want him to stay out of mine."

His basic concern about Jews, he said, was their dual citizenship.

He spoke calmly, but I recalled more rabid comments, as in 1974, when he brushed off his espousal of the Palestine Liberation Organization with, "I can remember fourteen years ago, when it was the Jewish guerrilla that was killing everybody in Palestine. So what's wrong with A-rabs killin' a few people to protect their land?"

"Have your views or feelings changed at all over the years?" I asked.

"Some," he acknowledged. "I'm more understanding now about the various conspiracies. In the beginning, the basic issue was the separation of the two races, black and white. Now that's just a mere knot in the wall compared to the many problems we're confronted with."

Smirking, he joked about his Jewish friends at the hotel, then resumed his usual brooding expression, his aura of bearing on his shoulders the future of the white society.

"Do you think you've mellowed?"

"I think I've hardened," he contradicted. "After a year in prison, after being involved in investigations, after seeing the brazen murders, assaults, the looting of businesses, and the disrespect for law and order, it's made me more harsh."

"You mean by blacks?"

"Right."

"What was your reaction today when the man who delivered my car turned out to be black?"

"To me, it was just a nigger."

"But what was your reaction to my riding in the car with him?" I pressed.

"It's just like the ol' saying 'It's ever'body's can of beans.' It would be no different if I went to the service station and I was going to leave my car and he dropped me off back home. The people having the car agency and being reputable people, I know they're going to have reputable employes working for them. Now there are some Nigras that I wouldn't allow my wife to get in the car with . . ."

"But if it had been your wife, would you have objected?"

"Not under the conditions, no."

When I returned alone to the rent-a-car office, the man at the counter smiled and chatted courteously as he checked the mileage, offering me a ride to the hotel.

"I thought you brought *him* to come after me!" He laughed with relief.

"Do most people around here know Shelton?"

He nodded. Also a native of Tuscaloosa, he emphasized that he didn't belong to the Klan.

"I don't think most people support Shelton or like him, but I think most folks are ready to join something. Things are getting bad. White people are losing all their rights. I don't like violence—mind you—but something is going to have to be done."

The next morning, Shelton met me in the hotel coffee shop for the drive in his Executive van to rally first at Amite, Louisiana, then in New Orleans' Rivergate convention center. A controversy had been raging over the second rally since the Klan put down its five-hundred-dollar deposit and announced an expected turnout of two thousand. A local black ministerial alliance and the city council had passed indignant resolutions, the afternoon newspaper had editorialized against the rental, and a bill had been introduced before the state legislature to prohibit the leasing of public buildings to organizations that would deny admission to events on the basis of race, color, or creed. The bill had made it to the legislative docket in spite of the threat it posed to the city's "old line" carnival organizations that still bar blacks and Jews. Ironically, only the state president of the NAACP—which had held *its* 1974 national convention at the Rivergate—backed the Klan, commenting, "I and my organization don't agree with the philosophy of the Klan, but we uphold their constitutional right to meet." Nevertheless, other blacks were threatening to picket the rally, tying it in with the case of a black teenager recently convicted of fatally shooting a white student during a racial disturbance at a nearby school. State and local police were preparing nervously for the worst, even bombs. Newspapers had published stories the week before that the rally was off because the Klan had failed to post the cash bond required to rent the huge facility, but Shelton assured me UKA's lawyers and local leaders were working things out. The rally *was* on.

In spite of the prerally turmoil, Shelton appeared characteristically calm as he settled into the driver's seat. The van itself was spacious and tastefully furnished, with shag carpeting, walnut paneling, a color TV, a queen-size sofa bed and two coordinated armchairs, and a kitchen equipped with an additional microwave oven and freezer. The back area converted into four more beds; in between was a bath and shower. Both Shelton's seat and the passenger's swiveled and reclined. Next to his, tucked in the map pocket, was a pistol. To keep him company on long drives, there was a CB radio, a tape deck, and a collection of cassettes by Brother Dave Gardner, for whom the Klan had served as bodyguards.

Shelton's reserve wore off as we drove through Tuscaloosa. At a busy intersection in what was once the outskirts of town, he nodded to the left. "When I was a kid, we picked cotton all out in there. My ol' home place—the house and the grocery—was up there on the hill."

The nostalgia was an unexpected departure from his matter-of-fact manner in Tennessee and even in his home. As the service stations and supermarkets gave way to rolling red clay and pine trees, he veered momentarily from the Klan to boast about his daughter Cindy's recent graduation from nursing school and her marriage and about how he had chewed tobacco until a few months ago but quit because "I like to do things that are a challenge to stop doing."

After a pause, his tone shifted to martyrdom. "I work better when I'm under pressure. I guess it's because things have always been so hard. You know it's not easy *just* being a member of the Klan, *particularly* being the leader of the Klan. You have three strikes against you going into the ballgame. Like at Rivergate."

When I asked if UKA's attempts to rent the Rivergate and New Orleans' Superdome were merely test cases, somewhat like those used by the NAACP in the sixties, Shelton said the Klan had used court cases long before this, adding that he wasn't too concerned about buildings because he preferred outdoor rallies, anyway.

"The person that's interested in the Klan will come to a function that's out in an open field much quicker than he would in a building downtown," he observed. "In a building, you can't have your cross-lighting ceremony. You don't have the stirring activity that you have in the open-type field, the formations, the ceremony of the cross. It's just a different atmosphere."

I thought about the rallies I had attended, the hard work that went into assembling the cross, and how, when the lighting actually came, many of the people were in their pickups and station wagons heading for the exit before the flames had licked their way to the top. Still, a veteran klanwatcher had likened the outdoor rally to a Wagnerian opera: "It has an overview of religious fervor. It has the dramatics, the theatrical, the passioned oratory, the pervading sense of violence and disaster. It's quite a dramatic show." But perhaps one klanswoman put it more poignantly, "This is pure Jesus."

Shelton's preference, however, seemed more for expedience than sentiment. "At least in a cow pasture—bein' an ol' country boy—I know exactly what to look for an' how high to raise my britches legs," he said, in an even more pronounced drawl. "But when you're in a buildin' an' in Washington, involved with the government, you can't see where you're goin' for all the political manure that's bein' thrown ever'where."

"Do you think if the Klan were to call itself something else, that would eliminate some of these hassles?" I suggested.

Shelton disagreed. "If you look at it on that basis, you could say since the Jews crucified Christ, why don't they call theirselves something else? You can look at the Nazis, and why don't they call theirselves something else? But people that are opposed to you are going to be in opposition to you regardless if you was the White Knights or the White Crusaders."

Nevertheless, in the sixties, many Klans, especially at a local level, did use cover names—such as the Delaware Birdwatchers and the Broward Fellowship Club—and Shelton acknowledged that some Klans still used such disguises, mostly, he said, for banking and to obtain loans.

"Like on the national level, we don't bank as the United Klans," he illustrated. "We bank as the 'Alabama Rescue Service.'"

"What's the difference between getting a loan or a bank account in the name of the United Klans and the Alabama Rescue Service?"

"Well, you've got to understand, you're dealing with liberal elements in many instances and more attention would be applied on any bank account or any billing or bills that come in as 'United Klans' than it would be 'Alabama Rescue Service.'"

"How did you choose that particular name?"

Shelton grinned. "We figgered it was about time *somebody* rescued some white folks!"

But the main reason for the cover names was to dodge the FBI harassment that Shelton and other leaders complained about and that most outsiders viewed as Klan fabrication until the U.S. Senate Select Committee's 1975 investigation into federal domestic intelligence. The hearings and continuing disclosures under the Freedom of Information Act had triggered several Klan lawsuits against the FBI, including one by UKA. Besides using the cover names, Shelton and UKA eventually invested in lie detectors and, according to one state leader, approved the use of "truth serum" to weed out informers. But the "purification" project had proven almost powerless against the FBI's Cointelpro, the shortened term for its counterintelligence programs aimed at sabotaging extremist groups in the sixties. The Klan still had to contend with infiltration and the FBI, Shelton said.

"If you're not doing or discussing anything wrong, why are you concerned about informers and why are you using lie detectors?" I asked.

"For the simple reason," he countered, "that informers are put there to provoke trouble."

Shelton shook his head disgustedly. "It's just been all types of harassment. I've been going through this for twenty-something years," he said, citing examples: a plot to assassinate him in a small plane crash; rumors that he was an addict and an alcoholic and was stealing Klan money; attempts to rent rooms from his neighbors in order to photograph his visitors; forging his signature on letters. But the biggest harassment had been the HUAC hearings and the resulting year in prison for himself, Bob Jones, and Robert Scoggin.

Even rank-and-file members had been targets of harassment and innuendos, Shelton continued, with agents sometimes visiting or telephoning wives and employers and/or sending cartoon postcards to expose their membership or to accuse them of running around. (During the 1975 Senate committee hearings into federal domestic intelligence activities, Gary Thomas Rowe, Jr., told investigators of FBI instructions to sleep with as many wives as possible in order to sow dissention. The story was corroborated by his control agent, who argued Rowe "couldn't be an angel and be a good informant.")

Shelton, like other Klan leaders I interviewed, claimed he had known the FBI was behind the harassment for at least eight or nine years. "But it was so unheard of that when you'd tell people, they thought you were crazy," he said.

"How did you find out? How did you get the FBI memos you've mentioned in various articles?" I asked.

"I had friends in Washington that would send the letters or be in touch with me and tell me some things that were going on, for me to be careful, what they [FBI] were trying to do. That they were trying to set me up, this, that, and the other. I have approximately a thousand copies acquired from friends in *key* positions in Washington, and they're very detrimental to me. And there's no telling how many families the FBI has caused divorces in, by harassing the wife and the husband."

The whole tale sounded bizarre, even in light of the Senate hearings. Then, nine months after my interview with Shelton, an Alabama truck driver and his wife filed a $250,000 suit against the FBI, charging that their marriage and sex lives had been adversely affected by "dirty tricks" conducted by the bureau against the husband because of his suspected membership in the Klan during the midsixties. The suit by Uriel and Laura Miles was the first of several that resulted from letters sent out in 1976 by a special committee established by Attorney General Edward Levi after the Senate investigation to inform three hundred persons they had been Cointelpro victims and could seek further information from the Justice Department. Twenty percent of the letters went to real or suspected members of white extremist groups, mostly the Ku Klux Klan.

When the suit was filed, John Mays, retained by Shelton to represent the Mileses and five other Birmingham klansmen, said the FBI dossier on the plaintiff contained two memos. One from the Birmingham bureau, dated August 25, 1966, indicated local agents had information that Miles was a Klan member, an excessive drinker, was not properly caring for his family, and was having an extramarital affair. Authority was asked to prepare an anonymous letter to Miles, with a carbon to Shelton. The memo included a suggested letter:

... I know what sorry things you have been doing lately and how you have neglected and mistreated your family. You and I are sworn to put an end to just such lowdown and sorry carrying on as you have been doing. I have put up with it as long as I'm going to. I'm letting the imperial wizard know about you. If he don't do something, or you don't straighten up and act right, me and some of your buddies are going to learn you a lesson.

In another memo, dated September 9, 1966, the Washington headquarters gave its Birmingham field office permission to begin its proposed harassment campaign on Miles:

Authority granted to prepare the letter proposed and to forward a copy to Shelton. The letter should be prepared with a manual typewriter on commercially purchased stationery and should contain a representative number of grammatical and typing errors. Post the letters in the area of Miles' Klan activity and take all the usual precautions to insure they cannot be associated with the bureau. Advise the bureau of any positive results and be alerted to recommend appropriate follow-up counterintelligence action.

At the time the lawsuit was filed, Mays noted that "not a single one of these individuals were suspected of having committed a crime or an act of violence." Some, he said, were not even members of the Klan at the time of the FBI actions.

UKA's fifty-million-dollar suit, filed in August 1977, sought remuneration for damages for "fraud, continued harassment and intimidation" and for loss of revenue during the FBI's 1964 to 1972 intelligence programs "aimed at hate groups." Attorney Mays indicated he had "evidence" that FBI agents broke into the Klan's national headquarters during 1964–65 to "steal membership lists, correspondence lists, and subscription lists to the Fiery Cross," UKA's publication. He said he also had evidence that two FBI agents, trained to forge Shelton's signature and handwriting, distributed phony letters claiming that various klansmen had been banished. Shortly thereafter, Shelton filed a personal lawsuit.

During my travels, various Klan leaders told me of unsigned letters they and other right-wingers around the country were receiving in the mail, accusing some of homosexuality, among other things. When I asked Shelton if he were being harassed now, he was positive the FBI still kept tabs on him and his members.

"When the Klan gets real active and starts mushrooming in an area, they'll go in—three or four agents--and start paying visits to members, even potential members. And there's been a lot of times when we have our conventions, the FBI would get down all the tag numbers of the cars. And they set up phony Klan groups, which they still have some of 'em operating today."

"You think that some of the splinter groups are financed by the FBI?"

"Absolutely. They're financed by the FBI and the government."

"Why do they do this?"

"It gives them an opportunity to attack us," he explained. "They can set up a phony Klan group that can go in and make us ineffective. If you've got the American Nazi Party—which most people despise—associated with the Klan and they go into an area and philosophize on their theories, people are going to say, 'Well, that's not what I thought the Klan was.' Then we gotta spend all this time patchin' up and redoin' what they tore down."

"Do you think David Duke is in that category?"

"Wellll," he hesitated, suspicious, "there's something very peculiar in that operation. I haven't been able to put my hands on it yet, but we're workin' on somethin'."

Shelton's accusation of phony Klan groups had been proven at least partially true during testimony before the Senate committee and in FBI documents released under the Freedom of Information Act. The long-standing feud in the sixties between North Carolina Dragon Bob Jones and the Reverend George F. Dorsett, and the latter's break to form the Confederate Knights of the Ku Klux Klan, had been orchestrated—and paid for—by the FBI, including help by the Bureau in drafting a letter to recruit members. The plot to sow dissension among the burgeoning

North Carolina ranks also had included circulation among klansmen of a letter from the "National Intelligence Committee" (NIC) that said Shelton and Jones had been suspended for mishandling of funds. At the time, 1967, Shelton, Jones and other key UKA leaders publicly swore no such committee existed, but Dorsett told the press NIC was a supersecret Klan intelligence agency that even the top leaders knew nothing about, one that had been formed in 1964 "by the people to protect them from the leadership." In 1975, however, a memorandum released with other FBI documents read:

> The so-called supersecret NIC referred to in these articles is a fictitious organization originated and controlled by the Bureau in our continuing program to disrupt the Klan on a nationwide scale. The purpose behind this fictitious committee is to circulate misleading information which will continue to neutralize and disrupt the Klan and discredit Klan leaders.

Dorsett was not the only informer to hold a high office in the Klan. Another set of released records showed that in the midsixties FBI informants held top-level leadership roles in seven of the then fourteen Klan groups and headed one state organization. At one time in 1965, nearly two thousand of the FBI-estimated ten thousand Klan members were its own informers. In letters written in September 1965 to Attorney General Nicholas Katzenbach and a special assistant to President Lyndon B. Johnson, J. Edgar Hoover boasted, "774 (informants) have been developed in just the past year—an average of more than two each day for every day in the past twelve months." Hoover was counting only FBI informants. There were also those planted by local and state law enforcement agencies and the Anti-Defamation League of B'nai B'rith.

Besides helping to populate the Invisible Empire, the records showed that the program to sabotage the Klan had included psychological warfare by pitting klansman against klansman in an attempt to create among them the fear that under every hood there might lurk an FBI informant. The records also documented the cartooned postcards Shelton and other leaders had described. One pictured a klansman saying, "I am an informant, color me fed!" Another, captioned "FBI Infiltrates Klan," showed two klansmen in a sinking rowboat with one exclaiming, "We seem to have sprung a leak!"

Hoover's letters to Katzenbach and Johnson's aide noted that the informants had helped the FBI not only to solve Klan murders and other crimes but also to prevent violence. He wrote:

> In one southern state, for example, the governor on one occasion expressed his great concern and fear of an outbreak of racial violence

because of the tense situation. But the head of the Klan organization in that state is our informant and we have had him warn every member of his organization that he will not tolerate violence in any form. As a result, we have been successful to date in holding Klan violence in the entire state to an absolute minimum.

Who was the Dragon? Bob Jones, Robert Scoggin, or Calvin Craig, who resigned in 1968 to join Atlanta's Model Cities Program? All three had held down violence, yet built up membership in their states. Any one of them could have been Hoover's fed.

There was no indication in the released documents as to the cost of the anti-Klan program or the money spent by the government on Klan dues, assessments, and robes.

Publicly, and in my own contact with the FBI, the Bureau vowed it no longer kept tabs on the Klan. Yet during an interview, one U.S. attorney thumbed through a just-released secret document on current Klan activity and confessed, "We are very concerned about a possible resurgence of Klan-type activity." A police intelligence officer also confided that the FBI was "trying to make a decision to actively investigate the Klan." When I filed a Freedom of Information request for the arrest records of eighty-three klansmen—accompanied with stories publicly identifying them as leaders and members—a spokesman claimed the Bureau had never received my parcel, even though I had hand delivered it to the J. Edgar Hoover Building. Five months later, after repeated calls, my letter and list surfaced; the clips no longer were attached.

As the interstate cut through Meridian, Mississippi, a Klan stronghold in the sixties, Shelton looked at the speedometer and announced the 1974 Executive camper had just passed the sixty-two thousand mark. The pickup truck used to haul his speaker's platform had been driven another thirty-four thousand miles, he said.

"I average about a hundred and thirty-five thousand miles a year. *That's* driving, not including air or anythang like that," he said, sounding both proud and put upon. "It's not so bad in the winter months. But in the summer, it's pretty constant. I'd say on an average traveling takes anywhere from three to four days a week at the height of rally season. In the sixties and early seventies, it wasn't unusual to have thirty rallies going on a Saturday night. I *have* made as high as sixty-two *continuous* nights."

"Don't you get tired of talking?"

"Well," he admitted wearily, "it gets kindy tiresome sometimes."

Thinking back to the Pulaski rally, I remembered a group of men crowding in front of the speaker's van after the cross-lighting, laughing and jostling one another. When I asked a teenage boy what was going on, he had answered, "Yellow Dog." Now, Shelton described it as both a "fun degree" and a test for mental attitude.

"Is this part of the initiation or for members?"

"Well," he said, looking secretive, "I can't go into a lot of detail of what transpires, but it's some pretty rough things. Kinda like a fraternity in college. It kinda gives you an idea of what kind of nerves a man's got. Blindfold a man, tie a string to an oyster, put it in his mouth, an' tell him to swallow it an' pull it back up."

"Why do you need a test like that?"

"It's just a fun ..." He gave a slight chuckle. "It gives you an opportunity to see how much he can take, if he's going to do what you tell him to do. Or if he's going to resist, if he's going to fight."

"When you say, 'If he'll do what you tell him to do,' do you mean dangerous assignments?"

"No, not necessarily," he replied. "You can tell if the man is going to work in the framework of the organization or if he's going to rebel."

The "fun degree" was unique to UKA, he added. There was also the Royal Order of the Purple Dog, "the granddaddy of the two." The Purple Dog was conducted only at national conventions; the Yellow Dog, at rallies and klavern meetings.

We rode silently a while, as Shelton looked ahead at the highway he had traveled more times than he could remember. His quietness seemed heavy with reminiscence, maybe of other trips, other rallies, other missions, perhaps of times when the Klan made travel through these same piney hills so dangerous for blacks and civil rights workers.

"Do you know what you're going to talk about tonight? Any particular issues?" I interrupted his thoughts.

"No, I get up there, and whatever comes to my mind is what I say."

"Do you get a speaker's fee?"

"No, it's part of my work," he said.

"What does it cost to put on a rally?"

Shelton shrugged. "Sometimes you can probably get the grounds for nothing; then again you might have to pay a hundred fifty, three hundred, five hundred dollars. You gotta take into consideration what you gotta have. Rent on the property. Some areas require you to have X number of toilets for the expected crowd you're gonna have, and there's a rental fee on that. It varies from a hundred dollars to a thousand dollars, two thousand."

"Do you make that back when you take up a collection?"

He shook his head. "That's all local."

"Do you go in the hole?"

"Well," he chuckled, "I've *always* gone in the hole."

At every rally I attended, robed klanspeople circulated through the crowd with upturned hoods and cardboard boxes, like church deacons taking up the offering. During the sixties, HUAC prosecutors and disgruntled klansmen made much of the final destination of similar collections. Their fate was no less mysterious or controversial today, with leaders like Shelton and Duke frequently being accused of "running with the money." But Shelton maintained most accusations were manufactured by the FBI, that neither he nor the Imperial headquarters made anything off the collections, Klan paraphernalia, or the sale of robes.

In the sixties, United Klans had operated Heritage Enterprises Incorporated, a thriving corporation that included Heritage Garment Works in Columbia, South Carolina, and Heritage Insurance Agency in Bessemer, Alabama. The Klan reportedly held fifty-one percent of the insurance company's stock, with the remaining forty-nine percent owned by personal friends of Shelton. During the HUAC hearings, investigator Donald Appell also introduced evidence that the Imperial Wizard received a commission on the sale of robes. To me, Shelton rejected any connection. "I'm not in the robe business. I don't care anything about being involved in it. We try to get them to push it on a local level, whether they get their wives or some widow woman that's a good seamstress." But William M. Chaney, Indiana's Grand Dragon until he was ousted by Shelton, attributed UKA's break with Heritage Garment Works to Shelton's suspicion that Younger Newton was passing the names of robe customers on to the FBI and to Newton's continuing business with Robert Scoggin after he was banished.

The Executive van left the interstate and headed down a two-lane highway that cut through Amite, a nondescript town of Dairy Queens and hamburger stands just northwest of New Orleans. Shelton let up on the gas pedal and crept through the sparsely-peopled streets, looking at each intersection for a ballpark.

"Let's try this one," he said, sluggishly steering the huge van over railroad tracks, still craning his neck at intersections until he saw a Little League stadium. He stopped even with the red-clay diamond and took stock of the drab bleachers and decrepit concession booths. Then, eyeing two tree trunks—one short, the other long—lying near second base, he wheeled the van behind the empty stands and parked.

Only the tree trunks hinted that a Klan rally was on the evening's agenda. No signs, no preparations, no people welcomed the Imperial Wizard. A two-story brick hospital faced the empty ballpark on one side, a trailer court on the other, but even they appeared vacant in the midafternoon heat. Faint sounds of laughter and splashing drifted from a nearby swimming pool. Yet Shelton didn't seem to mind his lonely entrance.

"I've held rallies ever' place you can think of and in ever' area," he said as he searched for an electrical outlet in which to plug the van. "Chicken houses. Gravel pits. Cow pastures. Banquet rooms. Hotels. Motels. Coliseums. You name it."

A smile crept across his face.

"What are you thinking about?"

"Yeah, we've been some places," he chuckled. "Rain. Sleet. Snow. I spoke in Michigan when it was twenty-six below zero."

"What kind of crowd did you get?"

"It was a pretty good crowd. 'Course it was inside."

When Shelton and the Klan were more acceptable to the segregated South, when he still called the shots from local klaverns to the Alabama governor's office, his entrances were carefully staged even if he had to circle the block several times to arrive at the most opportune moment. But there was no fanfare this day. Just one lone man who couldn't even pull strings to get into New Orleans' Rivergate. He kicked at the parched red clay, the sun steadily sucking sweat to his forehead and back. No hint of disappointment or anger altered his somber expression, although now and again he flashed the time on his electron watch and offered excuses: Friday was a bad day for a rally; people were just too tired after working all week.

Returning to the air-conditioned van, Shelton talked confidently about his lawyers working things out for tomorrow night. That rally *would* be held at the Rivergate. The Klan was being discriminated against. They were being required to pay a bond that other organizations weren't.

"Sometimes I sure wish that I'd went ahead and got a law degree so I could just go into the courts and give 'em headaches," he lamented. Shelton said he had studied prelaw at the University of Alabama for two years. The length of his education varied, according to past articles, from "a few courses" to a year. To me, he said that he had quit out of disgust with the teaching at the university; in old interviews, he had blamed lack of money and grades. HUAC investigators claimed the university dropped him after he had failed every course for two semesters.

About four o'clock, a car pulled up, followed by a pickup truck and the speaker's platform. Shelton ambled out to meet the men and to mull over the Rivergate dilemma and alternate plans to stage a parade in downtown New Orleans and to picket the giant convention facility and a black demonstration. The huddle—composed of Shelton, Pete Holden, the incoming Louisiana Grand Dragon, and Andrew Jackson Harrison, a stocky teenager who headed UKA's Junior Order—grew as cars trickled on to the grounds, and wide-eyed boys in wet bathing trunks congregated to watch.

Finally, Pete Holden walked away, calling back, "Where you gonna set up the trailer, Bob?"

"Behind second base."

A slender man with thick gray hair and piercing blue eyes, Holden—a service-station owner—began the arduous task of piecing together the rally, of unloading the speaker's platform and supervising construction of the cross, his work clothes becoming doused with sweat and oil and gasoline. All of the men took turns digging a hole for the cross until a photographer focused on Shelton and one of them grabbed his shovel, joking, "We can't have our Imperial Wizard photographed like *that!*"

By nightfall, the lights in the speaker's van and the ballpark were blazing. But the crowd consisted of fifteen or twenty people in the stands, two women in the concession booth, youngsters from the swimming pool, and the speakers, most of whom I had met in Pulaski: Holden, Andy Harrison, outgoing Dragon W. J. Kidd, Richard "Sky Boots" Toups, and George Higgins, Jr., the Mississippi Grand Dragon whose wife's election as a delegate to the National Women's Conference caused panic among ERA proponents. The men, I speculated, were perhaps Shelton's entire membership in the area.

Even the stirring marches on the public address system failed to arouse enthusiasm in the audience or the speakers. Here was none of the excitement or polish of the well-rehearsed Pulaski rally. None of the "show biz." Just a small group of weary people, the most faithful of Shelton's flock, who came out of obligation or for lack of a better way to spend a hot Friday night. Shelton spoke briefly, without bothering to put on his robe.

The next day, he and his followers neither paraded down Canal Street nor rallied in the Rivergate; instead, they settled for a small motorcade through nearby Covington and an indoor gathering at the local community center. A thunderstorm that washed out a David Duke rally in a wooded area thirty minutes away also dampened the spirits of the UKA affair. Except for a trio of state police officers, the faces—like the speeches—were leftovers from the night before. And while the white-robed klanspeople struggled to light a soggy cross in an adjoining playground, Shelton remained apart, inside the center, weary and alone, he and the dollar-apiece posters of him as a young hawk-faced Imperial Wizard in a purple satin robe.

11
G. T. Miller:
Taking on the Klan

Luverne, Alabama

On Highway 331, the one that goes due south from Montgomery to Luverne, past the welcome to "The Friendliest City of the South" sign, G. T. Miller pointed out an abandoned concrete foundation, creosote pilings rising above it like a monument to a broken dream.

"We was abuildin' a million-dollar warehouse when the Ku Klucks come after us," he said, explaining it was to have been part of a profit-sharing program for small farmers. Next to the foundation were Miller's Feed and Grist Mill and Miller's Service Station and Café and, on down the road, Miller's Supermarket. The café was "under new management," the supermarket was permanently dusty, and the mill had been bought out by his son and a partner when the banks threatened to foreclose.

For seventy-six, George Thaxton Miller was unusually burly. His hair was more black than gray, his browned arms firm. Moments earlier, he had trudged through his small truck farm, twisting off ears of corn and tossing them into a long cotton sack that he slung over his shoulder with the ease of a man half his age. Before he quit school in third grade to plow full time for his father, he fist-fought the three miles home every day, and, in his twenties, he was the champion wrestler and boxer of Crenshaw County. He could beat most anybody if he had a mind to. But the Klan had been something else, he conceded. He had been no more match for them during their first go-'round in the thirties than he had been since the beginning of an almost ten-year boycott of his mill—a boycott that the local Klan instigated because he refused to fire a black man whose son was among those to integrate Luverne's schools in 1967.

Before the boycott, that stretch of highway had been a bustling testimony to Miller's success at building the small gristmill he started with an old Buick motor into a dozen or so thriving enterprises. He figured the boycott had cost him $25,000 a year in business—$95,000, all told—and a good many friends who feared Klan reprisal if they so much as spoke to him. Still, Miller considered the warehouse's corpse philosophically. "Wellll, the good Lord ain't gonna let you take ne'er a penny with you, anyhow."

Now he spent most of his time tending the truck farm or puttering around the brick home that still, because of the boycott, lacked air conditioning. His usual attire—bib overalls, faded work shirt, and a well-worn felt hat—was no different from his more prosperous days or when he had farmed, logged, and cut hair to eke out a living.

Two oscillating fans shifted the heat from side to side in the den as he unraveled his Klan saga for me that August afternoon in 1976. His third wife, Clara, and Judy, their black cook, listened from the kitchen, now and then correcting a name or a date. Otherwise, Miller played all the roles in his version of a drama that began, he said, when his Uncle Ed invited him to a meeting over the Masonic Hall in the backwoods community where he lived. Then in his late twenties, Miller was married, with two children and a small piece of land. He had spent eight months in a federal prison for conspiring to make moonshine and for shooting a deputy in the scuffle that followed his arrest. But that experience was now no more than a good yarn he associated more with cutting Al Capone's hair than with serving time.

"I never heered tell of the Klan 'til then," Miller started, tilting his platform rocker. "But they said they was an awful good group an' they was he'pin' poor folks an' widow women, so I let 'em talk me into the notion of joinin'. It was 'bout six months when I began to find out what they *really* was. They was askin' for some volunteers to go out an' do what they call 'dressin' up.' I helt up my hand. I said, 'What'd you call 'dressin' up'? So they up an' tol' me. It was takin' you out an' beatin' the devil outta you! I said, '*Maaaaan,* you don't wanta git into beatin' up people.' They said, 'This fella got outta line an' we need to git him back in.' I begged 'em not to. So they eased on off an' didn't exactly let me know when they was gonna do it.

"Next time, then, when I found out they was goin' out to beat up somebody, I slipped out an' goes around a day or two ahead an' notified the man they was gonna take him out an' whup up on 'im. Somehow, the fella they was gonna beat up, when it was all over with, he said, 'You know, they would've got me last Frid'y night when the Klan met, but Mister Miller, he come out heah an' tol' me about it.' Well, he was talkin' to a Ku Kluck *an' didn't know it!*"

Miller's voice raced as he reconstructed how the Klan came after him, giving him a flogging and a threat: "You better never do that no more, *or else.*" And he didn't, not for maybe a year, not until he overheard plans by the Klan to flog some white folks in next-door Butler County. This time, Miller related, when he showed up to warn them, the Klan was laying wait for *him* and the original victims.

"Maaaaan, they give me about twenty-five licks with a big strop. Tore my butt up to where my britches jes' stuck to me. There was five of 'em beatin' me. One would hold this leg. T'other un would hold this leg. An' t'other un would hold this arm, an' another one would hold t'other arm. An' they'd lay you down on your face an' whup your back end with a strop about three inces wide. Give you five licks apiece. Wellll, I felt one of 'em—I didn't know which it was—give slack on my right leg, an' then I felt t'other fella loosen my arm, an' when he did, I jes' *wheeeeeled* over right quick—I was young an' pretty active then—an' when I jumped up, it surprised 'em by me bein' so quick! I kicked one of 'em in the groin. I *reeeally* kicked him, and, boy! he hit the doggone dirt an' commenced hollerin' and rooolled down the banks! Then I kicked the other un in the stomach, an' he leaned over, an' I hit him right there, on the neck! Down he went! An', boooy, I took off! I put to runnin', an' they hollered, '*Shoot him! Shoot him!*' Well, they hauled off then an' shot me with birdshot in the behind, and that didn't do a thang in the world but put me in high gear!"

His dilapidated hat sat on a nearby stool, captive audience to yet another rendition of the scrabble. Miller nudged it with his shoe and chuckled, the kind of chuckle that comes only after time turns a harrowing experience into an amusing memory.

"By that time, I was clear by the end of the bridge, an' I jes' slid down off the dirt bank into the water. An' swum down the creek a mile, I'd say. Near 'bout a mile. An' I jes' eeeased on down the creek. I was skeered to go home because I knowed they'd come git me. So I got close enough home to where I could see it, but I wouldn't go up 'til daylight. Sure 'nough, if I'd 've went home, they would've got me, 'cause they went that night lookin' fer me.

"By that time the police had done got word that we'd had a shootin' spat and a nigger'd gotten killed. Well, I'd recognized 'em that night. I'd snatched one of 'em's hood off, an' then I recognized two of 'em's voices because I'd cut their hair—shaved 'em, too—at my country barbershop. So by the time I got in the house, here come the klansmen. An' they said, 'If you tell on any of us,' they said, 'the next time, 'stead of the darkie gettin' killed, it's gonna be you!' "

Miller and the klansmen agreed to go their separate ways, he continued. He wouldn't bother them; they wouldn't bother him. He had, however, got some revenge: once he whipped one of the assailants outside his mill 'jes' to let him know to leave me alone"; another time, he gave a klansman a going-over in downtown Greenville. The police had fined Miller for that set-to, but now he beamed, "That was the best ten bucks I ever did spend." Aside from those incidents, he and the Klan had had no more than a hat-tipping acquaintance for more than thirty years, until the midsixties when the Civil Rights Movement reached Luverne.

Draining the sugary sediment from his iced tea, Miller set the next scene in his drama, a morning in 1967 shortly after a court ruling had peppered Crenshaw County's schools with their first eighty-five blacks, one of them the son of a mill employe.

"That night after they got all lined up for school," Miller recalled, "the Ku Klucks went out to Willie McDonald's house an' beat 'im up, run 'im off from home an' shot at him. But they missed, an' he out run 'em. Got away. He didn't tell me about it fer a day or two, but I could tell there was somethin' wrong, so one day I said, 'McDonald, seems like somethin's botherin' you. What's the matter?' He broke down an' went to cryin'. He said, 'Mister Miller, the Ku Klux Klan come out there, shot up my house, put KKKs in front of my door, an' tol' me if my boy went to school in Luverne with *any* class of whites, they're gonna beat me up an' run me outta town where I can't git a job.' So I said, 'Willie, if you come on an' go to work, I don't think they'll bother you no more.'

"Well, by George, he tol' me *this* mornin', and there was three of the Ku Klucks down there the next mornin'. They drove up out there an' said, 'Miller, I guess you know who we are, don't you? We your feed customers.' They said, 'The committee'—they didn't call theirselves Ku Klux—they said, 'The committee has asked us to come down heah an' ask you to fire Willie McDonald.' I said, *'What???'* They said, 'His boy's goin' to school with your boy.' I said, 'Well, he's going to school with the rest of the white boys uptown, too.' They said, 'Yeah, but he's in the class with your boy.' Anyway, they said, 'We're gonna turn it into the committee, an' we'll jes' give you three days to git shed of him.' I said, 'Nooooo, won't do it.' "

Miller sipped some tea and continued. "The second day they were back. There was six of 'em come that time. Two carloads of 'em, an' they had guns. They come up and ask if I made up my mind to fire him. I said, 'Nooo.' They said, 'Well, we're jes' gonna give you a choice. We gonna come down heah an' beat 'im up on your place, an' if you interfere, we're gonna beat you up, too.' Said, 'Remember, the Ku Klucks had you once or twice.'

"Next mornin', there was nine of 'em back. Drove up and got out with guns. An' Willie was workin' out there. We was pourin' cement. An' they all got out an' started towards him, and he broke to run. I run out there between 'em and tol' 'im, 'Don't run, 'cause they'll shoot you.' An' they said, 'Yeah, we come to shoot, 'cause we're gonna run him outta town.

You, too, if you interfere.' So I got in between 'em and went to beggin' 'em not to do it. But they said, 'Nooooo, we're gonna beat 'im. We're gonna git 'im right now,' an' they started around me. About that time, there was ten or fifteen cars that'd stopped, an' ever'body wanted to know what the excitement was. So the Ku Klucks got in their car an' went to hidin' their guns, an' said, 'Miller, we're gonna take other actions on you.' Said, 'We're gonna run him outta town, anyhow, but we'll take *other* actions on you.' "

At first, Miller considered the threat only talk. But by the next morning, he recalled, word had spread around town that the Klan was throwing a boycott on his mill. Customers were cautioned: "If I was y'all, I wouldn't grind feed there, 'cause they say they're gonna burn Miller's mill up. Or blow it up, one. An' they're gonna blow up the schoolhouse over yonder. Colored folks' schoolhouse."

"There was a lotta people wanted to grind feed with us, but they was skeered to 'cause they didn't know but what the Ku Klucks would do to them one way or 'nother. So then at noon, jes' as we set down to dinner, the phone rung, an' this same lady right here—you the one answered, ain't you, Judy?"

From the kitchen, the cook called back, "Yes, sir."

"She answered the phone, an' they tol' her she better come git her kids outta school. They was fixin' to blow up that place, and also they was gonna blow up Miller's place. It skeered her because she had . . ." Again he yelled to Judy, "You had three kids in school, didn't you?" The number confirmed, he went on. Judy and Miller's wife had hurried to the school to pick up her youngsters even though FBI agents, who had arrived a day or two before, assured him the Klan wasn't going to blow up the school or his mill.

"The FBI stayed on with me, then, all day," Miller recalled, "but that night, booooy, the Ku Klucks jes' rode this place all over an' shot their guns . . ."

"At the house?" I managed to interrupt.

"I can't say where they shot. They jes' shot. They didn't never hit the house. Anyway, me and my wife got up an' stirred around a little bit, half skeered to death. Then by midnight or a little after, they quit ridin' around through the place, and the telephone went to ringing. An' they was askin', 'Miller, the FBI's down there with you, ain't they?' I said, 'They was here today, but I understood they left.' They said, 'Naw, they here in town somewheres. We got our eye on 'em. An' you better never tell 'em nuthin' if you wanta live. We jes' givin' you a warnin'.' "

Easing back in the platform rocker, Miller sighed as though the mental melee had exhausted him as much as the actual midnight-to-morning telephone calls, the shooting, and the lengthy boycott that had stretched into a way of life. Clara, a fiftyish woman seemingly as strong-willed as her husband, had entered the den during his narrative. Now she added her recollections.

"God really looked after us. There's no two ways about it," she vouched. "Nobody 'round here would sell us corn an' stuff, 'cause they'd been told not to, but people off from a distance would sell us. An' we would think ever' time we'd send off a load of feed, well, 'the next order we git, we won't have corn and hay to fill it.' But we *never* ran out. It was always enough to fill the orders that we had an' still have some left for another order. An' it stayed that way allll the . . ."

"This was four or five years this went on?" I asked.

"Yes."

"So you were boycotted on both sides," I clarified. "The people around here wouldn't sell you corn and hay, and other people also wouldn't buy from you?"

"Right. They wouldn't patronize us in the grindin' an' the thangs like that."

Miller re-entered the conversation. "It was jes' like takin' a glass jug an' holdin' it to the handle an' fillin' it full of water an' takin' a pair of pliers an' hittin' the side of it. *Boomfff!* All of it went. Our business dropped from seven hundred an' fifty thousand dollars down to sixty-five thousand dollars gross business a year, an' that made us lose twenty-five thousand a year."

Then, the summer of 1968, when the U.S. Justice Department sought an injunction against the Crenshaw Unit of the UKA and its leaders to put a stop to their interference with school desegregation in the county, the Millers were among the blacks and whites called as government witnesses. The threats picked up with renewed vigor.

"After midnight our phone would go to ringin', an' they'd cuss us out an' ask us, 'You goin' to testify against us in federal court?' I said, 'Well, we're going up there an' tell the truth. Don't know whether it's testifying against you or not.' They said, 'Well, if you do, you won't never live to git back to Luverne.' Said, 'We'll guarantee you that.' So that went on 'til the federal court had a hearin' an' we went there and testified against 'em. Tol' the truth on 'em. An' they got a charge against forty-five of 'em an' put 'em under what we call a probation or injunction. If they harassed us or either the school or anythang like that, they would be subject to serve some time in the penitentiary. So they went along then with that pretty well."

There was a short moratorium. The shooting and the phone calls stopped, and business at the mill seemed on the rise. Then a CBS television crew, headed by newsman Ed Rabel, arrived from Atlanta to document Luverne's year-long quarantine of the Millers at the mill, on the street, even at church. The preacher had refused to allow cameras in the sanctuary but, Miller recalled, agreed the crew could film outside.

"So we come out an' was shakin' hands with the preacher an' they was takin' pictures. An' when we did, then what happened, there was a bunch that jumped on Ed Rabel. Kicked the camera down, pushed 'em over an' tried to turn the car over. Broke down a dogwood bush an' hit 'em with it an' stuck it in front of the camera. So we come back home an' et dinner an' Rabel said, 'What you think happened, Miller?' I said 'I jes' don't know. Ever'one of 'em is my friends. I been friends with ever' one of 'em.' He said, 'Suppose we call 'em an' see if we can talk to 'em?' So we called the preacher, an' he said, 'Yeah, some of 'em jes' got upset there an' done all that 'fore they knowed it. We really feel sorry that it happened.' Said, 'I'll go 'round with you to these folks myself.'

"So next mornin', the TV people come in here, but ever' time they'd go into a fella's place to talk with him about it, some of 'em took wrenches, hammers, and ever'thang an' *run 'em out* of there. Instead of makin' apologies, they said, 'We gonna run y'all outta town.' An' they had the polices an' ever'thang follerin' behind 'em. They was klansmen . . . If they wasn't klansmen, they'd be what you call honorary klansmen on the police department, an' they'd drive up behind 'em an' say, 'Y'all goin' to stay in town long, or y'all leavin'? We thought it might be best for y'all to go on.' They never would threaten 'em no way, but they'd ask 'em that two or three times."

Miller paused long enough to take a full glass of tea from Judy.

"So the Ku Klucks, then, they really put on a drive to push us out of business. They set my mill afire, but before that, I'd jumped in an' washed it down with water an' poured cement on the bottom floor in case some of them *did* throw some gasoline or somethin', it would be hard to catch. An' they piled some wood on in there—a li'l ol' pile of wood and splinters—set it on fire, but so much cement an' we had it so damp all 'round the mill till it went out."

Again, Miller recalled, the FBI visited him and insisted, " 'They ain't gonna do nuthin'. We went to the city polices, the county officials, an' the county sheriffs. Tol' 'em that we done seen enough, that if anythang happened, it looks like we're gonna have to involve y'all first thang.'

"That changed the picture a little bit. It came to look a whole lot better. But we knew that some of the polices an' all was honorary members of the Klan. We done found that out. So we rocked along that way until we liked to went broke, if it hadn't been for a young lawyer out of Montgomery an' the Koinea Partners in Americus, Georgia—what we call a Christian movement. They offered to help me if I wanted to stay, an' they lent us a little money to keep us goin'."

Miller added up their other losses: their regular income tax man quit;

most banks cut off their credit; a local merchant refused to install central heat and air conditioning in the brick house, which was then under construction; a cross was burned in the yard of his son's mother-in-law, and his widowed daughter-in-law closed the supermarket and fled to Montgomery.

"We had to git shed of a good bit of our property, an' then it kep' on so bad 'til we asked the United States Department of Justice if there was any way we could put a claim against the Ku Klucks to take care of some of our losses, an' they told us, said, 'We can't do it, but if you find the right kind of lawyer, he might bring 'em to light enough that they'll stop.' So we sued 'em in federal court, an' right after we filed suit, our business went to comin' back. In less than a year we had fifty percent back, and in less than two years, we had seventy-five percent of it back. An' finally they come to us an' wanted us to ... said, 'We'd like for us all to agree together to nol process [sic] that suit.' Said, 'We'll all—the klansmen an' ever'body else—will come back an' grind feed with you.' So the lawyer fixed up papers an' we dropped charges. But then, I was way past retirin' age, an' we sold the feed mill then to my son an' another young fella."

Miller's bottom lip normally stuck out in a little-boy pout. Now it quivered, and his eyes teared as he related the ordeal with friends and acquaintances, told how people would turn their head rather than speak, and when he attempted to shake hands, they would snatch theirs back and sneer, "I don't wanta shake hands with a nigger lover."

"What is it like today?" I asked.

"It's kind of easin' off," Clara Miller answered for her husband. "It's not completely gone yet, but it's startin' to ease up."

"Do you still hear people say they won't deal with you because they're afraid?"

"Oh, yeah," she nodded, "you can hear that all along."

Pondering the saga, from the boycott on back to the beatings, I asked, "Did you try to go to the police when they beat you?"

"I knowed better," Miller answered, "'cause I knowed the polices was honorary members and the judge, too."

Throughout Miller's tale, especially when the old man's lip trembled, I had waited for him to recall his own night riding. In a clipping from the 1968 hearings into Klan interference with the desegregation of Crenshaw County's schools, I came across an admission by Miller that he, too, had intimidated blacks "to the point of killing" during his own Klan membership in the twenties. Yet Miller had described to me only his own harassment.

"But didn't you go on some beatings?" I asked.

"Nooooo," he assured me. "Wouldn't go out on none of 'em. They got real teed off at me 'cause I'd go 'round an' tell on 'em. They called me a 'rat.' "

Had he been misquoted? Perhaps the clipping referred to someone else? Later, I looked up several more-recent newspaper articles that described the tribulations of the boycott and his earlier beatings. There was no hint of brutality on his part. When I questioned people from the area who had known him, their opinions conflicted. One man, reared in Luverne, knew him vaguely as "a nice man"; one woman, however, described him as "white trash" and accused him of using the boycott to cover his bad debts, adding, "I wouldn't believe anything he said."

CBS newsman Ed Rabel had encountered the same problem when he and the camera crew went to Luverne to do their story on the Millers. "There were a lot of bad feelings about him and a lot of conflicting stories," Rabel remembered. "As I recall, the minister said the people thought Miller was a charlatan, that all these things he was saying weren't really true. Then we interviewed G. T. Miller, who broke down and cried and recounted his past and said all he wanted to do now was help his fellow man, and he told about how they boycotted his feed-grain operation." There was no mention of his killing blacks. Rabel's own experiences in Luverne also conflicted with the story Miller had related to me. During the church filming, the members had snubbed the Millers, and one had broken off a tree limb and waved it in front of the camera. Another kicked the film crew's car as it drove off, but there was no attempt to overturn it, nor did the local citizens chase them out of town with wrenches and hammers.

"There was a confrontation there in which the local church people came out and were obviously upset with our presence," Rabel said.

"But they didn't try to turn over your car or anything like that?"

"Oh, no. I think parts of the story are true, but I guess other parts just don't hold up. I think it was true that members of the local community were hostile toward him and toward us because we were doing the story about him."

In Washington, the attorney who represented the Millers in their one-million-dollar suit against the Klan to recover losses from the boycott described Miller as "a very controversial, stubborn man." The boycott case had been dropped, the lawyer said, because Miller's books weren't good enough and because he lacked sufficient evidence to prove that the Klan boycott did all the damage. Cotton was no longer grown in the area after the late sixties, and some of the defendants had started their own grinding plants. These could have contributed to Miller's losses, the lawyer speculated. After staying with the Millers a week, the attorney was left with mixed feelings about his client. He both liked and disliked him. Although Miller had helped poor people in the community, the lawyer was not sure how much or how altruistic the deeds were.

"For a man with a third-grade education who can't read or write, G. T. went a long way," he commented, "but I'm not sure he was quite the wealthy man he is sometimes portrayed as."

The attorney loaned me a transcript of the school injunction hearings before U.S. District Court Judge Frank M. Johnson, Jr. I skimmed through Miller's testimony on the boycott and the Klan's orders to fire Willie McDonald, to his cross-examination by attorney Ira DeMent, whose role as Klan defender in the case caused a furor a year later when he was appointed a U.S. attorney:

Q. You used to be a member of the Klan, didn't you, Mr. Miller?
A. Forty-one years ago this fall.
Q. About how long were you a member?
A. About six months or a little better.
Q. Have you ever shot a Negro?
A. How is that?
Q. Have you ever shot a Negro with a weapon?
A. Yes, sir.
Q. How many times?
A. I wouldn't recall how many times.
Q. As many as six times?
A. I wouldn't think so, no.
Q. Have you ever killed a Negro?
A. Yes, sir.
Q. How many have you killed?
A. A couple of them.
Q. A couple of them?
A. Yes, sir.
Q. Were you ever prosecuted for that?
A. Yes, sir.
Q. And acquitted
A. I was.
Q. How many times were you prosecuted?

At that point, a government attorney objected, and Judge Johnson briefly took over the questioning, asking, "Were you prosecuted in Crenshaw County?"

THE WITNESS: I was.
THE COURT: A white jury?
THE WITNESS: Yes.
THE COURT: They turn you loose?
THE WITNESS: They did.

The questioning then changed directions. Under what circumstances had he killed the blacks? Had the explanation been stricken from the record? No one seemed to know or to remember, not even Ira DeMent. By phone, Miller himself denied the slayings, attributing the references to the black killed the same night the Klan flogged him. His wife said she didn't know the details because it happened before they met.

I reread the transcript and the clipping and thought about the afternoon with the Millers, about how he had laughingly described his family as "so po' the po' people called us po' " and how he had sobbed when he talked about being ostracized by the community for his work with poverty-stricken blacks. I remembered the details occasionally varying when he repeated stories. Was he senile? Was he lying? Or had the Klan orchestrated rumors that distorted fact with fiction? Why and when and *had* G. T. Miller killed those blacks so long ago that no one seemed to remember?

12

Ira DeMent:
The Defender

Montgomery, Alabama

For a time, it seemed, Ira DeMent's representation of the Klan
might be a stumbling block to his appointment as U.S. Attorney
for the middle district of Alabama. But now, after more than
seven years in the latter position, he could look back and chuckle. His
defense of the Klan during preliminary hearings into alleged interference with the integration of Crenshaw County's schools was just
another case. And yet, it wasn't *really* an ordinary case.

"They were just another client," he recalled by phone in early 1977 as
he unraveled the behind-the-scene story. "I quoted them a fee of a
thousand dollars to represent them, and they brought it in, in tens and
fives and ones. Some had to bale hay and sell it to get the money
together."

Most had taken the Fifth, and, as expected, they were enjoined against
harassing blacks and blocking school desegregation. The injunction was
posted in their meeting hall, and DeMent had considered the case closed
until the next year when his nomination as U.S. Attorney was challenged
because detractors claimed he was "a Klan lawyer."

Now, DeMent recalled, somewhat amused, how the Klan had offered
to come to *his* defense. "They wanted to go to Washington to get it
straightened out," he chuckled at the irony of the turn of events, adding,
"I wouldn't let them, of course."

"Did you find them to be different from what you had expected?" I
asked.

"No," he answered. "They were just ordinary people, close to the
earth. Ill-advised, to be sure, on some issues. But good ol' down-to-earth
Alabama rednecks."

He had no regrets for having represented them, he insisted.

"They were just another client, and I would represent them again for a
fee. That's what lawyers go to law school for."

13
The Birmingham Bombings

Washington, D.C.

The smirk on the face in the head shot in the September 29, 1977, *Washington Post* told the story. Before reading the news article or the headline, I knew that fourteen years of speculation and suspicion had ended in J. B. Stoner's arrest in connection with the rash of bombings that rocked Birmingham during the fifties and sixties. The photograph was no less haunting than the man at whom I had stared across the National States Rights party headquarters one hot afternoon in June 1976—the same eerie eyes, exuding a hate so compelling that even his soft, mannered drawl had not diminished it.

Before my travels through the South, several newsmen who covered the Civil Rights Movement had cautioned me about Stoner. "You be careful around him because he'll kill you," one warned. Another described him as "spooky, with cold, flinty eyes and sort of a heartless look about him. You get the feeling ice water runs through his veins." Most knew him as a man with an unquenchable hate for blacks and Jews and as the prime suspect in the 1963 Birmingham church bombing.

Gene Roberts, executive editor of the *Philadelphia Inquirer,* remembered that Stoner and his late cohort, Connie Lynch, "chased violence." Assigned to cover the South for *The New York Times* during the sixties, Roberts recalled questioning Stoner about the bomb rumors during a trial in Anniston, Alabama. "I asked if it were true that the FBI suspected him, and J. B. said, 'Yeah, they have me under surveillance.' I said, 'What do you have to say to the suspicion that you're the Birmingham Bomber?' and he just laughed and made no comment. Then I said, 'J.B., do you know anything about dynamite?' He said, 'Yeah, I know a lot about dynamite.' I said, 'Why do you know so much about dynamite?' and he answered, 'Well, you know how us lawyers are, you never know when knowing about dynamite will come in handy in a case,' and chuckled again."

I read the *Post* article, headlined "Church Bombing Denied By Gun-Toting Klansman":

MARIETTA, Ga.—The leader of the National States Rights Party, political arm of the Ku Klux Klan, was arrested here today on a charge that he dynamited a black church in Birmingham, Ala., in 1958.

J.B. Stoner, 53, denied in Cobb County Superior Court here that he was involved in the bombing. Wearing a small Confederate flag in his jacket breast pocket, Stoner—who once ran against Jimmy Carter for Governor of Georgia—said the statute of limitations had run out on the 1958 Birmingham bombing anyway.

Earlier, Stoner met with reporters here outside his party headquarters, a trim two-story brick building with a Confederate flag out front and two German shepherd guard dogs inside the fenced yard. Stoner, who was wearing a pistol in a holster on his right hip, called his indictment Monday by a grand jury in Birmingham the work of "nigger-loving" attorney general of Alabama, William J. Baxley.

Robert Chambliss, 73, of Birmingham, a retired auto mechanic, was accused on Monday of the 1963 bombing of the Sixteenth Street Baptist Church in Birmingham, in which four young black girls were killed.

Informed sources in Alabama said today that the Birmingham grand jury will return indictments against several more persons in the next two or three weeks. Alabama authorities believe that most of the racial bombings during the early desegregation struggle in the South were the work of two or three small groups of men.

Stoner was charged today with putting a dynamite bomb alongside the Bethel Baptist Church in Birmingham on June 19, 1958. The pastor was Rev. Fred L. Shuttlesworth, former Birmingham civil rights leader.

The bomb exploded after it was moved into an open area between the church and an adjoining house by a Bethel church employee. No one was injured.

The indictment against Stoner centers on the damage done to the house. By Alabama law the statute of limitations for bombing an uninhabited building runs out after 10 years, but bombing an inhabited dwelling is a capital offense with no statute of limitations.

The story conjured up memories of my interview with Stoner and another with aggressive thirty-six-year-old Attorney General Bill Baxley and revived the horror that jarred the nation's conscience when four black girls were killed September 15, 1963, in the bomb-shattered Sixteenth Street Baptist Church in Birmingham.

Mrs. Ella Demand had read the lesson for the day—"The Love That Forgives"—and dismissed her Sunday school class a little past ten o'clock. Denise McNair joined Cynthia Wesley, Carol Robertson, and Addie Mae Collins in the hallway, and the four scampered to a downstairs lounge to don satin choir robes. In spite of a three-year age difference between Denise, eleven, and the older girls, they were close friends. All but one were daughters of Birmingham schoolteachers. As they experimented with lipstick and makeup, a passing car slowed down near the north wall, then sped away. Moments later, an explosion thundered through the building, ripping it apart and showering the people with stained glass, plaster, and chunks of wood. The congregation—some screaming, some praying, some cursing—fled, their clothes torn and blood streaming from cuts and gashes. Blacks from nearby homes hurried to the church, where police with shotguns attempted to hold them back. Determined, some surged past, making their way through the blood-stained rubble to the downstairs lounge. *"Oh, God!"* one young man shrieked. *"My sister, she's dead!"* The crowd wailed and prayed as the four mutilated bodies were carried out. That night, the terror spilled over into the black section and into the rest of the city. Scattered bombings and fires lit the darkness like funeral pyres. Angered blacks roamed the streets, hurling rocks at cars that boasted Confederate flags. Police patrolled with dogs and shotguns, and five hundred National Guardsmen were called out to keep order. Yet, by daybreak, the city police—notorious for their "working relationship" with the Klan—had fatally shot a black teenager among the rock throwers and another riding his bicycle. Two others—one white, one black—were wounded. Governor George Wallace, under court orders to end the violence that had started with school-desegregation rulings, offered a five-thousand-dollar reward for the arrest and conviction of those responsible for the church bombing. No one claimed the money.

The bombing was the fourth in less than a month, and fiftieth in two decades, in what had become known as "Bombingham." Almost from the beginning, law enforcement officials were rumored to have known the bombers' identities but claimed to be unable to gather sufficient evidence to indict them. They—like law officials in much of the South— also faced the insurmountable task of finding a jury willing to convict a white man for a crime against blacks.

Robert Chambliss, a former klansman, was first charged along with two other men within days of the blast. At the time of those indictments, state troopers were reported to have information that would lead to the implication of an out-of-state man as the ringleader in the bombings. When the state failed to present ample evidence to link even Chambliss and the two others to the blast, the trio was convicted on the lesser charge of illegal possession of dynamite. They appealed the decision and were found innocent.

Born in Pratt City, a working-class section of Birmingham that was now all black, Chambliss had had a limited education and wrote only slowly and laboriously. Local police referred to him as "Dynamite Bob" because he boasted of his ability with explosives. Although he had an extensive arrest record, he had never been convicted of a serious offense. His first recorded arrest was for liquor-law violations in October 1935. Less than a year later, he was charged with desertion of his first wife and nonsupport of his children. He was also said to have a long record of violent confrontations with blacks, including a charge of "flogging while masked." His ties with two sons by his first marriage long severed, he had married a second time and now lived in a lower-middle-income section that was rapidly integrating. Neighbors described him as a poor, uneducated man who kept to himself. In spite of his record, several black residents had expressed surprise when he was indicted again in 1977 for the bombing.

Aside from a stylized black Christ on the cross and a memorial plaque with photographs of the dead girls, only the slightly mismatched stained-glass windows told of that fateful Sunday. Mortar had pieced together the seventy-two-year-old stone structure, now a state historical landmark, but the hearts and lives touched by the tragedy remained torn as the months stretched into more than a decade. "We don't even know if anyone is still working on the case," the mother of one dead girl lamented. "When you walk around in this town, you sort of have the feeling the people who did it are somewhere. I think people would like to forget. And they sometimes actually seem to think that we've forgotten." Her faith in justice—like that of much of the black community's—wavered even when Bill Baxley was elected attorney general in 1970 and announced plans to reopen the case. Baxley assigned his key investigators to it and wrote on his telephone credit card: Denise McNair, Cynthia Wesley, Carol Robertson, and Addie Mae Collins. "Every time he made a call," a friend recently recalled, "he wanted to be reminded of those four dead girls."

Bill Baxley was a law student at the University of Alabama at the time of the Sixteenth Street Church bombing. Lunch was being served at the Kappa Sigma fraternity house when he heard the news. Instead of eating, he wandered alone across the campus to the nearby Black

Warrior River, and that night, he had trouble sleeping. For him, the day was comparable only to Pearl Harbor and to John F. Kennedy's assassination.

The next year, when the Klan picketed Morrison's Cafeteria after it had agreed to comply with the Civil Rights Act, Baxley defiantly ate every meal there for three months.

"Made me so damn mad!" he fumed the July 1976 afternoon we talked in his office. "I hated 'em so much even back then."

Alabama's outspoken, somewhat flamboyant attorney general thoughtfully reflected on the day that was to shape his life almost as much as his late father had influenced his choice of a profession, and his mother, his social attitudes.

"It was a real traumatic thing for me. It's not totally accurate that I said then, 'One day I'm gonna solve it.' I was just hoping it would be solved and that some of those who did it would be punished, electrocuted, or whatever. But after I got elected attorney general—before I took office—I knew I wanted to solve it, because it had been with me over the years."

Reared in Dothan, just below the state's black belt, Baxley first encountered racism as a youngster when he wanted to take a black playmate to the town's swimming pool and his mother had attempted to explain why he couldn't. Years later, the former playmate, on a military furlough, visited Baxley and his brother—also a lawyer—and the three threw their arms around one another. "I knew then," his mother recently recalled, "my boys weren't racists."

The son of a state circuit court judge, Baxley got an equally early start at politics, campaigning at age twelve for Adlai Stevenson. In 1965, just after law school, George Wallace appointed him to fill the unexpired term of the district attorney in Dothan. He was elected to a full term a year later and served until he became attorney general, winning eighty-three percent of the vote and upsetting an established political figure. When he entered the race, few had given the twenty-eight-year-old any chance of success.

Baxley's aggressive, no-holds-barred style and vocabulary soon gained him a reputation as a formidable and controversial prosecutor. Besides his pursuit of Alabama's unsolved cases of racial bloodshed, he had cracked down on voting irregularities and utilities frauds, impeached three county sheriffs for misconduct, and convicted several other officials—including two legislators—for corruption. After some of his successful murder prosecutions, his life reportedly was threatened, and he sometimes was accompanied by a bodyguard.

He came across as a combination good ol' boy, tough-guy lawman, and another in the South's long line of colorful, one-of-a-kind politicians, as capable of grabbing headlines and cussing as were George Wallace and Huey Long. When Edward Fields, of the National States Rights Party, wrote to protest the reopening of the church bombing, the attorney general brashly answered on official letterhead: "My response to your letter of February 19, 1976, is—kiss my ass." Bill Baxley was a new breed. He was fighting *for* the cause most of his predecessors had bitterly opposed.

His detractors branded the widely publicized investigation into the bombing as politically motivated. Baxley denied the allegations. Nevertheless, many friends and foes alike saw him as Wallace's successor, both to the governor's mansion and to the tradition of keeping Alabama's chief executive in the national spotlight.

I looked at the just-married Baxley, whose life-style—like his upbringing—differed little from that of other Alabamians his age: he liked country music, attended church regularly, and was an avid fan of Coach "Bear" Bryant. "Why," I asked, "do you feel even more stongly about the Klan than most people do?"

He replied instantly. "'Cause they've gotten away with so much. By the authorities not enforcing the law as far as the Klan's concerned, it has made people in other parts of the country think they are representative of Alabamians or Southerners when that's not so. I would like to see that changed." He shook his head disgustedly. "What they do is so distasteful to everything America stands for, or should stand for. I just hate 'em."

Although Baxley passed off today's Klan as "so ineffective *I* don't consider them a force" and contended he no longer kept it under constant surveillance, the Hooded Order knew he was pursuing it with a vengeance.

In the Birmingham case, he often worked as many as a dozen investigators—including Jack Shows and Tom Ward, the former Montgomery city detectives credited with solving the bombings and beatings that became almost commonplace in the former Confederate capital during the fifties and sixties. The two men—ostracized by many of their fellow officers and the community in those days—shared the new attorney general's fervor in seeking the convictions they had never been able to win in a South both fearful of and sympathetic to the Klan.

Almost from the time he took office, Baxley dogged the men he and other investigators had long suspected. Some had since died, but when he reopened the case, the attorney general warned, it "ought to make some people in Jefferson County pretty nervous." Still, one lead after another came to a dead end. Even the U.S. Justice Department refused to share its extensive files on the scores of bombings across the South, many involving suspects from the same right-wing groups—notably Ku

Klux Klan splinter groups and the National States Rights Party (a neo-Nazi group once headquartered in Birmingham). Finally, in early 1976—four years after his initial request—Baxley was granted the files and again cranked up his floundering investigation. The FBI, which had assigned more that fifty agents to Birmingham after the bombing, later attributed its reluctance to assist him to a fear that the terrorists had direct pipelines to local and state law enforcement agencies. The files were opened to Baxley only after he had exhibited a marked break with his state's white supremacist political traditions.

The fear may have been well founded. Alabama had been noted for its political Klan liaisons, and during the Civil Rights Movement, some of the worst violence occurred within its borders. Besides Shelton's ties with John Patterson and George Wallace, current Lieutenant Governor Jere L. Beasley had opened his door to the Imperial Wizard and addressed UKA's 1970 Klonvokation. The late U.S. Senator, James B. Allen, whose signed photograph hung in Shelton's den, had sent a telegram to that same gathering. But the Klan's political influence long preceded those events. In 1926, hundreds of klansmen and Klan-backed candidates—including Hugo Black, Bibb Graves, and Charles McCall—were elected to state and county offices. Exalted Cyclops of a Montgomery klavern, Graves seated Imperial Wizard Hiram Evans and Grand Dragon James Esdale on the podium for his inauguration as governor. Attorney General-elect McCall, a member of Montgomery klavern number three, announced Esdale as his choice for assistant attorney general but soon withdrew the nomination in the wake of widespread opposition. Evans was said to have hosted a secret victory celebration during which he presented "passports"—gold-engraved lifetime plaques—to Graves and U.S. Senator Black, who voiced their appreciation for the Klan support. The latter was said to have given the Grand Dragon a letter of resignation signed, "Yours, I.T.S.U.B. (In The Sacred, Unfailing Bond)," to be made public, Esdale told him, if "you'll need to say you're not a Klan member." The need arose in 1937 when Black was appointed to the U.S. Supreme Court and word of his Klan affiliation circled Washington and the nation. At first, he refused to comment. Later, on coast-to-coast radio, he said he had joined but resigned before he became senator, insisting the passport was unsolicited. Many found the brief explanation unacceptable. Some, however, speculated he entered the Invisible Empire out of political ambition and because of an affinity "to join." His first tie with the Klan was as prosecutor in the case of a Klan organizer who came to Alabama and walked off with Klan funds. He next defended a klansman who shot a priest for marrying his daughter to a Puerto Rican, convincing the jury the circumstances constituted justifiable homicide. He himself became a Klan member in 1923. Eventually, he lost favor with the Klan by supporting Al Smith in 1928, taking a pro-labor stance in the Senate, and advocating black rights under the New Deal.

"We know the Klan was responsible for all the bombings and beatings that went on in Montgomery at that time," Baxley told me. "They had a committee that did all the violence and the head of the Klan would give instructions about some kind of dirty work to be done, and it would be passed on down to a committee that'd go out and do *allll* kinds of stuff. They just administered beatings around here all the time, to blacks *and* whites they thought were trying to do something about civil rights. 'Course, they had some 'in's' in the police department."

"Is this something you've documented since you've become attorney general?" I asked.

"Uh huh."

"When you say 'head,' are you talking about Shelton or the local head?"

"Local head. Name was Boyette. He's dead now. I don't think Shelton had anything to do with it around here, because the Klan is not nearly as regimented and structured an organization as they'd like for you to believe. It's a scattered group of thugs and desperates and bigots and nuts and people on the fringes of the law from each locale. And I don't think the left hand knows what the right hand's doing."

"Does the Klan still have that 'committee'?" I asked.

"Yeah, yeah . . ."

"Is that 'committee' still committing violence?"

"Not any more. It's been a long time since they did. It's not because they aren't capable of it. It's because now they know they'll get their ass hauled in court and be prosecuted and be treated like they should have been all along. That's why they quit. Hasn't been any real wakening."

"In the course of your investigations, were any of your investigators threatened or was there any point at which you thought they might be in danger?"

'*Noooooo,*" he bragged. "Most of these klansmen are the biggest cowards in the world. When we get them in on subpoena, when I question them sonofabitches, they *tremmmble* in the chair. Naw. It's the *other* way 'round. These klansmen, when you get 'em off by themselves, they're scared to death of my investigators."

The mere thought of the Klan and its violence made Baxley's temper and his husky voice rise. "When they claim they're nonviolent? Well, they damn sure are violent! They're just as damn violent as they have been, except now they know they can't get away with it!"

"No change of heart, huh?"

"Naw, hasn't been any new image or anything like that, 'cause it's made up of the same *sick, sorry* people. The same type people. But they know they're not going to be allowed to do this kind of crap."

"Did this start with you?"

"The attorney general before me was in with 'em, kinda," he charged hesitantly, "but I can't take credit for it. It was on the local level. They knew the public wasn't going to put up with it."

In the course of probing the Birmingham church bombing, Baxley's investigators had stumbled on what he called "a civil rights execution" by the Klan, one that for twenty years had gone unreported: the 1957 death of a twenty-five-year-old black man forced at gunpoint to jump from a bridge into the Alabama River when he was mistaken for another black truck driver who supposedly had smiled at a white woman.

That case first drew public attention on February 20, 1976, when William Kyle "Sonny" Livingston, Jr., thirty-eight; James York, seventy-three; and Henry Alexander, forty-six, were charged with first-degree murder after former klansman Raymond C. Britt, Jr., confessed. During a 1957 bus boycott in Montgomery, the defendants—and Britt—had been indicted but not convicted in the bombings of several black churches and homes, including those of Dr. Martin Luther King, Jr., and the Reverend Ralph Abernathy, now head of the Southern Christian Leadership Conference. In spite of the defendants' many scrapes with the law, only one—Alexander—had served time. In December 1964, he and two other men faced capital charges for an explosion near the Negro First Baptist Church in Montgomery. Recorder's Court Judge D. Eugene Loe reduced the charges to "disturbing religious worship." The men pleaded guilty and were each fined two hundred dollars and sentenced to six months in jail. All but ten days of the sentences were suspended.

In the bridge case, a tip from one defendant's disgruntled ex-wife and her even more disgruntled boyfriend initially had baffled a Baxley investigator. With no more to go on than a complaint that *a* black man had been forced off *a* bridge, the investigator at first assumed the complaint to be without basis, probably stemming from a lovers' triangle. Then another defendant—during an interrogation concerning the Birmingham church bombing—blurted out, "Man, I got out of the Klan when that guy jumped off that bridge!" The comment was casually passed along to the co-worker who had received the initial tip. The two then began the tedious work of discovering the identity of the "missing person." They finally arrived at Willie Edwards, who, three months after being reported missing, had been found floating in the Alabama River in adjoining Lowndes County—site of the Viola Liuzzo slaying and trial.

"Then maybe about a month after that, that's when we made Britt break down," Baxley recalled.

At a preliminary hearing in early 1976, Britt, a jowly mobile-home salesman in his midforties, told how he and the three accused had stopped Edwards' truck on the outskirts of Montgomery, "slapping him around a bit" and threatening to castrate him when he denied making advances to the white woman. After driving Edwards around the rural countryside for much of the night, they then forced him—"crying and sobbing and beggin' " for his life—to jump into the river. The men, Britt continued, returned to Alexander's home, laughing and joking about "that nigger going swimming in the river" in January.

Under cross-examination, Britt readily acknowledged his own role in the violence that surrounded the bus boycott—including the bombing of four churches less than two weeks before Edwards' death and firing shots at the newly integrated buses. Although he had been acquitted then, he said he was now cooperating with the attorney general because "I wanted to tell the truth after living with this thing for nineteen years." Britt said he had joined the Klan the same year as the bus boycott and the bombing "because I was young and fell in with the wrong crowd." He dropped out a year later.

Baxley smoldered. "But as it turned out, Britt was wrong about one of the damn people and has, I'm afraid, destroyed our case. At least it's destroyed his credibility as a witness. I think when it started out it was a very honest mistake. What he was wrong about was Sonny Kyle Livingston. He's a no-good thug."

"He has a record, doesn't he?" I asked, remembering details of Livingston's involvement in the bombings that rocked Montgomery on January 10, 1957. Along with Alexander and three others, Livingston had also been arrested for stirring up racial violence at a black college football game in 1960. His most recent brush with the law had occurred January 1976 when police said Livingston, a bail bondsman, had forced his way into the city parking lot to pick up a bond jumper. No charges were filed—not even for carrying a .38 caliber snub-nosed pistol—and the case was closed early the next month.

"One of the problems down there is Livingston's got a bunch of buddies on the police department, which is just shocking," Baxley complained. "Livingston's been in on everything the Klan's done and on every other kind of bad stuff you can imagine. *Ever'night* during that time—back in fifty-seven, fifty-eight—these klansmen were riding around the streets of Montgomery doing somethin' bad to somebody."

Baxley stopped momentarily, as though he were preparing for his final argument. "It turned out, I think, that everything Britt said happened is true, *except* there was another fella who was there in place of Livingston. If you just substitute his name for Sonny Kyle Livingson, then it'd be exactly like Britt said. And that's the only damn thing Livingston *wasn't* in on."

But the case had run into trouble even before the Livingston mix-up when State Circuit Court Judge Frank Embry threw out the indictments because they "did not sufficiently specify the cause of death." Livingston had also added to the problems by filing a million-dollar lawsuit against Britt and investigators Jack Shows and Tom Ward for violating his civil rights and conspiring to fabricate evidence against him. The case was eventually dismissed against Ward, a high-ranking detective, and Shows, assistant chief of police, before the two joined the attorney general's staff. Ironically, the same two lawmen had arrested Livingston, Britt, York, and Alexander after the 1957 bombings.

Momentarily subdued, Baxley expressed hopes of getting the case back in court, but his tone was not optimistic, nor was it when I asked the status of the Birmingham church bombing investigation.

"We know who did it," he vowed as he had since the day he reopened the case, "but making a case, we just don't know . . ."

"I've had several people tell me that J. B. Stoner of Marietta, Georgia, has been a prime suspect," I suggested.

"He was our first suspect," Baxley answered somewhat distantly, as though he mentally had returned to that September Sunday in 1963.

"Is he any longer a suspect?"

"No."

"Is that because you can't get the goods or the evidence on him, or is it because he has been cleared?"

"He was responsible for a lot of bombings, but . . ." Baxley stopped abruptly. "I don't want to talk about that, I don't want to talk about that bombing."

Except for a sign bearing NSRP and a stylized thunderbolt reminiscent of the Third Reich, the headquarters of the National States Rights Party looked like a typical two-story brick house, the lawn manicured and enclosed by a chain-link fence. Even Stoner hadn't seemed out of the ordinary when he answered the door. Once aptly described as resembling a fireplug, he was short and thick, with close-cut curly hair and narrow-slit eyes. But as the interview progressed, he impressed me as being as inwardly unattractive as he was physically, a man whose insides were a blackened inferno. In spite of his pathetic attempts to charm me with his hateful heroism, he seemed totally lacking in redeeming qualities. For almost two hours, Stoner boasted about his fight for the white race, his legal defense of klansmen accused of everything from flogging to bombing to murder, and his own arrests—including charges of interfering with the integration of Birmingham's schools. He brushed aside the bombings during the Civil Rights Movement with, "That's been mostly a long time ago."

When I asked about some of the racial violence klansmen had been accused of, he laughed, "Well I don't advocate it, but if somebody else does it, I never criticize 'em."

"But do you condone it?"

"Niggers are killing white people from one end of the country to the other ever'day, so if a white man kills a nigger, why I say more power to him!"

"But *would* you advocate it?" I asked.

"No, ma'am, I don't advocate it, but, uh . . ."

"You applaud it?"

"It's like the killing of Martin Lucifer Coon, I didn't shed any tears over it," he chuckled. Then he became serious, as though he were preaching the gospel. "Niggers are animals. They're *wiiild* animals. I don't have any love for niggers any more than they do for white people."

"You seem very jovial when you talk about this," I remarked. "Do you find your work and your interest in this entertaining?"

Stoner grinned. "It's a pleasure. I'd find life very dull if I didn't fight for the white race. I get pleasure out of it. I guess I'm what you could call a happy warrior."

He began his battle when he was sixteen, but that was as much background as he would divulge. Each time I tried to delve into his past, into what made him tick like a time bomb, he threw up a verbal barrier. Even when I asked his age, he subtracted twenty years and chuckled. "Thirty-two. I don't like to go into all that," he explained. "Usually when writers talk about personal things, they're trying to figure out some way to smear you." A reporter, attempting to learn more about his background, once asked if "somewhere along the line" a teacher or someone had influenced his philosophy, and Stoner cut him off. "No, sir, there's no 'somewhere' along the line. I've always been this way."

Born in 1924 in Walker County, Georgia, Jesse Benjamin Stoner, Jr., came from what, in the South, would be referred to as "a good family." One of three children, he was never as popular or as attractive as his sisters. An early case of polio left him with a limp, and his grades at McCallie's School for Boys were mediocre. He attended public high schools in Atlanta and Chattanooga for a while. His father died when he was five; his mother, when he was sixteen. That was about the time, many observers agree, when his all-consuming anti-Semitism surfaced and he reportedly worked out a method to communicate with Nazi-propagandist Lord Haw-Haw. At eighteen, he moved from Georgia to Chattanooga and shortly thereafter contacted Imperial Wizard James Colescott, who named him Kleagle for Tennessee.

Three years later, while still in the Klan, he named himself "Arch Leader" of his own organization, alternately known as the Stoner or

National Anti-Jewish Party. Its purpose, announced on postcards at the time, was "to obtain passage of proper laws or constitutional amendments making it unlawful and impossible for Jews to live in North America." Or, as he told an Atlanta newspaper reporter, "to make being a Jew punishable by death." The 1946 article quoted him as saying Hitler was "too moderate" and that he and his own men planned to be "more modern," using gas, electric chairs, shooting, hanging, or "whatever way seems most appropriate" to eliminate Jews. He was reportedly thrown out of what had then become the Association of Georgia Klans in 1950 for making a motion at a klavern meeting to put all Jews out of Chattanooga. The ouster did not deter him. He continued with his Anti-Jewish Party, renaming it the Christian Anti-Jewish Party when he moved to Atlanta in 1952 and joined forces with Edward Fields. That marked the beginning of a long association between the two, who had much in common: the then-twenty-one-year-old Fields also came from a fairly "good" family and had been infected with a hatred for Jews at an early age, having belonged to the Columbians—an Atlanta-based storm-trooper organization—four years before he and Stoner met.

In the years that followed—after Stoner's graduation from Atlanta Law School and Fields' from the Palmer School of Chiropractic in Davenport, Iowa—the pair began a right-wing migration, marked by the formation of the short-lived Christian Knights of the Ku Klux Klan by Stoner in 1959 in Louisville and of the National States Rights Party by Fields a year earlier in Knoxville. Eventually, the two—still keeping close ties with the Klan and other right-wing groups—concentrated their energies on the NSRP, shifting its headquarters from Knoxville to Louisville to Birmingham to Augusta to Savannah and finally to Marietta, just outside Atlanta. Fields soon gave up being a chiropractor, and Stoner limited his legal practice to fighting for his fellow racists.

Stoner's first official role with the National States Rights Party was that of legal counsel, beginning in 1959. He was then elected vice chairman in 1964—the same year he ran as vice president on the NSRP ticket with Tennessee agitator John Kasper—and chairman, his current title, in 1969. During the sixties, he popped up on the segregation battlegrounds across the South. Eventually, he and the late Charles Conley "Connie" Lynch—an itinerant rabble-rouser known for his rabid mouth, Confederate-flag vest, and pink Cadillac—formed a two-man "riot squad": Lynch would incite the crowd to violence; Stoner then would defend them in court. Together, they wreaked havoc from St. Augustine, Florida, to Bogalusa, Louisiana.

Ordained into the Church of Jesus Christ, Christian, in California by former Ku Klux Klan rifle-team instructor Dr. Wesley Swift, Lynch once challenged a Baltimore rally crowd: "I represent God, the white race and constitutional government, and everyone who doesn't like that can go straight to hell. I'm not inciting you to riot—I'm inciting you to victory!" His audience responded by chanting, "Kill the niggers! Kill! Kill!" After the rally, stirred-up white youths headed for the city's slums, attacking blacks with fists and bottles. At another NSRP rally in Berea, Kentucky, Lynch's verbal violence was followed by two fatal shootings. Again in Anniston, Alabama, he goaded his audience, "If it takes killing to get the Negroes out of the white man's streets and to protect our constitutional rights, I say, 'Yes, kill them!'" A carload of men left the rally and gunned down a black man on a stretch of highway near where a Freedom Riders' bus had been burned in 1961.

But it was in Florida—especially conservative St. Augustine—where the two caused the most bloodshed, moving in to counter demonstrations led by Martin Luther King Jr. Nightly, Lynch harangued in the normally peaceful Old Slave Market. During one rally, his audience attacked two hundred demonstrators parading through the plaza. On still another occasion—an outdoor Klan rally—Lynch bellowed : "They asked me if I advocate violence, and I say the niggers have declared all-out war. And in war you shoot. I don't know who bombed that church in Birmingham, but if I did, I'd pin a medal on 'em. Someone said, 'Ain't it a shame that them little children was killed.' But they ain't little—thirteen or fifteen, old enough to have venereal diseases. Besides, little niggers ain't little children. Children are human. So if there's four less niggers tonight, then I say good for whoever planted the bomb. We're all better off." Then he shifted to a subject closer to home. "You've got a burr-headed bastard of a dentist in St. Augustine that ought not to live. He ought to wake up tomorrow with a bullet between his eyes. If you were half the men you claim to be, you'd kill him before sunup." Shouts of "Niggers! Niggers!" suddenly came from the bushes. Pistols and brass knuckles appeared as four black men—one of them the dentist, known for his civil rights work—were shoved toward the platform. Prodded by the women, the at first uncertain klansmen stripped off the blacks' shirts and beat them savagely. "Castrate the bastards!" the women urged. "Kick their——out! Kill 'em! Come on, do somethin'!" One called to her husband, "Go get the head chopper . . . And the rope . . . And, for God's sake, take off your robe! I don't want to mess it up!" In the end, the klansmen were cleared, and the blacks were found guilty of trespassing and assault. Sheriff O. L. Davis, an avid segregationist, shrugged: "I don't know what got into them niggers, going down that dirt road when they knew a Klan meeting was going on."

At the height of Bogalusa's racial rioting, Charlie Christmas, Grand Dragon of the Original Knights of Louisiana, chased Lynch and Stoner out of town. Even Edward Fields finally dismissed Lynch as NSRP's

California organizer and official spokesman. "He organized his group with black belts and boots and helmets. This was not authorized," he told the press. "He raised more money than any other man we ever had. But he was too extreme."

Nevertheless, Stoner and Lynch—who worked as a plasterer in California whenever collection-plate funds ran low—remained cohorts until the latter died of heart trouble in 1972

"Connie and I had a lot of fun," Stoner remembered now nostalgically.

"Fun?" I repeated, not sure I had heard correctly.

"Yes, ma'am," he grinned broadly. "I enjoy fighting the niggers and the Jews."

When I asked why Stoner shifted from the Klan to the National States Rights Party, he explained, "I decided we needed a political movement more than a fraternal movement. And also, if we were going to reach the public and arouse and mobilize 'em to save the white race, we needed to be out in the open instead of secret or semisecret."

He limped across the room, past a large NSRP flag tacked behind his desk. Its design was almost identical to that of the Confederate flag except that it had a thunderbolt in the center and no stars. "The South might have won if it had had a more dynamic flag like that," he observed as he gathered an assortment of pamphlets and hobbled back to his chair.

"Let me give you some material that will help you understand us more," he said, handing me the issue of *The Thunderbolt* with the "revelation" about the Jimmy Carter-John F. Kennedy kinship, an "OIL YES—JEWS NO" bumper sticker, and a greeting-type card with the inscription "IT'S TERRIBLE THE WAY BLACKS ARE BEING TREATED! ALL WHITES SHOULD WORK TO GIVE THE BLACKS WHAT THEY DESERVE!" Inside was a caricature of a black African native dangling by his neck from a rope.

"Do you have an investigative reporting staff?" I asked, scanning *The Thunderbolt,* which was more commonplace than daily newspapers in many Klan homes.

"People give us information," Stoner answered. "We get newspaper clippings from all over the country about nigger crimes, and, of course, those kinds of news articles seldom get on news wires."

I stared again at the headline "Is Carter Illegitimate Brother of Kennedys?" and inquired, "Where do you get stories like this one?"

"Uh, somebody, uh, gave, uh, that information to Doctor Fields."

"Did he verify everything to make sure it's true?"

"Well, we verify ever'thing as much as possible," he assured me. "Of course, uh, we take it for granted—now something like that's a little more difficult—but, of course, now, I think it's pretty well verified that John Kennedy was married and divorced before he married Jackie."

"But something like Kennedy and Carter being related, you're really not sure if that's true or not?" I pressed.

Stoner conceded, "I think Doctor Fields checked up on that some—I don't know how much," and then quickly changed the subject to the clippings on "nigger" crime.

"Niggers don't belong in the United States in the first place," he said flatly. "They're trying to destroy the white race. The more I fight 'em, the better it is for the white race."

"How are you fighting them?"

"In politics, with propaganda . . ."

"You mean by running for office?"

He nodded. "And by stirring up white people to stand up for their rights."

Stoner had offered himself for political office a half-dozen times, first running in Tennessee's Third Congressional District in 1948 and then as NSRP's vice-presidential candidate in 1964. But it was in his home state that he had campaigned with vigor and, to the embarrassment of many Georgians, increased his votes with each bid: polling seventeen thousand votes in 1970 for governor; forty thousand in 1972 for the U.S. Senate, and seventy-one thousand in 1974 for lieutenant governor.

Each campaign had been used as a platform for his hatred of blacks and Jews, and each had been marked by controversy. During the governor's race, his campaign manager—Jerry Ray, brother of convicted assassin James Earl Ray, whom Stoner briefly represented—was charged with shooting sixteen-year-old campaign worker Don Black in the behind. At the time, Black—now David Duke's second in command—was sharing living quarters with Stoner and Jerry Ray, who, four months later, was arrested for a bank robbery in St. Louis.

In Stoner's bids for senator and lieutenant governor, his television and radio spots and his posters on city buses stirred up a furor that put the Federal Communications Commission and the courts in a quandary over where freedom of speech should end and censorship begin. Stoner, in the media spots, proclaimed: "The main reason why the niggers want integration is because the niggers want our white women. You cannot have law and order and niggers, too. Vote white."

Atlanta Mayor Sam Massell issued an executive order asking that the commercials be banned, the local branches of the NAACP and the ADL petitioned the FCC to modify its regulations so that Stoner's words could be stricken, and a prominent pediatrician publicly diagnosed the spots as "having an adverse effect on child development." The stations—which ran disclaimers before and after the spots—also turned to the FCC for relief, but in the end the commission ruled in Stoner's favor.

Four years later, Stoner won another legal battle allowing him to advertise on city buses in Macon, Augusta, and Columbus. On winning that point, he gloated, "I'd say this proves one thing—God loves me."

During most of his campaigns, Stoner spoke at Klan rallies, relying on the Hooded Empire's votes and its financial support. In 1970, announcing that he was prepared to spend fifty to one hundred thousand dollars to capture the governor's office, he boasted, "Not a dime of that money will come out of my own pocket." Most of it, he said, would come from subscribers to the NSRP's monthly *The Thunderbolt*.

Billing himself as "The White People's Candidate," Stoner's platform varied little from campaign to campaign. In the senatorial race, he ran on a twenty-five-point platform that included legislation "to pay and finance blacks to settle in Africa or elsewhere outside the United States"; "reduction in funds for WELFARE so only the needy and elderly will benefit and not the lazy drunken Blacks," and the repeal of civil rights laws, which "give special privileges to blacks and take rights, jobs, homes, and freedom from white people and give them to the black savages." As a candidate for lieutenant governor, he announced he was *for* "the death penalty for rapists so as to protect white womanhood from the army of black rapists" and "an end to busing and race-mixing insanity in the schools" and was *opposed* to all anti-gun laws, ratification of the Equal Rights Amendment and "women's lib," and to Martin Luther King, Jr.'s picture hanging in the state capitol.

Continuing our interview, Stoner grinned over the victories he had won in spite of never having been elected. "I'm somewhat candid in my advertising," he admitted.

"If you were elected," I ventured, "what kind of governor would you be?"

"I'd make things so hot for the niggers in Georgia that most of 'em would go ahead and move out."

Stoner attributed his escalating votes to a growing awareness among white people that "they need to do something to stop the niggers."

"What do you suggest?" I asked.

"I think we need to move 'em out of the country, some place like Central Africa."

"And what do you think should be done about the Jews?"

"I've always advocated sending 'em to Madagascar. Of course, if they'd rather be resettled at the South Pole, why I think the nations of the world could get together and settle it."

"You said that you differ from the Klan in that it is too moderate, and then you say you don't believe in violence," I started.

"Most of 'em in the Klan don't believe in violence," he interrupted, continuing, "I take an open anti-nigger stand that I advocate the repeal of all civil rights laws and that people fire niggers instead of hiring them. Some Klan members are strong racists like me and wouldn't hire niggers to work for 'em, but I know other klansmen who have nigger cooks, nigger maids and all."

"You wouldn't hire one to do housework or anything?"

"I wouldn't hire a Jew or a nigger, either one,"-he re-emphasized. "Or I wouldn't hire any of these Vietnamese refugees or anything because they have been brought over here to mongolize the white race. Most of 'em didn't want to come over here in the first place. They oughta be resettled somewhere back in Asia."

And the Chinese? The Japanese? The Mexicans?

"They should all be in their own country, or at least not here."

"How old were you when you first started feeling this way . . .? "

He cleared his throat. "When I grew up, I never did know of any nigger lovers because if there *were* any nigger lovers they didn't say anything. It wasn't popular. Ever'body I knew back at that time—relatives, where I went to school, church, ever'where—ever'body was opposed to associating with niggers. A lot of 'em believed in having niggers for servants. Some still do, even though niggers aren't willing to be servants any more." He chuckled. "My mother use to have a nigger maid."

"What did you think about her?"

"I always thought we'd be better off without having her around. I didn't like to smell her." He made a face. "When I was growing up, I used to talk to the niggers quite a bit—or listen to 'em, more so, because they did most of the talking. And I found out way back then that the nigger was dissatisfied with his position. I never been fooled like so many Southerners into thinking that nigger servants loved 'em. I know better."

"So your racial views haven't changed at all?"

He shook his head, and when I asked if they were possibly stronger, he laughed. "If they got any stronger, I'd have to start killing niggers."

When the interview was over, and Stoner walked me to my car, I asked if he devoted all his time to his work.

"Fighting Jews and niggers and chasing women," he chuckled.

"Oh, you chase women?"

Stoner blushed. "See, I'm trying to stop the aging process. I decided about twenty years ago to stop getting older." He laughed in a vain attempt at humor. Never married, he said he had "come close" a few times but had always decided against it. "I've handled a few divorce cases, and in court I've heard parts of others. That's why I'm afraid to get married." In the end, he insisted, he thought everyone else should marry, but in his case, it was better to only have girl friends.

"Do you find it hard to find women who agree with the way you feel?"

"No, ma'am," he assured me, "I know quite a few women that feel like I do. In fact, in places where there's been a lot of street fighting going on—like St. Augustine—women, generally, were better fighters than the men because they're not as much targets as men when it comes to fighting niggers."

"Have you had any girl friends, though, who were worried that you might get in trouble or hurt or something?"

"There's some that might. In fact, that's a problem that white organizations have had over the years. Men's wives are afraid they'll get in trouble."

"Would you say that's one of the reasons you haven't gotten married, also?"

"I know girls that wouldn't be worried about that at all, that would get out in the street and fight and all."

"To protect you?"

"Yes, ma'am. I've had women bodyguards at times."

When I asked if he always had bodyguards, he answered no, only when things got stirred up and he felt he needed them.

"You never know what some crazy Jew or nigger will do."

"Are you ever afraid?"

"I'm not afraid at all," he was positive.

"I never heard of anyone having women bodyguards," I observed.

He chuckled, "They're much more interesting than men," and slammed my car door.

As I drove off, he opened a pen and let out two German shepherd watchdogs: one the usual brownish-black, the other pure white.

After the news of Stoner's indictment, I again thought about the man I had studied that afternoon, hoping for a glimpse into his inner mechanisms, the psychology that ground out the hate he never shrouded with euphemisms or subtleties. He was no intellectual, but neither was he ignorant or uneducated, like so many Klan members and sympathizers. Although, unlike them, he didn't lack material possessions, he had suffered the early death of his parents, and he had endured the lifelong misfortune of the horrid limp. Had these factors unleashed the anger he aimed at others? Was he emotionally ill? Was he genuinely hateful, a thoroughly evil man?

One lawman had told me J. B. Stoner was *the* man behind all the bombings. After having spent an afternoon with Stoner, I found it easy to believe he was capable of the blasts that so unmercifully ripped the South and its people apart, needlessly taking lives and property and creating ill will and hurt.

His ties to explosives were extensive. He had admitted his familiarity with dynamite to more than one newsman; two months before the Sixteenth Street Church blast, he had instructed an audience at an NSRP rally outside Birmingham on how to make a bomb by using a candle to regulate the time of detonation, and he had legally represented, or was closely associated with, scores of men accused of bombings: Emmett Miller, charged with an attempted bombing at Philander Smith College in Little Rock in 1961; the four klansmen accused of a blast at the home of a black boy who integrated an elementary school in Jacksonville, Florida, in 1964; Robert Miles, the former UKA Grand Dragon of Michigan, currently imprisoned for the 1971 school-bus bombings in Pontiac; Byron de la Beckwith—twice tried but never convicted for the slaying of civil rights leader Medgar Evers—who, in 1973, was arrested just outside New Orleans with both a time bomb and a map tracing in red the route to the home of a Jewish leader in his car; Roy Frankhouser, the former Pennsylvania Grand Dragon and NSRP member whose career as an informer ended with his arrest for allegedly selling two hundred forty pounds of explosives to Miles' one-time body-guard; William M. Chaney, former UKA Grand Dragon of Indiana and Imperial Wizard of the new Confederation of Independent Klans, who, in November 1977, lost an appeal for an earlier conviction of fire bombing; and Richard and Robert Bowling—indicted but never tried in the 1958 bombing of an Atlanta synagogue—who once lived with Stoner and helped the Christian Anti-Jew Party and NSRP. (George Bright—tried for the same bombing and represented by James Venable—with whom Stoner briefly shared a law office, was also an NSRP member.)

According to a *Los Angeles Times* clip, Stoner also spoke at a rally sponsored by the Americans for the Preservation of the White Race in Meridian, Mississippi, in May 1968, at the height of a series of Klan-suspected bombings of synagogues and Jewish homes in that city and nearby Jackson. That same summer, after a shoot-out with the FBI and Meridian police, Thomas Tarrants—a member of the White Knights of Mississippi and formerly linked with NSRP—was captured with a time bomb like the one found in the car of Byron de la Beckwith, also an NSRP member.

During the HUAC hearings, Donald Appell questioned Stoner on his knowledge or involvement in the Sixteenth Street Church blast and in two explosions ten days later that, Appell contended, were intentionally set "to injure FBI agents and other law enforcement personnel in retaliation for their vigorous investigation of the church bombing, including the questioning of many Klan suspects." When Stoner refused to answer, citing his constitutional rights, Appell proceeded to "place" him in Birmingham "immediately prior to, and including, September 15, 1963," and in March and April of 1965 when a series of bombs were uncovered in that city.

Besides the bombing ties, one investigator also had commented, "You know Stoner's part of the conspiracy in King's death, don't you?" Over the years, Stoner had slithered from one right-wing group to another, speaking before meetings and rallies, representing their members in court, sharing offices. His ties were like a bowl of venomous spaghetti. Was there an underground right-wing network that perhaps had plotted King's assassination and other violence? On several occasions, Robert Shelton and Robert DePugh, former leader of the Minutemen, announced plans for such a network, and a meeting supposedly was held in Kansas City, Missouri, with Shelton and David Duke, among others, present. In 1976, Tony LaRicci also had told the press about the formation of a coalition of right-wing groups in Maryland. The FBI and many law enforcement officials scoffed at the idea of such a network existing, even in view of the Shelton-DePugh efforts and a coming together of right-wing leaders from around the world at an International Congress convened by Duke in New Orleans in September 1976. Were they wrong? Or were they concealing information? Was there indeed such a network? And could J. B. Stoner be the knot that tied the pieces together? Was he the key to more than the bombings? Was he part of a conspiracy? Was his tie to James Earl Ray more than that of attorney and friend of Ray's brother Jerry?

An overall look at clips and photocopies and newsletters and bits and pieces of information gleaned from interviews and conversations provided grounds for speculation.

In an article written less than two months after King's assassination, the *Philadelphia Inquirer* quoted the FBI as saying Ray had entered into a conspiracy "on about March 29" to kill the civil rights leader, the other party being "an individual whom he (Ray) alleged to be his brother." The article stated that the FBI had, itself, injected the word "conspiracy" into the case on April 17 when it filed its original complaint against Ray, then identified as Eric Starvo Galt—one of at least seven aliases he had been known to use—and noted that "a day-by-day reconstruction of the movements of James Earl Ray indicates co-conspirators were active both in Memphis, where King was killed, and in Canada, where Ray lived the next month."

Soon after his arrest in London on June 8, 1968, law enforcement agencies released a partial breakdown of Ray's movements from the time of his April 1967 escape from a Missouri prison—where he was serving a term for armed robbery—through the April 4, 1968, slaying of King. As a fugitive, he had flitted from Birmingham to New Orleans to Los Angeles and on one occasion had seemed to be in two places simultaneously. The *Inquirer* article said that Ray first assumed the Galt alias in July 1967 when he turned up in Toronto several days after two men robbed a bank in Alton, Illinois, his home town. A man legally named Eric St. Vincent Galt lived less than two miles from the apartment rented by Ray. The two were said to be strikingly similar in appearance, including scars on their noses and their right-hand palms. Two years earlier, the real Galt had vacationed in Tennessee. He insisted he had never met Ray, and the Royal Canadian Mounted Police could find no connection between the two.

Later that summer, the article continued, Ray used the Galt alias to check in at the Economy Grill and Rooms in Birmingham, to obtain an Alabama driver's license, and to register a white Mustang he reportedly purchased with cash. Next, he showed up in Atlanta on March 25 and five days later, according to the original FBI complaint, entered into the alleged conspiracy. The getaway car—described as a white Mustang— appeared in Atlanta the morning after the assassination. When neighbors finally reported the vehicle to police as abandoned, the registration was found to be in the name Eric Starvo Galt.

Ray returned to Canada on April 8 and during the month he lived in Toronto, before fleeing to London, assumed two aliases—both names of actual men who resided in Toronto, bore physical resemblance, and insisted they had neither met nor heard of him. On May 3, he flew to London as "Raymond George Sneyd"—the alias he used to get an easily obtainable Canadian passport.

During my research, I also came across a provocative article from the July 1968 issue of *Inside Detective* magazine about a Russian spy who— also using a Canadian passport obtained for him in Toronto—had posed as both a Canadian journalist and tourist in South Africa the summer of 1967. His true identity, the article claimed, was Yuri Nikolayevich Loginov, born in Moscow in 1933 and considered one of the Soviet Union's top spies. At the time of Loginov's arrest, South African authorities discovered a list he had compiled of boys born in 1933 and 1934 who died between 1939 and 1941, the information apparently intended for use in obtaining new identities and passports. After a long solitary confinement, Loginov broke down and told the South African authorities his ultimate destination had been Canada and the United States. He allegedly told Major General Hendrik Van den Bergh, South Africa's security chief, that Canada was to have been only his place of entry. His "real work" was in the United States. "I believe that it was to do with assassination," he reportedly told Van den Bergh. "I gained the impression I was to be a key man in an assassination plot not aimed at one particular man, such as the president of the United States, but at a number of big men simultaneously in order to confuse, dismay, and cause panic among the people if a number of their great men died suddenly." Seven months after Loginov's revelation, Martin Luther King, Jr. was assassinated on April 4, 1968, and Robert F. Kennedy, the following June 6. Loginov also stated that the KGB—Russia's version of the CIA—knew thirty-six hours in advance that John F. Kennedy would be shot in Dallas. "I was not involved in any plot," he told Van den Bergh, "but I was in the same room as a number of KGB officers, and I heard two of them discussing the death of the president. They were speaking as though he were going to die within a day or so. I did not pay attention to it. I heard the word Dallas several times. It was only after we heard the news of the assassination that I put two and two together and knew that my superiors in KGB had known well before not only that President Kennedy would die but almost to within the minute when he would die." An article in *Newsweek* of September 25, 1967—two months after his arrest—confirmed that Loginov's real mission was in the United States and quoted an anonymous U.S. official as saying "the interrogation is far from over."

Was Loginov's story all fabrication, or was it based on fact? In a telephone conversation, James Venable had confirmed a tip I had received from still another Klan source that a man fitting the description of Lee Harvey Oswald had visited Venable's Atlanta law office shortly before the assassination and requested the names of right-wing leaders.

Toronto seemed to play a key role in the stories of both James Earl Ray and Yuri Loginov. It was also headquarters for the far-right Western Guard and home of John Ross Taylor, the sharp-faced little man I first met at Dale Reusch's rally in West Virginia and later in New Orleans at David Duke's International Congress. The *Toronto Star* described Taylor as "Canada's High Priest of Hate." In 1965, the Canadian government terminated use of the mail by him and another man because of their distribution of *The Thunderbolt* and other anti-Semitic literature. At a hearing preceding the ban, Taylor and David Stanley said they were not members of NSRP but had agreed to represent the American group in Canada. Back issues of *The Thunderbolt* carried stories that Taylor had been a speaker at NSRP's 1973 convention, along with Buddy Tucker and Byron de la Beckwith. The Western Guard reciprocated by inviting Stoner to speak at one of its dinners in March 1974.

Could the Western Guard have lent a helping hand to a fellow right-winger? Could it have aided James Earl Ray in obtaining the falsified passport and his sundry "identifications"? As for the baffling question of where Ray got money for his extensive travels, Stoner himself had boasted that *Thunderbolt* subscribers would pick up the tab for his 1970 governor's race. Over the years, the tabloid also had carried letters of appreciation from various recipients—including de la Beckwith—of NSRP defense funds. Could the NSRP also have picked up Ray's financial tab?

When Ray escaped June 10, 1977, from the Bushy Mountain Prison, northwest of Knoxville, his last visitor had been his brother Jerry, Stoner's former campaign manager and roommate and guest of honor at a 1973 NSRP meeting in Chicago. At the time of his escape, prison officials acknowledged an inside conspiracy and speculated on the possibilities of outside help. The case bore similarities to that of one-time NSRP member Tommy Tarrants, who, after a 1968 conviction for his role in several bombings in Meridian, successfully escaped from Parchman Prison in Mississippi with the help and planning of fellow members of the White Knights, many of its members closely tied to the NSRP. Could the Klan or the NSRP or a coalition of right-wing groups have attempted a replay with James Earl Ray?

My speculations were bolstered in January 1978 when the House Assassinations Committee indicated it would subpoena Stoner—along with several NSRP associates—to testify in its investigation into the murder of Martin Luther King Jr. An unidentified congressional source told the press that the panel wanted to find out whether Stoner's activities "are in any way directly connected with the assassination of Dr. King." The source indicated the committee would question Stoner both about his allegations that an FBI informant had offered him twenty-five thousand dollars to have King killed and two thousand dollars to blow up the Birmingham church and about his relationship with James Earl Ray. A month later, *The New York Times* disclosed that Ray's brother, Jerry, was acting as bodyguard for Stoner, who announced he would again run for governor of Georgia.

Shortly after the official charges were brought against Chambliss and Stoner in September 1977, a source familiar with the bombing investigations told the press that the latter's indictment was designed as "psychological warfare" against the others as much as it was to convict the arch-segregationist. "Stoner is a symbol," the source explained. "A lot of these people look on him as the most hard-nosed guy of all. If we can get him, then it's a signal to all those other guys that we can get them, too."

At the time, investigators had narrowed the bombing suspects to no more than thirty, twenty of them still alive. There was also speculation that the suspects might have been part of Nacirema—"American" spelled backwards—formed in 1961 by klansmen who wanted "more violent action" in their fight against civil rights. During the HUAC hearings, investigator Philip Manuel had said Shelton and UKA Grand Dragon Calvin Craig were among the klansmen instructed by Nacirema in the manufacture and use of firearms and explosives. He described it as "an organization of black-robed klansmen suspected of participating in racial bombings across the South."

Meanwhile, the black community—reluctant to get its hopes up—adopted a wait and see attitude as the state prepared its case against Chambliss, and Stoner fought extradition from Georgia for the earlier Bethel Church bombing. Chris McNair, one of a dozen or so blacks elected to the Alabama House of Representatives since the Sixteenth Street bombing, refused to comment on the eve of the Chambliss' trial for the death of his daughter. And while Claude Wesley, Cynthia's father, expressed satisfaction that "some progress has been made," he, too, was guarded: "Of course, no one has been convicted. I've waited this long; I'll wait some more."

At the church, Pastor James T. Crutcher had remained quiet when *New York Times* reporter Wayne King asked his own feelings. "Ambivalence," he finally answered. "Always, deep down, there was the hope that justice would be done, that the climate had changed, that white Southerners, decent white Southerners who feel that they were degraded by this, can feel better. But there is also the pain of bringing up the bygone fear, the remembrance of atrocity and horror. You tend to forget; the mind blocks those things that are beyond remembering. But this is the time, the particular time." He picked up a worn Bible and read from the third chapter of Ecclesiastes: "To every thing there is a season, and a time to every purpose under heaven: a time to be born, and a time to die, a time to plant, and a time to pluck up that which is planted; a time to kill, and a time to heal; a time to break down, and a time to build up . . ."

In mid-November 1977, Robert Chambliss—who had angrily lunged at a black cameraman while leaving the grand jury room just months before—showed little emotion as the state unfolded the first of its four cases against him, the murder of Denise McNair.

Kirthus Glenn, a retired laundry worker from Detroit who had been visiting friends in Birmingham at the time of the bombing, identified a 1963 photograph of Chambliss as that of one of three men she had seen in a car parked outside the church during the early hours of the morning of the bombing. Another witness, Yvonne Young, testified that she had seen the defendant with several bundles of "oversized firecrackers" in his home two weeks before the bombing.

But the most damaging evidence had come from Chambliss's niece by marriage. In a soft, halting voice, Elizabeth Cobb, an ordained Methodist minister, recalled that her uncle told her the day before the bombing "he had enough stuff put away to flatten half of Birmingham." Then twenty-three, the Reverend Cobb remembered Chambliss as being "in a very angry and agitated state" over the recent integration of Birmingham's schools. She had urged him not to do anything violent, but "he looked me in the face and said, 'You just wait until after Sunday morning and they will beg us to let them segregate.'" She asked what he meant, and he answered, "You just wait and see." Six days later, she found him watching a television documentary on the bombing. "It wasn't meant to hurt anybody," he remarked. "It didn't go off when it was supposed to." Mrs. Cobb described Chambliss as "a racial fanatic" for as long as she could remember and said that when she was a teenager, he had paid her to sew blood-drop emblems on Klan robes.

After four days of testimony and cross-examination, the state rested its case. Chambliss sat quietly, almost dozing, during the final argument by his attorney, Arthur Hanes, Jr., whose father had been mayor of Birmingham at the time of the bombing and had since been legal counsel to several klansmen and, briefly, to James Earl Ray.

"Birmingham is not like it was," the younger Hanes told the jury. "Let's think back on Birmingham the way it was in nineteen sixty-three and a fairly rough, sixty-year-old white man on a weekend before the schools were to be integrated. Rough talk does not make a verdict. Mister Chambliss didn't have any monopoly on rough talk in those days. How would you like to be judged on things that were said then around your kitchen table? That was a normal, human thing to say." He urged the jury not to find Chambliss guilty simply out of a concern that a "not guilty" verdict might further tarnish the reputation of Birmingham, a city, he noted, that had made considerable strides since the days when Martin Luther King Jr. termed its race relations the worst in the country.

Birmingham—like much of Alabama *and* the South—*had* changed its racial attitudes. The jury itself—three blacks and nine whites—was symbolic of the change. Restaurants, theaters, schools, were desegregated. Blacks sat on the city council and in the legislature. But Bill Baxley was more concerned with cleansing the state's soul than with further tarnishing Birmingham's reputation when he gave his ninety-minute closing argument that left jurors and spectators weeping.

"You've got a chance to do something," he pleaded with the jury, holding up photographs of the four maimed bodies and the shattered church. "Let the world know that this is not the way the people of Alabama felt then or feel now. It's not going to bring those little girls back, but it will show the world that this murder case has been solved by the people of Alabama. Give Denise a birthday present."

Denise McNair—and the South—got that long-overdue present on what would have been her twenty-sixth birthday when the jury returned its verdict:

"Guilty."

14
The Warning

Vidor, Texas

A black man, thirtyish and sportily dressed, entered the coffee shop first. He was followed within minutes by a female companion, still another, and then two small girls no older than ten. The room grew quiet except for the rattling of dishes. The waitresses and afternoon regulars exchanged glances, then focused on the blacks as they occupied a booth between mine and the door. I watched anxiously, knowing that the Texas head of the Knights of the Ku Klux Klan would be arriving at any moment.

It was midafternoon of my second visit to Vidor during July 1976, and I had come to know enough about the all-white community to be apprehensive. Blacks had not been welcome when the town was settled at the turn of the century. As recently as the sixties, road signs had warned: NIGGER, DON'T LET THE SUN SET ON YOU HERE. The signs were gone, but the sentiments remained. Five Klans were headquartered here, with some leaders openly boasting of chasing blacks out of town. On Main Street, along with the usual businesses, a small book store brandished foot-high letters: KNIGHTS of the KU KLUX KLAN.

Bisected by Interstate 10 and surrounded by swamps, Vidor was less than ten minutes away from Beaumont, my early childhood home, yet I had known nothing about its racial makeup or reputation. I had passed through it but never stopped. Few outsiders did unless they had reason to. For it was an unattractive cluster of fast-food stands, gas stations, shopping centers, and working-class homes, with many lawns cluttered with jacked-up automobiles and worn-out refrigerators. Pickup trucks sprouting two-way antennae moved back and forth through its streets like passing lines of ants.

At city hall, a secretary had estimated the current population at thirteen thousand: twenty-five Mexican-Americans, a few Jews, the rest white Protestants. When I noted the uniqueness of Vidor's all-white population, she seemed proud. "Yeah, I don't know how we've managed *that.*" She, like most people I talked to, expressed little concern over the new book store or the assortment of Klans. When I asked a saleswoman at another Main Street business if the store's opening had provoked any reaction, she answered, "No comment," quickly adding, "and *that* doesn't mean there has been." A few doors away, the woman behind the desk at the public library said the building had been a burned-out pharmacy and philosophized, "At least they cleaned it up and it looks better."

As in most areas where Klans proliferated, the selection had grown out of the usual inner bickering. Each clash led to the formation of still another group, another choice, with the members shifting affiliations but seldom growing in number. Still, Robert Watts, in his second term as mayor and on the city council before that, labeled the Klans and the store "a disgrace to the city" and admitted they had "hurt the image of Vidor quite a bit." Most of the leaders lived outside the Vidor city limits, he complained. "Our local police will end up with the problem, and these so-called klansmen will be home in Rose City or Lake View or Beaumont or Port Arthur or wherever they're from." While the majority of residents preferred to remain segregated, he doubted they would support the Klan if it operated outside the law. He himself was neither a segregationist nor an integrationist, believing in a person's right to choose, but admitted, "I'd like to see my neighborhood stay the same as it is." He confirmed that "calling cards" had been handed out at school functions—even football games—and acknowledged that blacks had recently filed complaints of harassment. Indictments, he said, would soon be made. When I asked if they involved presenting Klan "calling cards" to blacks and then, if they refused to leave, escorting them by car on to the interstate, the mayor speculated, "This is probably where it started, but it led from that into a more serious charge." He refused to comment further.

Several days earlier, I had spent the evening with Dan and Pat Smithers, whom I had met at Scoggin's Greenville, South Carolina, rally. In the interim, the couple had feuded with James Venable and switched allegiance from the National Knights to the Invisible Empire, a loose association of independent Klans. They had, however, maintained their titles, as Grand Dragon and Queen Kleagle. Fifty-five, Smithers had belonged to UKA and then to the old Originals. He had worked five years as a Houston policeman, a claim an official police spokesman was unable to verify. Now he was a warehouse supervisor in Beaumont. He and his wife had met in 1957 through her first husband, also a klansman. They married in 1971.

He was a tall, solid man, his brown hair barely receding; she was a thin woman who sounded like a whiny child as she complained about the backbiting among the splinter groups and attempts by blacks to set foot in Vidor.

"We jist don't want the blacks out here," Smithers was blunt. "We've got a good community. We've got a good school. I really don't think they wanta come out here."

"What do you do to discourage them?" I had asked.

Pat Smithers answered. "Set up patrols. If we find any over here," she started, "actually, you know, shoppin' or any other wise, we find out what their purpose is. They don't live here. They don't go to school here. What are they doin' here?"

She shrugged.

"Do you actually go up to them?"

"Right," she said without hesitation, allowing her husband to explain: "Go up an' give 'em a 'You're Bein' Watched by the K-K-K' card. Hand 'em one."

Indignant, Pat Smithers resumed. "They have been escorted plum out of town if they have no legitimate excuse for bein' here. I mean, if a man is workin' over here, he's got a job over here, we don't bother him too much. *At least* he's not on the welfare rolls."

"What if somebody were down on Main Street in a drugstore buying a tube of toothpaste or something?" I asked.

"We'd find out why they couldn't buy it where they live," she answered firmly. "If they don't have any in Beaumont, and if that's where they lived, we'll write the comp'ny an' see why they don't have some."

"As long as they are not hurting you or socializing with anybody . . ." I started.

But Pat Smithers was obstinate. "The main and primary purpose of comin' in the drugstore in the first place to buy a tube of toothpaste is to see how far they can push themselves."

"See," her husband explained, "mainly, the blacks or Negroes that do stop in Vidor are mostly—I'll say ninety-five or better percent of 'em—are transients, that's jist goin' through. Now, they'll stop off to get somethin' to eat, or git gas or this, that, and the other, an' they go on. A lot of 'em are out of state, and *all* of 'em are out of county, or most of 'em. Now, there's a few that will venture in from Beaumont and from Orange, once in a while. This is the ones that we don't want . . . They don't have any business here."

"Besides giving them a card, how do you escort them out?"

"We jist ask 'em to leave," he shrugged nonchalantly. "That's all."

"What if they don't leave?"

"Well, somebody sort of stays on their back bumper until they do," he began.

Pat Smithers explained. "We have sort of a little secret there. I've used it quite a few times myself—actually, they fuss at me all the time—'cause I go out and do these things single-handed, see, without even somebody with me. But we all carry CBs. Well, any nigger that's not familiar with a CB, it sort of scares 'em. Jist like I ran into a whole carload of 'em down here at the shopping center one day. And, uh, asked 'em what they was doin' over there. 'We goin' shoppin',' she mimicked sarcastically. "Well, I jist got out of the car and handed her a card. She was standin' there outside her car. An' she jist looked at me an' tol' me she didn't have to leave. So I says, 'Well, 'bout five minutes from now, I believe you *will* leave, an' I got back in my car and jist picked up my mike. She decided she *was* goin' to leave. Well, I escorted her right up on the freeway, and she had her eyes right on me, boooy. I don't know who I scared the worst, me or her." She laughed, then continued to expand her image as a heroine.

The women didn't limit their patrolling to the shopping centers and public streets, Pat Smithers informed me. They also walked the school hallways to keep out black teachers and students.

"I hadn't got to first base with the principal of the junior high yet. We fuss an' fight all the time. He don't like me walkin' his halls to see if he's got any nigger teachers or somethin' down there, you know. But the one right down here, the elementary school, well jist the first part of last year, they had a whole bunch of 'em tryin' to enroll in school down there. So the principal called me, said 'I'm gonna stall 'em long as I can till you git here,'—'cause he knew I could git rid of 'em where he couldn't. So I got down there, and they was settin' there in the hall waitin' for 'im to do somethin'. Well, I jist walked in an' handed 'em a card. Started like I was goin' to open the office door, you know, an' walk in, and they . . ." Pat Smithers switched to a mocking tone, " 'Oh, we not in Orangefield?' I tol' her no, she wasn't in Orangefield. She was in Vidor. And I advised her, if she lived in Orangefield, she'd better travel on. When the principal came out of his office, he looked out the plate-glass window and said, 'What did you do with my enrollees?' I said, 'I didn't do nuthin' to 'em. I jist walked in, an' they walked out!' An' he laughed, you know. We have that in several of the schools here. We have a good working relationship, and the women walk the halls. Believe you me, when school starts, we're gonna see *they're* not there. An' we're not gonna take nobody's word."

Dan Smithers spoke up. "The stores and business places doesn't even employ any niggers."

"None at all?" I questioned.

"Not in any the business places, no," his wife vouched. "We had an ol' man that was employed at Dairy Queen. Sweepin' the sidewalks an' washin' 'em down an' takin' care of the trash. Thangs like that. He lasted about three days." She was triumphant. " 'Cause he was goin' to have to go, or Dairy Queen was goin' to have to go. Then Weingarten's had one in the meat department an' another one stockin' shelves at night after they were closed. They *locked* him in at night. Well that manager was called, an' he was met and talked with."

"By the Klan?"

"Right," she verified.

Originally a sawmill town, Vidor still relied on the timber industry, although it was becoming increasingly a bedroom community for workers at nearby shipyards and refineries. Local businesses were limited to pharmacies, groceries, and other stores that offered day-by-day necessities but little job opportunity for blacks or whites.

Now Pat Smithers further related the town's history to explain its personality. "Vidor has been a nigger-fearin' place for a long time. I mean, this is not jist a thang of now. This was back when Vidor maybe had jist a Main Street down there, an' the rest of it was woods. The ol' man that helped found this town did not allow a nigger around here. I mean, he carried two thirty-eights on his hips. And he made it law and order, and the town grew from that."

As I waited for Ray Booker, I thought about comments he and other Vidor Klan leaders had made. While most ridiculed the Smithers' brazenness, most told of issuing more "friendly" warnings.

"We don't actually warn 'em, tell 'em they gotta git out of town," explained Bobby Leland, named by James Venable as Smithers' successor. "We jist tell 'em that if they're new in town, it would be best, for their benefit, if they'd try to git out as soon as possible because there are some people here—not even the Klan—that don't like niggers. They hate 'em worse than anythang else. That's somethin' we don't want here. We don't want no killin's because killin's will bring the FBI an' ever'body else. All we want's a peaceful town."

Booker had described a similar procedure during an earlier interview at the book store he operated for David Duke. "A lot of times, we'll pass 'em a friendly visit card. An' some of our cafés—if you don't serve 'em you're gonna be closed down—so they put up a little sign 'Ten Percent of All Our Profits Go to the KKK Road Fund.' But you can't keep 'em out. Anytime you go to whup somebody, you go to jail, and you can't do your country no good in jail."

But now I wondered how he would actually react when he saw the blacks? Would he approach them in my presence? Were the claims mere talk? Or was I about to witness Klan intimidation firsthand?

A mustard- and cream-colored pickup parked outside the door, and Ray Booker climbed out and entered the coffee shop, followed by a stocky blond. At thirty-four, Booker was solidly built from years on construction sites. He wore cowboy boots and a straw cattleman's hat. One cheek was swollen with a plug of tobacco, and his clear-blue eyes looked slightly askance at the blacks as he and the other man ambled toward me. The customers' eyes shifted from the blacks to Booker as he confirmed an interview and then excused himself. He and his companion needed to sit at the counter to discuss some matters. A gray-haired waitress placed cups of coffee before them and snickered, her eyes straying toward the booth. She and the klansmen laughed, their conversation muffled.

Later, when I approached the cashier, Booker leaned toward me. "You better stick around. We may have a barbecue later." He nodded over his shoulder, toward the blacks, and chuckled. I drove several blocks and, discovering I had left my tape recorder at the restaurant, returned. The booth was empty; the blacks, gone. Booker explained they had been out of towners, unaware of the situation. He had given them "a calling card" and a friendly warning that, for their own good, it was best to leave. And they had, he insisted—willingly.

Lt. Gen. Nathan Bedford Forrest
(Photo courtesy Library of Congress)

A Reconstruction Klansman (Photo
courtesy of North Carolina Museum of
History)

Mrs. John B. Kennedy, widow
of one of the six Ku Klux
Klan founders, and Mrs.
Grace Newbill, former
Tennessee state historian of
the United Daughters of the
Confederacy, pictured at the
unveiling May 21, 1917, of a
plaque marking the site where
the organization originated in
Pulaski, Tennessee, in 1865
(Photo courtesy *Giles Free
Press*, Pulaski, Tennessee)

Colonel William Joseph Simmons, responsible for the Klan's 1915 revival and its phenomenal growth in the twenties, studies in his Atlanta office (Photo courtesy James Venable)

Imperial Wizard Dale Reusch speaks from the Statehouse steps in Columbus, Ohio, to a Labor Day 1977 gathering

Sign-wielding demonstrators protest against the Klan at a Labor Day 1977 gathering of Dale Reusch and a handful of his followers on the Statehouse steps in Columbus, Ohio

Bob Jones and Robert Scoggin
(Photo James Denning)

Robert Shelton, in full regalia as head of the
Alabama Knights in 1961

For many, the Klan heritage begins young (Photo © Mitchel L. Osborne)

Robert Shelton and his traveling speaker's podium (Photo © Mitchel L. Osborne)

Opposite left: The Night-Hawk (Photo © Mitchel L. Osborne)

Center top: Jesse B. Stoner, chairman of the National States Rights Party, with the Thunderbolt flag in the background (Photo Al Clayton)

Center bottom: Klan security guards oversee the dismantling of a UKA billboard near Smithfield, North Carolina (Photo courtesy *The News and Observer,* Raleigh, N.C.)

Below: A member of the invisible empire in the thirties, G.T. Miller of Luverne, Alabama, found himself the victim of a Klan boycott when local schools were integrated

Above: Alabama Attorney General William J. Baxley, putting the Klan on trial

Center: Louisiana's David Duke blends intellect and charm to win converts to his new version of the Klan (Photo © Mitchel L. Osborne)

Opposite right: David Duke at monument to the confederacy and white supremacy in downtown New Orleans. He had just been released from jail on inciting to riot charges (Photo © Mitchel L. Osborne)

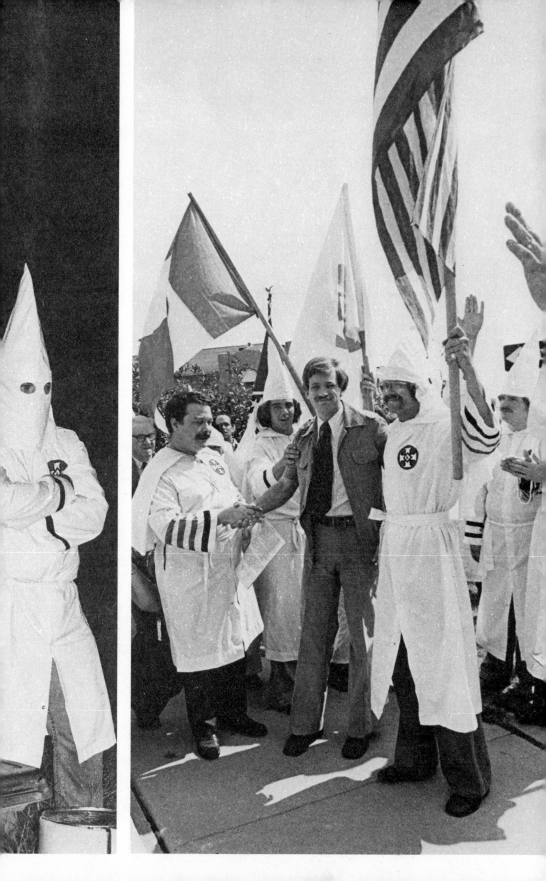

David Duke leads a crosslighting ceremony (Photo © Mitchel L. Osborne)

The eerie beginning of a David Duke crosslighting (Photo © Mitchel L. Osborne)

Veteran right-winger James K. Warner speaks at a Duke rally (Photo © Mitchel L. Osborne)

Armed Security Chief Clara "Bip" Pecoraro confers with a guard during a Duke rally in Louisiana (Photo © Mitchel L. Osborne)

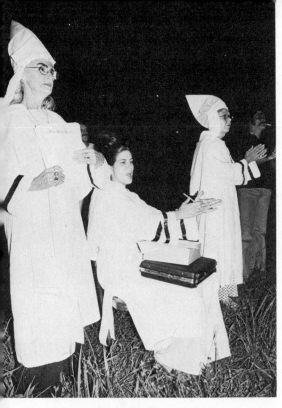

A trio of Duke's female members lend vocal support (Photo © Mitchel L. Osborne)

UKA rally, Amite, Louisiana, 1976 (Photo © Mitchel L. Osborne)

"Colonel" Rene LaCoste at the controversial White Monument in downtown New Orleans (Photo © Mitchel L. Osborne)

Klan rally, 1977, Chalmette, Louisiana, Knights of the KKK (Photo © Mitchel L. Osborne)

Klan members, Stone Mountain, Georgia, 1977
(Photo © Mitchel L. Osborne)

Paying homage to the old rugged cross
(Photo © Mitchel L. Osborne)

Imperial Wizard James Venable visits the birthplace of the Klan on its hundredth birthday in December 1965 (Photo courtesy *Giles Free Press,* Pulaski, Tennessee)

Right: Former Klan terrorist Thomas A. Tarrants III is photographed on the campus of the University of Mississippi where he has been a student since his parole from Parchman Prison in December 1976 (Photo John White)

Below left: Calvin Craig, speaking from a flatbed truck

Below right: Will Minton of Baltimore poses with two officers before losing the struggle for the Maryland Grand Dragonship to KKKK veteran Tony LaRicci (Photo Bill Snead, *Washington Post*)

Maryland Grand Dragon Tony LaRicci supervises the rigorous task of erecting a cross for a rally near Baltimore (Photo Bill Snead, *Washington Post*)

An unidentified security guard acts as bodyguard for Maryland Grand Dragon Tony LaRicci, Imperial Wizard William M. Chaney of Indiana, and Pennsylvania Dragon Ray Doerfler during a rally in Gamber, Md., in September 1977 (Photo Bill Snead, *Washington Post*)

15
David Duke:
The Image Maker

New Orleans, Louisiana

An hour before the march, the crowd in the river corner of Jackson Square was already thickening: forty or fifty men, women, and children, not counting police intelligence officers and Richard "Sky Boots" Toups, who was snooping for Robert Shelton. Some arrived with rolled-up American, Confederate, and Klan flags; others, with drip-dry robes in laundry bags.

Colonel René LaCoste, clutching his own yellowing satin robe in a Woolworth sack, had established himself on a bench where he could see and be seen. Eighty-nine, he was dapper in seersucker slacks and navy sports jacket. His white mustache and goatee had been home trimmed that September morning to perpetuate his likeness to the Kentucky fried-chicken magnate, which was how he came to be called "Colonel" in the first place. That origin long since forgotten, he nevertheless commanded the esteem associated with the actual rank even when he made his rounds as proprietor of the American Specialty Company, selling tear-gas guns and pocket combs. Now he was captivating a small but admiring audience with a tale of the day in January 1972 when he and Roswell Thompson had their run-in with a black group at New Orleans' Robert E. Lee monument.

"I'm the only one that *evah* put the Black Panthahs on the run," he told them in a dramatic baritone, which, in younger days, had performed for a New York City opera company.

"The Black Panthers?" an awe-struck teenage boy asked.

"That's right," the colonel boasted. "We were celebrating Robert E. Lee's birthday. There was me and Mistah Thompson and several other klansmen. And also Jake was there. Jake was the United Cab driver." Until Roswell Thompson passed away several months ago, the colonel digressed, he was Imperial Wizard of his own Klan in New Orleans: the Universal Klan, or the Fraternal Order of the Klan, as Thompson sometimes had preferred to call it. The colonel had been his Imperial Kludd, bosom friend, and personal adviser right to the end, right through Thompson's fourteen bids for mayor, governor, and assorted political offices.

This particular day, the colonel said, they had set out in their Klan robes to pay respects to the general. They draped a Confederate flag at the foot of the monument and were marching back and forth when some blacks began hurling bricks at them.

"Jake drove up in his cab, and when he did, he told us, he looked around and he said to himself, 'They're in trouble!' So he didn't do a thing but *riiip* out his thirty-eight, and when he did, he said to himself, 'Well, I cahn't shoot because I'm liable to hit an innocent person.' His second thought was to shoot in the air. And the Black Panthahs thought there was *even more* klansmen than were there! So *then* what happened, they didn't do a thing but arrest *Jake* for having a gun—the police did—and put him in one of these police cars. And I told him, I said, 'Don't worry, Jake!' I said, 'We'll get you out before you get in jail!'

"Then I *gashed* a niggah that threw two bricks at me . . . I gashed him and he went *allll* the way down the steps and he ran *into* the police. If there was one car, there must have been eleven police cars. And the captain of the police said, '*Which* one of these men threw bricks at you?' I said, 'Men? You call that niggah a man?' "

His audience chuckled, and the colonel, still mentally dwelling in the past, continued. "*Ahhh,* Roswell was a wizard. There was no two ways about that. He was one of the braaavest men I knew." He sighed and shifted his performance to the present. "You know, I want to tell you this." He leaned forward in a confiding attitude. "Maybe you don't know. Your mayor, Moon Landrieu, is a niggah!"

"I didn't know that," a woman murmured.

"His grandmothah was black as the ace of spades," he assured the listeners, "and if you don't believe me, you ask . . ."

His story ended prematurely as a robed man climbed onto the colonel's bench and cupped his hands to his mouth. "Can I have y'all's attention, *pleeease*!" He waited while the crowd quieted. "We're out here fightin' for white people! Right now, Jim Warner and David Duke are in jail! Are we gonna stand here and put up with things like this?"

The crowd thundered "*No!!!*"

"So what are we fighting for?"

"*Whiiite power!*" the people roared.

"White power!"

"*Whiiite power!!!*"

The announcement was made more to whip the crowd into a frenzy than as news. Already, word had spread about the arrests of Duke and

Jim Warner, his second-in-command, after last night's rally and cross lighting. As often as anyone would listen, Duke's wife, Chloe, had raced through her version of the incident: the State Police—acting on warrants issued in Jefferson Parish (county), adjoining New Orleans—had stopped cars driven by Duke and Warner and arrested them on charges of inciting to riot, plus "simple battery" for Warner. Chloe Duke and twenty-five others had spent most of the night attempting to get them out on bail. Now, she was confident, "David *will* come to the parade."

The arrests were the finale to a day-long exchange between the police and Duke's Knights of the Ku Klux Klan outside a motel where the Knights were hosting simultaneous national and international conventions. By Klan estimates, the meetings had attracted six hundred: rank and file members, leaders, and heads of other right-wing organizations, including Warner's California-based New Christian Crusade Church, the Western Guard of Canada, the People's Movement of West Germany, and the European-wide League of St. George. Enough delegates were known to police for their previous violence here and abroad to bring out plainclothesmen armed with telescopic lenses and cameras. When delegates complained about the picture taking, Duke and Warner readily agreed to a confrontation with the lone police unit then on the scene. The encounter soon grew to a hundred or so delegates against five police units—four cars and a paddy wagon. The crowd allegedly rocked a patrol car, jammed the car door on an officer's foot, and snapped off a radio antenna. The police countered by arresting three klansmen. Duke and Warner retreated just ahead of the handcuffs, only to be nabbed later that night.

Warner had been arrested the day before for failing to appear at a zoning hearing on the Knights' operation of a printing press without a permit. Even that was not the first arrest for the combination National Information Director-Louisiana Grand Dragon, whose long right-wing career at one time earned him a spot on the Secret Service's list of persons considered a threat to the president. In the course of migrating from the American Nazi Party and the NSRP to his own creations—the Sons of Liberty, the Odinist Religion, Inc., and the New Christian Crusade Church—he had been arrested for numerous clashes, especially during his days with George Lincoln Rockwell. In 1963, both he and Jerry Dutton—who also recently had moved from California to New Orleans to become one of Duke's leaders—were charged with conspiracy to interfere with the integration of Birmingham's schools.

Nor was it the first arrest for the twenty-six-year-old National Director, the title Duke used in preference to "Imperial Wizard." In January 1972, he and two members of the National Party—an outgrowth of the White Youth Alliance, formed during his student days at

Louisiana State University—were charged with making Molotov cock-tails. That following June, he and several others were accused of theft by fraud and contributing to the delinquency of a minor while supposedly collecting funds for George Wallace's presidential campaign. During the 1971-72 school term, police blamed Duke's National Party for fanning the already inflamed race relations at two New Orleans high schools. Duke, however, had never been tried for any of the charges.

Along with Chloe Duke, the "Reverend" Rick Norton, who was affiliated with the New Christian Crusade Church, shook hands and expressed appreciation for offers of money and help. "I certainly appreciate your courage in staying with us," Norton comforted one man. "I know it's been a very traumatic experience." The "Reverend" Norton, forty-three, earlier had described himself to me as district superintendent of three of the organization's Los Angeles "churches," a retired air force captain, a political science graduate of Occidental College in California, and the son of a former Methodist minister.

"Oh, God—bow your heads, please—Oh, God, we ask that You'll have Your blessing today on all the people gathered here—especially Jim Warner, Dave Duke, who are still in prison. We know that You've said where two or more are gathered together in Your name, there You'll be also." His soft voice grew loud. "We know that You're the God of the *white race! And we ask that You'll be with us and guide us through this march and let no harm befall ANYONE ELSE HERE! IN JESUS' NAME. A-MEN!*"

"A-men!!!" rumbled through the crowd as Norton hopped down and Sandra Bergeron, the Giant—or top officer—for Jefferson Parish, warned: "There will be *no* violence from the Klan. I expect all our people to obey this. If we see anyone doin' anything wrong, you *will* be asked to leave. *Do not* give us a hard time. Smile. Many people will wonder what's on your mind."

At ten thirty, Duke and Warner were not among the hundred or so klanspeople who filed out of the square. Half of them in robes and peaked hats, the rest in street clothes, they marched solemn-faced, led by Jerry Dutton, the Knights' new Grand Wizard, and the Giants for St. Bernard and Orleans parishes. In front of them, one hand on the steering wheel, the other gripping a CB mike, Clara 'Bip" Pecoraro guided a convoy-green jeep toward Canal Street. Their destination: the Liberty Monument, erected in 1874 in honor of white New Orleanians killed during Reconstruction.

"Break one-four for Triple K," Bip Pecoraro barked into the mike. A heavy-set young woman seated beside her scanned the rooftops and balconies with binoculars.

The CB crackled, "This is Triple K, Diamond Girl. Come back."

"What's it look like down there?" Bip Pecoraro asked.

The female voice at the other end of the CB reported a few cars and pedestrians headed for the nearby Mississippi River ferry landing. From the rear of the marchers, Security Two reported another "All's clear."

At first, it was quiet. Just the rhythmic *right-left-right-left* of the marchers' footsteps. Then the shouts exploded into the Sunday-morning quiet like rounds from a machine gun, slamming back and forth again and again across Decatur Street until the echoes dissolved into a silence as deafening as the shouts. A hoarse male voice led the litany:

"Whadda we want?"

"White power!"

"Whadda we got?"

"WHITE POWER!!!"

"White power!"

"WHITE POWER!!!"

"One—more—time!"

"WHITE POWER!!!!"

Each round grew louder, more piercing, more frightening, with children and women—even Chloe Duke—slinging their voices into the verbal barrage. Only Dutton and his partners marched stoically, neither chanting nor, like the others, extending their left arms in Nazi-type salutes. The three stared straight ahead, oblivious to the motorcycle police escorts, wide-eyed tourists, and tittering blacks. One small girl, robed like the rest, clung to her father's hand, her face reflecting none of the arrogance of the other marchers. In spite of the humid September heat, the child and a man on crutches kept up as the block-long parade turned on to Canal Street.

The colonel and a stout, gray-haired man, whose sandwich billboard was a montage of right-wing mastheads and slogans, waited at the monument. Waving the current issue of *The Thunderbolt,* the sturdier man encouraged onlookers to *"Buuuy your literature here!"* His cries soon were drowned out as the marchers reached and circled the monument, still shouting *"White power!!!"* The klanspeople milled aimlessly until a car pulled up, and Warner and Duke—the latter, in a fashionable corduroy safari suit—emerged to a hero's welcome of cheers, applause, and a bugler's taps.

"This is the best part of the march!" one man yelled.

"Best part of the whooole march!" a young woman echoed.

"How 'bout Duke for preseeeedent!!!"

Swirling pasta and talking about the time he sold Kirbys door to door, David Duke bore no more resemblance to a vacuum-cleaner salesman that he did to a national Klan leader when we met for lunch at a suburban New Orleans restaurant in July 1976. His blond hair was tousled but styled, his bush mustache trim, and his lanky six-foot-two frame sported a rough-textured white suit, pleated and belted in back with detailed finesse. Over the summer, the suit had become a respectable stand-in for his robe and hood. Today, it was mated with a white shirt and paisley tie, and Duke scrunched under its slightly padded shoulders as he extolled the virtues of the Kirby vacuum.

"I sold about seven the first week," he boasted. "At first, I was very much taken by the Kirby. It's certainly the best vacuum cleaner on the market. There's no doubt about it. It has a good vibration. Great suction. Just a *treeemendous* cleaner." His fork took a slow swirl and stopped as abruptly as his sales pitch. "But the people we were trying to sell them to were the middle class or lower-middle class. Well, it *is* the best vacuum cleaner you can buy, but most of them didn't really have the carpeting or the floors. They didn't really need such a thing. So eventually I got this through my thick skull. I stopped believing in them. I thought I was really doing something really kind of wrong. So I stopped selling them."

"Are you a good salesman?" I asked.

"Sure," Duke acknowledged, "if it's something I believe in. I can't sell something I don't believe in."

The stint with Kirby and another plotting curves for a New Orleans stockbroker were summer jobs to put himself through LSU and earn the history degree that had made him a novelty among Klan leaders and a sought-after guest on television talk shows.

"My father could have afforded it," Duke quickly added, "but he said, well, he paid his way through school and it'd be good for me to pay mine. I don't feel bitter about it, but I'm not especially glad I did."

The university degree and his physical appearance were not all that set him apart from the rough-hewn nightrider image usually associated with the infamous KKK initials. Articulate, charming, sexy, Duke was boyishly sophisticated, his vocabulary encompassing "gosh" and "golly" and *vis à vis;* his accent worldly. The son of an engineer, Duke was born in Tulsa, attended kindergarden in The Hague and a private military school in Georgia, and had lived in sundry other places before his parents moved to New Orleans in the early sixties. He interrupted his college studies, he said, to spend part of 1971 in Vientiane teaching English to Laotian army officers in what he described as "a special government program" conducted by the State Department's Agency for International Development.

"How did you come to join the Klan at seventeen?" I asked.

Duke sighed philosophically. "The whole family has always been oriented toward education. My grandmother was a chemistry professor at Kansas University, and my father used to make me sit for an hour a day and read. So I developed a habit of reading when I was about seven or eight. When I was very young, I was really oriented toward science. I read everything I could get my hands on. Science Digest, every month I would devour it. And Popular Mechanics. I wanted to be a natural scientist. Maybe an anthropologist or an archeologist, or some sort of biological science."

A wistful note had crept into his voice. I studied him and his white suit and manicured nails. A ring seemed to be his only tie with the Klan. He looked very much the young man on his way up. Even detractors conceded he could probably succeed in almost any profession. Why had he chosen the Klan? He had had none of the disadvantages and liabilities that drove many people to the Hooded Order. His family was educated, economically comfortable, and fairly close knit. He could have majored in science as easily as in history.

"Why *didn't* you go into science?" I asked.

"Because," Duke explained, "I came to believe that race was the most important thing to civilization in building a society and a nation. In fact, I came to believe the most important thing in the world was people—the quality of people. I came to feel our race was being overcome by the nonwhite world."

"At what point did you start to feel that way?"

"Not until I was about ... that was, uhhh, sixty-two. I was about thirteen." He leaned across the table. "Now here's the shocker. By the time I was twelve, I imagine I'd already read as much as people twenty-five, and I was becoming a liberal. I really was. I had read some of these books that were very much pro-black and trying to instill a guilt complex in the white people for being white. You might say I was committed reasonably and emotionally to liberal ideas. And then something changed." Duke paused suspensefully. "What changed was entirely a reasonable thing. My emotions followed later. One book started me off. One single little book. It was called Race and Reason: A Yankee View." Almost nostalgically, he repeated, "A Yankee View. It was the first anti-integration book I'd ever seen."

"That one book changed your mind?"

He buttered some bread. "No, it didn't change my mind, but it started me out. I wasn't even half convinced, but I was convinced enough to say, 'My gosh, this man does have some reasonable arguments.' So then I started reading everything I could get my hands on, on race and things like that."

After his four-year metamorphosis from liberal to racist, Duke said, he had never veered from his chosen path: every book he read, every course he took in school had been aimed at helping him achieve his philosophy of life. He had joined the Knights of the Ku Klux Klan, headed by a man who—before his murder in June 1975—had led at least a double life: to the Invisible Empire, he was Ed White, leader and financial backer; to the New Orleans establishment, he was Jim Lindsay, owner of a prosperous real estate firm and resident of the "social" uptown section of town. (Police knew him by still another alias, James Lawrence.) Most who attended Lindsay's funeral did not connect Duke's role as pall-bearer with any affiliation between the dead man and the Klan. Even his widow—separated from him at the time of his death and acquitted of the murder—acknowledged that she knew her husband had been associated with Duke and had given him money but claimed she was unaware that he was head of the Klan. She said, however, she was not surprised at my disclosure during a telephone interview. "I'm sure that's how he met his fate," she charged, "and I just became the 'patsy.'"

At the time David Duke joined, the Knights was composed mostly of high school students and did little more than meet. But young Duke believed in it. When he entered LSU in 1968, he promised his father he would join no right-wing organizations. And he didn't. At first, he limited his activities to distributing literature printed by right-wing groups and monopolizing the campus' Free Speech Alley. In 1969, he formed his own White Youth Alliance at LSU, eventually spreading it, he said, to about forty, mostly Southern, universities. Based on Klan principles, the Alliance, which he later broadened into the National Party, existed primarily to hand out white racist literature, including its own newsletter. These activities, plus his picketing—in a storm-trooper uniform complete with swastika—of activist attorney William Kunstler, soon earned Duke the dubious title of "the Nazi of LSU."

Now he attacked the fairness of the "Nazi" label. "I was really politically active at school. I was passing out all sorts of literature just trying to get the campus acclimatized. I must have passed out a hundred thousand pieces of literature by different groups, you know, which included . . ."

"The American Nazi Party?" I interrupted.

"Yeah, but it wasn't anymore . . . It wasn't *for* them. It was just stuff on the race issue, and it might have had their name on it. Something like that."

"But if you didn't want to be identified with the American Nazi party, wasn't that a bad thing to do?"

Duke's tone was a mixture of controlled outrage and martyrdom. "You're very naïve when you're starting your political activity, and you don't realize the lowness of these people. I've passed out all sorts of stuff, but that's the kind of thing they pick up on. They say, 'Well, you're a Nazi.' Or you make a statement like I did about World War Two that we should have fought against Communism instead of with Communism. You could have said a hundred other statements, but they pick this out and call you a Nazi, which is an age-old Jewish thing, anyway. But I *didn't* have a name at LSU as a Nazi. Like I say, that was just the first semester."

Indignant, Duke rested his defense momentarily while he swirled his fork through the pasta. Then he took the verbal stand again. "Now, here's another thing they've tried to use on me. I've written many, many articles that have been picked up by many, many publications. So if they have an article on me or something that refers to me, people say, 'Oh, he's a member of this or that,' you know. Of course, they could say I was everything. They could say I was a Minuteman, which I've really never been. I've worked with them a little bit," he conceded. "I've worked with *all* of 'em, but I've never joined anything except the Klan. And the White Youth Alliance and the National Party." He hesitated, then continued somewhat uncertainly. "I might've joined the National States Rights Party. I don't remember . . . it's been so long. But that's all."

Brightening, his tone became somewhat swaggering. "And because I've passed out literature, different groups have taken credit for things that I do. I had a lot of energy. I passed out a lot of literature. But that doesn't mean anything."

He shrugged, and reached into the bread basket.

The *National Socialist Bulletin*—official publication of the National Socialist White People's Party (NSWPP) and edited for a time by Jim Warner—took note of Duke's activities in Louisiana. One item, in the August 1, 1970, issue, referred to "local National Socialists led by Dave Duke, a student at Louisiana State University. . . ." That fall, a special edition of the White Youth Alliance's *Racialist* included a "White Power Program" in which Duke, under his own byline, copied verbatim passages from the already published "Goals and Objectives of the NSWPP." The back page carried a boxed coupon captioned "Membership Application for the White Student Alliance, 2507 N. Franklin Road, Arlington, Va. 22201," the address of the NSWPP. The *National Socialist Bulletin* also ran accounts of Duke's heckling of Dr. Benjamin Spock when he spoke at LSU on September 30, 1970, and his picketing of Kunstler at Tulane University a month earlier. Photographs from the latter event showed a lean, expressionless David Duke toting signs: "Kunstler Is a Communist Jew" and "Gas the Chicago 7."

When I asked about the picketing, Duke scoffed. "That was clear back when I was eighteen. Maybe I was twenty. I was just a kid. I just didn't know how to combat William Kunstler."

"Do you regret any of those things now?"

"Wellll, yeah," he said cautiously. "In a way, and in a way not. I regret it because people might take it wrong. I just don't like for people to hold something against me when I was a kid for the rest of my life. I can't quite understand that, but that's the facts of life." He sighed. "It doesn't have any reflection on my approach or my politics, but any sort of handle they can use to discredit you, they will. It's as simple and clear as that. And people's minds . . ." He stopped, disgust in his voice. "People are not basically open-minded. People are bigoted, and I think I am open-minded."

Duke described the National Party as "kind of a jump from just college students to general," although its membership still remained mostly young people.

"It was basically a . . ." He studied the ceiling. ". . . What's the word for it? A Klan that wasn't called a Klan. It really wasn't deceptive. It was just basically an organization that was based on Klan principles, Klan symbols."

"Why did you call it something else?" I asked.

"Even though I had been in the Klan, I wasn't entirely convinced that the Klan was the way to victory. Another thing," he continued, "I was disenchanted to a point with the leadership—not the one I was with—but around the country. There are some leaders in the Klan or groups that are called the Ku Klux Klan who are very ignorant. I'm not saying that to put down the Klan. I'm just saying that's a reality."

But after a year—during which he married, lived briefly in Seattle, and returned to LSU to get his degree—Duke decided to "drop any pretense and just be right out in the open as a klansman."

"I realized that no matter what you call yourself, if you stand up for these principles, you'll end up being called the same thing and you'll get all the bad publicity. Another thing, there is a tremendous press blackout in this country of any organizations or groups that are basically right-wing, unless . . ." Duke sat up excitedly as he went on with his argument. "The press, you see, built up the Klan as a boogeyman, as a foe, to push the Civil Rights Movement. So the Klan got a lot of publicity. The Klan was an organization worthy of publicity. People knew it existed. People knew it was sizable. It had a lot of interesting characteristics—from a news person's point of view. The fiery cross. The robes make good copy. Good pictures. So even though it had these negative connotations, at least the Klan had the ability to break through the media's silence."

The restaurant had emptied except for the two of us and an occasional waitress, yet Duke showed no sign of winding down.

"The biggest thing is the effect it has on your own people. The Klan has all the effects of a mass movement. It's got the banners, the badges, the history, the heroes, the martyrs. It's got all the right things that can bring out the sort of dedication and religious fervor that any sort of movement needs to be ultimately successful. Second, I came to realize that the image of the Klan as a radical—in fact, an image which was not really inaccurate—a very strong antinigger image, a very strong anti-Jewish image in the long run may not be a political disadvantage. That, in effect, it may be an advantage. If, indeed, America is headed toward more, quote, radical times, if its people really feel threatened, they're not going to want some kind of half measure. They're going to want something strong."

Having attained almost podium fervor, Duke resumed his smooth façade as he concluded, "I reached the point I was tired of half truths, I was tired of insincerities. I reached the point where I said, 'You got to stand up openly and honestly, and whether you win or whether you lose with that method, you've got to do it.' "

That decision made, Duke said, he began working more closely with Klan leader Lindsay—alias Ed White—first, as an organizer in the New Orleans-Baton Rouge area and as editor of the official publication. He quickly worked his way up to Grand Dragon of Louisiana and National Information Director and, finally, about the time of Lindsay's death, to National Director and Grand Wizard—positions he had since held separately or simultaneously, depending on the outcome of inner feuds. It was in 1973, when he became National Information Director, that he emerged as the Hooded Empire's media personality, appearing on local and national talk shows, such as "Today," "Tomorrow," and "A.M. America," and traveling the college lecture circuit. Magazines profiled him, newspapers interviewed him, and gradually he became as well known as, maybe better than, Robert Shelton.

Duke exchanged greetings with the restaurant owner before returning to our conversation. He would gladly yield the spotlight to someone else, he said. "I don't *need* the notoriety. I don't *need* the people to know who I am. I don't need *any* of that," he vowed not too convincingly. "I would be tickled to death for somebody to come along who knows more about history than I do, that can argue with these people better on the radio, that can put forth a better image, that can build the Klan better. I would give it to them. I would support them. I would get behind them. Then, maybe I'd have more time for myself."

"But do you enjoy people knowing 'This is David Duke'?"

He tossed aside any enthusiasm for fame. "I don't necessarily enjoy people knowing 'David Duke.' At first, it was kind of nice going into a place and people knowing who you are, getting special treatment at restaurants or if you went to a bar. It's nice seeing your name in print. But! after a while, if you're normal—and I'm afraid I'm normal—after a while, it wears off and gets like anything else."

He gave one of his snorting laughs.

"Do you ever get tired of it?"

"I'm not gonna let myself get tired until the work's done," he said defensively, "until my work's completed."

Music played in the background, and as our conversation meandered away from the Klan to books, travel, exercise, and education, the interview seemed like a lunch conversation with a pleasant acquaintance. Duke was interested and interesting, always ready with a reasonable-sounding answer, always smooth and controlled.

"You're very different from what people think of as the average klansman," I observed.

"Maybe the media stereotype hasn't been accurate," he countered.

"Which do you think it is? Do you think you're an exception or do you think you're a new breed? Or do you think the media *hasn't* been accurate?"

"I think I'm a traditional klansman. In some ways the media has had a lot to make fun of. I would closer resemble the *early* leaders of the Klan, people of the caliber of Nathan Bedford Forrest, than what we've had before."

"Do you think you could be a leader in another area?" I asked. "Some people have commented that Klan leaders—and I think they were probably talking about the more typical Klan—are people who could lead only . . ."

"Misfits or something?" he finished the sentence.

"Yeah."

"Well, I think if I wanted to be a traditional politician, I could do it. I think I could be governor of this state. I really do. Because if I wanted to play the game, I think I could be very successful." He paused and laughed. "But I don't."

Nevertheless, he took credit for attracting high-caliber people—even well-known people—from all walks of life who, before, wouldn't have considered joining the Klan. His image, he said, had even been a boost to other Klan groups.

"See, a lot of the media now talks about Klan resurgence in the last couple of years, and that resurgence, I think, is basically an offshoot of our work."

"Of your work?"

"Yes. Exactly. *Specifically.*" He was emphatic. "The Klan was *dying* in a lot of ways. Not because it didn't have appeal. Because the leadership was poor. And *we've* completely turned it around. If you just scan local and national newspaper clips from the last two years, *at least* eighty percent of them is going to be stuff from either myself or our members around the country."

But when I asked if he had any well-known members who might be willing to divulge their names, Duke became publicity shy. "We had a policy a few years ago of encouraging our people that are well-known to come out and support the Klan, because we think that it is important to show the average person in America, 'Look, this is not exactly the way the media had portrayed it. There are some outstanding individuals that are active in our organization.' But a couple things have happened that's affected that. And today, we don't encourage it.

"A good example is Mary Bacon. She was on the cover of a number of magazines. She was one of the first big successful lady jockeys in the United States. She came to us a couple of years ago, and since that time, her whole livelihood has been attacked. It certainly did us some good when she went public, but we think we have more responsibility to people like her now than they do to us."

"Is she still a member?"

He hedged. "I'd rather not discuss it. She, uh, was on the 'Tomorrow' show a while back, and she said a few things that were very untrue, and it really actually caused her—Tom Snyder had to come on a few nights later and say, 'She did lie to us. ' "

"Do you have members in all states?" I asked.

"Uh, every state," he confirmed, and added, "We've only got organized units in about forty, forty-two, maybe."

"Would you have as many as three thousand members?"

He retreated to secrecy, "I'm not going to give you any membership figures."

"You can't say 'less' or 'more'?"

"I'll just tell you it's a lot more than that, but I'm not going to tell you anything more than that. But it's growing fast," he wavered diplomatically. "We're just about doubling our numbers every two years."

Throughout most of my research, the FBI stubbornly maintained the Ku Klux Klan was all but dead, that its total membership added up to less than two thousand. Then, in November 1977, the Anti-Defamation League conceded what I had suspected throughout my travels: after a decade of decline, the Klan's major factions had grown by about twenty percent, from ADL's estimated sixty-five hundred klansmen in 1975 to eight thousand. Director Irwin J. Suall credited David Duke for the increase. "Duke is extraordinarily clever in manipulating the media," Suall said at the time. "He tones down his views for public consumption, and he is being given platforms all over the United States. The impression has been spread around that there's been a national resurgence in the Klan and that it is now respectable to be a member of the Klan." But it was more than that. Duke was, in his own words, doing things that had not been done before by the Invisible Empire: he advertised in newspapers and on radio; he often hired rock bands to appeal to young people; he opened his ranks to college students and women; he replaced many of the preposterous-sounding titles with more acceptable ones, such as National Director and Chaplain; he never wore a hood, not even for cross-lighting ceremonies, and he shed the colored satin robes for stoic white cotton. He had, in essence, put together an organization that was the Klan in name only. His competitors—even once-solidly entrenched Robert Shelton—viewed him as a threat and began altering their own procedures to keep up with the newcomer.

Now, when I asked Duke if he thought the splinter groups would ever merge, he scoffed. "I don't think it's important. I think we're way ahead right now. I mean, we're growing so fast that it's just not going to be important. I think our group is definitely emerging as *the* Klan group. When people think of the Klan in this country, I think *my* name now is as well known, or *better,* in many places—on campuses. A lot of people nowadays are just growing up, you know—freshmen, sophomores, juniors in college never even heard of Robert Shelton."

As he coolly put down the veteran Klan leader, I remembered Shelton's accusation in Tennessee that Duke had attempted to join UKA on two occasions: once years ago, again earlier in the spring.

"Shelton said you had approached him about becoming a member," I started.

The smooth veneer vanished. "This is an old ball of garbage! I know the whole story. Heard it before. Last year, in Kansas City, we had a meeting with DePugh—a bunch of right-wing groups. Doctor Warner was with me, and we visited Shelton. To our face, he was very nice and everything . . ." Duke's show of anger did not seem genuine as he offered his side of the story. "Years ago—I never once saw him in Tuscaloosa—I stopped at their offices, that big Imperial House, but nobody was in. Anyway, he made up the story that I came to Tuscaloosa and that I wanted to join his organization and have some high rank. I don't even know what the whole thing was. But he says that I—what does he say?" He creased his forehead, trying to remember. "He says he wouldn't do it. If I would join the ranks, I'd have to start at the bottom like everybody else and work my way up. This is the story he tells everyone. Well, it's totally untrue. First of all, I never was in Tuscaloosa . . ." He corrected himself. "I never saw him in Tuscaloosa *once.* Second of all, it's ridiculous, you know? Third of all, probably if I would've come to him like that, it seems to me it probably would have been a pretty good deal for him, although I would refuse."

"How long ago would this have happened?"

"He says three years ago," Duke answered, still perturbed.

"And you haven't talked to him recently?"

"I saw him about a year ago . . . I talked to him on the telephone a month and a half ago . . ."

"And you didn't ask to join then?"

"Absolutely not!" he stopped. "Oh! Is he talking about that?!!"

I nodded.

"I can't believe it! You know what I said? I talked to him and I've always . . . like I say, I try to go along with all Klan groups, and I called him the other day, and I talked to him about some kind of rumors he was putting out on me and on Don Black, our chief organizer in Alabama. But I talked to him about that, and I told him specifically that we would be willing to work any way we could and if he would be interested . . . This is what I said. Of course, Shelton puts out that I tried to join him. This is ridiculous."

Duke quickly regained his composure when the subject changed to his parents' reaction to his emergence as a national Klan leader.

"It's kind of a shock," he acknowledged. "They're expecting their son to follow some sort of traditional line. But my father always said, 'Look, if you go into a field—I don't care what you do basically—if you go into the field, get to the top.' His family has always been oriented toward excellence."

"He probably didn't mean the Klan," I ventured.

Duke looked sheepishly at his plate. "No, I don't think so."

One Sunday afternoon later in July, Jim Warner slouched in one corner of an oversized sofa, reading *Newsweek;* at the other end, David Duke watched a team of East Germans scull across the TV screen.

"They're winning everything!" he cheered.

Uncharacteristically reluctant to discuss Klan philosophy, Duke concentrated on the rowers, ignoring even the shrill screams by Erika, his not-quite-year-old replica. Her toys and some still-boxed wedding gifts cluttered the living room of the future home of Warner and his fiancée, Debbie Coleman, a shapely brunette who had given her bikini-clad endorsement to Duke's Klan in magazine photographs. Chloe and David Duke had spent the night there after a rained-out rally. Now he was trying to persuade his wife to postpone the hour's drive to their Baton Rouge residence so he could continue watching the games.

"I enjoy sports," Duke explained when he finally flipped off the TV and led the way upstairs. "I'd rather be out participating than watching, though. I like competitiveness. And I like the outdoors. To go out some place and swim, lay in the sun, and be pure animal for a while. I might play a game of tennis, handball, and I run a little bit and play some basketball. I try to keep fit. It's important. I work out about three times a week. Pressing weights. I press about two fifty on the bench."

"You're strong?" I asked, eyeing his slender silhouette.

"Very strong," he confirmed. "I'm going to stay strong. This is one leader that's not going to have a potbelly. I've always been slim and trim and fit, and I'm gonna stay that way."

He said he especially watched his diet and exercised while traveling, the way he spends half to three-quarters of his time. Just back from a tour of Europe, he boasted of successful meetings with Klan members and other right-wing leaders abroad.

"One problem the Klan has had in the past, it's been very parochial," he complained as we sat down at a small dining table in a room whose only other furnishings were a shelf of books—mostly on Hitler—and a typesetter. He leaned across the table and mimicked a redneck accent. " *'Where you from, you from the next county, boy?'* You know? *'We don't need nobody's help down here in this county.'* That kind of attitude and approach is not going to make any political changes. We see the struggle not just on the county level or state level or regional level, the South, or even the national level. We see a worldwide struggle that's being waged."

"Klan leaders are always on the go," I observed. "What keeps you so busy? Meeting people?"

"What do you mean, 'What am I doing'?" he countered suspiciously. "You know my background. I feel like being busy. I have to have eight hours sleep, but when traveling, I usually get four. But the point is, I don't like to sleep, and I want to go. Now what causes that drive? I don't know."

His legs jiggled under the table, rattling it.

"You can't sit still."

He laughed. "I know. It's terrible. This is part of the way I am. I'm not that nervous. I'm just . . . it's energy. That's why I'm not ever going to get fat."

Serious again, Duke, like most leaders, was convinced that the Klan was the solution to this country's—and the world's—problems. But unlike the others, when he referred to the Klan, he meant *his.*

"We're really the only group that doesn't follow the Simmons' Klan," he explained snobbishly. "That's the one that became the largest. It became more of a fraternity. *We* go back to the original for the basis of our philosophy, for the basis of our action, for our formulations."

"What do you consider yours, more military?" I asked.

"No, political," he retorted. "We see this as a social movement in the traditional sense. The same way that the Sons of Liberty were. The same way the Communist Party was. The same way the Fascist Party was. In other words, a movement for social change and not just as a fraternity for people to get together and have fun or salute the past."

Duke sounded older and wiser than his years as he expounded on his Klan's goals. "We want political power in our country for our philosophy of life. This means we've got to get involved more and more in politics. We're going to start running more candidates openly. I ran for state senate, you know."

"You came in third, right?"

"Second. Well, there were only two candidates," he laughed. "I got a third of the votes, which wasn't bad. I was the youngest candidate, running in the most educated and the most wealthy district in the state. And I was running against a guy who was the former student body president of LSU, forty-five, member of every fraternal and service organization, in the height of his power."

"Did anybody use your Klan affiliation against you?"

"Yeah, he had an ad out with a hood and two eyeholes, and it said . . . the eyeholes were part of 'Don't Be Hoodwinked.' In other words, because I sounded so reasonable and because I made such a good appearance, 'Don't be hoodwinked, he's actually a rat!'" He gave another snorting laugh. "That's the thing, you see, I never talk radical on television or in person. But the image the media presents of the Klan leader, people expect you to have cow manure on the bottom of your shoes, chewing tobacco in your mouth, and be unintelligent and rough and mean and discourteous. It's just terrible."

In November 1975, when Duke polled more than eleven thousand votes in Baton Rouge's Sixth Senatorial District against incumbent Ken Osterberger, even the press conceded the then-twenty-five-year-old National Director "showed surprising strength." Duke predicted that voters were "just about ready for us" and pledged, "We've just begun." In the campaign's closing days, Osterberger—described as "a middle of the roader"—took a more conservative tone, pledging opposition to gun-control laws and forced busing. Duke himself had made race an issue, veiling it in respectability and reasonableness. Reflecting his political savvy, he appealed to his white suburban middle-class constituents in well-put-together brochures that listed his "stands": he was "staunchly" opposed to forced busing and plans to force the merger of LSU and Southern University (at one time, the state's separate white and black university systems); he was against the reverse discrimination "going on against white people in employment, promotions and scholarships"; he believed "public schools should reflect the heritage, traditions, and ideals of our nation, and should not become vehicles to degrade and debase that heritage through false history meant to affect social change." The brochure noted he was *against* gun-control laws and tax increases and *for* stronger state criminal laws and free enterprise. It also argued the need for representation of white people. Still another leaflet pictured him and a pregnant Chloe Duke, the caption noting that she was an LSU graduate with a degree in home economics and that they were expecting their first child two months before the election. The text included among Duke's qualifications "National Director, Knights of the Ku Klux Klan—who has brought on the greatest period of Klan growth since Reconstruction," and credited him with "leading the anti-busing fight across the nation." Much of his fund raising was handled by Jim Warner, who sent out letters addressed to "Dear Christian Friend" and signed "May God Bless You."

The state senate race was not Duke's first political activity in Louisiana. In 1974, he and a colleague appeared before the Louisiana House Judiciary Committee to protest its consideration of anti-discrimination legislation, leaving the usual Klan calling cards: "You have been paid a friendly visit by the Knights of the Ku Klux Klan. Should we pay you a real visit?" The committee later deferred action on the bill, in effect killing it. Shortly after my first meeting with Duke in July 1976, he made two appearances at the state capitol: first, he testified against a bill aimed at preventing the Klan from barring blacks from meetings that were held in public buildings and advertised as being open to the public; the second time, he and a black-faced colleague showed up for the unveiling of a bust of the state's only black governor, P. B. S. Pinchback, who served briefly between 1872 and 1873.

Now Duke insisted it was not the form of government but the people running it that dissatisfied him. On attaining political power, he emphasized he was referring to appointed as well as elected positions. "We have a lot of people in government in D.C. who are members. They work in some government agency or some government office or some part of the armed services."

"Members of *your* Klan or *all* Klans?"

"I think we have more than anyone else," he said positively, "because we're the only ones that are really into the college grads and so forth."

When I asked how he would encourage his members to preserve the white race, Duke was emphatic. "The most important thing they could do is to have children. White people *better* start having children, otherwise we're just going to die out."

"We've got to encourage economically those that perform best. Democracy and equality is or [sic] completely opposed to this. Every-thing today is equality, mass, equal." He grimaced. "What about quality? What about excellence?"

"How would you support these people?"

"It's very simple. Today, the more children you have, the less money you're going to make. There's a small tax break, but it doesn't even make up for the kids. So I'd say tax credit for kids for people who are most productive in certain areas."

"Who's going to determine this?" I wondered.

Undaunted, he answered, "Somebody's got to. It's being determined right now by chance. I don't even think it's being determined by chance because I think the people are antiwhite. I don't believe in suppression, but I think those low on the totem pole—IQ-wise, intelligence-wise, ability-wise—I don't think they should be encouraged to have kids."

"They would have a tax the other way?"

"Sure," Duke answered. "I imagine this all sounds harsh, but its not meant to. I don't think you can have a high society without high people."

Duke seemed confident that government-determined birth control was the answer to a better world, although some of his own members, I felt, probably never would pass muster under such terms.

"In a society in which this came about, where the emphasis *was* on raising quality people, what would happen to the black people in that category?" I asked.

"I don't think anything would happen because basically they would be in their own country. Someday, it's going to be possible. In the meantime, I'd say they'd have their own communities and call their own standards within them."

And Jewish people? "The same thing goes for them" he started. ". . . except, the Jews that have been working against our national interest—I mean treason against our race—I think they should be punished under the law. Those who have not, I don't think anything should be done to them."

Exactly what was the philosophy of life the Klan wanted implemented? Duke's delivery suddenly became succinct, his points made like well-aimed bullets: "Specifically, we're totally opposed to integration. We think integration has only caused hatred and violence between the races. We think the races should be separated—whether in this country or even outside the country is something time will tell. We're staunchly anti-Communist. In terms of foreign policy, we think we should actively support any anti-Communist regimes and especially any white nations of the world. The white people are outnumbered nine to one, and we've got to start sticking together. Other special political ideas depend on the area. You say the area, and I can tell you our position." He eased back in his chair with the air of a veteran politician.

"Some people say the Klan varies the issues according to the area . . ." I started.

"We do that, definitely."

"Do you do that to get in and interest the people and gradually . . ."

"We never lie," he cut in defensively. "We don't compromise our philosophy. But we are a social movement, a political movement, and naturally when a subject—if it fits with our basic philosophy, then naturally if this is what the people are interested in, then naturally we talk about it."

"But you do use the issue that's currently at hand as a drawing card?"

"Of course—if that's our issue, too."

When we arranged the interview, Duke had insisted he could spare two hours, at most. But now that he was immersed in Klan philosophy, he showed no signs of wanting to stop.

"Why don't we go over to one of our book-processing centers and get you some material?" he suggested. "I've just talked about external things on the periphery. I haven't given you any of the reasons behind the philosophy. I haven't given you any of the facts or any of the studies or any of the evidence or research that goes into the reason why I feel like I do."

We got into his car, which was cluttered with clothing, and headed through the suburbs to a large two-story frame house within blocks of the Patriot Book Store, the Knights' official headquarters. "You've got to promise not to tell where it's located," he admonished. An American flag folded lengthwise was tacked over the door. Next to the bell, one sign bore instructions for making an appointment; another simply said to knock. When no one answered, Duke led me to the back of the house and rapped on the door. A gray-haired man peered from behind the window shade before opening the door. Duke instructed him to let us in the front entrance. Upstairs, the walls of the three main rooms were lined with partially filled bookshelves. More books were still boxed, waiting to be unpacked.

"This is our library of right-wing books," Duke explained as I scanned the titles, most of them on Hitler, World War II, and the Jewish question. The older man—introduced as "Tom"—followed us from room to room, finally leading the way downstairs to what he described as "our mail-order book headquarters." Books and printing equipment filled the main room and two behind it.

"We have more than four hundred different books," Tom told me while Duke selected random volumes.

"This one should be good," Duke muttered. "And you really ought to read this."

Tom eyed him and the accumulating stack of books. "Even though I'm National Director, I'm going to have to ask you to give me the money for these books," Duke informed me. "We'll give it back when you return them." I squirmed as the pile grew and explained I needed enough money to pay the ten-dollar cab fare back into town. The selecting process halted, and he began replacing hard-cover editions with paperbacks. Even those added up to eleven dollars. I reluctantly removed the contents of my wallet, twenty dollars, and again emphasized I needed *at least* ten for a taxi. Tom interceded, allowing me to take the books without paying. Before we left, Duke browsed some more, picking up a cassette of his appearance on the Tom Snyder show—the selling price, five dollars—and several books, including *My Friend Hitler.*

Back at Warner's house, we returned to the upstairs room and played the tape. Duke listened with childlike delight, commenting on the discussion and taking special pride whenever he outpointed Snyder. I looked over the bookshelves and asked, "You got a book on Hitler and I notice there are some here. What are your feelings about him?"

"I don't have that many actually," he protested. "The Klan certainly doesn't have any affinity with Nazi Germany. There are some points I think they would be in agreement. There are some points you have to agree with Communism and with Mao Tse-tung. We're not the laissez-faire Catholics, you know. The point is, the media is so controlled by the Jews that we owe it to—like intellectual honesty—to read and investigate any side of the question that they suppress from us."

"So your reading is not because you admire Hitler?"

"No," he said thoughtfully. "In some ways it's not admiration, but certainly there's some knowledge that can be gained from it, because Germany was one particular case—and Italy and Spain to a degree—where Jewish powers were supplanted. We're certainly not in favor of every program they put through on their side—the Socialists—but there is something to learn there in terms of how to fight and how to overcome the Jewish power that exists."

As Duke gravitated to the "Jewish question," his arguments were monotonous retreads of other Klan speeches on a slightly more intellectual level—his words bigger, his feelings better expressed—but the charges were the same: Jews dominated the media and money, taking everything from society and giving nothing.

"Now you say, how can I criticize them for being racist when I'm a racist? Well, I'm a racist but I think I'm much more of . . . of . . . I define racism kind of differently than they do," he hedged.

"How *do* you define it?"

"The Jews are a racist of a variety that hate. They *hate,*" he said strongly, "because they see the whole rest of the world as persecuting them. They're paranoid. And when they look at other racists around the world—like white racists—they define us by their own definition. They say *we* are the haters. We *are* the ones with hate in our hearts, when we're not that way at all. We are racists because we *love* our own people. It's as simple as that."

Robed figures edged the thoroughfare shouting *"White power!"* and encouraging motorists to pull into the gradually filling parking lot of the St. Bernard Civic Center. Late-model Cadillacs and Chryslers, instead of the usual pickups and campers, mixed with the vintage Fords and Chevys. Aside from scattered AKIA decals, the gathering could have been any one of the community functions staged at the modern glass and concrete structure. But, tonight, the occasion was an indoor rally to climax what Duke and the Knights had billed as an "International Patriotic Congress." Men, women, and children, some in Klan robes—

mingled out front. One group gathered around a sturdy gray-haired man, who—for the benefit of a television crew—recounted the arrests made earlier that afternoon after the confrontation between delegates and Jefferson Parish deputies outside the motel where the congress was held.

"They came in with riot helmets, billy sticks, and all this stuff! Grabbed a seventy-one-year-old man with heart trouble, threw him up against a car, and *I* saw them hit him *at least* three times myself with these billy clubs! And they had him cuffed when they was hittin' him! Another man said, 'Stop hittin' that man!' and they grabbed *him* and threw him in jail. . . . And then they grabbed another man who was *just* standin' there. Okay, then they picked up two doctors, two chiropractors who *didn't* even know what was going on!"

A young woman, her voice racing the narrator's, interrupted, "Didn't have nuthin' to do with us at all. Right. They were comin' out of their convention same time we were comin' out of ours. Anyhow . . ."

The man regained his audience. "The *sixth* one was the best of all. They picked up a Negro and threw *him* in the police car, too. I assume they were so stupid they couldn't tell he was colored!"

The crowd laughed appreciatively.

"What were they charged with?" I inquired.

"Resisting arrest was one of them. Assault or something like that. The thing is, there was *no* assault on the police officers."

Outside the entrance, two men—one in his midthirties, the other with thinning gray hair and a walking cane—wore sandwich billboards and waved copies of *The Thunderbolt, The Crusader,* and other right-wing papers. The older man's billboard was covered with mastheads and slogans: "What is Communism?" "Who Shot Presidents?" "Who Will Bury Us?" "True Answers 25¢," "OIL YES, JEWS NO." As I read the latter—a bumper sticker—aloud, he chuckled and in a thick accent exclaimed, "Yews! Yews! Thees ees Stoner's."

He introduced himself as Joseph Dilys and his partner as John Kay. Both originally came from Lithuania and now, Chicago.

"You sell the literature of David Duke's group?" I asked.

"That and Vanguards, Thunderbolts, Cross and the Flag from Los Angeles, and National Christian News," John Kay listed.

Dilys interrupted. "Many, many. Publications that addresses people, organizations. Papers who we think ees goot."

"Do you belong to any group?"

Kay ignored the question. "We just pass out literature of all the groups that are represented here tonight."

"Do you do any other work, or is this a full-time . . ."

"No, no. On the side, I do this," Kay assured me. "I'm a barber."

"How did you get started?"

"First of all, I'm a victim of Communism. And I was always wondering what is behind Communism. Wondering why all these people ran away from Europe and why there was such a big revolution in nineteen seventeen. And so I kept searching and searching, and I'm actually a DP, too, myself. And I finally met Mister Dilys on a trip to Washington. We were demonstrating against Brezhnev. He was here to sell out this country, you know, by détente and all that."

Dilys added, "We met on the bus," and handed me a photocopied sheet with his picture in the billboard and a biography that said he had been born in Lithuania in 1903, shot a policeman when the Communists occupied his country, and in 1944 lost his left leg when the Communists machine-gunned him shortly before he escaped to Germany. He migrated to the United States in 1951 and began hawking right-wing literature in Chicago in 1958.

As I turned to go, I spotted John Ross Taylor, the Canadian I had met in June at Dale Reusch's rally in Charleston, West Virginia. He wore the same gray suit and dark shirt as before. Only the Western Guard armband was missing. Since our first meeting, I had learned of his reputation as Canada's "High Priest of Hate." In 1964, the Canadian government had revoked his right to send or receive mail because of his distribution of racist literature, including *The Thunderbolt.* According to the *Toronto Star,* his grandfather had been an alderman, and his father, a prominent attorney. Educated in private schools in Canada and the United States, Taylor toured Europe for a while and returned to Toronto in 1930 to work as a salesman. He first gained notoriety in 1937 when he ran for political office on an anti-Jewish platform, his leanings said to have grown out of an admiration for Hitler and a friendship with Quebec Fascist Adrian Arcand. In the sixties, his farmhouse was reportedly used as a training camp for military-minded young rightists. Both he and Jack Prins, his traveling companion in West Virginia, had been in numerous skirmishes with the law.

At the ticket window, a hand-printed sign requested a "donation": "Adults—$2; Teens—$1; Children, 50¢." In return, a robed klansman stamped "Paid" in red on each person's hand for entry into the auditorium. Inside, banners of the various groups represented at the meeting decked the balcony, and recorded music created a festive air. To one side, several middle-aged women handed out applications, and, at still another table, younger women sold the familiar assortment of Klan paraphernalia—some emblazoned with the blood-drop emblem; others, with the crosswheel, the insignia used on costumes in *Birth of a Nation.*

The plush red seats gradually filled with a more prosperous people than I had seen at other rallies. Chloe Duke arrived, pushing Erika in a stroller. Much of the attention centered around the toddler, who wore a miniature robe over her blue-checked dress, and the elderly, stooped Colonel René LaCoste, who resembled a dwarf in his yellowing-satin hood and robe.

Security guards—most with handcuffs, billy clubs and fold-up knives dangling from their belts—darted in and out of the auditorium. They conscientiously eyed the spectators and kept in contact, via walkie-talkies, with their commander, Bip Pecoraro. Five feet of muscle, she appeared worthy of Jerry Dutton's earlier warning: "I wouldn't want to tangle with her!" Tinted gold-rimmed glasses added to her aura of authority, and although no gun was visible, I had been told she was usually armed.

Olaf Poter, Giant of St. Bernard Parish, welcomed the crowd with, "You don't know how good it is to look out at the auditorium and see all them white faces. You can't go too many places an' do that." He then relinquished the microphone to Don Black, Duke's Alabama organizer. Now in his midtwenties, Black had been a member of the White Youth Alliance and the National Party before joining the Knights. His earlier association with J. B. Stoner and Jerry Ray—brother of James Earl Ray—who shot him during an argument, seemed incongruous with his clean-cut, educated image as he introduced a parade of speakers led by conservative radio commentator Richard Cotton and Sandra Bergeron. The thirty-one-year-old mother lashed out at busing and textbooks as "Communist plots." But it was when she recognized her parents in the audience and thanked them for *"raising me with racial pride and courage to stand up and fight for the white race!"* that the crowd's mood soared to her feverish pitch.

Returning to the podium, Black stoked up the fiery enthusiasm. "Everybody knows what we want—*White power,* right? Let's hear it. *White power!"*

"Whiiite power!!!"

"We're not going to win this by being the silent majority, so let's hear it," Black chided. "What do we want????"

"White power! White power!! White power!!!!" The auditorium vibrated. Jerry Dutton, the lanky Grand Wizard, gripped the podium as he waited for quiet. In an earlier interview, this fourth-generation klansman had seemed bland and ineffective. He had refused to discuss his long right-wing career except to say he had started the Knights of the Confederacy while he was still attending school in his native Georgia. But now, his verbal strength lifted the audience as he, too, harped on the "white power" theme.

"What we have in America today is Jewish power voted for by black power!" he shouted. "These people did not get their black power and their Jewish power overnight. They organized this very effectively, subverting our Constitution and our great white race over a period of years! When we have white power again, let me tell you, you'll be not only able to look over this audience tonight and not see a black face. You'll be able to look over this nation and not see a black face!"

"White power!!!"

"The white people have to unite if we are to save ourselves. *There* is no other organization. *There* is no other hope. We are not going to be saved by the powers in Washington who tell us they will support a constitutional amendment against busing. We want a constitutional amendment *against niggers!"*

The audience went wild. In the midst of the outburst, David Duke, in the familiar white suit, strolled on to the stage. "This afternoon," he started coolly, "I wasn't quite sure I was going to be here. But I'm here, not in jail." He waited for his accolades. "It's a tough fight, but it's a fight that's got to be done. The American white people are searching ... are reaching out ... for a movement to carry forth their ideals, their values, the dreams they carry in their hearts. And the Ku Klux Klan is their movement!

"Integration came upon this country in a massive scale in nineteen fifty-four. They told us, 'We're going to have Utopia! We're going to mix the races! We're all going to get along!' And what happened? All we have—and the liberals can't argue with it and the race mixers can't argue with it—all we've had is more violence in the schools and *more* racial hatred."

At first, his delivery was paced and reasonably punctuated, but as he progressed, his suave demeanor gave way to shouting, and to the audience's delight, he switched from "black" to the more inflamatory "nigger." Verbally, he attacked reverse discrimination, Henry Kissinger, black welfare, oppression of the white race, and Jewish control of the media. "I say if the Jews can have their state in Israel, we can have our state right here in the United States! We have a right as the white majority to run this country as we see fit!"

Standing, Chloe Duke led the applause. A voice from the audience urged, "Give 'em hell, David!"

Then, inciting the crowd almost to the point of riot, Duke again related the earlier arrest scene. "We rented the hall. We paid for it. We preached Americanism and the ideals, the way this country must go. And the delegates went down and told them exactly what they thought of 'em. These, these ... pimps! And that's the only way I can put it!" The word ignited the audience. "They arrested three of our people, and what did they charge them with? Criminal mischief?" he asked mockingly. "Criminal mischief? And interfering with a police officer on private property?" The mock questioning disappeared. His voice deepened. "They wanted to charge me with inciting to riot." The people chuckled. "And looking back on it, I think I should have incited a riot!"

"Yeaaa, Dave!" a male called out.

Another shrieked, "Give 'em hell, Dave!"

"Are they down at the N-double-A-C-P meeting?" Duke asked, his question engulfed by *"Nooooo!"* "The N-double-A-C-P is run by fifteen Communists and one . . .," he hesitated, ". . . black, nigger, whatever you wanta call him."

"Nigger!" the crowd enticed. *"Nigger!"*

"Do they harass the Anti-Defamation League?"

"Noooo!"

"In the last twenty years, the FBI has made *not* one arrest or one conviction of a Communist spy in the United States of America. But down in Mississippi and Louisiana, they throw klansmen in jail for fighting for the white race!"

Again, the people cheered. Duke's tone changed to that of a preacher seeking converts. "All over America, white people are beginning to band together and fight for their rights. A new wave is sweeping, and it's rising fast. We are coming to a situation in this country that the federal government now can recognize the Klan as the true enemy of the race mixers, the *true* enemy of Communism throughout the world. They have made every effort to try to destroy our movement. But the more that they try to put us in jail and the more they try to cut down our leaders and cause dissension in our ranks, the stronger and more determined we will be!"

"White power!"

"The more our faces become ground into the dirt, the bloodier the bodies of our warriors become, the more restless we will be. We are not quitting in this fight! We are just beginning! The Klan is not something of the past! It is something of the future! *All* of you will see its victory!"

The audience burst into cheers as Duke strode off stage. The enthusiasm simmered only when Don Black introduced Jim Warner. In spite of his short, solid build, the former Pennsylvanian contrived a resemblance to *der Führer,* perhaps because of his mustache, perhaps because of his curt, militaristic delivery. He strove to outdo his more attractive cohort in his quest to please and arouse the crowd. Portraying himself as hero and martyr, he once more related the afternoon's confrontation and his personal encounters with the law during the Civil Rights Movement.

"I've been in this fight a long time. The FBI must have a file on me this big." He spread his hands apart. "And I'm *proud* because I've stood up for my white race and I've fought for years!"

He became almost incoherent as he shouted, "The federal government puts Jews in power in Washington. They give blacks special privileges. They don't give a hoot about the white race! If you're hurt by blacks, they don't say a word. We'll just say to white people everywhere—from now on, whenever a white man is killed by a black or a Jew, we're going to scream bloody murder and we're going to fight back!"

"Woooo-weeeeeee! Yeaaaaa!"

"We saw what happened in Jefferson Parish today. One man came to this convention from Pennsylvania. He's seventy-one years old. He's sitting in the jail over in Jefferson Parish right now!"

A wave of voices crested, *"Let's go git him! Let's go git him! Git him out!"*

"We need twelve hundred dollars for bail for this man," Warner challenged. "He had the guts to come down here and stand up for this! Will you people put it up?"

"Yeaaaaa!!!"

"We *must* get this man out! If you believe in white power, then put your money where your mouth is! Let's hear it: White power!"

"White power!"

"White power!"

"Whiiite power!!!"

The auditorium was silent as robed men and women swished from row to row with box tops and upturned hoods. Then a single male voice cried out, *"We want our country back!!"* As the collection continued, Duke stepped to the microphone. "We of the Klan are devoted to political solutions which are constitutional and legal. But when they step on the white race, when they threaten our constitutional rights, then we'll fight back any way possible. They can have their choice: it'll be ballots or bullets. And if they stop us with the ballot, they're going to get the bullets!"

As I watched Duke, wholesome in his white suit, I thought of Buddy Tucker in his militaristic black boots and epaulets. Each, in his own way, had whipped his crowd into wanting to march in the streets and fight. Now he grinned boyishly, stopped for a financial accounting, and then announced, "We're halfway there. Anybody who would like to help us some more, push us over the top, we'd appreciate it most sincerely."

From the sidelines, Louis Beam, Duke's Texas chieftain, waved a bill and yelled, "I got some more!" in a manner reminiscent of the shill games of the sixties when Klan leaders planted people in the audience to entice others to make heftier donations.

"Very good," Duke acknowledged. "Thank you. White power!"

"White power!"

"You can do better than that!" he teased.

"White power!"

"What'd you say about Moon the Coon???" he attacked New Orleans' mayor.

"Whiiiite power!!!"

Duke exited but returned to announce instructions for reaching the cross-lighting ceremony's undisclosed destination. Gradually, the people filed out of the hall and into their automobiles, forming a caravan. Led by a car with a Klan banner, the procession slowly wound its way through shopping centers and suburbs to a dark tree-edged highway. The lead car pulled on to the shoulder of the road, the others parking behind it. The people walked along the shoulder to a path that led to a clearing. Torches silhouetted the towering cross and moss-draped trees and cast eerie shadows on to a nearby bayou and the robed figures. Overhead, whiffs of clouds drifting past an almost-full moon created a Halloween mood. Farther back, where tall reeds narrowed the clearing, the masked klansmen gathered. There were no patriotic marches or mimicking Amos 'n Andy records, just the rustle of robes as they lined up and proceeded toward the cross. The klanspeople formed a seemingly endless circle inside the ring of spectators.

Duke, with neither a mask nor a hood, looked as saintly as an altar boy as he stood between them and the cross. Torches in their left hands, they obeyed his instructions: "Salute. Up. Right. Left. Down. You have made the sign of the cross, and now we'll proceed." He walked slowly to the cross and laid his torch at the base. A klansman supported Colonel LaCoste's arm as the old man hobbled forward with his firebrand. The others followed. Flames swept up the cross, crackling and turning the sky orange. Again in their widened circle, the klanspeople extended their left arms in Nazi-type salutes. Then, the chaplain read a prayer from a printed sheet.

"By lighting it," Duke preached, "we are not destroying the cross. We are illuminating it. Showing the way to the white world. May we be victorious in this struggle for our race and our freedom! White power!"

The Monday after the rally and the Canal Street march, I visited the Patriot Book Store. Wedged into a hodgepodge of small businesses, the brick building offered no outer clue that it was national headquarters for the Knights of the Ku Klux Klan. The sign mentioned neither the name nor the initials, and a plate-glass window was curtained to conceal the interior. A woman peeked out, then opened the locked door.

Inside, a teenage girl slouched at a desk, more engrossed in conversation than with guarding the entrance. A .38 lay in front of her; a rifle was propped against the wall. Copies of *The Crusader* and *The Christian Vanguard* only partially filled shelves at one end of the L-shaped room. Behind the girl, a display case contained Klan merchandise, and a charcoal portrait of Duke hung on the wall. In the adjoining "naturalization" room—for initiations and special ceremonies—votive candles studded a wooden cross, and American and cross-wheel flags stretched across the wall. A rear door was secured by six bolt-action locks and a chain.

Bip Pecoraro was there when I arrived. At twenty-seven, she was tomboyishly attractive, her hair cut in a short shag and her large brown eyes framed by gold-rimmed glasses. Born and raised in New Orleans' Ninth Ward, she spoke in the Brooklyn-Southern mélange common to that working-class section of the city. Her father, a retired pipefitter and now a taxi driver, had taken a second job selling razor blades on the street to help put her and a slightly older brother through Catholic schools. Her mother had adhered to the Italian tradition of staying in the home. Bip Pecoraro had hoped to become a veterinarian but, unable to afford the schooling, had settled instead for a job as a lab technician. She also had worked as a long-distance operator, a warehouse shipping clerk, and, until two weeks ago, a store detective. A member of the Klan three years, she achieved her position as security head because of her detective work and training in Kung Fu.

"Kung Fu?" I marveled as we sat alone in the "naturalization" room. "How did you get into that?"

"More or less with all the problems that's happenin'. Livin' by myself and all," she explained importantly. "I do know a little bit how to protect myself, but I think besides a gun or knife or regular street fighting, a method of martial arts is more or less what's needed at this time and age."

"Are you very good at Kung Fu?"

"I can handle myself," she was confident. "I was studyin' to be an orange belt, which is only your second highest—your punches, your kicks. The flipping never came yet. I never had to use it. In fact, I don't think I would really use it because I wasn't all that experienced. But I feel like if you're right an' you're mad and someone's tryin' to mess over you—gun, knives, Kung Fu, nuthin'—I have done thangs I never thought I could do."

She attributed her solid build to the Kung Fu training and to high school sports. "I carry all kind of letters in basketball, volleyball, baseball, football—touch, tackle, the *whole* bit. Any type of sport they had, I went all out for it. I was always interested in horses and motorcycles and football. Just the average things as you're going through high school." She shrugged her broad shoulders. "I wasn't the type to care to sit down and write poems. I'm not an indoor person. Strictly outdoors. And I'm not the lipstick and the makeup type. A woman has more beauty without all that."

Her ability to look out for herself also grew out of her upbringing. "My daddy always said, 'If you have a problem, I don't care who it's with, if you can't whip 'em, I'll whip you.' So that was more or less our situation." She laughed. "I even took care of my brother in those days. He was just never a fighter like I was. I hit one boy with a school bag."

"How good a shot are you?" I asked.

"I would say average for a woman," she assured me. Although she wasn't armed now, she said, she usually carried a gun in her car and when she was on bookstore duty.

"Is that a loaded rifle by the desk, against the wall?"

"It's supposed to be," she said, insisting, however, there were never any problems at the store. "I don't know if it is. It's supposed to be used in case someone was actually breakin' in. It would be used in self-defense."

"What were some of your more exciting cases as a store detective?" I asked.

Bip Pecoraro swelled with professional pride. "I've had to chase people throughout the parking lot. I've chased 'em for blocks. Jumped in my car. The most I've ever apprehended at one time was nine black males."

"At one time?"

"At one time," she confirmed.

"How did you do that?"

She laughed with bravado. "I haven't the faintest idea. I've always looked at it with the attitude that this is the job for me to do. The employees see me every day walking around makin' busts. If I don't do the job, they're gonna lose respect for me and I'm gonna lose respect for myself. I've always faced it, whether it was one or ten. My tallest man was six foot six, and I never had no problems with him."

A member of the security guard since shortly after she joined the Klan, she was first assigned as Chloe Duke's bodyguard. She had been elected chief six months ago. To join, she said, a person was interviewed and, if approved, taught to use walkie-talkies and CB radios. He or she had to agree to purchase a uniform and to attend weekly meetings and serve on bookstore duty.

"How do the men feel about having a woman in charge?" I asked.

"I lost a lot of members due to that reason," she conceded. "They would not take orders from a woman. And when I was nominated, I was running against a man at the time, and him and I—not talkin' about another klansperson—but we still don't see eye to eye on things. Now if *he* would've won—because I do believe man is superior to woman, I was brought up that way—I do believe I would still have stayed in the security unit and worked under him."

Nevertheless, she was positive a female had advantages over a man. "A woman could do more because there is less suspicion. We can get into a woman's bathroom, whereas a man couldn't. We can also go in a man's bathroom by asking a man real politely, 'Watch the bathroom, I have to go in there. The lady's bathroom is out of order.' Whereas a woman wouldn't do that for a man."

"What's the purpose of that?" I asked.

"Okay," she confided, "say we want to go check out a man's bathroom and there's no men to check somethin', whether someone put an object in there . . ."

"A gun or a bomb?"

"Yeah, anythang," she confirmed. "Also we can pat a man down, where a man—a policeman, also—cannot pat a woman down. We've only frisked a few," she hurriedly added. "But just in general, a woman can do a lot more, I think, mentally than a man can."

"At the rally the other night, what did you do?"

"We checked out the whole place. The exits. The entrances. The bathrooms. Everything. Doors. Where do they lead to. How many flights of stairs. The capacity of the place. We just more or less walked through the whole thing. Observed it. Asked questions on the management's part. Can we have this door locked? What purpose does it serve? Where does it lead? We checked out the whole place."

Her tone and manner were in the best detective tradition, or at the very least, the very best mystery-book tradition, as she elaborated.

"Would you say you operate like the Secret Service?"

"I don't know how the Secret Service works. I just do what I think would be best to secure somethin'."

Besides her security work, she said she conducted the den's weekly meetings and encouraged her people to do target practice.

"What do you do, drill and train?" I asked.

"No, we discuss functions that are comin' up and how we are going to handle them. We don't march or drill. It should be more on a military basis," she admitted, "but there's no time for that right now because we are growing so fast. We hope to. We have headquarters with weights and some mats to exercise and practice judo."

"Where?"

"That's secret."

As we talked, a half-dozen or so members trickled into the bookstore. Women of assorted backgrounds and ages, they—unlike those in other Klans—were eligible to hold the same offices as men: Sandra Bergeron was the Giant, or top officer, for Jefferson Parish; Shirley Garcia and Ethel Segui were organizers; Ellen Cusimano was the security guard secretary, and Ethel Kuzina served as Jerry Dutton's secretary and helped edit *The Christian Vanguard,* a tabloid published by Jim Warner's New Christian Crusade Church.

Sandra Bergeron, a "NEVER" button pinned to her orange sweat shirt, lavished upon Ethel Kuzina the additional title of "Heartbeat of the National Office." The others cooingly agreed.

"Without Miss Ethel, we would be wading in seas of orders and everything else," Sandra Bergeron explained as eyes focused on the sixtyish woman whose cultured appearance matched her taste in art and classical music. The mother of three grown children, she had moved recently from Seattle to devote her time to the Klan and the *Vanguard* after having worked two summers in California with Warner. Her father had been born in England and moved to Australia where he met and married her mother. The two then migrated to the United States. "Miss Ethel" had studied languages at the University of Washington but after two years was forced by family finances to drop out and to enroll in business school. Even after she married and had children, she worked as a secretary.

Now she credited her interest in the racial movement as part of the reason for her recent divorce after thirty-one years of marriage. "I felt so strongly about what I wanted to do," she said softly. "I've been studying the identity of the white race on my own for a long time—fifteen years or more. My husband didn't want me to leave him, but there was no tie. His interests were so divergent from mine. I just wanted to get where I could put my whole life into what I believed."

"Did you feel these differences before?"

She nodded genteelly. "For many years. When you have children, you have to do the best for them. They were my purpose for years. Now they are on their own. I don't owe anybody anything. I have my own life."

"The work," she said of her summers with Warner, "satisfied my soul. I *know* this race issue is the key, the answer to everything that we have a problem with."

Ethel Segui sat next to her, quietly listening. She was a short, plump woman, her face creased in a permanent grimace. Never married, she had worked twenty-five years as an accountant for the same firm because she hated change. She moved to suburban Jefferson Parish from her native New Orleans neighborhood and dropped out of the Episcopal church when "they got a little too black for me." She became a member of the Klan almost three years ago when a friend introduced her to David and Chloe Duke at a parade in nearby Waveland, Mississippi. Now she worked three or four nights a week for the organization.

"What about him made you join?" I asked.

"I don't know," she pondered. "I guess it was just his personality, and I knew they were a young couple that believed in what they were doing and that they were doing something good. I just wanted to be a part of it. I have two sisters living out of town. They know but don't approve. They think maybe I should talk to someone about it, like a minister or somebody, because 'everybody's created equal.' And most of my friends think I'm kind of crazy," she said sourly, but brightening somewhat as she added, "But my father was a boilermaker, and if he were living, he'd be a klansman!"

Sandra Bergeron spoke up. "Either you get tremendous respect from your family or they just turn off." In her case, the reaction had been supportive, partly because her paternal great-grandfather had been a member. Now she and her husband—Titan, or head officer, for southern Louisiana—were teaching Klan history and racial pride to their two young daughters.

In spite of the age difference, the five women shared a dislike for blacks and a fervid belief—or hope—that the Klan was the answer to all their problems. They also saw a need and a role for themselves as women, although they labeled the Equal Rights Amendment as "for the birds" and "Jew-inspired."

"The men need the support we can give them in little details, like office work, answering letters," Ethel Kuzina explained. "The men don't have the time to do this type thing."

"Besides time, can a woman reach people better than a man?" I asked.

"Oh, definitely! Oh, yes!" Shirley Garcia beamed. "She can talk a whole lot better than a man. She will just keep at it. She'll show you all kinds of angles."

Unlike her heavily penciled eyebrows and canary-yellow hair, the enthusiasm of the late fortyish divorcee was genuine as she again answered for the others when I asked if people were more receptive to a woman. "Yes! I've had men call, and I'll say, 'Would you like to talk to one of the gentlemen?' 'Oh, no, I would rather talk to one of the ladies.' "

"How do the men in the Klan react to the women?"

Sandra Bergeron insisted, "They all love it. I don't think we have one man that's jealous of any woman. They all love it, boy! I'll be truthful, if you can get a woman, you've got the husband. But if you can't convince the woman to join, forget the man." Looking somewhat like a high school cheerleader with shoulder-length auburn hair, she smiled smugly. "They protect us. Chivalry is *not* dead in the Klan. They are *true* knights."

When I asked about cattiness among the women themselves, they maintained they got along "beautifully." "They call us a hate organization, but I think you can see there's a lot of love here," Sandra Bergeron purred as she glanced around the table. "We're not friends. This is our family."

But when the topic shifted to the possibility of a future female National Director, the agreement ended.

"I think there might be," Sandra Bergeron speculated, her low-key answer overcome by Shirley Garcia's enthusiastic, "I think so, yes!"

But Sandra Bergeron went on to reason that a married woman with children could not devote the time required by the job and by a family. Besides, she was doubtful that a woman could safely handle confrontations such as when demonstrators sometimes booed Duke and refused to allow him to talk. Nevertheless, she saw women's future in the Klan as bright and elaborated on the roles they were already playing: females headed local dens; at least forty percent of the Knights' national membership was female, and the breakdown was fifty-fifty in Louisiana. She took credit for holding the highest national office for a woman, having responsibility for Klan organizers in two parishes and outranking, she noted, Bip Pecoraro, whose title was head of security for the southern province of the state.

I turned back to Shirley Garcia. "How would you like for a woman to become National Director?"

"Oh, yes! Absolutely! I would *love* to see that, wouldn't you, Ethel?" She elbowed Ethel Segui, who frowned. "That's a man's job!"

The next morning, when Chloe Duke met me at the bus station in Baton Rouge, the back seat of the dusty Montego was still crammed with luggage, crumpled-up clothing, and toys. Yet she herself seemed as unruffled by the constant shuttling between cities as she was by most of life. Like her husband, she appeared emotionally detached, even from her Klan beliefs. A petite young woman, she was, in her own words, "a typical home ec major": her face without makeup, her mousey hair straight, her often homemade clothes neither fashionable nor eye catching, her conversation uninspired. Both her appearance and almost shy manner contrasted with the more gregarious Duke, whom she had met at LSU.

"He was passing out literature on campus one day," she recalled as we drove toward their suburban home, "and a friend of his lent me a White Primer. I didn't have the money with me, so I later called David to send him the money, and he asked me out to dinner. I had heard of him, but I hadn't met him before."

"What was your reaction?"

"Oh, I liked him, all right," she laughed blandly. "He took me out to eat. We dated three years. A long time. We were married four years last week—September ninth."

The daughter of a Florida used-car-lot owner, she had been taught to oppose integration and had attended a few traditional Klan rallies. Even though her family agreed with her husband's principles, she conceded, "I've learned a lot in the last seven years."

"What was your parents' reaction when they found out what David did?"

Chloe Duke stopped briefly to remember. "They liked him, all right. They were just concerned about our safety because my parents think if you attack the blacks and the Jews enough, they're gonna blow up your car or shoot you or something like that."

"Do you worry about that and about David?"

"A little bit," she shrugged, "when he goes to colleges or makes speeches like that. A lot of times they'll call and say, 'There's a bomb in your house,' or at meetings or the office. We don't worry about that."

"Did you at first?"

"Not very much. I'm not much of a worrier."

We had entered a subdivision of small, neatly kept brick homes. In the driveway Chloe Duke glanced at the slightly overgrown lawn, uttered a housewifely groan, and continued talking about the three months she taught at an all-black New Orleans school for girls shortly before she married.

"Did you hesitate to take the job?"

She shook her head. "I learned a lot. It was a real good experience. They were all black girls, but some were as light as I am. I didn't have *one* example of a true Negro. I was teaching biology and chemistry. They were divided into intelligence groups. One class was morons. Another class was a little higher." She giggled. "The other was about average."

Inside, the house was as cluttered with toys as the car. Near the front door were a vacuum cleaner and a partially opened umbrella. The furnishings differed little from those of other young couples except for a framed sketch of Nathan Bedford Forrest over the sofa and a proclamation, signed by George Wallace, naming Duke an "Honorary Colonel in the State Militia" for his work in the Alabama governor's 1972 campaign for president. Besides a couch and two straight-back rockers, there were a spinet piano, a stereo with earphones, and two cases of books that reflected both the couples' schooling and their beliefs: *The Magic of Thinking Big, The Art of Persuasion, White Power, Art Through the Ages,* sets of *Family Circle* cookbooks and *World Book* encyclopedia, and the 1973 LSU yearbook. A volume entitled *George Washington Carver* seemed out of place.

His shirttail out, his eyes puffy from his late-night drive home, Duke entered the room with Erika toddling beside him.

"Who plays the piano?" I asked as he settled into one of the rockers.

"Both of us a little bit," Duke answered, fatigue in his voice.

"Neither one very well," Chloe Duke contributed.

"I took when I was very young," he explained. "I was going to take it up again, but I don't have time for it."

"What do you like to play?"

" 'Faith of our Fathers' . . ." he started.

"Oh, come on," I chuckled, thinking he was joking.

He protested. "I like stuff like that! I like 'A Mighty Fortress Is Our God,' 'Born Free,' that kind of stuff."

Erika reached for my tape recorder, and he yelled, "Hey! Erika! *NO! No!* No!" His voice lowered as she looked at him wide-eyed, cried briefly, then quieted. "That's better," he told her, and resumed discussing their life-style.

Unlike other leaders, he said, they often put aside the Klan and become just plain Mr. and Mrs. David Duke, participating in sports, dining out, and occasionally barbecuing with their neighbors, most of whom were not shocked by his line of work.

The conversation turned to money, to accusations by other leaders, law enforcement officers, and disgruntled former members that he was a con artist who would sign up anybody for the initiation fee. He scowled. "That's ridiculous. You've been around the country and . . . first of all, you've seen a higher quality—generally speaking—among our members than anybody else. *That's* one point right there. And specifically on money," he squinched his shoulders, "you see how I live. I have very little needs. I put a lot more money *into* the organization than I've *ever* taken out of it. So I've been a financial plus. I personally have *and could* make good money, but I haven't because it's gone to the Klan. I wouldn't object to making a higher income. I just feel the organization needs *everything* now. I used to draw a little bit—between three and four hundred a month—but I don't draw anything now, not for the last nine or ten months. I'm not even going to draw travel expenses from the organization pretty soon."

Midway in an argument that echoed Shelton and other Klan leaders, he reconsidered. "I don't want people to think I'm so poor because they'll think our organization doesn't have much money. I don't make any money, but in terms of the organization, financially we *are* aware and we are going to stay strong. You have to have money to expand and to get these projects and keep our publications going and recruit new people."

He returned to his own financial situation. "I've gotten eight and twelve hundred dollars a speech—per college. Last year, I didn't speak to as many as I usually do—and I don't get paid for all of them. I'd say about forty a year," he figured aloud. "It's all gone to the Klan except for travel expenses."

"Don't you have to keep a little money to live on?"

"Yeah, I've kept some," he admitted. "But see, some of these other leaders . . . Shelton, he draws fifteen thousand dollars a year and lots of expenses. It must run thirty, forty thousand a year. You've been to his place. You've seen how he lives. He's got about four or five cars. A Cadillac. Plus he's got the twenty-thousand-dollar camper and a good piece of property—and that's not too cheap out there." He stopped. "I'm not making charges, but . . . Now *I* don't draw a penny. Doctor Warner draws nothing from the organization. And Jerry Dutton is not drawing anything right now, although we hope to put him on some kind of salary."

I surveyed the room and its furnishings. Granted it was modest, but I thought about the impeccably tailored clothes and his constant travels from coast to coast and abroad.

"How do people like you and Warner and Dutton make it?" I puzzled.

"I have an advertising agency. Jerry's got a printing business, and Doctor Warner has a book business. So we've got some of the top talent. All of us are interested in building up the organization." With Erika climbing in and out of his lap, Duke looked and sounded convincing. Yet at least two of his former top leaders—including Bill Wilkinson, who had formed his own Klan in August 1975—had accused Duke of living off the Klan. And later, when I checked, his alleged business—known, he said, both as the Patriot Advertising Agency and the National Advertising Agency—was listed neither in the Baton Rouge telephone directory nor with information. Warner's "book business" turned out to be the Sons of Liberty, which churned out right-wing literature pushed in his *Christian Vanguard* and other sympathetic publications.

"Don't you have a contract requiring people to sign over their money and worldly possessions if they leave?" I inquired, remembering a copy of a two-page document passed on to me by a Texas Klan leader. Apparently for Duke's paid organizers, the document provided that anyone who lied or violated the oath agreed that the Knights of the Ku Klux Klan, Louisiana Realm, "is entitled to all my real estate, personal property, bank accounts and everything of monetary or sentimental value" and to turn them over "upon written demand of the National Director."

Duke met the issue head on. "Exactly. What this is—that's not really holding, I don't think, binding and legal—but what basically it is, if they go to another group for some reason, it is a protection for our members." He backtracked. "The only reason we did this was after Kentucky . . . This is to protect our organization from opportunists. This is to be sure if a person takes part in this organization, he can't run off with the money, he can't run off with the members."

The Kentucky reference was to a feud between Duke and Phillip Chopper, head of one of the many Klans that sprang up like wild mushrooms during the Louisville busing demonstrations. After the two staged several rallies in August 1975—sharing the podium with Jim Warner and Robert Scoggin of South Carolina—Chopper publicly accused Duke of running off with four thousand dollars. In the press, Duke countered that the accusations were "completely untrue" and that Chopper was an FBI informant giving false information to the media to "spread dissension within the Klan." To me, he claimed he sent Chopper fifteen hundred dollars for rally preparations; when he and Warner arrived, nothing had been organized. In the course of swapping insults, Chopper labeled Duke a "fraud" and a "self-appointed" National Director; Duke called Chopper a "self-appointed" Grand Dragon, adding: "Chopper's a throwback to the Klan of thirty years ago. The man's a weirdo." A month later, Chopper was extradited to Louisiana on past charges of passing bad checks.

To defend his policy of accepting members by mail—referred to sarcastically by Shelton as a "Sears, Roebuck Klan"—Duke described his two membership categories: regular members and mail recruits, known as "associate members," who do not receive the rituals and secret instructions until they have been personally interviewed and approved.

"There are *millions* of people who would like to become part of the movement," he argued. "We've got to have high standards—which we do. Our standards are higher than any other group in terms of activities and actual commitment. But the key to winning this fight is not just using what we have, but to grow. So we are oriented to growing."

Before a mail applicant could recruit, he said, one of his organizers was sent to the area to administer the oath and to assist in setting up a unit. As far as keeping out infiltrators, Duke portrayed the people with the best credentials as "often agents," noting that the *very* groups that accused him of operating a mail-order Klan had had far more cases of infiltration than his.

"How can you determine if a person *is* an agent?" I asked, because in my own travels I had often wondered if I was interviewing a legitimate klansman or an informer.

"We have our own people in government," he said, intrigue in his voice. "And we have our own agency, so to speak. We *have* to, for self-defense. People who join our group understand we have to have security because of the nature of what we do. They know they will be investigated if we have any reason to suspect them as agents."

"How do you know you are successful?"

"We use the lie detector, and we have men working with us who used to be detectives—both private and with the police. That's the only way we can be confident."

His self-assurance was amusing. Two days earlier, at the Canal Street march, a plainclothes detective I knew discreetly informed me he was aware of the interview I had scheduled with Duke's female members. Yet I had discussed the appointment only with the five women, considered his top female officers.

When I asked the outcome of the convention in New Orleans, Duke told of the formation of a seven-person board of directors that would elect and monitor the activities of the National Director, the National Information Officer, and the Grand Wizard and, if it saw fit, vote them out of office. The same detective who had learned of my interview also tipped me off that a move was under way by Dutton and Warner to form the board and eventually ease Duke out of power. Yet Duke, at least outwardly secure, expressed excitement over the new board. As for internal bickering, he vowed his group was an exception to the Klan rule.

"Every group, every organization has gossip, but I don't think we have quite as much," he insisted. "Our people are so dedicated and they believe so much in the ideals—they really and truly believe in brotherhood."

When I asked if, in addition to Don Black, he had an Alabama Grand Dragon, Duke hesitantly answered no.

"Do you have Grand Dragons in *any* state?" I asked, having heard the title used in his organization only in reference to Jim Warner.

"We've got some Grand Dragons, but it's not something we publicize much." Again he hesitated. "A lot of times, we just have state organizers. It just depends on the basis. We go entirely on what a person puts out. What he does. We're not like some of these other groups, where if they go into an area they select an individual and make him a Grand Dragon or some officer. It's not as easy to make rank in our group as it is in the others."

"Do you try to choose leaders—especially state leaders—who will give a good image?"

"I don't think we select anybody *strictly* because of image. But usually a person that's effective and a person that's a good person usually has the right kind of image. It's just a natural thing. We select people for what they do and how they perform."

"While we're talking about image, I have noticed you have very good taste in clothes." The three of us looked at his shirt tail and old slacks and laughed. "This will be an exception, but do you like clothes?"

"It's important to look right, you know. All this comes into being. I think any professional person notices this. I've never spent very much money on clothes, but I try to—my wife picks out most of my stuff—I try to pick things that I feel will set the right kind of image and something that looks neat and right. I'm trying to get an idea over. I don't want to be 'way out,' because that might stop some of my ideas from getting over."

"At the rally, you spoke in your suit—most of the people did speak in their suits, right?"

"Yeah, I just think it's part of the professionalism. This was a formal meeting. Occasionally I speak in my robe. It just depends on what kind of meeting it is."

At one point, Chloe Duke slipped out to run an errand, leaving Erika in her father's care. We moved into the kitchen, the counters cluttered with containers of vitamins, cereals, and powdered milk. Duke mixed some milk and poured it into a baby bottle and, as he handed it to the toddler, boasted, "She's smart, intelligent, beautiful, healthy."

Chloe Duke returned with an armful of legal transcripts from court battles currently being waged against the U.S. Department of Health, Education and Welfare (HEW), East Baton Rouge Parish school board, and a New Orleans motel—all for refusing to rent space to the Knights for rallies. The HEW suit, pending in the U.S. Fifth Circuit Court of Appeals, and the one against the school board, in state court, stemmed from the board's cancelation of a November 1975 agreement to rent a local school gymnasium to Duke's group after HEW threatened to cut off more than eight million dollars in federal funds if the rally was held. At the time, Duke labeled the cancelation "a violation of our civil rights." Even HEW admitted the legal tangle raised questions of a possible conflict between the First Amendment guarantee of free speech—including those of unpopular views—and the department's obligation to foster desegregation of public schools.

When I suggested he show me his latest book, Duke left the room and returned with a paperback entitled *Finders-Keepers* and watched excitedly as I skimmed its advice to women on how to find and keep a man, including everything from sexual exercises, to diet, to makeup tips. By "James Konrad"—actually Jim Warner's first two names—the book had been printed by Arlington Place Books, a publishing house operated by the National Socialist White People's Party (NSWPP), the renamed American Nazi Party. Duke explained "Konrad" as merely a "pen name" picked at random and identified the printer as "a friend." Although he said he had placed an ad in a fashion magazine and was already receiving orders, he was confident the book was destined to make bigger money. He asked me to act as a go-between with my literary agent, offering me a cut of the sales. He also asked that I not reveal his identity because no one else knew. Later, however, I learned that the book—like many of his off-the-record requests—was no secret. Several people—including the police—were aware both of the book and that Warner was "furious" about Duke's use of his name.

That day, as we headed back to the bus station, Chloe Duke drove, and her husband sat to my right, happily bouncing Erika on his knee.

"We," he boasted unabashedly, "are the Klan with sex appeal!"

On my way back East, I stopped in Washington to meet Duke's father. Aside from gray hair and a slight midwestern flavor to his voice, the elder Duke looked and sounded remarkably like the youthful Klan leader, especially as the private meeting room at Fort Myers' Officers Club darkened with the day, and the father's views surfaced. A graduate of the University of Kansas and a retired colonel in the U.S. Army Reserve, he had been employed as an engineer for twenty-five years by Shell Oil Company and, for the past ten, by the U.S. State Department— mostly in Southeast Asia, overseeing the planning and construction of hospitals and schools for the Vietnamese government. Back in this country less than two years, he had followed his son's career in letters from home and the military's *Stars and Stripes.*

"I didn't encourage him any," the father insisted. "He was over twenty-one, and what he did was his business. I just wasn't sure that this was the right way to get his views across, the right kind of an organization. But that was his way of doing it."

Slowly, calmly, he diplomatically tried to express his feelings. "I would have preferred he'd gotten a professional education—law, engineering, something like that—rather than just a more or less general course," he admitted. "However, the first thing was to finish, to get a degree. Of course, he did go to the University up at Baton Rouge, and that's probably where he got associated with the group, where he got a little bit more of his present ideas."

When I mentioned David Duke's Klan affiliations in high school, the father hesitated. "I don't know about that . . . It didn't surface much until he went to Baton Rouge. There, he was on the conservative side against a bunch of radical students."

"But what was your reaction when he emerged as the Klan leader?"

"At first," the father answered simply, "I was a little worried for his safety." Then, as though rethinking the situation, he started again. "Let's put it this way, I didn't encourage him, and I didn't discourage him."

"Now that he has been in it longer and you've had a chance to hear more of what he has to say, have your feelings changed?" I asked.

"He's gotten a tremendous lot of good experience out of it," he said with a touch of parental pride. "Whatever you may say about the organization, he's gotten a lot of speaking experience, a little organizational experience. It's been a seasoning process for him to handle an organization like that, which could be used in other lines of work. And it certainly shouldn't . . ." He paused. "If he branched into something else, it shouldn't disqualify him because he has once been a member of the Klan."

"But do you think it *will* hurt him?" I pressed.

"It's just like anything else," he rationalized. "In some groups, it would; with others, it wouldn't." Outwardly, the father was unconcerned about his son's future and, in some ways, even proud of his achievements as we discussed the positive effects of young Duke's wholesome image on the Klan.

"Do many people know he's your son? What kind of reaction do you get as his father?"

"Selected few know. The people who know don't object at all," he assured me. "I'd rather nobody much know, but a few, I don't mind. I don't want to offend anybody because I deal with all kinds of people, and I have no personal animosity toward the Jewish people or colored people, and so I don't want to have an image . . ." He stopped. "Like, why should this disqualify me because of what he is?"

He remembered David as a serious child and good student who attended the Methodist church regularly and, from high school, held part-time jobs. He also recalled seeing *Race and Reason* around the house and reading passages from the book that was to influence his son's thinking. "No doubt there's some good research and some truth in it," he observed, "but it didn't move me to any great action." It was, he agreed, fairly serious reading for a thirteen-year-old, but then "David's always been serious."

"What did you teach him about black people when he was growing up?"

The elder Duke was thoughtful. "Always to treat them with respect. And not to be rude to them. But that they *were* different. They're different *because* they are black, and nobody can argue with that. They're a lot different." His easygoing tone became firm as he illustrated with his own observation that blacks and whites rarely shared tables in the cafeteria where he worked. "There is a natural segregation that's taking place."

"Have your feelings and views changed because of David's affiliation? Has he influenced *you* at all?"

"No."

When I asked if he shared any of the Klan's beliefs, he answered, "No, not insofar . . . I wouldn't say I share any views or feelings with the Klan." He wavered. "Everything has good and bad, and some of these things the Klan stands for, in general, are sound politics, are the feelings of the great middle class." But as the topic shifted to race, the elder Duke's tone became vaguely reminiscent of that of klanspeople I had met in my travels. "I only feel in harmony with the Klan on two things: antibusing and anti-reverse discrimination." His halting selection of words had long vanished. "Busing is absolutely asinine. It's the greatest misconception and the greatest bill of goods this country has ever been sold. It's a waste of energy, and the ideas of raising the quality of education of the blacks is very remote."

"What are the things you are against? You said there were some good things and some bad in the Klan," I reminded him.

"I'm against any kind of rabble-rousing or any kind of violence. And David's part of the Klan—so far as I know—has no violence. I'd be against speeches talking about 'niggers,' talking about Jews and 'niggers,' things like that. I presume some of the other branches do."

Although the police acknowledged that Duke had held down violence, many of his cohorts had arrest records. Both Warner and Dutton had admitted to arrests for stirring up trouble during the civil rights turmoil in Birmingham; David Wydner, who had traveled from Boston to operate one of Duke's bookstores, was currently wanted for armed robbery and escape from the Baton Rouge jail; and Phillip Chopper, who had recruited in Kentucky, was serving time for passing bad checks. Nor were most of his leaders above ranting and using "nigger" to inflame their audiences. And although Duke had described his platform delivery as "emotional, but I never really say things that are radical and I try to refrain from 'nigger,' " at the St. Bernard rally, he had teased the audience with mock hesitancy, "black, negro, whatever you wanta call him," and at the Canal Street march, he had proclaimed, "We're right in the heart of nigger NuAwleens, and Moon the Coon notwithstanding, we'll be back here again!" He had grinned, and the people had cheered at the slur aimed at blacks hired by the mayor.

"Have you been to his rallies?" I asked the father, baffled at his unfamiliarity with his son's delivery.

"I only went to hear him speak, and I never heard the word 'nigger' used by him or anybody in his group," he maintained.

When I asked his views on the Nazi arm salute and the "White Power" slogan, Duke's father sounded uncertain. "I don't think the White Power slogan does any good. And the arm salute . . . very neutral. I guess it's not much different from the sign of the cross or the salute like this."

He raised his right hand to his brow in the traditional military salute, then paused. "Well, the arm salute, that's not the Klan anyhow, is it?"

"I was only asking your reaction."

"I'd react against the hand salute because that would be more Nazi," he reconsidered. "I would be against any Nazi group, certainly."

I studied the man who was becoming as puzzling as his son as he voiced his own racial and political views. How had he missed the mimicking use of "nigger," the Third Reich salutes, the newspaper photographs of his son picketing William Kunstler and the accounts of his affiliations with George Lincoln Rockwell's NSWPP? Even Duke's book had been printed by NSWPP's Arlington Place Books. Was the father innocently unaware of the full extent of his son's activities? Was he trying to conceal them from himself? Or was he, too, in some way equally involved?

"What are your feelings when you see David on TV, is it pride or . . . ?"

The father chose his words carefully. "I wouldn't say I feel proud." He stopped. "If he handled himself well, I would be proud of him, yes. And if he was able to get any points across that were not rabid or anything like that, I'd be glad to hear it. It's a mixed bag with me. It's kind of a dangerous thing in a way."

The father described his relationship with his son as "close." They talked often by phone, usually about the family or general politics—never about the Klan, he insisted. Nevertheless, he took stock both of his son's accomplishments and the need for his work. "A good old schoolteacher one time said, 'The white Americans and the Europeans have over five thousand years of cultural development, and these people are three and four generations out of being completely heathen savages. How can we expect them to compete and come in and develop and be everything we are, to live in our society and be together in our society?' Errrrrr, he's got a point. Right or fair."

The father shrugged. "I'm not antiblack. I'm just trying to talk facts."

During the remainder of 1976 and 1977, Duke and I exchanged telephone calls and occasionally had lunch or dinner on his frequent trips to and through Washington for speaking engagements. Sometimes his calls were to follow the progress on my book, asking, "How much will be devoted to us—most of it?" And, "Will I like it?" Often, the lengthy conversations centered around the most recent news events inspired by him or his members. But sometimes the calls were merely to chat, to tell me he and Chloe were expecting a second child and then, in June 1977, to announce it was a girl named Kristy.

At first, he called almost nightly to check on the fate of his own book, always positive it was destined to be a moneymaker. When I reported no interest by my agent or a publisher, the suave, confident David Duke of talk-show fame suddenly sounded like a small boy who hadn't made the Little League.

Then, in November 1976, after fourteen black marines broke into what they thought was a Klan meeting at Camp Pendleton and stabbed six white enlisted men, I called Duke, who pridefully confirmed that the intended victims were members of his Klan.

"The white guys are really getting a rotten deal," he said of the seventeen identified klansmen whom military brass scattered to bases across the country in an effort to break up Klan activity.

"The camp people already admitted the Klan has done nothing provocative or illegal on the base that they know of, yet the whole focus is on the Ku Klux Klan and . . . and the newspaper, other articles have just practically said, 'Well the blacks are perfectly justified because they thought that was a Ku Klux Klan meeting.'"

An extensive study by the Naval Investigative Service was to disprove Duke's allegations that the attack was unprovoked. It indicated that race relations had long been a problem at Camp Pendleton and other marine bases and that some commanders had failed to discipline—and sometimes even promoted—klansmen who systematically harassed black marines. The same study, and one by *New Times* magazine, established that the Klan had been active at Pendleton since 1973 and that hundreds more belonged on bases in Japan, Okinawa, the Philippines, California, Texas, North Carolina, and other locations around the world. To retaliate, blacks had formed their own groups and begun countering white harassment, "signaling," *New Times* suggested, "an incipient race war within the Corps." Meanwhile, Marine Corps brass down-played the Camp Pendleton incident as both "isolated" and "small," and Duke portrayed the klansmen as martyrs.

"Dozens are getting retribution on the base," the latter charged. "They're being transferred. They're being hurt. Many of them were rounded up in the middle of the night and held incommunicado and threatened with retribution and court-martialed."

Nevertheless, he didn't hesitate to take credit for infiltration of the armed forces. "The soldiers themselves see reverse discrimination as much as anybody. Probably more. Promotions, treatment, and so forth. So the Klan's been active there. We get letters from main APO numbers around the world and bases in this country, especially the army and the marines. Both of them have a very bad racial problem—more so than the navy or the air force. That's where our biggest response has been. There must be a *million* Klan calling cards distributed on military bases a year—*just* on military bases. These go like wildfire. That's just one barometer of how things go."

The Klan had attorneys advising its marine members, Duke said, and in a couple of weeks a public meeting would be held. Then he laughed. "Those blacks are fortunate they broke into the room they did, because if they'd broken into the room with the klansmen, they wouldn't have gotten off so lightly."

Shortly after Duke was attacked by sign-wielding protestors when he showed up that December in California for the pretrial hearings of the fourteen blacks, we again talked.

"I was whopped!" he snickered. "Did you see that?"

When I told him the *Washington Post* had carried a five-column photograph of him ducking to miss the blow by a member of the Progressive Labor Party and the Committee Against Racism, he seemed pleased with the coverage.

"Whop!"

"Did it hurt?"

"A little bit," he laughed again.

"Did any of those people get arrested?"

"Of course not," he said indignantly. "There were about thirty news people there. They had it on film. The MPs were right there. But the people who did it—they weren't arrested, naturally."

In October 1977, after he dreamed up a special Klan patrol of the Mexican border to prevent the entry of illegal aliens, Duke exulted, "It's the biggest thing in five years." Many aptly labeled the patrol another of his publicity gimmicks, especially when it attracted more reporters than klansmen. But there was probably equal truth to Duke's admission to me: "It gave our people something to do."

The conversation then moved closer to home, to New Orleans. When I attempted to get the correct titles for his various leaders, he hesitated.

"Jerry is not with us anymore . . . right now," he said of Dutton. "He's doing silk screening and stuff."

"Why did he drop out?" I asked, curious if the detective had been correct about the move to oust Duke.

"Well, a few things. I'd kind of rather not go into it," Duke hedged. "You know, personality conflicts and things of that nature. I came to believe that he was dishonorable, and the people here did, too. So our association ended. There's no Grand Wizard. It's like it was before, basically, when I was National Director *and* Grand Wizard. Jim's still Grand Dragon."

He informed me he had sold his house in Baton Rouge and moved permanently to New Orleans. "I needed to be close to the business end of it," he explained. "It's really the best move I ever made. Things are moving along so much better now. I've never seen us make any better progress."

"It was my understanding Jim and Jerry were good friends," I probed. "Did this break up their friendship?"

It was late, and Duke sounded tired and uncharacteristically foggy. "I don't think they're very good friends anymore." He seemed uncertain. "In fact, I'm sure they're not. Apparently Jim didn't know him as well as maybe he thought. I hate to even discuss this with someone like you . . ." He hesitated again but went on, charging that Dutton had stolen the Knights' mailing list, attempted to change the post office box into his name, and had begun steps to have the corporation name, Patriot Press, registered with the Louisiana secretary of state so he could cash incoming checks. But Duke had caught him in time, he said, and no harm had been done.

"This stuff goes on . . . ," he vouched. "The N-Double-A-C-P has had *thousands* of splits. This wasn't even a split. It was just a situation where he took the stuff and then he wouldn't go along with the Council, so that was it. He was dismissed. Everything is the same. Nobody's gone. They're still in their offices. Everything's perfect. It's a very small pinprick in the life of the movement."

The detective attributed the split to Dutton's discovery that "Duke was making a living off the Klan." Dutton had confronted him. According to the detective, Warner and several others had not pulled away only because they were afraid of losing large sums of money Duke owed them. Sandra Bergeron's husband Ed was said to have put up the fifteen-hundred-dollar bond to get Duke out of jail after his arrest for inciting to riot at the New Orleans conference; Warner was believed to have loaned him a hefty amount toward the purchase of the house where the book-processing center was located. When I contacted Dutton—who had joined another Duke ex-patriot, Bill Wilkinson, as editor of *The Klansman*—he wrote back, "Yes, I left the Duke organization November 8 [1976]. Have you noticed how, when some one departs another, it is on a last name only basis?" He didn't give his reasons, saying he preferred to discuss his resignation in person.

That spring, Duke passed through Washington on what he described as his "most ambitious undertaking" in terms of recruiting members. He would visit twenty-five states in four weeks and appear on more than fifty radio and television programs. Traveling with him in the Montego was Don Black, his Alabama organizer. In the next issue of *The Crusader* Black's name replaced Jim Warner's as National Information Director. Several months later, when I asked about Warner, Duke nonchalantly said he now held only a membership position so he could work full-time for his own New Christian Crusade Church.

During the spring trip, I watched as Duke again emerged on television as a hero of racists, coming across as reasonable and calm while his unprepared interviewers became ruffled and enraged. When black columnist Carl Rowan turned up as one of his interviewers, I was certain Duke had met his match. Instead, while Duke coolly punctuated his answers with "ma'am" and "sir," Rowan grew increasingly agitated: "You think you are superior to blacks, but the mental processes you are showing are just the opposite." When Duke politely refused to divulge the size of his membership, Rowan charged, "Roughly it's so small, you're ashamed." Neither Rowan nor Ed Mutter, the moderator, questioned Duke about his Nazi ties, his notorious members, or his own arrests.

After the show, when I telephoned Mutter, he glowingly described Duke as "absolutely fascinating. I find him articulate, bright, unassuming. He makes a lot of significant points. However, the heritage of the Klan makes anything he says suspect. If I just said, 'Here's David Duke who will give some views on integration,' people would listen a lot more carefully." Mutter said many viewers had called to complain that Rowan and a black newswoman had been rude to Duke. "He's a media person," Mutter continued. "He knows how to manipulate the interviewer. Frequently, he's better informed because the interviewer hasn't done any homework." I asked Mutter about his own homework, and he informed me he watched a tape of the "Tomorrow" show and had read a recent interview in *Oui* and several other articles.

Gradually, Duke's relationship to me became almost that of an old friend whose views and actions I didn't share or condone but whom I found likable and interesting. The more we met and talked, the more I watched him relax and veer away from the Klan and racial philosophy, the more difficult it became to view him as a legitimate Klan leader. I found it increasingly hard to believe he sincerely hated blacks and Jews when he persisted in wanting my agent—whose name is obviously Jewish—to represent him and when he confided that he bought most of his wardrobe from a Jewish clothier. Away from the crowds, from his followers, he became just David Duke, a fellow New Orleanian and an engaging young man with an eye for women, fashionable clothes, and a good time.

Initially, he used the "now I'm only telling *you*" line as a ploy to warm up to me, perhaps to ensure himself more space in the book, but as time passed, as the masthead of his *Crusader* reflected the inner struggle by Dutton and Warner to topple him, he seemed to be seeking a sympathetic ear or to bolster his ego.

I wondered about the real David Duke. One writer had asked, "Is Duke a blond comic opera character doing Adolf Hitler, or is he for real?" I thought about his boyish grin, how he often looked as if he were playing a joke on somebody. But on whom? The public? The Klan? I toyed with the accusations that he was a con man or a rip-off artist, as he bragged about his numerous speaking engagements at colleges and on talk shows. The colleges usually paid from eight to twelve hundred dollars; some television and radio stations footed his plane fare and expenses while he often squeezed in as many as thirty shows a trip, traveling in the Montego and staying at cheap motels. Was this to make money for himself or for the Klan?

But I pondered even more the possibility that he was an agent, for somebody. At his Baton Rouge home, he had scoffed when I confronted him with insinuations made by Shelton and other Klan leaders. "That goes back to some sort of weird thought process, where they say, 'He's getting on national television, and he's hitting 'em so hard and so forth— he can't really be doing this. He can't be getting away with this. He must be working for the enemy,' because they themselves have been failures in their own approach."

Earlier in my travels, a detective who had monitored right-wing groups for six years—the last two, assigned exclusively to the Klan—had offered his own theories:

"There are two ways to look at David Duke—either he has been working for somebody an awfully long time or he's making money. Look at David as being CIA. He's taught in Laos. His father is with the State Department. David, being associated with right-wing groups, he's anti-Jewish. Any anti-Jewish propaganda would be supported by an Arab faction. So, consequently, an Arab faction may want to talk to David in order to keep the fires burning on the Jews. It's hypothetical. But he travels a lot more than what we think his expenses would allow him to. And he's just been around so long.

"Also," the detective continued, "another very, very good reason that makes me think David is working for somebody is that none of the federal agencies have ever come to us for information on him. Everybody else, they do. But not for him. They don't ask us for Klan information. On the other hand, ninety-five percent of the FBI information on the left comes from local law enforcement. This is only theory," he cautioned, "but . . . ."

I had my own reasons for suspecting Duke's role as agent. He popped up everywhere, in places the government would want someone on the inside: Boston and Louisville during the busing demonstrations; the Marine Corps infiltrations; taking on the illegal trafficking of aliens at the Mexican border; meeting nationally and internationally with other right-wingers. He was in the Washington area at least ten times in the course of a year. Once when I met him at his motel, he showed me what looked like a small block of wood, explaining that it was a bug detector "a government friend" had given him and walked around the room to test it. I speculated the agent role could possibly explain an "attack" manual on how to kill white people that he surreptitiously wrote under the pseudonym of "Muhammad X," in order, he insisted when confronted by *The New York Times* in early 1978, "to compile a list of blacks . . . involved in racist activities against white people." It could also explain how he managed to slip past London customs in March 1978 after the British government had banned entry by him and other Klan leaders and then play hide-'n-seek with Scotland Yard when it attempted to find and deport him.

Obtaining information on him from the government proved impossible. Duke repeatedly claimed he could remember neither the name of the teaching program in Laos nor of his supervisor and suggested I call the State Department or its Agency for International Development

(USAID). For days, my calls were transferred from department to department, in both the State Department and USAID. No one could remember such a program. People who had been in Vientiane in 1971—the time Duke supposedly taught there—could not recollect anyone by his name or description. I then tried the Pentagon and various branches of the military and again came up with nothing. When Hodding Carter, III, was named deputy press secretary for the State Department, I renewed my efforts, hopeful another journalist could help. Carter returned my initial call within fifteen minutes even though he had been in his job less than two weeks. He sounded anxious to help and asked me to put my request in writing. A year later, the letter—written February 3, 1977—had not been answered, nor were subsequent phone calls to Carter.

Shortly before deadline, when I renewed efforts to clarify the story, the wife of a former administrator for USAID in Laos was the first—and only—person to place the younger Duke in Vientiane. She recalled his visits to his father but was unaware of his teaching job. At her suggestion, I contacted a woman who had taught there during the same period. The latter said she knew no one by that name or fitting Duke's description and offered to ask her daughter. Sometime later, she called back to apologize that neither knew him. One man who also worked in Laos during that time described the chances of Duke having taught there without him and others knowing it as "possible, but highly unlikely." When I resorted to a formal Freedom of Information Act (FOIA) request, the State Department replied that my previous letter was possibly never answered because it and the current one "are not valid requests under the terms of FOIA, in that they do not reasonably describe existing records." A few days later, a USAID public information officer reported no indication in that agency's records of Duke ever having been employed.

My FOIA request—like the earlier letter—had merely asked the name of the program, Duke's supervisor, and what security clearance Duke would have needed for the job. To a lay person, it seemed incredible that an individual who had publicly brandished a swastika and been associated with the NSWPP could have passed clearance when he had been refused an ROTC commission at LSU "because he was a racist." And what about his father? Certainly he must have needed clearance for his work with the State Department in Vietnam, Cambodia, and Laos. He had returned early in 1975, shortly after his son began making the national television circuit. Could the father have been called home because of his son's activities? Had his security clearance been revoked? Could the younger Duke have been sought out to be an agent for the government through his father? In the course of my inquiries about the

Klan leader's need for security clearance to teach in Laos, I received answers varying from "definitely" to "something below top secret but above confidential."

Duke also kept in contact with most right-wing leaders: J. B. Stoner, Dr. Edward Fields, James Venable, Robert Scoggin, William Chaney, Robert DePugh, Robert Shelton, even foreign leaders like John Ross Taylor of Canada's Western Guard—people, it seemed logical, the FBI and the CIA would be interested in following. Could his frequent calls to me and his repeated offers to read my transcript for technicalities to make sure I didn't make "any embarrassing mistakes" also be to keep tabs on me?

But it was when our conversations and our visits drifted into the casual area that I found it most difficult to consider him a true believer, when I wondered whether he was an agent or a con artist or merely a young man seeking adventure.

The last time I saw Duke, before finishing the book, was September 1977. I drove up to his Arlington, Virginia, motel as he and his father were returning from dinner. We exchanged greetings, and the elder Duke left. David and I went to his room so he could change shirts.

As he slipped out of one shirt and into another, he talked excitedly about the Klan's prosperity, his talk-show performances, and the day's events. He picked up a pair of light-weight plaid trousers thrown over a chair. "Look what I did to these today," he digressed, exhibiting a slit in the crotch. "You've seen this suit before."

"David," I said, laughing both at the scene and the familiarity, "I think I've seen most of your clothes."

Then we laughed together, like long-time friends.

"C'mon," he urged, "let's put the top down on your MG. I want to show you something at the Jefferson Memorial."

It was a pleasant night, the temperature between summer and autumn, the sky a navy background for the stars and the moon. As we headed across the Potomac toward the lighted monument, I conjured up mental images of Duke in his white robe, ranting on the podium. Then I glanced at him; exuberant, his blond hair blowing in the wind. Who, what was the real David Duke?

He sucked in the air and sighed contentedly.

"Don't you think I belong in a sports car?"

16

Bogalusa: A Battleground Revisited

Bogalusa, Louisiana

The town seemed visually unchanged from what had been among the major civil rights battlegrounds. When blacks—led by James Farmer, then head of the Congress for Racial Equality (CORE)—launched a drive in 1965 for voter registration, desegregation of public facilities, and better job opportunities, Confederate flags sprouted from automobiles, and the Original Knights announced their presence with threatening leaflets and telephone calls. Almost daily, there were marches and countermarches; at night, whites gathered by the thousands in a vacant lot at the edge of town to hear J. B. Stoner and "Connie" Lynch harangue. A black deputy was fatally shot in nearby Varnado, and many more blacks were beaten and their houses burned as the war of nerves stretched into months. Klansmen patrolled the streets, and blacks formed the armed Deacons for Defense to protect themselves and their homes. The trouble eased only after a federal court in New Orleans ordered the police chief to protect the demonstrators and the Original Knights to end their harassment.

Now, along Columbia Road, the shoppers—like the store mannequins—were integrated. The marches and open clashes had faded into history, and so, for a while, had the Klan. Yet racial tension still hovered over the town like the omnipresent paper-mill haze. Blacks seemed no less leery of whites; whites, no more accepting of blacks nor any less inhibited in expressing their feelings. Laws and federal court injunctions had opened the cafés and movies to blacks but not the white citizens' hearts.

Thus, on Good Friday 1976, when the Klan returned in its modern-day trappings for a parade and ribbon cutting to mark the opening of its Sixth Congressional District headquarters, Bogalusans—black and white—turned out to watch. A lone, robed klansman on horseback led a contingent of fifty or more in cars and pickups past blocks of black-power salutes to the dedication ceremony. Mayor Louis Rawls snipped the ribbon and accepted a hood and certificate making him an honorary member. That night, a hundred spectators returned for a cross lighting and a speech by Imperial Wizard Bill Wilkinson in front of what had been a Lutheran church but now sported a thirty-two-foot sign: LODGE W-27—Invisible Empire—Knights of the Ku Klux Klan.

Several months later, the parade leader, Paul Pierce, Jr., the district's Grand Titan, sat in the cinder-block ceremonial room with Hulon Dunaway, who had been one of the old Originals named in the court injunctions. Pierce, twenty-seven, listened quietly as Dunaway reminisced about the racial turmoil and rallies, which were childhood memories for the younger klansman.

Dunaway was a grandfatherly looking man with gray hair and a freshly ironed sport shirt, its breast pocket lined with pens and a pocket comb. A former carpenter and construction worker, he had managed a hardware building-material company until he retired. His own father had been a carpenter and farmer; his mother, "a fine Christian woman" who raised him and his four brothers and sisters in the Baptist church. Still religious, Dunaway had served as Sunday school superintendent and church deacon. He saw no conflict between his religious beliefs and his membership in the Klan, which dated back to the early sixties and the impending arrival of the civil rights workers.

"We've been misrepresented," he said gently. "The Klan was accused of things in Bogalusa that they weren't guilty of. This bunch came in here and brought all this agitation. It wasn't our people. I think some of the blacks were as fed up with 'em as I was. But we realized we couldn't go down there and beat 'em up, shoot 'em up, kill 'em off an' drag 'em off and such as that. We never had any plans to do any of that."

"But you were accused of trying that," I ventured.

"We *were* accused of tryin' that," he agreed. "We didn't teach it to our people. Our purpose was not with guns because we realized that day and time was gone. You can't get out there and kill people to get your way. I feel like anybody else is entitled to their thoughts as much as I am to mine."

"What about the guy with the radio station?" I asked, remembering news accounts of the Klan's intimidation and economic boycott against Ralph Blumberg and five other men who, in early 1965, invited former Congressman Brooks Hays to speak in Bogalusa on integration. All six had been harassed, but Blumberg, operator and half owner of a radio station, had borne the major brunt of the attack. His radio transmitter had been fired on, his life threatened, his car windows smashed, and most of his advertisers withdrew as sponsors. The intimidation continued long after the meeting was canceled.

Dunaway readily acknowledged, "I'm reasonably sure that was true even though I didn't have any part in it because it was strictly out of my jurisdiction. But I would believe that he was harassed by the Klan because of some of the derogatory remarks he made. The news media would pick up a word here and a word there, and they'd twist it and put it in print to suit theirself, and ever' bit of it was against the Klan." Nevertheless, he insisted, the Klan would not have intimidated anybody for speaking out in an objective way. "But an untruth they wouldn't stand for."

As he spoke, I remembered the articles on public apathy at the time and the community's reluctance to speak up for fear of Klan reprisal. "The difficulty," one resident had said, "is that nobody knows for sure who's in the Klan. The next fellow who walks through that door might be a member. It's a shame, but people can't speak their mind freely in Bogalusa today." When the three-judge federal court held special hearings before issuing its injunction against Bogalusa klansmen, Mayor Jesse H. Cutrer, Jr., gave a harrowing account of attending a Klan meeting to try to persuade its members against a demonstration. Some hundred and fifty klansmen had sat hooded and quiet as he entered the meeting hall without protection.

"All I could see was their eyes," he told the court.

"Were you frightened?" a government attorney asked.

"I was frightened, yes," the mayor admitted. "You can't be too comfortable talking to a group of eyes."

Now regret turned to thoughtfulness as Dunaway pondered those turbulent days that contributed to the Klan's already infamous reputation. Yet in his own, quiet way, he was adamant that the Klan did not deserve the blame.

"The only thing the Klan tried to do was to indoctrinate the general public as to what this was goin' to lead to an' what was takin' place and try to get it over to the colored people they were being used by outsiders to accomplish a purpose that would not involve them in the end. I don't think it's advanced their cause one bit."

Dunaway grew agitated as he relived the experience. "I think that bein' this was a Klan town, it was picked for a demonstration area, *because of* the Klan. That's why we had so much of a problem here. I think the outsider said, 'We gonna come in here and we gonna show you that we can tear that Klan up.' And they brought lawyers and ever'thang else with 'em when they came. They brought *all* kinds of people with 'em. And they stirred up strife and hatred, and when it came up to the boiling point, then they moved out and went back to New York, they went back to California or where have you and left the thang brewin' an' stewin' down here."

The outsiders had torn apart people who had gotten along before, he argued. "I don't think Bogalusa has gotten over it yet. It's goin' to be with us many more years."

"Would you say that Bogalusa today would be considered a Klan stronghold in Louisiana?" I asked.

Paul Pierce entered the conversation. "It probably is. It's nationally known throughout the country for its Klan activities, even stemming from the sixties and going on with the new publicity that we've been gettin' in the past six months."

"Would you say, because of the Klan in the sixties, that it is easier to recruit here than perhaps in other places?"

"I wouldn't say so," Pierce insisted. "I would say it's harder. When the Klan was disbanded and busted up by the FBI, the people felt let down, and they're reluctant to get started again—*those* people. We're attracting a newer generation."

Many of his members, Pierce noted, had relatives who had belonged to the Klan in the sixties. And Dunaway himself had had a Klan heritage. He remembered, as a small boy, discovering his grandfather's robe in an armoire. "He was one of the original klansmen, back in the Pulaski, Tennessee, days, back when it was organized," he boasted. While, as a child, he had loved to look at the white robe with its bulky hood, he had never considered joining the Klan until the early sixties when a friend invited him to a lecture that turned out to be a Klan meeting. Eventually, he became a Kleagle and helped to organize the Originals in Mississippi, the group that later spawned the White Knights.

In spite of the old Originals' reputation in the Bogalusa area and nationally, Dunaway insisted he had never taken part in night riding or violence.

"Nuthin' except burning crosses," he vowed.

"You *did* burn crosses on people's lawns . . ."

He quickly corrected me. "No, not in people's yards. Out through the countryside. Diff'rent places. We never—that I know of—burned a cross on anybody's private property."

"What was the purpose of the ones you burned on the countryside?" I asked.

"Advertisement," he answered. "Just to let the people know the Klan was active."

In late 1965, when the Original Knights publicly dissolved to resurface as the Anti-Communist Christian Association in an effort to evade the FBI and federal court injunctions, Dunaway was among the more than thirty members ordered to discontinue harassing civil rights workers and blacks. Even the cover name had not saved the Original Knights. Dunaway estimated the dummy organization lasted six months before it disbanded. "There wasn't enough interest in it. People were afraid. The FBI began to come in and harass people who belonged to that just like they did the Klan." He dropped out of the Klan in 1969 and didn't rejoin until Paul Pierce's group formed.

Initially, he was shocked by the new Klan's openness and its penchant for publicity. "You can't help but wonder why," he ãdmitted. "But it's under new management. You have to accept the fact that those old days are gone and you got new people comin' on that have slightly new ideas."

As the older man stood up to go, I asked, "Would you say you have to be brave to belong to the Klan?"

At first, he shot back, "No, because I *know* I'm not brave." Then he became thoughtful. "No, you didn't have to be brave. You just had to have a little common sense. And if you saw someone tryin' to get brave, you tried to teach them that bravery's a thing of the past."

After Dunaway left, Pierce, a member for seven months, reconstructed his own childhood memories of the Klan. He credited growing up during Bogalusa's racial turmoil and his mother's and stepfather's membership in the Klan for his own decision to join in December 1975.

"What do you remember from those days?" I asked.

Paul Pierce thought back to age sixteen. "I remember a lot that should have been done and wasn't. The Klan in those days was a good thing, but it was organized wrong. There was a lot of good people, but they took in people who couldn't care anything about furthering the white race. They were just in for the glory or to knock some nigger on the head."

Pierce agreed that the violence had given both the Klan and Bogalusa a bad name and that last spring's ribbon cutting had renewed the controversy. Many blacks heckled him along the parade route. Still, he persisted, "The Klan has a good name in Bogalusa, even though all the violence and ever'thang that happened back in the sixties. People respect the Klan, and they come by our headquarters and blow their horn an' wave. They're glad to see it. I've had several business people and different city officials say they were glad to see the opening of the headquarters."

Later that day, I talked to another man who, like Hulon Dunaway, had been among the Original Knights enjoined by the courts in 1965. Gray-haired and retired now, he seemed incapable of violence, even as he recalled those angry days. Unlike that of most klansmen I had met, his defense was touched with regret, with admission that the Klan had committed acts it shouldn't have.

He watched quietly as I thumbed through a Konstitution, which described the Original Knights as "military in its government" and dedicated to teaching "a pure Americanism; to protect the oppressed; to relieve poverty among its own members; to aid widows and orphans; to help in building and maintaining segregated institutions of learning." The back page had been torn out because, he said, there were things he felt should not be made public, things that might hurt others.

"The Klan worked together throughout a given area," he explained. "It was divided into districts, and each district helped the other. When we'd get a call from Slidell that they had trouble, we'd go in force because we were always expecting trouble." He paused, continued thoughtfully. "Those were scary times. It got to the point that there'd be groups that would come in uninvited and they'd cause the problems. The Negroes would be picketing, and one of these 'renegades,' I call 'em, would go knock one of them up aside the head, and then you'd have problems. Most of the trouble was caused by outsiders."

The man paused and looked from his air-conditioned car at the afternoon shoppers. He seemed torn, as though he wanted to talk but wasn't certain as to whether he should. He spoke calmly of being known all over the country and about his nocturnal visits to courthouses to initiate sheriffs and city officials, but there was much he wouldn't tell me.

Then he handed me a typed sheet that he said had been distributed by the Klan to every house in Washington Parish. "I want people to know," he muttered, although I wasn't sure what it was he wanted known. "I want people to know." I recognized it as probably the original draft of the mimeographed sheet circulated after Congressman Hays had been invited to speak in Bogalusa. Headed "PUBLISHED BY THE ORIGINAL KU KLUX KLAN OF LOUISIANA," I scanned what I already had seen excerpted in news articles and the HUAC testimony:

On Sunday, December 27, 1964, the Bogalusa Daily News announced that a "renowned layman" Brooks Hays is to speak in Bogalusa, on January 7, 1965. His subject will be better community relations. The Bogalusa Daily News stated, "A group of civic, religious and business leaders of Bogalusa have invited Hays to speak here at the St. Matthew's Episcopal Church Parish House. Due to limited seating facilities, the meeting will be by invitation."

The Daily News did not tell you the whole true story concerning this meeting and it is the purpose of this leaflet to give you the full story concerning this meeting . . .

The man pointed to a passage. "I wish they hadn't've said that." He shook his head and read aloud. " '. . . will try to convince you that you should help integration by sitting in church with the black man, hiring more of them in your businesses, serving and eating with them in your cafes, and allowing your children to sit by filthy, runny-nosed, ragged, ugly little niggers in your public schools.' I regret that. I wish they hadn't included that."

On another day, Charles Christmas, the Original Knights' Grand Dragon since before the Bogalusa turmoil, had also insisted, "The Klan didn't actually do anythang other than make an appearance over there. At one time, we could've taken the town of Bogalusa. We had enough men and we had enough guns. But it's like I explained to the fellas, 'Why take it? We can't hold it. It won't do us any good to take it . . .' "

"But you *did* talk about it?" I asked.

Christmas bypassed the question. " 'What we gonna wind up with is a buncha widows and orphans and families with their husbands in penitentiaries. It just doesn't make sense to get out there and take it when you can't hold it.' See, they had the Guard and ever'thang right up there at Jackson, Miss'ippi. They were ready to drop 'em right in there. It could've been—now really, if the Klan hadda been *near* 'bout what they tried to paint it, it would have really been some bloodshed."

In 1965, when the federal courts ordered Christmas and Saxon Farmer, the Grand Titan, to produce a list of officers and members, the two had sworn the Original Knights had disbanded. But now he acknowledged that its successor, the Anti-Communist Christian Association, was merely a front group created to get around the courts. The membership and the officers were the same. Unlike Dunaway, Christmas said the Knights had never ceased to exist.

"How soon after that *did* you resume being the Klan?" I asked.

"We never did stop, really," he confessed.

"When did you drop that name?"

"Right after we came out of New Orleans. We saw it wasn't goin' to do any good, so we just dropped that."

An automobile salesman in Amite—west of Bogalusa—Christmas had been born in Meridian and raised by a grandmother after his mother's death when he was twelve. He moved to Louisiana in 1956 and three years later joined the Original Ku Klux Klan of America. After a split in 1964, he was elected Grand Dragon of the faction whose membership was concentrated in the Sixth Congressional District. Before the splintering, the Original Knights had gained considerable strength in the areas around Bogalusa, Shreveport, and Monroe. Its membership had far outnumbered that of the United Klans.

The afternoon we talked, Christmas conceded the Knights were no longer big or active. "The Old Originals is just quiet. I did have six thousand people in the Sixth Congressional District. Now I got about fifteen hundred. We're not havin' any meetings. No dues payin'. No nuthin'. I just know where they are. If it comes a time people need a rallyin' point or somethin', I'll call 'em together and they'll band together."

At the Poole Funeral Home where he works part-time, Mayor Louis Rawls brushed off the critical editorials and comments that followed the Klan's ribbon cutting. "Ever'body's entitled to their opinion."

A native of Bogalusa, Rawls was tall and slim, his face lined in an eerie seriousness befitting his second job. Rawls said he received a call from a UKA member urging him not to cut the ribbon and a couple of out-of-town unfavorable letters "cussing more or less," but most commended him for standing up for what he thought was "democratic constitutional government."

"Why did you cut the ribbon?" I asked.

"For the simple reason, some of the members were citizens of Bogalusa, and I won't do for one citizen what I won't do for another," he emphasized. "When I see a citizen, I don't see black or white."

During the sixties, he insisted, there was no real problem in Bogalusa. The news media had exaggerated. "I worked for the post office at that time—right where all the blacks gathered for their marches—and it was just blown out of proportion. You were just as safe here as you were anywhere else. When I'd come home and look at it on TV, if they hadn't 've said 'this is Bogalusa' then I never would've recognized what was going on. They filmed the marches from all angles and made it look like a lot more than it really was. When I was out at night, I saw nothing unusual going on. I don't say that some didn't get telephone calls and things like that. But I really saw nothing to get excited about."

In his sixth year in office, Rawls insisted the Klan's presence had not scared away new out-of-state businesses and industry. "I'm questioned more about the black organizations." Thirty-five percent of the town's eighteen thousand citizens were black, he estimated. To date, none had served in the city government.

"I have no problems with blacks in any shape, fashion, or form," he said. "They won't vote for me, but I don't have any problems with 'em."

"Why won't they vote for you?" I asked.

"Welll, I get a few. Now, when I first ran, there was two blacks run, also. And one of the blacks labeled me as being head of the Klan. And what good would it have done for me to go to the blacks and try to tell 'em I was not a klansman?" he shrugged. "So, I just ignored it. I've run twice, and, as a rule, I get beat three to one ever'where they vote."

While the Klan had never endorsed him, he said he wouldn't object.

"It'd be all right with me if the Klan endorsed me next time. It'd be hard to say what effect it would have. But, as I said, the blacks don't vote for me, anyway."

Before leaving Bogalusa, I pulled into a service station and, as I signed the charge slip, asked the teenage attendant what he thought of the new Klan headquarters.

"It's just great!" he beamed. "I'm a member myself."

17
The Agent

I knew I would see him at the rally. Still, I was surprised when I recognized the police intelligence officer circling the flaming cross in a white robe, the sleeves marked with red stripes to denote his klavern rank.

"What office do you hold?" I joked by telephone the next day.

He laughed and diplomatically evaded the question by relating the difficulties posed by his two identities—as undercover agent and klansman; of having to conceal his robe from neighbors as carefully as he hid his law enforcement role from the Klan.

"Fringing" was the way he had first described his work with the Klan, refusing to divulge whether he was a member or merely a bystander. Now he told of seven years of precariously juggling his dual lives. It was, he admitted, a difficult assignment, one that involved more than a change of clothes and vocabulary, one that encompassed an entire way of life.

"Everything enters into this type case," he explained. "You've got to look at everything. Plus you're undercover, your activity has to be conducive to the environment you're in. Your language has to be adjusted. This isn't like buying drugs, where you go in and cop a deal. This is an ideological thing. This is actual beliefs. This is your culture, your life-style, your background. You've got a lot of variables that enter into the whole thing."

"Don't you also have to be very careful about what you discuss?" I asked.

"Yeah," he admitted. "You have to be very careful about what you say about your family. You've got to keep your stories straight, and you have to be careful not to plant ideas in anyone's head so that you've got the entrapment problem. You want to avoid all that. You don't want to take on the posture of any kind of provocateur. To prevent that, you have to keep alert as to what's going on around you and know when to speak and when not to."

"Don't you worry about driving into police headquarters?"

"Definitely."

In appearance and dress, the officer looked like many of the young men I had seen hanging out at rallies. How many of *them* were agents? I suspected some, but that was only speculation or intuition on my part. How would I—or *could* I—know when I was interviewing an informer and not a genuine klansman?

18

The White Knights of Mississippi

Jackson, Mississippi

The man had been identified by three sources as the White Knights' interim leader while Sam Bowers was serving six years in a Tacoma, Washington, prison for conspiracy in the murder of three civil rights workers in 1964. Yet, on the telephone, he politely insisted there was some mistake. He had never belonged to any Klan. I apologized, but the man continued to talk.

"I'm not a member of any of 'em, but if I was, it would be the White Knights. They're the only *real* Klan. The others . . . I wouldn't give you a dime for any of the other groups. They like to stand on the corner with their hands in their pockets and talk about the niggers."

He hesitated, as though torn between wanting and not wanting to talk. "If you want a story about the *true* Klan, what you need to do is talk to a leader of the White Knights." He paused again. "If you could talk to a couple of their top leaders, that'd be all you needed." Another pause. "Sam Bowers would be the one. Don't know he'd talk to you, though."

I thanked him and was about to hang up. "Ma'am," he stopped me, "I'd say if a man's a good klansman, you won't know it."

The phone call was one of many I made as I crisscrossed the state where, after the headlines and horror stories of the sixties—I had assumed klansmen blanketed the countryside like pine trees. I had anticipated no problems in getting interviews. Due to my Southern writing and travels, my contacts in Mississippi were extensive. But even top newsmen were of little help. They had gotten no closer than I had to the notorious White Knights of Mississippi, the Klan described by the FBI as the most violent in history and once suspected of almost three hundred acts of terrorism. Even an unorthodox Baptist minister, who described himself as "tight" with the White Knights, had refused to help me make contact. He described the group as "extremely closely knit, like a family, and very secret." He was confident that "Two days after Bowers got out of prison they were back in business."

I was left with only a collection of old clippings and the telephone book. During July 1976, I made countless calls, countless excursions down winding dirt roads. The answer was always the same, always Southern mannered: "Ma'am, wish I could he'p, but . . ." I had expected the turndown by Sam Bowers, released from federal prison four months before. Bowers had never courted the press. He had, in fact, shied away from flashbulbs and television cameras and had never granted an interview.

But what about the others?

I thought about the men whose trials had ended in acquittals and hung juries and had focused the nation's attention on Mississippi, men accused of bringing a reign of terror to the Magnolia State, of making even veteran newsmen leery about traveling its highways after dark.

Where were they?

The men, who like nature itself had reddened the Mississippi soil, must still be there, among the pines and rolling hills and Delta flatlands. Most, I speculated, had neither died nor had a change of heart. Why were they—unlike other klansmen I had met—unwilling to talk, to give *their* side of the story? Where were the rallies and cross lightings that filled the weekends and the people's lives in other states? Was the alleged leader correct: was I actually talking to klansmen who—more than any since Reconstruction—were guarding their membership by their silence?

Bill Wilkinson's Mississippi leader, Gordon Gaille, had made headlines when his group applied for a state charter, and the United Klans had opened a "public lodge" in Picayune. I had interviewed twenty-seven-year-old George Higgins, Jr., who differed only in age from Robert Shelton's other state heads. I had also talked to former UKA Grand Dragon E. L. McDaniel of Natchez, whose friendship now with his former black adversary, Mayor Charles Evers of Fayetteville, often made news. No longer a member because "the Klan has served its purpose," McDaniel nevertheless accepted credit for helping to organize the White Knights and recruiting Sam Bowers before Shelton lured him to UKA. But when it came to reaching the White Knights themselves, I drew a blank.

And yet they were there. I could feel it: driving along interstates, passing pickups with rifles in the gun racks, walking in almost-deserted downtown Jackson, even in my motel room with the curtains drawn. It was as though someone I could not see was staring at me. An eerie, uncomfortable feeling. Perhaps it was leftover apprehension from the sixties; perhaps they were watching. They weren't talking, but I felt they *were* there.

On my first stop in Meridian, Obie Clark, president of the town's NAACP chapter, had told me the Klan was still around. Actually, he had confirmed the Knights' current existence the summer before when we talked long-distance about the mysterious deaths of two black men in Kemper County, next to Neshoba County and Philadelphia. Both, he was confident then and now, were lynchings and both, the work of the Klan—or of former Klan members. The October 1974 deaths of a thirty-three-year-old father and his three children had been classified as being caused by carbon monoxide poisoning; the second death, in July 1975, by an epileptic seizure. But Clark and the mortician who prepared the bodies for burial were convinced the adult males had been lynched. Reared in what had long been known as "Bloody Kemper," Clark had known better than to turn to local authorities. He had contacted the U.S. Justice Department and Congress's Judiciary Committee. There was, the Justice Department informed him, no indication of federal violations nor a basis for federal action. But the afternoon we met in July 1976, Clark persisted in his theory. "I have a strong feeling they've developed a knack up there for breaking folks' necks without hanging them."

Clark, forty-two, had good reason for his speculations. He remembered black people disappearing and never again being heard from during his youth. Even though he described the Klan as "so weak now that it's not even noticeable," he said that the same men, the same Klan mentality, existed in the area and that many blacks remained fearful of standing up to them. The lynchings, he theorized, had been committed by "individuals who at one time were klansmen."

Now he reconstructed what it was like for a black growing up in Kemper County, home of Senator John Stennis. The same as many blacks in the South, he had been reared among whites, one family in particular. He had played with their children, even been close friends, *up* to a certain age. And he—like his white playmates—had been counseled by his parents in the racial "do's" and "don'ts."

"As late as nineteen fifty-eight, when I got out of school and followed the only profession that a black could follow in Mississippi at that time— I got a job teaching at a school there—I bought a new car, and my people were scared to death for me to ride around in the county in a new car. That was based on their personal knowledge of past reprisal by whites who saw blacks doing things that weren't guaranteed them. Black people in Kemper County even now to an extent live by that old rule—'you stay in your place'—because it's been instilled in them by their parents as a way of life."

"And as long as they do, there's no problem," I commented.

"No problem," Clark concurred.

After World War II, when the military was integrated, the black-white code of ethics had remained in Mississippi because of those parental warnings. It changed in the sixties only because of outsiders, Clark speculated. "It was a national-type movement. I still don't think it would have happened in the sixties had Mississippi been isolated. A lot of white Easterners and Northerners who came in and conducted workshops and led these kind of movements, they sort of opened the eyes of people. You found a lot of black churches, a lot of blacks who *wouldn't* join in the movement because they *knew* what was going to happen. It just took people like Michael Schwerner and Goodman to come down here and do it. And they found young people who were ready to join the movement."

"Was it pretty well known who was in the Klan and who wasn't?"

He nodded. "Yeah, it was *very* well known. But the kind of violence that my people knew about was conducted by whites who were not organized *as* a Klan. It was a *Klan* mentality. Now, it became popular to organize in the early sixties, and I remember when Ku Klux Klansmen stopped a black man for something he did that they didn't like and poured gasoline on him and burned him up. They set him afire. That case happened when we were *civilized* enough in Kemper County to get N-Double-A-C-P lawyers in, and we sued. Of course, they acquitted."

"It was very hard to get convictions." I observed.

"Yeah," he agreed. "In those days."

In the late fifties, Clark had moved thirty miles south to Meridian, the scene in 1871 of a Klan-led riot triggered by the trial of some black leaders accused of making inflammatory speeches and disturbing the peace. As other freedmen gathered for a show of force, someone—black or white—took a shot at someone else. Gunfire erupted, and within minutes, numerous blacks were dead or dying; only one white was injured.

Mississippi had been among the nine most active states in the Reconstruction Klan. Yet its 1915 successor never received the response it did elsewhere. In 1922, when the Klan attempted to move into Greenville and the Mississippi Delta, Senator LeRoy Percy, a member of a long line of aristocratic planters, successfully led the opposition, including blocking the election of klansmen to public office. Even Governor-elect Theodore Bilbo, once a klansman himself, helped short-circuit a move by the Grand Dragon to form a delegation to oppose Al Smith's nomination at the 1928 Democratic convention. After that, there was little Klan activity in the early days of the Civil Rights Movement, with Mississippi relying on its Citizens Councils and state government to hold the status quo. But that changed in the spring of 1964 as the Magnolia State—like much of the South—girded for the arrival of rights workers bent on pushing voter registrations and equal access to public accommodations.

Obie Clark had been away at college during what became known as "the long hot summer of 1964." But he vividly remembered the years after that, when the Klan regularly published a "Black List" of black leaders, white activists, and civil rights organizations. He also remembered standing guard over black homes and churches.

"Police Chief Gunn, he had some people inside the Klan in the *early* stage," he recalled, "and we were ready for them in most instances. Now, they would go out into the county, and shoot in mailboxes and shoot in houses and things like that. But when they were going to do something in the city, a lot of times we knew about it, and we were there ready with our shotguns and *we shot back*. We foiled a lot of their plans here in Meridian because of that. Then, also, a lot of times we just didn't take any chances. Like First Union Baptist Church and Saint Elizabeth, where the ministers were in active roles, we just—on a routine weekly basis, seven nights a week—we stood guard in those facilities."

"Did they ever shoot at your house?" I asked.

"Oh, yeah," he answered softly. "Threats. Now one thing. I refused to have an unlisted number. My wife had a tendency to talk back to these people, but when I'd get one of them kind of calls at one o'clock in the morning, as soon as I discovered it was a prank call, I hung up and dialed two."

"What was two?" I asked.

"The number on the phone so it wouldn't buzz when I took it off the hook." He laughed now at what he had not allowed to harass him even then.

He had been chairman of the NAACP's education committee during that period, from 1965 through 1967. He still received calls, but he never stayed on the phone long enough to find out whether they were from the Klan. And he received threatening mail that often included the familiar warning "The Knights of the KU KLUX KLAN Is Watching You" as well as literature published by the NSRP and the National Socialist White People's Party.

Roy Gunn's crackdown earned the police chief a place on the Klan's "Black List," and his home was among those targeted for bombing, a fact his own assistant knew but never warned him of, Clark related. "Chief Gunn fired him, and then the man asked for a hearing with the Civil Service Commission, and at that hearing he stated he just didn't believe in segregation and got reinstated."

"Wasn't there a period when people—white people—were afraid to say anything against the Klan?"

"Oh, yes. A lot of whites were victims of that stuff, too. I know some public officials became victims. When these sixteen guys, or eighteen guys, were arrested in Philadelphia," he said, referring to the murders of the three civil rights workers, "some were almost *obligated* to come to the rescue of these people in posting bond. And I guarantee you've never seen the legal community—like *our* legal community—every lawyer in town became associated with the defense of those guys. You know, lawyers now who are serving as judges. There was *one* white lawyer who walked the streets of Meridian with his pistol on, like he was a police officer. Bill Ready. Now, Bill stayed with us, and every time there was a planned assault on the black community, Bill Ready was with us. We had to stake someone at his house, too, because they had him tops on their list."

Overall, Clark looked back with disappointment on the community's response to the terrorism aimed at blacks, especially at their leaders and their churches. Not until the late sixties, when the Jewish leaders and synagogues were hit by a series of bombings, was serious action taken to curb the Klan.

"I got frustrated really with the city and the power structure, because within a period of six months prior to the capture of Tarrants, some twelve or more black churches had been burned, and they had homes, too, that had been shot into. But the white community—including the local elected officials—just sort of stood on the sideline." He shook his head. "I'm *sure* they were in sympathy with us. Matter of fact, there was a biracial committee formed. Called themselves Concerned Citizens, or something like that. Their mission was to rebuild these churches, and a lot of white preachers got run out of town because of that. Now when Temple Beth El in Meridian was bombed and I drove out there the next morning, I saw the local TV cameras, I saw the mayor, the city manager and all ... That made me so angry, I didn't stop. I just circled back, because the thing in my mind was that when Savannah Grove had been burned down, they didn't lift a finger. And I knew that that church—even though maybe it was substandard—it meant as much to its poor members as that Jewish synagogue did to the businessmen who were members."

"So you think that had they not made the Jews targets, the Klan might still be going?" I asked, referring to a series of bombings of Jewish homes and synagogues in Meridian and nearby Jackson that ended in the June 30, 1968, shoot-out between Meridian police and Thomas A. Tarrants, III, a young member of the White Knights.

Clark agreed. "When the Klan mixed that up, when they started making a target out of white, out of the Jewish community, that's when you started getting some convictions. That's when you started getting some action. In Meridian in particular, the Jewish community really controlled the economics, *substantially.*"

"So that's why there was so much emphasis put on Meridian?" I pondered.

"Yeah," he confirmed. "When that Jewish synagogue ... it really was the crumbling of the *whole* Klan kingdom, because the system came down on them. Because, really, prior to that, the black community and the Jewish community were just like black and white. There was complete separation."

"Did the blacks and the Jews then work together?" I asked.

Clark, tall and solidly built, spoke softly and without bitterness. "There was really no opportunity," he explained. "This marked the end of the terror—the bombing of that Jewish synagogue here and then also in Jackson. It was the end of a campaign, you know, and there was no need—or no cause, I guess you'd say—for a coalition."

The "campaign" to which Clark referred had begun during the spring of 1964 in reaction to newspaper accounts that warned of what journalist Don Whitehead later described as a "massive assault" by the Council of Federated Organizations (COFO), a confederation of civil rights organizations. The South—notably Alabama—had attempted to fight off an influx of Freedom Riders in 1961 and the scattered integration of public schools. But it was not until 1962 and 1963 that Mississippi became the primary target of the Civil Rights Movement. Its goal there was to break down the voter registration barriers largely responsible for the rolls including only twenty-four thousand of the four hundred thousand blacks of voting ages. Hundreds of young people, trained by COFO, were due to converge on the state in late June.

In the meantime, a group of white men had decided to revive the Klan to counter the voter registration drive. Early in 1963, the men—one of them E. L. McDaniel—organized a branch of Louisiana's Original Knights of the Ku Klux Klan just across the state line in Natchez. The new Klan was barely nine months old when it was torn apart by the familiar accusations of money grabbing. Among those to pull away and form still another group—the White Knights of Mississippi—were McDaniel and Sam Bowers, who was credited with drafting the constitution, bylaws, and organizational structure. McDaniel's stay with the organization was short-lived. He soon moved on to become UKA's Grand Dragon, taking with him most of the White Knights in the Natchez area. After a brief struggle over leadership, Bowers allegedly was elected Imperial Wizard and set out to recruit, concentrating on his hometown of Laurel. Located between Meridian and Hattiesburg, in a portion of the state referred to by one writer as "a brutal place," the town proved fertile ground. The Masonite Corporation was located across the street from Bowers' combination vending machine-real estate business and living quarters. He frequented the workers' hangouts, preying on their fears of a black takeover. Between March and June of 1964, membership swelled from three hundred to approximately two thousand. By fall, HUAC estimated membership at six thousand.

By June, when the COFO workers arrived, the White Knights were ready, both in numbers and strategy. Don Whitehead related the scene that took place in his book, *Attack on Terror.* On the Sunday morning of June 7, 1964, armed white men had traveled by dirt roads and highways to an abandoned church near the town of Raleigh, 40 miles southeast of Jackson. They came from all directions, guided not by road maps, but by prearranged signals—a Coca-Cola carton on a car fender, another hanging from a tree limb—gradually winding their way deep into the woods, where they were stopped by two guards with shotguns. One jotted down the license-plate numbers; the other demanded the occupants' county and unit numbers. No one gave his name, only the number assigned after he had been sworn into the White Knights. After the guards were satisfied the men were klansmen, the drivers were instructed to proceed to the church and to leave their guns in the cars. The road ended in a clearing, where the weathered frame church stood on a sandy knoll. Two small planes circled overhead, maintaining ground contact by walkie-talkies. Still more guards, .45s on their hips, kept watch at strategic points, and six men on horseback patrolled the woods. By midmorning, about three hundred men were summoned inside the church, where some sat on the worn benches and others leaned against the walls. The Kludd, a thin, red-faced man, read a ritual prayer. Then, amidst a chorus of "Amen!" a tall, sandy-haired man stepped to the lectern and delivered a prepared speech later recorded in the HUAC reports. Sam Bowers began:

Fellow klansmen, we are here to discuss what we are going to do about COFO's nigger-Communist invasion of Mississippi which will begin within a few days." "I have here an Imperial Executive Order which must be understood by every member of this organization. Please listen closely.

It is absolutely necessary that each and every member of this organization stand fast and remain calm at this time, while he is working deliberately to prepare himself and his unit for effective combat against the enemy. Our best students of enemy strategy and technique are in almost complete agreement that the events which will occur in Mississippi this summer may well determine the fate of Christian civilization for centuries to come. Within a very few days, the enemy will launch his final push for victory here in Mississippi. This offensive will consist of two basic salients, which have been designed to envelope and destroy our small forces in a pincer movement of agitation, force by Federal troops, and Communist propaganda.

The two basic salients are as follows, listed in one-two order, as they will be used: One, massive street demonstrations and agitation by blacks in many areas at once, designed to provoke white militants into counter-demonstrations and open, pitched street battles, resulting in civil chaos and anarchy to provide an excuse for—Two, a decree from the Communist authorities in charge of the national government, which will declare the state of Mississippi to be a state of open revolt, with a complete breakdown of law and order, and declaring martial law, followed by a massive occupation of the state by Federal troops, with all known patriotic whites placed under military arrest. If this martial law is imposed, our homes and our lives and our aims will pass under the complete control of the enemy.

The small planes hummed overhead. Otherwise, the church was quiet except for Bowers as he continued reading the document:

Our situation calls for the highest degree of combined intelligence and courage, combined with a sincere, Christian devotion. We can not permit ourselves even one mistake in combating the enemy. All of our actions must be disciplined, precise, courageous and intelligent. There is no margin for error. When the first waves of blacks hit our streets, we must avoid open daylight conflict with them, if at all possible, as private citizens, or as members of this organization. We should join with and support local police and duly constituted law-enforcement agencies with volunteer, legally deputized men from our own ranks. We must absolutely avoid the appearance of a mob going into the streets to fight the blacks. Our first contact with the troops of the enemy in the streets should be as legally-deputized law enforcement officers. It must also be understood that there are many different local police situations. Where we find corrupt and cowardly police, obviously, our members cannot submit to their control, but we should still try to work with them at arms length in every reasonable way possible to avoid being labelled as outlaws.

In all cases, however, there must be a secondary group of our members, standing back away from the main area of conflict, armed and ready to move on very short notice who are not under control of anyone but our own Christian officers. This secondary group must not be used except in clear cases where local law enforcement and our own deputized, auxiliary first groups are at the point of being overwhelmed by the blacks. Only if it appears reasonably certain that control of the streets is being lost by the established forces of law can the secondary group be committed. Once committed, this secondary group must move swiftly and vigorously to attack the local headquarters of the enemy, destroy and disrupt his leadership and communications—both local and Washington—and any news communication equipment or agents in the area. The action of this secondary group must by very swift and very forceful with no holds barred. The attack on the enemy headquarters will relieve the pressure on the first group in the streets and as soon as this has been done, the second group must prepare to withdraw out of the area. They will be replaced by another secondary group standing at ready. It must be understood that the secondary group is an extremely swift and extremely violent hit-and-run group.

When the black waves hit our communities we must remain calm and think in terms of our individual enemies rather than our mass enemy. We must roll with the mass punch which they will deliver in the streets during the day, and we must counterattack the individual leaders at night. In our night work, any harassment which we direct against the mass of the enemy should be of a minor nature and should be primarily against his equipment. Any personal attacks on the enemy should be carefully planned to include only the leaders and prime white collaborators of the enemy forces. These attacks against these selected, individual targets should, of course, be as severe as circumstances and conditions will permit."

Bowers surveyed his audience, sweat beading their foreheads and darkening their shirts, but their eyes, all their attention, focused on him as he ended:

We must use all the time which is left to us in these next few days preparing to meet this attack. Weapons and ammunition must be accumulated and stored; squads must drill; propaganda equipment must be set up ready to roll; counterattack maps, plans and information must be studied and learned; radios and communications must be established; and a solemn, determined spirit of Christian reverence must be stimulated in all members. May Almighty God grant that our arms be guided to success in this, our greatest trial.

By the time the men filed out of the old church and made their way through the maze of dirt roads home, they were, as Whitehead wrote,

committed to a campaign of terror that was to leave a tragic trail of death and destruction, bring shame to Mississippi, challenge the Federal government's enforcement of civil rights law, and plunge the Federal Bureau of Investigation into a four-year underground fight against klansmen the like of which the South had never seen.

The fight was not a clean one, not even on the FBI's side. The Klan fought with everything from bullets to rattlesnakes. The FBI opened a field office in Jackson in July when its files bulged with two hundred unsolved Mississippi cases. While the Bureau suspected some cases involved UKA members, it was virtually positive the White Knights were responsible for most of the violence. In addition to the regular agents dispatched to the state, the Bureau sent a special detachment that came to be known as the "Big 10" because of the agents' size and their readiness to overlook such niceties as "due process" in getting answers from Klan leaders. The fight also signaled the beginning of Cointelpro, the Bureau's controversial counterintelligence program, which came under fire when special Senate hearings in 1975 focused national attention on the FBI's "dirty tricks" against the Klan and other radical groups.

In early 1964, crosses had blazed across the countryside, hailing the Klan's return to Mississippi. Most people—even law enforcement officers—credited them to "pranksters" or ignored them. On the night of April 4, that year, the Klan announced its return to Philadelphia with a dozen flaming crosses, one of them erected in the courthouse square and allowed to burn to a charred skeleton. Crosses burned in sixty-four of the state's eighty-two counties on April 24. Still, nothing was done, just as thousands of posters, listing twenty reasons for joining the White Knights, remained untouched—including one tacked to a bulletin board in the Philadelphia courthouse lobby not far from the sheriff's office.

The White Knights had claimed their first victim—a black male accused of sexual involvement with a white woman—in February, and scores of black homes and churches were burned or bombed. But it was on June 21, two weeks after the clandestine church meeting, that the Klan's presence could no longer be ignored. Three COFO workers, Michael Schwerner, Andrew Goodman, and James Chaney, vanished while they were investigating a black church burning near Philadelphia. Their disappearance attracted the attention of the nation, the president, and J. Edgar Hoover. Hoover himself, accompanied by agents, flew to Mississippi to open the field office in Jackson. The latter, along with men from nearby Keesler Air Force Base and the state's highway patrol and Game and Fish Commission, fanned out into the muggy swamps and pines, looking for the trio. Forty-four days later, the workers were found in an earthen dam, their bodies so decomposed that the fingers had to be removed and sent to Washington for print identification. On December 4, 1964, twenty-one men—six identified by the FBI as White Knights—were arrested and federally charged with conspiring to violate the civil and constitutional rights of the three slain men. The case was then thrown in and out of court during almost three years of legal entanglements that ended when a grand jury reinstated the conspiracy indictments in February 1967, finally clearing the way for a trial. By then, the accused had shifted to include Sam Bowers and Ethel Glen

"Hop" Barnett, a former Neshoba County sheriff who was re-elected to the post later that year. In the interim, Bowers had been indicted in the January 10, 1966, fire bombing death of Hattiesburg NAACP leader Vernon Dahmers. State murder charges were never filed.

In the case of the three civil rights workers, the accused also included Neshoba County Sheriff Lawrence A. Rainey, his twenty-seven-year-old deputy, Cecil Ray Price, and Edgar Ray Killen, a Baptist minister and sawmill operator, who was credited with masterminding the Hitchcock-like plot.

The task of finding witnesses was tedious. Few were willing to talk. One disgruntled klansman told FBI agents: "Anyone who would testify against the characters you had indicted in that Philadelphia case is asking to be killed. If for any reason I'm called as a government witness, I'll deny knowing anything about the Klan."

At the trial in October 1967, in the Federal District Court in Meridian, U.S. Assistant Attorney John Doar drew upon confessions and the testimony of paid informers to piece together a conspiracy that began shortly after Michael Schwerner arrived in Meridian from New York. Labeled "Goatee" because of his beard, the COFO leader had been marked for "elimination" as early as March. At a secret meeting in Meridian, a klansman had suggested, "We ought to get him." But a visitor from Philadelphia warned, "Don't bother Goatee. You'll just mess things up. The state organization already has approved his elimination, and another unit is going to handle it."

According to Doar, Deputy Sheriff Cecil Price arrested the three on the night of June 21, 1964: James Chaney, for speeding; Schwerner and Andrew Goodman, for "investigation." "After they were released about ten thirty from custody," Doar told the court, "they were chased by three cars, one of which was driven by Cecil Price, deputy sheriff, in an official state law car, and as they got fifteen or sixteen miles south of Philadelphia, they were stopped on a side road, and again placed in custody of Price, who was accompanied by some of the other defendants. They were taken in Price's car, four or five miles back up towards Philadelphia in Neshoba County. The deputy sheriff turned off the side road, stopped his car. The boys were taken out of the car and shot and killed at close, contact range."

Doar singled out Bowers as the one who conceived the plot but also linked Price and a third man, Edgar Ray Killen—nicknamed "Preacher"—as central figures in the conspiracy. He cited testimony that a black church where civil rights meetings were held had been burned intentionally on June 16, 1964, to lure Schwerner to Neshoba County from Meridian. The Reverend Delmar Dennis, a former top aide to Bowers who turned paid informer, identified nine of the defendants as

White Knights and told of a meeting at which an announcement was made that Bowers had ordered the "elimination" of Schwerner. He, too, tied Price, Killen, and several others to the conspiracy.

Defendant James E. Jordan, later tried in Atlanta, testified that the trio had been jailed while the executioners assembled. Then they were released, overtaken by Price, transferred from Schwerner's station wagon to the deputy's car, and driven down a lonely country road, where he said he was posted as a lookout. "I heard car doors slam, some loud talk that I could not distinguish, and then I heard several shots." Moments later, Jordan walked down the road, he continued, and found the three youths sprawled on the ground. Burial by bulldozer came later. Still another defendant, Horace Doyle Barnette, in a written confession corroborated the broad outline of Jordan's testimony with one dramatic exception: he swore that Jordan actually fired one of the fatal shots. By Barnette's account, just after Schwerner and Goodman had been shot, Jordan came up yelling, "Save one for me." Then, sighting Chaney, "Jordan stood in the middle of the road and shot him," Barnette said in his statement, adding that Jordan complained, "You didn't leave me anything but a nigger." No one testified as to who shot Schwerner and Goodman, although Doar speculated it would have had to be a large man who could have pulled both men out of Price's car and shot them at close range. In his closing argument, Doar repeatedly described Alton Wayne Roberts, a two-hundred-eighty-pound former night-club bouncer, as the most vicious of the group.

Doar acknowledged that the government had failed to prove its case against Travis Maryn Barnette and could link Sheriff Rainey to the conspiracy only by citing evidence that he was a klansman and in Philadelphia at the time. The prosecutor also conceded that the government's case was built on circumstantial evidence but added, "Midnight murder in Neshoba County provides few witnesses."

In spite of the confessions, the defendants boisterously laughed and talked in the courthouse hallway.

"Hey, violent man, let me have your autograph," one of Roberts's friends ribbed him.

Only Bowers remained solemn and apart.

When the jury returned, the courtroom was quiet. The foreman handed the verdict to the court clerk, who began to read what sounded like a roll call of the Last Judgment:

"... We, the jury, find the defendant, Cecil Ray Price, not guilty ..." he called out, then quickly stopped, looking at the judge. "I'm sorry, your Honor, may I start over?"

"Yes," Judge Harold Cox nodded, and the clerk proceeded, proclaiming Price and six others—including Sam Bowers—guilty. The jury had been unable to agree on the guilt or innocence of Edgar Ray Killen, Ethel Glen "Hop" Barnett, and Jerry Sharpe; the others were acquitted. After two years of appeals, the guilty seven reached the U.S. Supreme Court and were turned down. Bowers and Alton Wayne Roberts were sent to prison for ten years; the other five were given sentences ranging from three to six years. State murder charges were never filed.

By July 1976, most of them were out, and many still lived in the Meridian-Philadelphia area. Only Lawrence Rainey, who had fit the movie image of the mean, tobacco-chewing redneck sheriff, had faded from sight and memory. In spite of his acquittal, he had been stripped of his badge and had become a migrant security guard, moving from job to job, as his past caught up with him.

Cecil Price was a truck driver for an oil distributor. The year before, Price had told *Washington Post* writer Richard Cohen, "The people here thought they were being invaded, changing the way of life they had been used to for so long. I felt that way at the time. I don't know how to explain it. You're born and raised in a certain society and you have your beliefs and here comes a group which is trying to change you overnight. It upsets you." He had, of course, proclaimed his innocence to Cohen, but shrugged. "It was just something that happened in the sixties." He no longer wore the khaki uniform, the straw cattleman's hat, and the six-shooter on his hip. He had changed. He was bearded. And he even said "black" instead of "nigger."

When I visited Philadelphia in July 1976, Price was making deliveries. Most of the others were "out," too, or preferred not to talk, trying to forget the past. Blacks and whites passed on the sidewalks, patronized the same stores, sat at the same lunch counters. Yet I sensed an underlying tension between the races, an unspoken remnant of the past— a black should not get *too* far out of his place. There seemed still a hostility in the town's visible effort to forget.

I passed the jail but didn't stop. I had been there the summer before on another assignment, visiting the peeling gray cells where Schwerner, Goodman, and Chaney had spent their last hours. In the booking room, arrests were still designated by "N" or "W" or "I," a vestige of Neshoba's three-way segregation that once had forced the Choctaw Indians to travel as far as Oklahoma for a high school education.

At city hall, Mayor Allan King swore, "If there's any Klan around here, I don't know about it." But that was what residents said in the sixties. A car dealer then, King said he didn't know much about what had happened to the three. He hadn't kept up with "local politics."

"We're not people with two heads," the fiftyish mayor protested politely. "We're nice people. We integrated our schools, and *Boston* hasn't. We appointed a black to the school board, and *Boston* hasn't. We got two on the police department, one in the fire department, six or eight in the street department, and a number in sanitation." He shook his head. "I just think some time it ought to be over with. Some of these days, they're going to decide this place isn't as bad as they think."

When Richard Cohen had visited Philadelphia, the local editor told him, "There is nothing to be afraid of here." But another resident who knew the town warned, "Be careful of who you say you're a Northern reporter to. Some of them rednecks have not forgotten. They don't like reporters."

I thought about that now—just as I had the summer before—as I headed out of town on Route 19 toward Meridian, eyeing the dirt roads that cut off from the main highway. Which one had led the three to their fate? Could it happen again? As I drove, I remembered the summer before when I had left Philadelphia and DeKalb, in neighboring Kemper County. I was on assignment then to do a story on jail conditions. Sheriff Bud Jarvis had focused his eyes on me when I asked to see the inside of Kemper's jail, two stories of crumbling concrete and bars: "Not lessen you git locked up." When I persisted, he snarled, "Lady, why don't you tear up them notes and forgit you ever was in DeKa'b." I drove carefully that day, too.

Back in Meridian, I still had no interview with a White Knight. Only one seemed on the verge of talking. The one John Doar had called "Preacher," "the man with the plan," who was described by Don Whitehead as Exalted Cyclops of the Philadelphia klavern. Each time I called, Edgar Ray Killen was apologetic: he really *would* like to talk to me, but he didn't know when he would have time. Pastor of a Baptist church every fourth Sunday, he operated a sawmill by day and was a private detective by night. He was currently working on a case that had him tied up. Later, when I was in Montgomery, on my way East, I decided to try again. This time, he said he just might be able to see me the next night. It was worth a try, I decided, and headed back to Meridian. But he neither came nor called. When I telephoned early the next morning, he assured me he was almost positive he could make it *that* evening.

Around six thirty, the motel desk called. A man was in the lobby to see me. I asked that he be directed to my room. Then I panicked. The man accused of perhaps the most malicious of civil rights crimes was on his way to *my* room. I was alone and afraid.

When I opened the door, I faced a wizened man, lost in a too-big brown suit and Stetson hat. A "WALLACE" clip held his tie, a Shriner's emblem was pinned to his lapel. He peered at me through black-rimmed glasses and removed his hat as he entered the room. His brown hair was as sparse as his brows were ample. I imagined that at the time of the murders, when he had been thirty-nine, his hawkish face with its humped and pointed nose could have been menacing indeed. Now he seemed quite harmless.

He eased into an arm chair, removed his glasses, and rubbed his eyes as he began his story. He talked in a soft drawl, his statements often ending with question marks, his I's wide, and his syllables sometimes swallowed. He was relaxed, as though it were a friendly visit, even when I ventured from his family background to questions of racism, then to the events of June 21, 1964. His simplest, most innocent-sounding statements often contradicted one another, and he chuckled, "I talk two ways."

The oldest of eight children, Killen had graduated from high school and studied agriculture at a junior college until he quit to buy a sawmill. His family had logged, milled, and farmed at least as far back as his grandparents. When I asked if his people had been of low or medium income, he laughed. "Wellll, we knew a little about both." He told me he was pastor of Zion Baptist Church in Kemper County, where he held services once a month.

"What, racially, were you taught when you were growing up?" I probed.

"Really wasn't mentioned," he pondered.

"Was it just the typical Southern accepted . . ."

He started before I finished. "When I first remember—you did say race?—The first . . . I'm tryin' to think of what age . . . My uncles joined us on part of the ol' property my granddaddy had, and they had colored families. We played with the children. Never did know any differ'nce. We thought a lot of those nigger children. If any the ol' ones livin' now, if I see 'em, it's still the same feelin'. But that didn't last but too many years." His eyes circled the ceiling, his brow accordioned. "I've never known why. There was never no problem. No trouble. It might have been that they began to kinda mechanize the farm. But they drifted out. Maybe the young ones grew up an' got jobs." He tried all the possible combinations. "But, now, there was *never* any problems. Really, I never thought of the word 'race.' Maybe we missed that in bein' educated, but we didn't even think about race."

"When *did* you first think about it?" I questioned him.

"I suppose the first thang that ever created any differnt feelin' was when they began to tell us we *had* to do this. I'm not an extensive traveler, but I've been in several cities. First time I recall 'em eatin' in public places was in Washington, D. C. That was before they integrated the South."

"What were your feelings about that?"

"Well, I ignored 'em, to be frank with you," he answered softly, then quickly continued, "*However,* I don't mind tellin' you, when they started, you know, comin' in and sittin' down in the booth next to ... I would almost choke to death." He chuckled lowly. "I still do to some extent, but I've tried to become adjusted. I have no hatred for 'em, I mean, if you would like to ask me. I have no hatred for the race."

He had worked among blacks and accepted them as individuals. It was the Northerners coming down and telling the Southerners what to do that he resented.

"Far as any sudden uprisin' in my feelin's, they never was," he assured me. "I think the very sin of all the problems of America lay at the door of our ancestors for buyin' the slaves. That was the real wrong. The thang that I hold aginst 'em today is they are bein' used more. Most of our churches—the old dilapidated colored churches—they were burned not by the Klan, as the newspaper said, but most of 'em were burned either by outsiiiders or some of the leaders in the Civil Rights Movement."

"Why would they have done that?" I asked.

"Well, I never did read this in the paper, but I observed it from personal observation." He was suspicious. "But most of the whiiite business people, the people in our community, rebuilt 'em new brick churches. I never did see *that* in the newspaper. My hometown made money up to help *rebuild* one. It got blown up, for why *I do not know.* I never did know. Usually I checked out to see, because I was accused of bein' in the know on ever'thang."

"Did you read the book, The FBI Against the Ku Klux Klan?" I started, attempting to maneuver the conversation toward the White Knights and the murders.

"Uh, truthfully it is *so far* from anythang close to the truth that I never completed it," he answered. "Momentarily, I couldn't think of one sentence in it ... But it made my blood pressure real high, because it's not true."

"The author mentioned a church called Mount Zion, where klansmen went in and beat up some black people and then returned and set the building on fire. Do you know which one I'm talking about?" I asked.

"Yessum," he nodded. "I thought until the day the FBI made the arrests, I thought the church was on the *other* side of that highway. Naturally, they would assume ... Well, they even said I led the people out that did that. But I didn't even *know,* really ..."

"So you're saying the Klan did not do that?"

"I do not ... if I knew anythang about it, I wouldn't ..." He started, backed up, started again, each time moving in a different direction. "Now, *probably* the FBI *paid* someone to make the statement that they gave. I can assure you that none of my associates or friends that I know of *ever* made any plans to burn that church, even though they [FBI] spent probably fifty thousand dollars tryin' to prove that ... Myself, I have always been *bitterly* opposed to burnin' a nigger church. For several reasons, and one was, had I burned it, my neighbors would have given 'em a large brick church back."

He leaned forward to emphasize his sincerity. "But I never did. I never advocated it. Had I been in the Klan and the Klan planned to burn a colored church, if it'd been in my power, I would have stopped it."

The phrase "had I been in the Klan" echoed in my head. News articles at the time of the trial had identified him as a member, and in our telephone conversations, I had repeatedly said I wanted to interview Klan members. I also remembered a passage from Don Whitehead's book:

> From Philadelphia the Klan moved southward thirty-eight miles, into Meridian, the Lauderdale county seat and hub of commerce for eastern Mississippi. Again The Preacher was the organizer, and his first recruit was Meridian Police Sgt. Wallace Miller, a longtime friend. Sergeant Miller was chubby, gregarious, middle-aged, and a sixteen-year veteran of the police force. He also was a segregationist bitterly opposed to COFO's planned student invasion of Mississippi.
>
> The Preacher went to Miller's home one night in early April to tell him of the White Knights of the Ku Klux Klan. They sat in their shirt-sleeves at the dining-room table drinking coffee. They talked of their boyhood escapades in Neshoba County and of the later years when they had shared tragedies.
>
> At last The Preacher said, "Wallace, you're against integration, aren't you?"
>
> "You know I am," Miller said.
>
> "Then you should be a member of the White Knights of the Ku Klux Klan," The Preacher said. He went on to describe the Klan as a "Christian organization" of men dedicated to fighting integration and communism. Many of Mississippi's "best people" were joining— businessmen, oilmen, doctors, lawyers, and ministers of the Gospel. Their goals were those in which Miller himself believed. The Klan could do things to help Mississippi and the nation that the police themselves could not do officially—and the Klan actually wanted to work with the police.
>
> "You help us," The Preacher said, "and we'll help you. Would you like to become a member?"
>
> "Yes, I'd like to join," Miller said.

Perhaps I had misunderstood Preacher Killen, I speculated, so I asked, "When did you join the White Knights?"

"I never did join," he answered almost inaudibly.

"You did not?" I repeated,

"The FBI paid informers to say . . . See, they have a boy—the assistant chief of *poleece*—he came on the stand as one of the last witnesses they put on, and he said he went with me to meetin's and he said he planned, you know, he was there when I planned to git these three."

"So you never were a White Knight?"

"I never . . . Under no circumstances was I ever at liberty to say I *was,* that I *ever* was, that I *ever* would be, or that I even wanted to be."

"In the book, they refer to "The Preacher." Was that you?"

"Most people use it," he admitted. "'Round the sawmill, from the time I was licensed to preach to this day, they call me 'Preacher.' "

"Whitehead said that you were head of the Klan in that area and that they held meetings at your house . . ." I started.

"Yessum, they said, but that was wrong." He was emphatic.

When I asked why the FBI would have wanted to picture him as a klansman and a murderer, the Preacher unwound a tale: he had been implicated by a man from the area in an attempt to get even with him for refusing to go to the governor on his behalf and ask for a pardon. The man, Killen explained, was a known Communist who lost his citizenship when he challenged a newspaper editor to a duel for printing articles alluding to his Communist activities. According to Killen, Mississippi law provided that anyone who challenged another to a duel could lose their citizenship

"But how would he have convinced the FBI you belonged to the Klan?" I puzzled.

"It didn't take any convincin'," Killen sneered, "because they was desp'rate. They wanted anyone they could. They were *very* desp'rate."

While Killen insisted he had never been a klansman, he admitted he had belonged to the Americans for the Preservation of the White Race, described by law enforcement officials as a Klan "front" and that he was acquainted with some Knights.

"I'm sure that I would have known all of 'em. I'm sure." He reconsidered. "That's a broad statement. I'm thinkin' I would have known most of 'em, without knowin' right off who. Some of the men they arrested, I was not *that* acquainted with, but through a process of court for more than three years, I got real acquainted with most of 'em. None of the men that *I* know of that they arrested on that thang would've shot in a house."

"Did you know Sam Bowers?" I asked.

"Only . . . I knew Sam, let me see, how many months? You know, I can't even remember *how* I met Sam. I possibly met him . . ." He paused again. "I knew Sam before they arrested him on this. See, he was one of the last ones to be arrested on this Philadelphia case. They spent an awful lot of money to git false testimony on Sam Bowers. To the best of my knowledge, Sam Bowers wouldn't have had any more to have done or to be any more in a conspiracy or to have actually done the deed than *you* or I as of *this* moment."

"You are saying he would *not* have taken part in the con . . ."

"But they brought him to the courthouse under arrest. That's the reason I was tryin' to think. As I said, I'm tryin' to be honest. I don't recall if I introduced him to the other people who were arrested for conspiracy. Of course, they called it a conspiracy trial, but they tried 'em for murder, which they *never* proved. But Sam Bowers was brought in, and *I could* have been the one that, soon as they were where they could associate, introduced him to these people. They didn't know 'im. Now they knew him well *after* the arrest."

"None of them?" I challenged.

"Not to my knowledge. I'm talkin' 'bout my neighbors now. We'll git a conflict of statements here. See, now, we all became close and if there'd been any way to have committed a conspiracy *after*—and when I say conspiracy, I say a lotta thangs that might be in a jokin' way, but the conspiracy where two or more conspire?—Well, we would have certainly conspired to have defeated the government in that case, certainly, honestly and all."

"Do you think the White Knights did any of the things they were accused of? They have a reputation for being a very violent group," I noted.

He started slowly. "I think what really happened, some outside radical, someone took advantage . . ."

"You mean, framed them?"

"Yes," he nodded. "That's why I would not . . . the U-nited Klans—what I do know about 'em, if that is really what they believe, I'm for 'em—but I never joined for the simple reason, when they'd counter march on the streets, they had the *entire* fed'ral government opposed to 'em. In most of the marches, you had Communist leaders."

When I maneuvered the conversation to the actual murders, Preacher Killen vowed, "I never did see a one of the three. Never did. But *after* the arrest . . . I did a lot of research at that time, and if you can look at the files, J. Edgar Hoover had a file that Mister Schwerner was an *underground,* active agent for the Communist Party. So was Mister Goodman. He was young, but he was recruited and he was trained. They were recruitin' young blacks throughout the South, especially, particularly in Mississippi."

"For the Communist Party?"

"Well," Killen dodged. "they wasn't usin' the word, I don't think. But they were recruitin' them and makin' 'em sign a card at these meetin's they would rape a white woman once a week throughout the hot summer of nineteen sixty-four." He paused, then continued with uncharacteristic zeal. "Because never before have I told, but *I saw* some of the cards. I know what I'm talkin' about. We had to burn 'em because they, uh, and the FBI did but they will deny it . . ."

"Why did you have to burn them?" I challenged.

"They would have used it that we . . . we obtained those even *after* the arrest, but they would have used 'em and said that we got 'em off them. We didn't git 'em off 'em."

"What do you feel happened with the Philadelphia killings?"

"You mean . . .?" He sounded as though he had temporary amnesia.

"The ones you were accused in," I prompted.

"Martin Luther King visited Lyndon Johnson, and he promised that they would arrest someone and the . . ."

"You mean after the bodies were found?"

"I don't recall before or after . . . They *never did* prove they found the bodies. 'Course, I'm most certain they found somethin', but they never would even let the local coroner—which is *strictly the law*—if the federal government believes in law right down the line, why would they not go according to the law? They had the force here. No one—if they had three bodies out there—no one would try to break in there and steal three decayin' bodies. It wasn't out of fear of that."

"Do you remember when you first found out they were missing? Do you remember what the people's feelings were about that?"

"I don't remember exactly . . . you know," he said. "A lot of people really didn't believe it. At that time, ninety-nine percent of the people were, well, they just didn't believe it. And frankly those that *would* believe that anythang could've happened, were not too bitter about it."

"How many would have thought if you *had* done it, it would have been a good thing?"

Preacher Killen stopped twiddling his thumbs and cocked his head slightly. "I really don't know, but the majority at that time, because feelin' was high, real high."

"How were your feelings?" I pressed.

"I didn't have any children to have to go to school with 'em. I never would invite 'em to church with me," he dodged.

"I mean when *this* was going on?"

"I wasn't *all* that *up*set. I didn't have any reason to just really, you know, uh . . . Now feelin's got high *after* the FBI moved in. They didn't move a *few.* They moved hunderds. I counted fourteen of 'em in my front yard at one time. So, feelin's got high then, but at the time I did not have a lot of emotions about it. No high feelin'."

"When did they first start coming and talking to you? When did you first start knowing they suspected you or were going to implicate you or whatever?"

Killen stretched out his legs until his body was rigid like a board, pressed his fingers together to form a steeple, and stared at the ceiling. "Tryin' to think of the date ... Some time in July. The first time they approached me was there in Philadelphia, I well remember. They asked me if I would go out to the motel, to their headquarters and take a polygraph test. And of course, I said, 'No, sir, I would not.' I mean, what business did I have goin' with him? 'Course I knew ... They had asked an awful lot of people if they had seen me around town. A lot of 'em had told me they were huntin' me. I went out and stood on the street, 'til they ... 'cause they were jist buzzin' thick."

"But," I wondered aloud, "wouldn't it have been better for you to take the test to prove your innocence?"

Preacher Killen shook his head. "There is a possibility of that, but if you are innocent, anyway, and at the time, if I took it and *you didn't,* they would have accused you. But they came to me and told me, said they're trying to git ever'body to take one. You know, anyone, if your name was called. They were desp'rate. The record says they wrapped the case up. They got some convictions, but they probably have people that knew *more* than anyone that went to prison that they never questioned. They never got *as close* to that case as they thought they did."

"Do you know who did it?"

"I don't know," he said guardedly.

"Do you think the Klan was responsible?"

He stalled. "I'm not sure that I even know what I ...."

"Do you think the ones who went to jail did it, were in on it?"

"Really, I don't ...I don't know that the ones who went to prison could give the names for certain. 'Course, in the courts, John Doar said I was the man with the plan and said these men carried it out."

"You planned it?" I repeated.

"He had witnesses who testified to that, but one testified also to how much money they gave 'em. They did not have any honest witnesses that could truthfully say that 'I conscientiously come here today to tell the truth.' They had to tell that some got fifteen thousand dollars."

Preacher Killen next told about how the FBI agents had hounded him, about how they had come to his house "possibly a thousand" times, how they drove back and forth in front of his house at all hours.

His trial had ended in a hung jury and the charges, along with those of "Hop" Barnett and Jerry Sharpe, eventually were dismissed. In the long legal maneuvers, he had never served a day in jail. "It will break their heart," he chuckled. "They never *did* git to lock me up. Never got in jail."

"How do you feel now about the three guys getting killed?" I probed. "Do you think they had it coming? Are you glad it happened?"

Preacher Killen didn't answer immediately. His thumbs stopped mid-circle, and he looked at me, eye to eye. "I have a lot more feelin' about the boys we lost in Vietnam fightin' the same characters as the two white boys." He continued in his soft, unfettered drawl. "I have a feelin' for any human bein'. I don't exactly know how to answer you because I don't know exactly if I really understand the question. In other words, if you are sayin' would you have planned it, well, I didn't and I wouldn't. After knowin' the thangs I know today, had I done it, I wouldn't have any regrets."

"Would you condone *any* of the violence that the Klan was accused of during the civil rights times?"

"No," he assured me. "Not really. I would—in other words, if you are quoting me—I couldn't tell you that I condemn the Klan for bombin' a Jewish home when I conscientiously wouldn't know that they did. I am not sayin' that I would condone it if one of my friends did it. I am saying I have not." He stopped and started again. "Well, what I don't mind bein' quoted, after they moved in in force, any acts of violence that was done was either by an agent if they had one that had the nerve or by one of their cohorts." Preacher Killen's answer gradually wound its way into a lambast at the agents and paid informers and the television version of Don Whitehead's book.

It was almost eleven o'clock when Preacher Killen put on the gray Stetson and started toward the door. He got into his faded green Buick and turned the key, but the engine wouldn't start. He turned the key again and again, pumping the gas pedal, but there was only the grating sound. We walked to a next-door service station, where the mechanic was off, and the attendant knew of no others on duty in town. Preacher Killen tried the car again. Inwardly, my mind raced as the car refused to start. It was almost midnight. What would I do with the Preacher? I had never allowed fear to interfere with an assignment, yet I could not bring myself to offer him a ride, to travel with him on that same infamous stretch of road between Meridian and Philadelphia. Finally, he telephoned a friend, and a tow truck arrived to haul him and the car away. I watched as they left, relieved and also amused as I envisioned the two of us in the motel lobby and at the gas station. Had he, as John Doar accused, been the man with the plan? I still wasn't sure I had talked to a White Knight.

Back in my room, I thought about the White Knights and Sam Holloway Bowers, Jr. Who was this man accused of masterminding such hideous crimes, of being so persuasive that one agent insisted, "He can get these people to do near anything"? Veteran reporters could offer only glimpses from their memories and from clips, mostly of a man who remained aloof both when he was on trial and in his day-to-day life. He once told a newsman who tried to question him, "I don't intend to cooperate with you and you don't have permission to use my name in any way." One article described him as "a voracious reader and a prolific and quite literate writer." And his life story had appeared in print frequently, but its facts had come from scattered sources, not from him.

Even from afar, most agreed he was not the stereotyped redneck Klan leader. Born in New Orleans on August 6, 1924, he was the grandson of Eaton J. Bowers, a distinguished Mississippi attorney who served four terms in Congress, and a direct descendant of the first president of the Virginia House of Burgesses. His parents were divorced when he was fourteen, and he then followed his father to wherever his sales job took him: the Tampa-Fort Myers area of Florida, Gulfport, and Jackson. Former classmates at Fortier High School in New Orleans remembered him as a bright student who made fairly good grades but worked below his capacity. He seldom socialized and never associated with girls. Shortly after Pearl Harbor he left school and enrolled in the navy, serving until 1945 when he was discharged as a machinist mate first class. The next year, having secured his high school diploma through an equivalency test, he enrolled in Tulane University in New Orleans. He transferred after a year and attended the University of Southern California School of Engineering before moving to Laurel and setting up a vending-machine operation known as Sambo Amusement Company. From that time until he went to prison in 1970 for the civil rights slayings, he and his partner shared living quarters behind the business.

Even as an adult, the bachelor was described as a loner and a fanatic on guns and explosives by acquaintances. They told the press of Bowers' habits, such as wearing a swastika armband, clicking his heels in front of his dog, and saluting, "Heil, Hitler!" He was also said to have warned acquaintances against a Communist plot to train blacks in Cuba and invade the United States by way of the Mississippi Gulf Coast. They quoted him as saying the president would then federalize the National Guard and force loyal white Mississippians to evacuate, leaving the state to blacks and sympathetic whites.

Both friends and enemies viewed him as extremely intelligent. Dr. Ken Christopherson, Bowers' religion professor at Pacific Lutheran University during his incarceration at McNeil Island Federal Penitentiary, described him as "a talented writer." "Sam is without question the most interesting writer I've had in eighteen years of teaching," Dr. Christopherson told the press, upon Bowers' early release for good behavior. "Overall, he is definitely among the top five percent of the students I've had."

In spite of Bowers' indictments in the Philadelphia slayings and the 1966 fire-bombing death of NAACP leader Vernon Dahmer, several of his former associates insisted he was more misunderstood than ruthless, that he was not guilty of the things for which he was blamed. Yet one disgruntled klansman told FBI agents: "Bowers don't have the guts to kill anyone himself, but he's not above getting others to do the dirty work. I don't know whether or not this happened in the case of those three COFO workers. But Bowers was the only person who would have the final say-so, and who could authorize the killings of anyone by Klan members." After his building was bombed in 1964, J. W. West, editor of the *Laurel Leader-Call,* commented, "Anything we write about Bowers will be strictly from the court record. We don't want to fool with him." Still another Laurel resident told the press, "We don't talk much about them (the White Knights) around here because we never know who we might be talking to. You don't know who all the members are."

During the HUAC hearings when investigator Donald Appell asked Bowers, "As Imperial Wizard of the White Knights of the Ku Klux Klan of Mississippi, did you ever authorize the extermination of a human being?" Committee Chairman Edwin Willis looked at the witness and remarked, "You seem shocked by that question. Why don't you say 'no' under oath?" The Imperial Wizard conferred with his counsel and then invoked the First, Fifth, and Sixth Amendments, as he did to every question. According to the official testimony, the response was the same when investigators produced a "Black List" and a "Schedule of Jones County Violence," which, for a seventeen-month period, included two bombings, seven assaults on civil rights workers, twenty-three burnings of homes, churches, and businesses, an attempted house burning, six shootings, a barn explosion, and nine cross burnings.

Billy Roy Pitts, a young klansman who pleaded guilty in the Dahmer case, told the court of a meeting at which Bowers allegedly "beat on a table" and insisted that "the nigger Dahmer" be dealt with by the Klan for his role in a voter education project. Pitts testified that Bowers had "wanted a Project Three, and if possible, a Project Four on Dahmer." A Project Three in Klan terms meant the burning of a building, he explained; a Project Four, "annihilation or death, or, you know, murder." According to Pitts, Bowers was not among the eight men who slung a bomb into the black leader's house and store and then riddled the buildings with bullets. However, the Imperial Wizard "was to serve as one of the backup men if anything went wrong." The state and federal trials resulted in life sentences for murder for three klansmen and a ten-year prison term for arson for a fourth. Pitts was given five years after pleading guilty to federal charges of violating Dahmer's civil rights and implicating himself, Bowers, and nine others. Bowers' own trials for murder, arson, and conspiracy ended in hung juries, and, in 1973, the federal charges against him and eight other defendants were dropped by U.S. District Court Judge Harold Cox.

During the Philadelphia and Dahmer trials, Bowers was described by the press as sitting grimly quiet, sometimes chewing gum and occasionally sharing a private word with a friend. He always appeared in a business suit and tie, his trousers held high by suspenders.

After I returned East, I renewed efforts to meet Bowers or to at least interview a White Knight. I wrote directly to him at his amusement company, describing the book and asking that he reconsider talking to me. In return, I received a reply from his attorney, who politely chastised me for contacting Bowers directly and yet sounded vaguely hopeful. ". . . All serious communications with Mr. Bowers should be addressed to him through this office. Your propriety and polish last summer in formally communicating through this Firm was duly noted and approved by Mr. Bowers. Your letter of January 12, 1977, while noted as being friendly and courteous in tone, was improperly addressed. Mr. Bowers is unequivocal on the point of not replying directly." I acknowledged the letter with an apology that led to continuing communications between the attorney and me but—by deadline—not to an interview.

In the interim, during a trip back South, I arranged a get-together with a couple acquainted both with a friend of mine and Bowers. The day we met, the husband and I spent the afternoon discussing the White Knights and the Civil Rights Movement. He and his wife, both college graduates, were proud and fiercely defensive Mississippians. As we talked, he gently took over the questioning, probing my knowledge of the Civil War and the Reconstruction period?

"Do you see any similarities between any particular Klan and Reconstruction?" he asked me.

"Because of their secrecy and because of the conditions and causes that brought them about, I would say the White Knights," I answered.

The man, impeccable in a three-piece suit, seemed pleased. "And when did the White Knights start?"

"I'd say the spring of sixty-four. That was when they had the meeting at the old church, when they talked about the civil rights workers coming down for COFO," I started, then backtracked. "But as I understand it, the Original Knights of Louisiana moved over into Mississippi in sixty-three, and six or eight months later, a group broke away and formed the White Knights."

"What happened *before* sixty-three?" he pressed as he began unraveling what seemed a justification for the White Knights and their alleged deeds.

I was stumped, and he answered for me. "Ole Miss. The thirty thousand troops when James Meredith enrolled." He likened the troops and the later announcements of the impending arrival of the COFO workers to Reconstruction, to modern-day carpetbaggers. "A lot of Mississippians thought, 'Seems like we've been through this before,'" he said, adding firmly, "There have been two occupations and two Reconstructions."

We continued to discuss the similarities between the original Klan and the White Knights: the secrecy and the motive—to drive off invaders and fight for a cause. I noted that Bowers seemed more akin to the Reconstruction leaders because of his education, his family background, and his low profile. The man agreed.

"Would I like him?" I asked.

"I think so."

"I take it you like him?"

He simply grinned, then continued the questioning. "When it was over, what did the Reconstruction Klan do?" he asked.

"They burned their robes," I answered.

The man smiled.

"Are you saying that's what the White Knights did?" I asked.

He nodded slightly.

"And that's what the other Klans should have done?"

Again, he nodded and then sympathized with the opposition that Pulaski citizens expressed when UKA returned to their town for its 1976 rally. "I'm not so sure I don't agree with the people of Pulaski," he commented.

I studied the man, polite, educated, nicely dressed. "You notice, I haven't asked if *you* are a White Knight."

He grinned. "I know."

That evening, his wife joined us in the discussion. A student at Ole Miss when Meredith enrolled, she remembered the Sunday the troops arrived *en masse*. It was a sunny day, the leaves in fall colors. Most students had been at a football game; their partying mood soon sobered when they confronted the beefy U.S. marshals.

"Have you ever been searched?" the woman asked me, resentment still in her voice fifteen years later. "Try it three times a day. Every time you went on or off campus." She thumbed through her college yearbook to a photograph of a trooper armed with a tear-gas gun. "How would you feel if you were twenty-two years old and confronted by him? I *didn't* like being invaded. I *didn't* like bayonets pointed at me. I didn't like seventy FBI agents coming into Mississippi! I'm anti-Establishment, antifederal, *not* antiblack," she fumed. "They didn't have anything to do with it. They were being used."

Her husband repeated his earlier observation, "'Seems like we've been through this before!'"

The two attempted to explain Mississippi. The state's population—unlike that of others—included more native-born residents. Even those who left kept close ties, returning home often. And, until recently, few outsiders moved into what had been perhaps the least industrial of states, especially into the smaller towns.

"The civil rights workers were probably the only outsiders," the woman said. "What was there to go there for?"

She looked back on the summer of 1964. "There was a feeling of protecting your home, your state, your culture. People might not have known *why* they felt it, but they did. They wanted to be left alone."

There was suspicion, too, they agreed: "Is this going to go farther?"

"The climate was supercharged," she remembered. "Under other circumstances, a good many of these people would not have done these things."

When I asked if they condoned the murders of the civil rights workers, the couple was unsure. "I don't know what I would have done or would do," the husband admitted.

"It would be like me walking through a ghetto at night and getting assaulted," the wife reasoned. "I shouldn't have been there in the first place." She opened Hodding Carter's *The Angry Scar,* and read, " '. . . the North has remembered so little of Reconstruction . . . and the South has remembered so much.' " She closed the book and added, " . . . and Mississippi has remembered most of all."

Before that Sunday in September 1962 when the troops moved into Ole Miss, she had considered herself moderate to liberal. "Now, I'm bigoted. I assiduously strive . . . I'm an unreconstructed rebel." She paused, then lowering her voice, added, "Mentally, I seceded that night."

19

Tommy Tarrants:
A Repentant Rebel

Parchman, Mississippi

The young man did not recall hearing police yell, "Halt!" He remembered dashing toward the Buick Electra, into a barrage of bullets and the high-speed chase that, for him, ended at Parchman Penitentiary. Before the July 1976 interview, I had been told that Tommy Tarrants had renounced the Klan, that he was no longer what some had referred to as "a mad dog." Even so, I had not expected such a complete transformation from the fatigue-clad guerrilla whose bombings had pockmarked the Jewish communities in Jackson and Meridian during the late sixties.

He looked like a college student. Instead of prison stripes, he wore white-duck trousers, a neatly ironed sport shirt, and well-polished loafers. His brown hair was cut just below the ears, and when he smiled, his face dimpled. A three-inch scar on his right arm was the only outward clue to the gun battle, eight years before, that critically wounded a police officer, felled the only woman publicly known to have participated in Klan violence, and tainted the reputations of the FBI and the Anti-Defamation League with still-persistent accusations of entrapment.

During the Sixties, nightrider attacks in Mississippi—as in most of the South—had been directed against blacks and civil rights workers. Then, in September 1967, a synagogue and a rabbi's house in Jackson were bombed. Alarmed Jewish leaders, with the help of the ADL, began raising reward money. Between 1967 and 1968, the attacks on Jewish and black communities numbered seventeen—all unsolved. Frustrated by their failure to stop the bombings, the FBI and Meridian police decided to use the unclaimed reward money to solicit the help of informers. They chose Raymond and Alton Wayne Roberts, the latter free on appeal of his conviction in the 1964 slayings of the three civil rights workers in nearby Philadelphia. The FBI and ADL later insisted $36,500 was paid to the brothers to gain advance warning of the next planned bombing. Evidence gathered in 1970 by Jack Nelson of the *Los Angeles Times,* however, indicated the informers enticed Tarrants and another suspect into a plot to bomb the home of a Meridian Jewish businessman. Policemen who staked out the area surrounding the targeted home told Nelson they expected a shoot-out and thought neither klansman would be taken alive. "We had in mind killing him, I don't mind telling you," one commented. What police had not anticipated was a last-minute switch in bombers. Instead of the Jackson man law officials hoped to nab, Kathy Ainsworth, a twenty-six year-old wife and school teacher, accompanied Tarrants on the mission.

Except for the police warning, every moment of that early June 30, 1968, was etched on Tommy Tarrants' memory. Now, in a prison office, he carefully reconstructed the incident with no show of bitterness: the plan had been coordinated and approved on "higher Klan levels"; he remembered arriving in Meridian before midnight and meeting Raymond Roberts at a bus stop east of town; he, Roberts, and Kathy Ainsworth talked, then drove to a wooded area where he prepared the bomb.

"I activated it to where it'd be a simple matter to plant it, and we made one pass by the Meyer Davidson home. Then I took Raymond back to where his car was at and told him to stay there in the lounge of the Holiday Inn to have him a good alibi when the bomb went off. Kathy and I went back and circled the house a couple of times. One of the times we were circling it, a car came right up behind us real quick, you know, as we were fixing to turn, and then he turned the other way. I feel sure that was a police car checking us out to make sure who we were. Then we came back and stopped on the street adjacent to the house. Kathy stayed in the car. And I got out. I had a pistol in the waistband of my trousers, and that bomb under my arm in a little box about ... I'd say twenty inches by maybe twelve by eight inches deep or so. Cardboard box from a grocery store. The bomb had twenty-nine sticks of dynamite and a timing device."

He paused briefly, his brown eyes vivid with memory. "I walked about halfway up the driveway of the Davidson home, and when I did, some shooting started. The police said they told me to halt, but I certainly didn't hear them say it if they did. They did shout *after* they started shooting. Perhaps they fired warning shots first because I wasn't struck by the first ones. Maybe they fired warnings shots and then hollered. I don't know." He gave them the benefit of the doubt.

"They started shooting," he continued. "And what I did—I was headed right toward the house—I immediately dropped the bomb and spun around and was running back toward the car. As I did, the pistol fell out of my belt or out of my trousers. And I ran back to the car. They claim I fired a shot at them and that was why they shot up the car and everything and killed Kathy, but I didn't fire a shot a'tall there."

Again, his statement was more matter-of-fact than accusatory. His tone remained controlled, his words spaced, punctuating the action. "The bomb just fell there on the driveway. They charged me with planting, placing a bomb at a residence. That's what they charged me with. But actually, I never got around to placing it because when they started shooting, I dropped it and it just fell there.

"Anyway, I ran back to the car. Kathy was still alive; she was sitting in the car. The police were on a little hill overlooking the car, and I was actually running right toward them, toward the position that they were firing from. When I got in front of the car, I was hit by a load of double-aught buckshot in my right leg. It stunned me for just a second, but I kept going. My momentum was such that I could continue. I got to the door—the driver's door—and Kathy leaned over to open the door and then she was hit with a three-fifty-one rifle round in the neck." He spoke haltingly now. "She ... uh ... told me as I was speeding off that she had been hit ... she fell over ... on the side of the seat, beside me ..."

"Was that the last thing she said?" I interrupted.

Tommy Tarrants nodded slowly. "Yeah ... She said, 'I been hit.' That's all. All she said. And she fell over on the seat beside me. And, uh, I didn't know it at the time ... I didn't know how badly she was hit. I saw, I think, a single bullet hole—I forget what side of her neck it was on—and she lay there on the seat.

"And of course the police got a squad car behind us." He sighed as though fatigued by simply verbalizing the event. "Mike Hatcher was hanging out the window with a shotgun, shooting all along the way. I was driving a Buick Electra, which was a heavy, awkward car, and they were driving a light Ford Custom, so they were able to stay on my tail pretty close. And, well, one of the tires was hit, and I pulled over to the curb, and Mike was hanging out, still shooting, you know. Hanging out the window with that shotgun.

"And when I stopped, I just ... I don't know ... I guess I figured that it was all over with and I might as well end it. And so when I came to a stop, they skidded up behind me and kind of rammed into the back of my car. I was able to get out first. I had a submachine gun in the car, and I just turned around—Mike was getting out with a shotgun—and I turned around and just sprayed their car. Hit him in the chest twice. The other officer ducked down below the dashboard, and he didn't get hit. I had emptied the clip in the gun, so I dropped it in the street, and there I was, standing there ... didn't have anything in my hands. And the guy that was driving the car—his name was Tucker—he apparently had one round left in his shotgun. He stood up after he saw I wasn't still shooting and took a shot at me. Maybe three or four little pellets struck me in various places. Really didn't disable me. Then he got back on the radio to call for help for Mike. And I ran around the corner of the house to get out of his line of sight and . . . I'd lost a lot of blood by then, and I tried to climb over a fence to get further away, but I didn't have the strength and it was an electric fence. So I fell into the bushes and then, uh, I guess about five minutes passed and a lot of police units converged on the area."

Although the two of us were alone in the small prison office, the room seemed to fill with armed officers and gunfire, with tension. "They came up on me in about, oh, five minutes more. I was entering a state of shock. Still conscious, though. Aware of everything that was going on. I was laying there in the bushes, and they shined the lights around me, saw me there, and they turned off the lights. Some of them said, 'Here he is.' Another said, 'Watch out . . . he might have hand grenades or something.' They were shining the light on me all the time and saw my eyes were just barely open. I was just laying there. Didn't have a gun or anything. And I was laying there on my side and they turned off the light and four shots were fired—about as far as from here to that wall. Ten feet, I guess . . ."

"They kept shooting at you?" I asked.

"No, they *started* shooting then," he corrected me. "See, the shooting stopped, been stopped for ten minutes or so because Tucker was on the radio and I had gotten out of sight and in those bushes and was just laying there bleeding. And after they found me, then they turned the light off and four shots were fired, shotgun rounds. Two of 'em hit me here in this arm." He held out his right arm so I could see a three-inch scar near the inside of his elbow. "Two loads of that double-aught buckshot. Nearly tore this arm off. I was laying on this right side and there was about six inches of space between my chest and my arm and the two rounds went in between and hit the dirt. It was a miracle I lived through it. Then they pulled me out of the bushes, and they said, one of them said, 'Is he dead?' and the other one said, 'Naw, the S-O-B's still alive.' "

Tarrants chuckled.

"You can laugh about it now?" I observed.

"Yeah," he chuckled again.

"Can you remember what you were thinking during all this?"

"I was just thinking it was about over for me and that I was just about dead and that I would soon . . ." He groped for a better way to verbalize that moment. "It was just like you turn your adjustable rheostat down on some lights in a room. You can adjust it to where they're bright, to dimmer and dimmer and dimmer, down to a low haze, you know. That's the way it was. Things were just getting dimmer and dimmer. All my sensory perceptions were becoming less and less acute. It was just sort of like life was ebbing away. Flowing out of me."

"You thought you were dying?"

"Yeah, certainly did. And that was fine with me. I thought, Well, boy, everything's lost. Kathy's killed. And here I am, captured, and 'course I've done so much I'd go to the penitentiary for the rest of my life. And so I thought, well, that would be the best thing."

"Were you sorry or regretful at that point that you had done these things?"

"No, not a'tall." He was honest. "The only thing I was sorry about was that Kathy was killed."

At the time, the parents of her fifth-grade students and close friends expressed surprise at the double life of Kathleen Capomacchia Ainsworth. Her husband, aware of her Klan connections but not of her deep involvement, described her as "an angel." Adon Taft, the *Miami Herald*'s religion editor, for whom she had often baby-sat, portrayed her as "an ideal girl from all we knew, the kind of girl we had long told our daughters we would like for them to grow up and be like." Born in Chicago to an Italian juggler and a dancer of Hungarian parentage, she had been reared in Miami, where her mother did domestic work after divorcing her husband. Most remembered young Kathy as a devout churchgoer who taught Sunday school and sang in the choir at Coral Baptist Church in Miami before attending Mississippi College, a conservative Baptist institution near Jackson. If she had any racist or anti-Semitic leanings as a girl, she—unlike her mother—had concealed them. The initial shock of her involvement in the shoot-out grew as the full extent of Kathy Ainsworth's other life came to light. Her purse contained a .25 caliber automatic and membership cards for UKA and the Original Knights. She also belonged to the White Knights of Mississippi and the Americans for the Preservation of the White Race, a Klan front. In her desk at home were manila folders labeled "Klan," "APWR," "bombings," "segregation," "conspiracy," "integration versus segregation," "Cuba," and "civil rights." A Minuteman manual, entitled "We Will Survive" contained hate messages and voluminous instructions for making bombs and firearms. There were also Klan reports and newsletters and assorted racist periodicals, including *The Thunderbolt*.

Now Tommy Tarrants indicated the bombing was not the first Klan violence Kathy Ainsworth had taken part in. The two had met at the Mobile home of Sidney Crockett Barnes to listen to anti-Semitic records with a group that often included her mother. He remembered Kathy as "a real worthwhile human being who was just misguided."

"She was a covert member, involved with the leadership there in Jackson," he recalled. "We had some previous involvement with this sort of thing."

"She had gone on other bombings?" I clarified.

Tarrants hedged. "Well, she had been involved in other radical activity, let's put it that way. I don't want to go into too much detail about her life. She's dead. But she had been involved in more than just a vocal way."

"Would you say that Kathy was willing to do anything for the 'cause'? Was she *that* committed?"

"You might say that. She was about as committed as any."

Although Kathy Ainsworth had been the only woman to participate in overt harassment in the Jackson area, Tommy Tarrants said many had been actively involved in the White Knights. Most were wives of male members.

"I don't want to create the impression that there were as many women as men willing to participate in the violence," he hurriedly added. "But there were a few that were just as willing to go along with violence. Kathy was rare, but she wasn't the only one."

Charged with attempted murder and the attempted bombing, Tommy Tarrants reluctantly agreed to plead not guilty by reason of insanity when it appeared his attorney lacked sufficient evidence to use the entrapment issue. On the stand, Mrs. Doris Tarrants testified that her son had had a normal childhood until the 1963 desegregation of Murphy High School in Mobile, which she said, mentally disturbed him. She said that police officers on horseback and carrying submachine guns at the school appeared to create a disturbing impression on young Tarrants, then a junior. He later joined the NSRP because, she insisted, "he didn't feel he had been treated right."

"He became completely absorbed with fighting Communism," she told the court, and he shied away from former friends, associating more with NSRP members. The family sought psychiatric care, but he refused it because he felt there was nothing wrong with him.

Shortly after the shoot-out, a news story identified Tarrants as the leader of a violent student demonstration. He and fifty-three others had been charged with disorderly conduct. The next summer, when he was seventeen, he was arrested with NSRP's Mobile representative, Bob Smith, and charged with possession of a sawed-off shotgun.

In spite of the testimony of his mother, and of a psychiatrist who described him as suffering from "a severe case of paranoia . . . a form of schizophrenia," the court ruled Tarrants sane. He was convicted of the attempted bombing and sentenced to thirty years' imprisonment. (When he appealed the conviction in May 1970, a state-appointed panel of psychiatrists reiterated the finding of "no evidence of insanity.")

"Even before I got here, I had no intentions of staying," he admitted now. "It was just simply to try and get in as good a position as I could to escape and resume my activity. When I arrived here early in December of sixty-eight, I had my eyes open, evaluating the situation. In July, I had a fairly workable escape plan designed."

"And this was done with the help of the Klan?" I asked.

"Right," Tarrants nodded his head. "Within the institution I needed two inmates to help me accomplish what was necessary to *get* to where the Klan would be waiting. I coordinated it and had a car waiting over there with monitoring equipment to listen to the prison radios and highway patrol frequencies. They were heavily armed, just had *all* kinds of armaments. They were waiting there at a prearranged time. We subdued the guards at the hospital [where Tarrants worked as a lab technician] and went over there, met them and went to a wooded area outside of Jackson. Stayed there about two days. The FBI somehow found out that we were there—probably through an informer—and we—were apprehended. One of the guys that went with me tried to shoot it out with them, and they killed him. Then we were brought back to the penitentiary."

Tarrants leaned forward, his forearms resting on his knees. He was quiet as he ended the chapter that had added another five years to his sentence.

"You were thought of as a dangerous man then, weren't you?"

"Oh, yeah!" he agreed. "The *most* dangerous criminal in Mississippi. They placed me in the maximum security unit. Beefed up their security measures. I stayed there three years by myself in a six by nine cell."

"Were you bitter?" I interrupted.

He studied the question. "More frustrated than anything. Caught in a situation where I couldn't go where I wanted to, do what I wanted to. Didn't have the liberty to move beyond two, three steps in any direction. But I realized I had to make the best out of a bad situation. I started reading a lot. Actually, the way I came *out* of right-wing philosophy and radical ideology was *through* it.

"I developed more than an average interest in philosophy, and I came to see that the explanations the radical right gives for problems are not at all defensible and substantial. The heart of their philosophy is the conspiratorial theory that the Jews—through international banking and what have you—are exerting pressures first here, then there, to bring about revolution and movements, all designed to achieve world domination. But it became more and more obvious to me that you can't just attribute it to a conspiracy. It's an easy answer to a complicated question."

Tommy Tarrants, now twenty-nine, talked with little prompting or questioning by me. He seemed as anxious to discuss why he had repudiated Klankraft as others had been to praise it.

"But then something happened that has really been the major thing in my life, that's changed it so much. I started reading the Bible. And God just really opened my eyes to see how foolish I'd been and I'd ruined my life by breaking His laws and doing my own way, doing my own thing. Sort of rebelling against Him. And God took away a whole lot of stuff that was in my life, like hatred for blacks. Hatred for Jewish people."

"So the easygoing person I'm talking to came about after this," I observed.

He smiled, the gap between his teeth showing. "Right. What I am now is the outgrowth of what happened in that cell when I came to know Jesus Christ."

Was the transformation genuine? I wondered. Or was it expedient? A way to rid himself of the cumbersome sentence? A ticket to the outside? Two ministers had expressed belief in his sincerity. Prison officials, also viewing the change as real, gradually relaxed the tight security. For a time, Tarrants had been allowed to live unsupervised in a guest house behind the superintendent's residence so that he could have privacy to work on college correspondence courses. Now he worked in the prerelease center, teaching classes aimed at helping outgoing inmates readjust to society. He also worked in the chaplain's office and often spoke outside at churches and other institutions.

Not eligible for parole before 1980, Tarrants said he could get out in three months, in November 1976, under a work release program. Whatever the date, he already had plans: he wanted to attend college; he hoped to marry one day; to live a normal life.

How had this clean-cut, soft-spoken prisoner ever been the hardened young man captured that June 30, 1968, a youth once suspected of more than a half-dozen such acts of terror and charged numerous times for illegal possession of firearms—mostly submachine guns and sawed-off shotguns—and with holdups in Jackson and Pine Bluff, Arkansas?

The son of a Mobile, Alabama, real estate agent, he had been reared in what he described as a typical, middle-class home and in the Baptist church. He remembered himself as an average youngster. Mischievous, but no more so than other boys his age. He had been somewhat of a loner, with little interest in extracurricular activities and dating. Yet even his mother—by her court account—had not considered him a problem.

At the time of the Meridian shoot-out, acquaintances told the press that Tarrants had viewed John Dillinger as a hero and by age thirteen was a proficient bomb maker. As a teenager, he was said to have openly boasted that he could take "rubber bands and a little wire" and convert an M-1 carbine into a fully automatic weapon. Some also told of overhearing him mutter, "Damn Jews, I'm going to kill them!" Now, Tarrants refuted most of those claims but freely admitted that at an early age he was known to local police. After the capture, Mobile Police Chief James J. Robinson told the press: "He has been a thorn in our side ever since he was seventeen years old."

While still a teen-ager, he had made regular trips to Birmingham, to the then NSRP headquarters. NSRP leader Edward Fields had reservations about him and his rabid statements. Once, Fields reportedly had a party functionary drive Tarrants to a bus station with instructions not to let him out of sight until the vehicle pulled out for Mobile. Yet Tarrants was soon back, making his regular visits to party headquarters. His first arrest, and the last before the attempted bombing, had been with right-wing leaders: the one with NSRP's Bob Smith; the latter, with Sam Bowers, the reputed Imperial Wizard of the supersecret, superviolent White Knights of Mississippi. When stopped for reckless driving with Bowers one day after his twenty-first birthday, Tarrants was charged with possession of a submachine gun like the weapon allegedy used in the Meridian shoot-out.

Now Tarrants speculated that his path to Parchman had begun in 1963, while he was working in Barry Goldwater's presidential campaign and became associated with members of the John Birch Society.

"I began reading their literature, and I said, 'Wow, this big conspiracy that they're talking about. Communists in the State Department and trying to eliminate the government and all these things.' I began to wonder why something wasn't being done. And I didn't have much confidence in the government because the Birch literature suggests that the government itself is undermined. So I started thinking some kind of decisive action might be more appropriate than letting things be undermined by creeping socialism. And that made me more susceptible to organizations that proposed force and violence as an alternative rather than pursuing the political alternatives that were available. I thought things had gone too far to work it out politically. Of course, in retrospect, I can see that was not accurate."

"Do you think that had anything to do with your age?" I wondered.

Tarrants reflected. "I don't doubt that it did. I had a very limited perspective from which to view things. And having somewhat of a compulsive nature, I think that contributed a lot. It did set me in a frame of mind where I was much more willing to consider force and violence and clandestine activities as a proper way of dealing with the problems at hand. I started soaking up, absorbing the literature of the States

Rights Party and the Klan and kindred movements, and I developed more and more a hatred of the blacks and a hatred of the federal government for excluding the states' rights."

'What about Jews?' I probed.

"That came later," he explained. "The way these things work . . . most white Southerners can be appealed to on the basis of racial prejudice. Just like blacks. They can get your attention with the integration issue. And then once a person is gripped by that, he can be given 'insights'—they would call them—into the *real* problem behind this, and they begin to introduce the Jewish thing. They say, 'Now the blacks aren't really the problem. It's the Jews who are behind them, who are inciting and instigating all this and they remain in the background and are using the blacks as pawns.'

"I don't think the people on the radical right are themselves deliberately seeking to deceive people and lead them," he speculated. "They believe this themselves. But the people who write the literature have been very selective in the data they include in order to present the picture that coincides with what they want to believe. And to me, it's not a matter of deliberate, willful misrepresentation. It's rather a question of those persons becoming so blinded to truth, by virtue of hatred and prejudice, that they are incapable of objectively assessing a situation."

Tarrants seemed to be mentally taking apart the biased reasoning he spoke of and examining it as if it were one of his former time bombs. "The rationalizations of the radical right are intriguing to me. They almost have it down to an art, where they can hold the Jews responsible for everything from crop failure in Siberia to an earthquake in Equador. It's a very difficult delusional system to penetrate. They have every little answer to every little question, to the exclusion of a great deal of other truth that would change things a great deal if it were taken into consideration."

His own transformation to the radical right's thinking took several months, probably a year at most, he speculated. His hostility shifted from blacks to Jews and grew in intensity.

"It wasn't but a small distance to make a transition from strong hostility to overt action," he continued. "The people I was involved with had a strong propensity for violence, for clandestine things, and I fell right in with it wholeheartedly. When something was to be done and I was asked—some minor act of terrorism like shooting a window out of a house late at night to scare the occupants—well, I volunteered."

"Without being asked?"

"Initially, these things were discussed and I'd volunteer. But I came to the point where I'd just volunteer without being asked and *even* conceive different plans and strategies to accomplish the objectives of the organization. I began to distinguish myself, so to speak. I had a rather adventurous spirit. Enjoyed a lot of excitement and was daring and whatever along with all of this."

The thrill-seeking trait became more pronounced as he became more deeply involved and met people considered "influential" in the movement. When I asked him to name names, he deferred politely, saying that it would be unwise, that he preferred to speak in generalities, before continuing. "Having distinguished myself by various acts of daring, I soon came to be highly trusted."

"Were you somewhat of a hero?" I asked.

Tarrants tilted his head. "Among certain segments, I would say this. I was a very dependable and resourceful and committed member of the radical right."

"And you felt you were doing something good?"

"Right. I thought in my own mind, in my own way, in view of the belief system I held, this was appropriate action. As time went on, I became acquainted with people that were responsible [for planning the violence]. One was a high-ranking military officer, and I was impressed. . . ." He reconsidered. "I don't want to paint the picture I was a poor victim of circumstance. That all these people influenced and made me do things. I was a very willing participant."

His parents had been unable to discourage his activities, and even police warnings went unheeded. For three or four years, he continued his acts of harassment and violence. Law enforcement officers never were able to nab him but gradually closed in, until finally he was forced to transfer his area of operation from Mobile to Mississippi, "commuting" for a time between the two, even enrolling in Mobile Baptist College. He had been loosely associated with the Klan in Alabama but never became a member until he met Sam Bowers and joined the White Knights. Free at the time on appeal of his conviction in the murders of the civil rights workers, Bowers initially was suspicious. But as Tarrants proved himself as a terrorist, the two became close.

"How would you describe Bowers?" I probed.

"He is very intelligent. I have no question about that." He was emphatic. "And I believe he was—like I was—indoctrinated, brainwashed, whatever. I don't know the proper word for it. Absorbed into an ideology that took on the awe of a holy cause and blinded his mind to everything else. I think Sam believes what he is doing is right and has the sanction of God and all the rest. But I think he's deceived in this. He is wrong."

"Was he sort of a hero to you?"

"You might say that," he agreed, then altered his response. "I don't know if hero would be the best word for it. I had a great deal of admiration for him and stood somewhat in awe of his position, I guess. I didn't follow him blindly, but I had good respect for his intelligence. He was cunningly clever, a cunning individual," he said thoughtfully. "He had that about him."

When I asked for examples of Bowers' shrewdness, Tarrants became somewhat nostalgic as he remembered the intrigue and adventure that, for most people, exist only in movies and books.

"Different ways he would devise to evade the FBI in their attempts to follow or tap phones. He was very resourceful. Probably the best around. He had a compass in his automobile, and he could just about go from one end of the state to the other on dirt roads without ever traveling on a main highway very far, so his car wouldn't be spotted."

"How did he bypass phone tapping?"

"That's something difficult to get around. You just use the telephone as little as possible, and you have prearranged signals, phrases, words that have a certain assigned meaning to both parties."

He grinned remembering. "One night we were at his place discussing some matters of business, and I don't think we spoke over a half-dozen words. Most of it, we were writing notes to one another. I'd write out a question, and he'd write down an answer. When we finished, all the papers were bundled up and burned, and the ashes—you know you can reconstruct from a burned piece of paper sometimes, the FBI can—and so he took them and crumpled them up and put them in some water and poured them out. That's going to an extreme, but there certainly wasn't anyway for *that* to fall into the hands of the FBI."

Tarrants laughed, caught up in verbally reliving those clandestine meetings that were to lead him to Parchman and Bowers to a federal penitentiary near Tacoma, Washington. "We used to meet a great deal in deserted areas. I'd come in from Mobile. We'd have a prearranged time and place of meeting and alternate places and times. And I'd come in from wherever I was—Mobile, North Carolina, or Jackson—and come to the appointed place at the appointed time and meet deep in a wooded area, on a pig trail that turns off an old dirt road and goes way down. That kind of stuff. We used to meet a great deal like that. And we'd take care to look over our cars and make sure there wasn't any transmitters concealed—the FBI used to use crystal transmitters to bug cars with sometimes. Of course, we'd use various evasion tactics, too, when we were coming to the meeting place to make sure that there weren't any cars following us for far distances. Then, oftentimes, we wouldn't sit in the car to talk, lest we had missed something, you know, that was there. So we'd get out of the car and maybe walk twenty-five, fifty feet away from it and talk in low tones. Planning, discussing, various things." He chuckled. "He could teach the CIA some things in covert operations if they'd listen to him."

For the most part, their conversations revolved around "business." Occasionally, they discussed their mutual interest in guns and history—the South, the Confederacy, the Klan—but mostly, it was "the cause" and fighting "the enemy."

"Radicals aren't like other people," Tarrants theorized. "Their interest patterns are not balanced. Their minds pretty much focus—at least the ones I've been with—on seeing the world through radical eyes, and everything is interpreted or discussed in light of that set of lenses that one sees with. It's terribly boring. Everything was geared around that kind of stuff. There was never anything on a cultural or social nature. It was all . . . just a lot of people with a one-track mind."

In the days before his capture, which signaled the end to the White Knights' reign of terror, Tarrants estimated the group had units in the southern two-thirds of the state. He described it as "well organized."

"When you say organized, do you mean the leadership, that Bowers knew about things beforehand?" I asked.

"Not all things," he speculated. "I think some Klan units undertook certain projects on their own, assuming that it would be all right and, of course, it was. The things that were done were agreeable to Klan leadership, but I don't think the leadership knew everything that happened before it happened. It wasn't that tightly knit, tightly run. Sam probably got credit for more things than he actually had his fingers in. But as far as masterminding different things, I believe he's capable of doing it, even now. In the past, I suspect he had a good deal of involvement. I know he's certainly *had* some. I wasn't privy to everything."

In its final report, the HUAC had indicated that the White Knights' Bureau of Investigation could authorize and participate in acts of violence, but that a murder—or "Number 4," as it was referred to within the organization—had to be approved by the Imperial Wizard, who was supposed to obtain the advice and counsel of the chaplain.

"What about the night that led to where you are now? That particular bombing? Can you recall when that was set up and the details of that?"

"Two of the Klan members down there in Meridian," Tarrants started, indicating he meant the two informers, "were in with myself in doing the actual planning. But it had been coordinated previous to that—the idea and the approval of it—on higher levels, which I'll say without going into any . . ."

I interrupted. "Are you talking about higher Klan levels?"

"Right. There had been a conference and it had been discussed and approval was given. It was just a question of arranging the details, and the details were arranged in conjunction with the Roberts brothers. And I'm sure you know the rest of the story, that Jack Nelson brought out in the L.A. *Times*. He was very accurate in his investigation of it," he ended quietly.

"Did they sort of encourage and entice you to do it?"

"Welll, lot of people have asked me about the entrapment issue. My feelings on it—and I'm very comfortable with those feelings—are this, that I was a willing participant. And if I were an FBI agent faced with the situation there in Mississippi at that particular time, I would not hesitate to use the same methods they used to get me."

While Tarrants hadn't heard from Bowers since his own trial, he nevertheless was skeptical of news articles that said his former cohort—who had earned a college degree in religion before his prison release on March 21, 1976—had changed. "I feel he's the same person as when I knew him before. I don't have any reason to change that judgment. He's still intelligent and has a lot of ability and talent and is good at influencing people. These things remain true always. He's had six years to arrange and organize and refine his thinking, plus he's had the advantage of being able to get some college training in areas of religious studies, which could weld to his strong racial views and give him a stronger grip and influence on people."

"So he's much more of a threat?" I summarized.

"If you wanted to put it in those terms, yes."

Another source close to the White Knights had told me that two days after Bowers got out of prison "they were back in business," and Tarrants agreed. The other source had estimated the White Knights had never numbered more than twenty-five members—"That's all it took to do what they did"—and was now down to probably a dozen. Tarrants could not confirm the figures.

"But it still exists?" I probed.

"Yeah, all the people that were in it are still around. The organization never does completely evaporate, and if the conditions were right, it could be just as strong, or stronger, than it was in those days."

Contrary to what others told me, Tarrants said the White Knights had held rallies, but always under tight security and in secluded pastures. "They were pretty much like ordinary Klan groups, except they were more violent, more openly committed to the use of violence."

Although he had joined the White Knights *after* the murders of the civil rights workers and black leader Vernon Dahmer, Tarrants was certain the White Knights were responsible for most things they were accused of. He said the organization had a number of small "commando" groups responsible for the violence.

"Do you think there are still those types of inner circles?"

"Let's face it, I'm the only one that's here in the penitentiary that used to be in it, and the rest of them are still out there. And whether they are welded together in an organized unit right now or not, the raw material is still there and if they came together—if events precipitated it—they could come together in just a short while and once again be a functioning entity."

"What made them different?" I wondered aloud. "Why were they more violent than other Klan groups?"

He pondered the question. "You have some people in Mississippi that have some very violent feelings toward blacks, and some, toward Jews. But I think the thing that made the White Knights so violent is they sought more to recruit that type of person and to control him, you know, to have them organized into a unit where they could use his potential for violence. It was the leadership, more, and the organizational structure. The basic philosophy that they had was more that way; therefore, they attracted people suitable to looking that way at things."

He described the bombings in Meridian as "part of an overall campaign to inspire terror against the enemies of the Klan all over . . . Meridian, Jackson." When I asked if he were in on all of them, he politely explained he did not want to incriminate himself, but conceded, "I was not unaware of what was going on and was involved in some of it, planning it, or directing it, or participating in the execution of whatever the project was."

"How did you learn about dynamite and bombs?" I probed.

"Studying and reading," he answered simply. "It was a challenge to me, to enter into an unknown situation and be able to gain a bit of understanding and expertise. And as far as explosives and stuff like that, I went to the college library, to Spring Hill College, and did some studying on it. The public library in Mobile, I think, had some field manuals. And so I got a pretty good idea, and then I started experimenting. Dynamite was easy to get. All you had to do was go order it."

"Nobody ever questioned you when you went to buy it?"

He shook his head. "I used a very circuitous route in obtaining it, but it was the easiest thing in the world to get dynamite, if you knew where to go."

"Can you recall any of your feelings after a bombing, say, after the first time you bombed? Did you feel any guilt?"

"There was no feeling of guilt," he acknowledged. "The sense of accomplishment would be a more accurate description of it. I felt like I was doing the right thing by carrying out clandestine activities against a segment of the population that was a menace to the American way of life. To start off, it was sort of random violence—shooting out windows at the home of a civil rights leader, civil rights lawyer, people like that. Agitating, you know. The only feelings I can recall back then would be a certain amount of nervousness and apprehension at the thought of possibly getting caught. But as far as any moral feelings about the rightness or wrongness, I felt like it was right. I was completely indoctrinated, brainwashed, willingly so."

Tarrants considered himself fortunate that no one had been killed in the violence he participated in and resented news stories that portrayed him as an assassin.

"But would you have done it if you thought somebody was going to get killed? Would that have stopped you?" I pressed.

"I don't think so," he answered softly. "I don't think it would have stopped me because I had so much hatred in my heart for black people and Jews that it wouldn't have deterred me."

Looking back on those years between ages sixteen and twenty-one, Tommy Tarrants pondered what had made him "Mississippi's most dangerous criminal."

"I think there is a certain personality structure peculiar to radicals, and I believe I had it—a combination of those traits. Because of my cultural setting being what it was, it took the expression of a klansman. But I believe it's the same basic personality type you'd probably find in Mark Rudd and the SDS guys and Bernadette Dorn . . . the people on the other side of the fence. I believe that more people get into radicalism more from inner needs. There are a lot of psychological factors that cause them to become so wrapped up in it. A need to belong. Feel like you are a part of something. Accepted. A need to feel worthwhile."

"So you felt you didn't belong?"

"Yeah," he admitted. "There are some frustrations along the line that you feel you haven't accomplished what you should. Strong ego needs play a definite part in it. And a need to be recognized. All these things are put together in different degrees in radical personalities and a certain compulsiveness and nonconformity. Nonconformity is one of the main characteristics."

"Where do you think these things came from in your life?"

"I think along the way I developed an inferiority complex, and that gave rise to various other problems. By the time all this came up in high school—this integration thing—there were needs there for recognition and for acceptance that were better met among the radical fringe than were being met in the social setting I was in at the time. It was very reinforcing when I was in that. The more I'd do and get patted on the back and be accepted by my peers in the radical movement, that was more esteem that came to me, more recognition and a sense of worthwhileness and belonging that . . .

"If you want to tack it down and nail it down to one thing, that'd be the foremost thing, I think it's a problem that all of us have in one degree or another—and deal with it in various ways—which was simply ego and self-centeredness, wanting to glorify me and make me look better. We all have that within us and it comes out in various ways. And that, I suppose, was at the heart of it."

Across the state, in Meridian, Mike Hatcher—the patrolman critically wounded by Tarrants—was now assistant police chief. It was night, and the station was quiet as he related the shoot-out as he remembered it. The details were much as Tommy Tarrants had described them. Thirty- .
one at the time, Hatcher had been in one of the patrol cars assigned to seal off the area to prevent the bombers' escape. Shortly before the confrontation, when it was too late to change their strategy, the police had learned a female was in the car.

"We weren't expecting a woman," he recalled. "We didn't know what the heck she was doing there, whether she was innocent or what. He could have picked her up and brought her along for the ride. She could have even been a hostage." He had hesitated to shoot, queasy and unsure—like the other officers—about firing on a female. But looking back, he was positive he wouldn't be hesitant again.

"I go by that house every day," he continued. "I look over there, and most of the time I do think about it. Not to the extent that it bothers me. Mostly, I think of it as an experience . . . something I learned something from. I don't look at it as something I'm sorry for or that I lost anything. My instinct of survival is going to be much better if anything like that happened again."

Tommy Tarrants had told of Hatcher stopping by his hospital room and shaking hands after the police officer was released. "I don't think he holds any hard feelings toward me." Tarrants had been confident. "I don't toward him."

But Hatcher did not share that forgiveness. He had visited the man who fired on him to show "I was a much better man than he was, and that I was up and ready to go." He pointed to his left breast pocket. One bullet was still lodged near his heart. "I have no use for him."

In February 1977, I received a letter from Tommy Tarrants. The return address was a box number at the University of Mississippi. Released from Parchman on December 13, 1976, a week before his thirtieth birthday, he was preparing to teach New Testament Greek at a church school or a seminary.

20

James Venable: The Wizard of Stone Mountain

Stone Mountain, Georgia

The men were out back under some shade trees letting their dinner settle when I drove up. A screen door banged, and three women crossed the yard toward my car. The larger one, a narrow ribbon holding red curls away from her face, met me halfway.

"Come on," she ordered in a hospitable but firm tone. "We're going to feed you, then you can talk to Mister Venable."

I declined the invitation, but Bobbye Kinnard—James Venable's long-time secretary—hustled me inside. The large kitchen was fragrant with Sunday dinner odors typical of the South I grew up in: ham and roast, a half-dozen fresh vegetables, hot rolls and iced tea. A dog that looked part German shepherd slept on the floor, along with two "mixed breeds," and a Siamese cat curled up on a chair.

Bobbye Kinnard introduced Venable's elder sister, Margaret Langley; his niece, Corribel; and a neighbor who had come by after church. Then she resumed washing dishes, talking nonstop about her boss's role as defense attorney for the Black Muslims and of Gary Steven Krist, convicted of the 1968 kidnapping and live burial of millionairess Barbara Jane Mackle. Behind her back, Corribel, a sturdy gray-haired woman, complained, "She talks too much." Long after my plate was emptied, I sat with the women, captive to Bobbye Kinnard's monologue. Finally, she led me into the yard past the men to a small, blond-brick building she said was Venable's office.

Inside, the National Knights' seventy-two-year-old Imperial Wizard stood to greet me. He was short and frail, and his ears, like his bulbous nose and cheeks, were red, more from age or alcohol than the sun. He wore baggy trousers and, in spite of the outside heat, a long-sleeved sport shirt buttoned to the neck.

Venable introduced a dapper man seated at a desk as Gene Hall and another, opposite him, as Pete Lumpkin, former Grand Dragon of Georgia and now Imperial Klaliff. Then he sat in a straight-back chair, occasionally twiddling his thumbs as he boasted about his family lineage, which included ancestors who migrated to England with William the Conqueror, the first man operated on under ether, an uncle who practiced law with Woodrow Wilson, and another who was president of the Georgia senate. Venable, in his own right, had served three terms as mayor of Stone Mountain. After graduating as a civil engineer from Georgia Tech, he had helped lay out the nearby Atlanta airport before he switched careers and entered law school. He spoke in rambling sentences, linked together in an unending chain, relying on down-home phrases—sometimes scorching, sometimes colorful—to express what seemed to be the opinions of a cranky old man as much as a diehard segregationist. Some had described his courtroom manner as similar, yet at one point he had been called "the most experienced criminal lawyer in Georgia and a master of court procedures." One writer had noted his "super-sensitivity to discrepancies in testimony" and that he had "the obvious cunning of a fox."

The old man was equally proud of his Klan lineage: his father, several uncles, and a now-deceased brother had been members, and his maternal grandfather was one of several Reconstruction klansmen credited with ridding Milledgeville—Georgia's capital at the time—of carpetbaggers, scalawags, and freed blacks. His uncle, Samuel Hart Venable, had allowed William Joseph Simmons to use Stone Mountain, then owned by the Venable Brothers' granite business, for the cross lighting that marked the Klan's 1915 revival. Jimmy Venable had been initiated into the Hooded Order in 1924 and had been personal friends of the procession of Imperial Wizards that followed Simmons. He had also served as legal Klonsel to Robert Shelton until Venable formed his own National Knights in 1963. In the sixties, he and his followers— estimated by ADL at between seven and nine thousand, most of them in Georgia—were viewed by newsmen and the law as more violent and chaotic than UKA. But now even officials conceded that the Klan, for Venable, had become little more than a hobby and a fraternal organization that consisted of maybe two hundred members, possibly fewer since he and five of his Grand Dragons—including Dale Reusch— parted ways in 1975. In spite of the dwindling numbers and the fact that Stone Mountain belonged to the state, the National Knights continued to host annual Labor Day rallies around its base on land still owned by the family. And what the Klan now lacked in size, it more than made up for in memories for Jimmy Venable, who fondly recalled the Thanksgiving night rally Simmons staged on the mountain "because it was the largest solid rock in the world." While his uncle had not attended the inaugural rally, he had joined the Hooded Order soon thereafter.

"The number of men there was only sixteen," Venable said. "All of them were merchants, doctors, lawyers, ministers of the gospel, people of *allll* walks of life. And two of the *original* Klan members of eighteen sixty-five and sixty-six was along. I've forgotten their names. But they was friends of Colonel Simmons, and on that occasion they knighted him. His uniform and all his things were quite different. No other klansman, no other Imperial Wizard has ever had the regalia he had."

"What was he like?" I asked.

Venable went into an adjoining room and returned with a stack of oversized photographs. He pointed to a figure in a funny-faced mask and regal robe and crown. "That's William Joseph Simmons, right there," he said. "He was a tall fella. Wore a Texas hat. The man, he was a *very* brilliant fella. Perhaps the most learned klansman that ever lived. He wrote all the ritualistic degree work of the Klan ... And that's Nathan Bedford Forrest the Second, there."

"That's the son ..." I started.

"Of *General* Nathan Bedford Forrest," Venable answered proudly. "He was the Grand Dragon of Georgia from about nineteen hundred and nineteen to nineteen hundred and twenty-four. See, history don't record these things. They *don't* want it to be known that Forrest Avenue in Atlanta was named after General Nathan Bedford Forrest. *I* went to school with Nathan Bedford Forrest the Third at ol' Tech High School in nineteen twenty-one, two, and three. So I knew the whole family except the original general that died long before my day."

"You really grew up knowing the Klan," I remarked.

Venable beamed. "That's right. Fact, all my life I been closely related to it. I was initiated over at the mountain, on the side of it over here. I was with the Klan when it was the *most* powerful organization in America, politically. We had nearly seven million members. It dominated the U-nited States Senate and Congress. Councilmen. State officials. Many governors. We had *four* presidents that belonged, but they ain't gonna tell ya that. Ain't gonna print it. In nineteen hundred and twenty-three, the Klan *itself* conducted a ritualistic burial ceremony in Marion, Ohio. I got pictures. Seein' is believin', ain't it?"

"For whom?" I asked.

"I could tell you, but you wouldn't believe me," he grumbled before he gave in. "Conducted the funeral of Warren G. Harding. *He* was a klansman. Woodrow Wilson was a klansman. Tell ya two more, but they'd be an embarrassment."

Pete Lumpkin contributed "Harry Truman," and Venable sneered, "Ol' Harry Truman was a traitor to the Klan."

"Don't forget Hugo," Gene Hall offered sarcastically.

"Yeah, well, ol' Hugo Black. He was a damn traitor," Venable fussed. "The Klan, under Roosevelt, they were *so* powerful they supported Roosevelt and got Hugo Black nominated as a Supreme Court justice. Then he turned against the Klan."

Venable held up a photograph of a group of men, pointing to one. "He was sheriff—James I. Lowery—sheriff for *over* fifty years of Fulton County, Atlanta, Georgia. This gentleman right back of him, Judge Paul Etheridge, he represented the Klan. He was on the Imperial Board and judge of the Superior Court. He used to be county commissioner. This picture was taken nineteen hundred and twenty-one. This is governor of Georgia, Clifford Walker. Better known as 'Whisperin' Cliff'."

"Was he in the Klan at the time?"

"Oh yeah, he was on the Imperial Board. Georgia had *six* governors in the Klan. Governor named Ed Rivers. Ol' man Gene Talmadge was in the Klan—Herman Talmadge's daddy. Three others, I've forgotten . . ." When he couldn't remember, he moved on. "Six mayors of Atlanta belonged to the Klan."

Although I could find no evidence to back the story about Harding's burial—repeated by several Klan leaders—Venable's information on the Hooded Order's involvement in Georgia politics proved accurate. Paul S. Etheridge had served simultaneously as Imperial Klonsel and a Fulton County commissioner, and Clifford Walker—eventually nick-named "Kautious Kleagle Kliff"—had promised that if the organization or its members got into trouble, he would not report it to the press. The Invisible Empire also helped to elect as governor E. D. Rivers, a former Klan lecturer, as well as Eugene and Herman Talmadge. The father's membership made national news in 1941 when he pardoned eight klansmen found guilty of flogging. At the time, the governor recalled that he himself had once flogged a black and added: "I wasn't in such bad company. The Apostle Paul was a flogger in his life, then confessed, reformed, and became one of the greatest powers of the Christian church. That proves to me that good people can be misguided and do bad things."

Now Jimmy Venable grew nostalgic about the old days, when the Klan's national office took in forty thousand dollars a day, when Simmons dreamed of establishing a university system "to teach patriotism and Americanism," and when the Invisible Empire owned millions of dollars worth of property, including the elaborate Imperial Palace in Atlanta. The universities and the palace, like the Klan itself, had been victims of the move by Hiram Evans to oust Simmons: only one university ever became a reality, and the Imperial Palace—"in the most swankiest, the highest-priced property in Atlanta"—had been sold to the Catholics and replaced with a church.

Bobbye Kinnard, who had entered the office, urged Venable to tell me about Bishop Gerald O'Hara inviting Evans to the church dedication but related the story herself. ". . . He invited Hiram Evans and his family to come hear the first services that were preached in American tongue, not Latin. And Hiram Evans told him that had he known that the Catholic services were that beautiful, he never would have said ugly things about 'em and that he wanted to apologize to the world. There was a writing in the paper about it."

The versions I read had not had such a pleasant ending. Many klansmen, it seemed, were furious about Evans' attendance at a Catholic ceremony, and he soon relinquished the Imperial Wizardship to James A. Colescott. But neither Evans' own downfall nor Bobbye Kinnard's story appeased Jimmy Venable. "Ol' Doctor Evans was a fake. He was from Texas. When he got control of the Klan, he abused it. He was in it for money and publicity and to sell its political influence. Why they begin to take in undesirables jist for votin' purposes." His voice lowered. "They *stole* the Klan away from Colonel Simmons. I never will forget it. It was a terrible thing for Colonel Simmons. He finally survived, but he never was the same man after that."

"I read that one of the problems Colonel Simmons had was with Edward Clarke and . . ." I started.

"E. Y. Clarke was a damn renegade—'scuse the language," Venable barged into my sentence. "He and a woman named Tyler were in advertisin' business. Colonel Simmons picked him up with some of the other people as his advisers and entered into a contract to go over this country and to organize and solicit membership. They built the Klan real good. Of course, they were paid large sums to do it, but they were lax in taking in membership. People who was really not qualified. Had we been careful, our country would not be in the shape it is today. *Never* would there have been any integration. There would have been the separation of the races, that is, the Negro element there." Venable seemed unfazed by the disclosure in 1965 that his own Great Titan of Idaho was a black Catholic.

His ranting shifted from the past to the present. Things weren't like they used to be. The two-room brick building in his back yard served the purpose of the once-grand Imperial Palace. The thousands who once flocked to Stone Mountain had been reduced to a mere handful. Even the leaders were not of the stature of Simmons and the governors and mayors and other officials he had grown up with.

"Most of our Klan leaders today are in it for publicity and money, and not for the sake of this country and the white race," he accused. "There's very few dedicated klansmen in this country left. Real dedicated white people. I don't know of a Klan leader in this country that would sacrifice and give his time and his money and his life to save this country and our flag and our race. I don't know of a one."

"Not any?" I asked.

He reconsidered. "Probably I'd be the only one. I've got some dedicated people in my organization that feel as I do, would sacrifice their life and their money and their time. But you take the Shelton group. He's in it for money and publicity. He was kicked out of the Klan for stealin' money. Edwards kicked him out for it over in Alabama. He's an unworthy klansman. You take that Duke, young upstart. He's a *dis*grace to the Klan. He's in it for money and publicity. He's not in it to save the race or to save the country. Most of the leaders don't know anything about the Klan. They didn't come up in the ol' school like some of our ol' people. Now like up in Pennsylvania, Ohio, there's a few ol' klansmen left. Gene, over here, and Pete's been in the Klan for years. But there's very few of 'em left, from the old school."

As Venable hurled the familiar thievery charges at one klansman after another, it occurred to me that he had been branded "senile" and "disorganized" but never "a money grabber." Even competitors and adversaries had described him as generous and told of being his house guests. During the HUAC hearings, he had told investigators the National Knights were "in the hole" and *owed* him seven hundred dollars. Venable had been one of the few Klan leaders to talk instead of taking the Fifth. Now he ridiculed those who had ended up in prison for contempt of Congress.

"Wasn't no need in any of 'em goin'," he swore. "They didn't have sense enough . . . Their lawyer didn't keep 'em out of prison."

"How did you keep from going?" I asked.

"There wasn't nothin' to it," he shrugged. "The only thing they was interested in was violence and where'd the money go. My books was nineteen thousand in my pocket in the red."

Recently, several disgruntled klansmen had accused him of turning his membership records over to the committee. However, in the testimony I read, Venable had identified a few of his leaders but claimed ignorance in terms of names and numbers, insisting his organization was "young" and not well organized. Now, when I asked if he had given the HUAC his records, he repeated his disclaimer.

"Don't keep a membership record for that reason. Somebody could steal it and expose the Klan. I only know a few of the leaders, that's all. *Don't* wanta know anything."

His excuse of not knowing was easy to believe. On a later visit to his law offices, I asked Bobbye Kinnard if he had been a good organizer in his younger days, and she answered, "No, he couldn't even organize his own family." Now, when I asked for people to contact during my travels, he pulled out a worn address book and thumbed through it, reading from bits and pieces of paper tucked between the pages. He estimated the National Knights had Grand Dragons in about forty states, although the FBI knew of organized units in only eight. As for actual size of his membership, Venable vowed, "I couldn't tell. Never try to keep numbers."

"Is your group smaller than it used to be?" I asked as he scanned business cards and scraps of papers.

"Naw." He looked up momentarily. "It's growin' all over the country because of this racial trouble. It's growin' *faster* in the North than the South. The South has fell back."

As he scoured the address book, Bobbye Kinnard chatted. "I'm real sorry Ginger didn't come today and bring her little girl. He's got the nicest daughter and granddaughter," she informed me. "He's got a nice daughter, too, that lives in Pennsylvania. She's got a darling baby."

". . . Here's a name," Venable interrupted. "Ingram. I-N-G-R-A-M. He's in Hibbs—H-I-B-B-S, Pennsylvania . . ."

"Jim," Bobbye Kinnard tried again to get his attention. "Little Bonnie's real sick."

"Here's another one. K-I . . ." He looked up, toward Bobbye Kinnard. "What?"

"Little Bonnie's real sick with a bad throat."

He returned to the address book. "K-I-L-L-I-A-N. Killian. George Killian."

"What does your Klan stand for today?" I changed the subject.

"Well, only two weapons we can do is to advocate . . ." he started, then backed up. "We're doin' *more* things. The Klan of eighteen hundred and sixty-six had only about three things they could fight: the carpetbaggers, the scalawags, and the nigger element. 'Course, we had Catholics. They've always been against us. But they were minor things. The Klan of nineteen hundred and fifteen, we had many, many things to fight, but we got a *thousand* now today to fight, where they only had a hundred."

The redness of his nose and cheeks spread as he lambasted the Jewish control of the banks and news media, the ADL and kosherized food. The ADL was "the most deadly enemy to this country today," he said, his voice growing sinister, then callous. "Ever' one of 'em oughta be shot and killed for spying on the white race, the Christian white people of this country."

Unlike most modern-day Klans, Venable still held equal fury for Catholics. "We don't accept 'em under *no* conditions," he said, emphasizing they excluded themselves because "they owe allegiance to the pope." Jews could not belong, he added, because they did not believe in Christ. Nevertheless, he boasted, "I hold no ill will against any race, color, or creed. I sent my two daughters to Catholic schools. They got the best schools in the world. Fact, I got a niece that married a Jew. Some of the finest clients I got are Jews, you know. They know how I feel. Some of the best friends I got are Jews and Catholics."

Bobbye Kinnard offered, "Mister Venable never had a greater friend than Sam Rothberg."

"One of Atlanta's richest Jews," Venable noted. "He thought I was walkin' Jesus. He and I've done many favors. In fact, I had a Catholic partner one time. Trained him." Venable defended himself with the help of Bobbye Kinnard, the two of them talking at once about a Catholic orphan from New Jersey he took in four years ago and helped get started as a lawyer.

"Never charged him a cent," she concluded.

Venable also insisted he never let his feelings interfere with his legal practice. "If a Jew hires me, I'll fight for him jist as I would my own race. Same way with a nigger. He's entitled to legal representation whether it's a civil or criminal case. I don't think about race when it comes in a court of justice." But even if he did not allow his racial beliefs to interfere with his legal practice, other people did. He had, he said, lost many lawsuits because he was a klansman.

Besides defending numerous klansmen—including Robert Shelton when he and the Klan were enjoined from interfering with the Freedom Riders in Montgomery—Venable boasted of representing a Communist and the Black Muslims. In the late fifties, he had also served as the attorney for J. B. Stoner, now chairman of the NSRP, and for George Bright, one of five NSRP members accused of bombing an Atlanta synagogue.

"You represented James Earl Ray, didn't you?" I asked.

He shook his head, explaining, "Art Hanes—used to be mayor of Birmingham—was supposed to, then Percy Foreman got in the case. He finally pled him guilty, but that's a foolish thing. In my opinion, if he'd 've tried that fella, I don't believe they'd have had twelve men or women that ever would have convicted him under that evidence there, 'cause Luther King, he had a bad reputation for disturbin' the peace, especially in Alabama durin' that Selma march. That's a man in prison, an' he done the world a favor by killin' that nigger," Venable ranted. "He's the worst troublemaker the nation, the world's ever known, and yet they honor him as the great emancipator of the nigger race."

"But do you feel murder was legitimate?"

"Well, I don't know whether it was legitimate . . . ," he stalled.

"I mean, do you condone it?"

"Under this, I would have to condone it, because he done the world—not only his own race—but he done the white man and the red man and the brown man, alllll races of the world, a favor!"

Venable's thoughts were as unorganized as his Klan and his book-keeping. His racialist blasts were scrambled with boasts of his own good deeds. "Over here, when I was mayor, I gave the city a piece of property for a nigger cemetery and put in there they couldn't charge none of them for diggin' the grave. *Ever'* nigger over there respects me. Same way in Atlanta. I got *worlds* of clients there. I've always respected 'em, but I don't believe in social equality.

"The one thing the Klan has carried the banner for is the white race. Had it not been for our forefathers—the Klan of eighteen hundred and sixty-six and the Klan of nineteen fifteen—we would have been a mulatta race in this country today. They—all of their acts and doin's and their belief is based on the Holy Writ. *Ever'thang.*" He handed me a brochure entitled "The Bible Answers Racial Questions" and nodded toward Gene Hall. "He wrote that book. Now I want you to study that."

Gene Hall grinned as Venable peddled his booklet.

"When you go to mixin' this inferior blood, intermarriage of the black man, you're goin' to destroy both races," Venable reasoned. "The nigger has the animal instinct in him. He wants to kill and destroy. You put him in the finest housing project in the world, and in six months, it'll look like a monkey's den. Now there's a few exceptions, where the bloodline of the nigger race is a half-breed, a white man with a nigger woman or vice versa. There has been some intelligence because of the crossbreeding, because of the mentality of the white man. Like ol' Brooks. Like ol' Julian Bond here in Atlanta. And ol' Young here, a congressman. And like ol' Maynard Jackson, the mayor of Atlanta. He's a half-breed. He's got more white blood in him as he has nigger blood, and he's intelligent."

"You say, you consider him intelligent?"

"Well," he hesitated, "I mean, he's got the intelligence. He's not . . . The characteristics stays with ever' nigger. Whether he's three-fourths white and one-fourth black or vice versa, he's got the animal instinct in him. Jist like the *po*leece dog, he's a half cousin to the wolf, and he wants to kill, destroy. And he's the greatest germ bearer in the world, his race."

For the most part, Lumpkin and Hall sat quietly, occasionally punctuating Venable's crotchety rampage with an opinion or prompting him with a name or date. A textile-mill foreman, Pete Lumpkin was born in Alabama and had lived in Georgia for forty years. He joined the U.S. Klans when he was eighteen, transferring briefly to the Alabama Knights, finally affiliating with the National Knights. Lean and late fortyish, Lumpkin was Venable's right-hand man and perhaps most constant member.

"My grandfather was a klansman, and my father before me was a klansman. But really, when I first joined the Klan, it was in Alabama, and, uh, if you know anythang about Alabamians, you know why I joined the Klan." He chuckled and turned to Gene Hall. "There's an ol' Alabamian, too."

Hall blushed.

"You're from Alabama, Mister Hall?" I turned to him.

"Well, naw, just lived there for a little while." He fidgeted.

Lumpkin jokingly interceded. "But he lived there long enough to *know.*"

The perpetual grin remained pasted across Hall's face, yet he seemed anxious to change topics.

"You're in the Klan?" I asked.

Again, Hall hesitated. "Oh, I've been to several of their rallies. Actually, I've spoke at a *few* Klan meetings, I'd say, but it would be on the basis of the Bible and this book tied in. Mister Venable, when he read the book, he decided that book was very much . . ."

"That's how you met, or got to know each other?" I asked.

Hall nodded. "I had heard of him before that, but that's about when we met."

"We're sending this to ever' member of the Congress and Senate," Venable informed me. "If you read this book, you'll see why. One of the very things the Klan has advocated since its conception is it's contrary to the Holy Writ to integrate these races."

A short, round man in cord suit and bow tie, Gene Hall had the look and manner of a patent-medicine salesman, although he was, he said, retired from the real estate business. He beamed as Venable praised the book and then finally lauded himself. "Took me years to do that book, as you'll realize when you get into it. But the Bible says you should have racial separation. From the very beginning, in Genesis when God created ever'thang, He said, 'We produce after their kind.' And the fowls and the beasts of the field and all obey God's command more than the so-called civilized man. You got only one animal, and that's the mule and man created the mule by crossbreeding a jackass with a mare. Yet, God in His wisdom controlled that. A mule cannot reproduce."

"Are you active in a church? Is that how you got interested in the Bible?" I inquired.

He stalled. "Well, in my heart I've always been opposed to race mixing. I, uh, didn't have to go to school. Knowing the Scriptures was obtained from studying the Bible, not merely reading the Bible. You have to go back and search why . . ." The answer gradually evolved into more interpretations, with Hall offering Scriptures from Genesis through Revelations as though they were racial elixirs.

He then explained his version of the biological differences in the races:

if a black man skinned his arm, it healed black; if a white skinned his, it grew back white. "There's something in your blood that's different."

Venable picked up the argument. "That's the characteristic of the white and the black. These doctors will tell you, 'Just pump the same type blood from a nigger to a white man.' They say, 'Ooooh, it's no difference.' Well, I don't want any that nigger blood pumped into me."

"How are you going to know the difference?" I challenged.

"I'm not gonna take it." Venable refused to budge. "I'm gonna git some from Gene or somebody else."

To support their argument, Gene Hall noted that for years the Red Cross had indicated race on its donor cards. He pointed out that Louisiana even had a law that the Red Cross had to segregate blood. When I informed him the law had been changed several years ago, he fumed. "Well, the only way to fight that is to refuse to give blood to the Red Cross. I wouldn't give 'em a drop!"

Each time I attempted to curb their racial meanderings, Hall and Venable rammed my verbal road blocks. Finally, I detoured to the subject of violence. In the early sixties, before Venable merged his Defensive Legion of Registered Americans Inc., the Committee of One Million Caucasians to March on Congress, and the Christian Voters and Buyers League into the National Knights, he had circulated a leaflet that recommended guns and ammunition approproate for home owners. It had warned ". . . Blood will surely flow in the streets. Let if flow! Let us arm our homes to make sure that Negro-Jew blood flows—not ours."

Now, even though Lumpkin felt everyone should have a gun, he and Venable stressed their opposition to violence and bragged that no National Knight had been convicted of a felony.

"During this investigation in the sixties, Shelton, the States Rights party, and many others were mentioned in there," Venable boasted. "But our name was not even mentioned in there. That's why we try to keep a clean record. We always . . . ever' officer of our Klan at ever' meetin', we advocate the do's and don'ts, what to do and what not to do. You can't take the law in your own hands. It's out of the question. You wouldn't have a ghost of a chance if you went into the federal court where you got niggers on the jury. You'd be convicted. Liberals and pinks, and therefore it's out. The Shelton Klan has caused more headaches and more embarrassment, and Duke has followed in his footsteps. The two things that caused the investigation in the Congress of the U-nited States was the killin' of this ol' sorry white woman that participated in the Selma march, and the klansmen over in Athens, two of 'em, in the killin' of the nigra soldier and the officers that were passin' through there at nighttime. It was uncalled for. And it caused the investigation."

Venable had leveled the same criticism during his HUAC testimony and in interviews at the time of the killings. He told one reporter, "Shelton's ruined the Klan. He shouldn't have killed Lemuel Penn. That nigger wasn't bothering anybody. Shelton caused an investigation of the Klan." Shelton, however, had insisted the men accused of the sniper shooting of Penn—returning to Washington from military reserve training with two other black officers—had been banished from UKA before the incident on a highway outside Athens, northeast of Atlanta. While the HUAC report had identified two of the accused—Howard Sims and Cecil Myers—as UKA members at the time of the murders, they were said to have also belonged to the Black Shirts, a small violence-prone group organized within the National Knights by Colbert Raymond McGriff and Earl Holcombe. The report said McGriff and Holcombe had been expelled from UKA after a shooting incident in Griffin, Georgia.

Now, Venable said, the latter had been members of his group for only a short term because they were "undesirable." He admitted it was a mistake to have accepted them but placed the blame on the Barnesville klavern.

"They have infiltrated the Klan, our enemy has," he said. "That's the reason that if we were mean enough to do somethin', we certainly wouldn't do it. I've always told my people, 'If you got anything to do, always remember two's a crowd. If you talk on your own self, you oughta go to the penitentiary or electric chair if you're mean enough to do something.' "

In spite of his repudiation of violence and his folksy talk about grandchildren and family lineage, I remembered articles that described him as "a fiery, red-faced, fist-shaking orator" and told of his ties to men who were considered dangerous. Another klansman had told me of a visit by Lee Harvey Oswald to Venable's Atlanta law office shortly before John F. Kennedy's assassination. When I asked the Imperial Wizard to verify the rumor, he confirmed that a man who fit Oswald's description had come to see him.

"It favored him," Venable recalled. "I'm positive it was him. He told me he was goin' to Chicago. He wanted names of right-wing leaders, but I wouldn't give him our Grand Dragon's name."

When Venable walked me to my car, we passed the copper-colored Pacer of Gene Hall, who, I later learned, was the same Eugene S. Hall arrested in connection with a series of bombings in Montgomery during the late fifties. The front license plate read "Governor's Staff" and bore a slogan about "Standing Up for Alabama."

"Do you think the Klan could ever be built up to what it was in the twenties?" I asked Jimmy Venable before I drove away.

The physically feeble Imperial Wizard became verbally forceful. "Long as there's a white man in this country, there'll always be a Klan. I've been in all of 'em, 'cept the Knights of Columbus. I've been an Elk, Moose, Odd Fellas, Junior Order, Red Man, Masons, name it. I quit 'em all. I've stayed with the Klan from the day I joined, and I'll *die* a klansman."

21
Calvin Craig:
Once a Klansman . . .

Atlanta, Georgia

Several people had told me Charles Weltner, the Atlanta congressman who called for the HUAC hearings, and Calvin Craig, former Georgia Grand Dragon, were now friends. The liaison seemed incongruous, but no more so than Craig leaving the Klan in 1968 to work with blacks on the Model Cities steering committee and then rejoining UKA eight or nine months ago.

The evening I visited Craig's Riverdale home, outside of Atlanta, he confirmed his friendship and political support of the man he once blasted as "our little white-face nigra" who was strictly after the black vote. After Craig was called to testify, he told a rally crowd: "I'll feel like Christ as He toted the cross for being persecuted for what I believe. Are we going to get justice in Washington? We've got as much chance for justice as Martin Luther King would coming to a Ku Klux Klan rally and expecting justice. I assure you as long as there is a white man in Georgia, there'll be a Ku Klux Klan in Georgia." And Weltner had responded in the press: "He's right. You can't.stop people from believing what they want to believe. But you can eliminate violence and killing, and that's what we intend to do."

Now, in June 1976, Craig came across as Average Man, U.S.A. A faded green Malibu was parked under the carport of his modest brick home in an all-white, suburban neighborhood. The living room was neat and tastefully furnished. On the coffee table was a large family Bible embossed with a gold Liberty Bell; a smaller Bible rested on an end table. Craig, forty-eight, was large and likable. His sandy hair had outgrown its crew cut. And his eyes, like his mind, were constantly inquiring, constantly searching, for another viewpoint, another observation that might expand his mental stature. In spite of his size and unpolished grammar, he matched the description of *The Washington*

Post's Paul Valentine, who, from his reporting days in Atlanta, remembered Craig as "the most courtly nineteenth-century gentleman." When I arrived that evening, he formally introduced me to his son Fred and to his wife Leona who quickly returned to the kitchen, where she remained throughout the interview.

The youngest of nine children, Craig and his four brothers had worked afternoons to supplement the family income from his father's produce business. He dropped out of high school to enter the merchant marine and then, after obtaining his diploma, briefly attended a night law school. For a time, he and his wife, a registered nurse, operated a laundry-dry-cleaning business and, later, a nursing home. He then went into construction, his current occupation.

Like many Southerners, Craig had become concerned about integration after the Supreme Court's 1954 decision. His mother, also alarmed over racial problems, encouraged him and his wife to join her in the U.S. Klans in 1960. After Eldon Edwards' death, Craig was instrumental in forming UKA and encouraging Robert Shelton to take over as Imperial Wizard.

It was difficult to imagine the soft-spoken Craig as the same man who had encouraged his robed klansmen to butt heads with civil rights demonstrators at the sit-ins and marches of the sixties and as the man arrested for assaulting a black teenager who attempted to board a school bus in Crawfordville, Georgia. News accounts described Craig as twisting the youth's arm behind his back and throwing him over the hood of a patrol car while onlookers shouted, "Kill him! Kill him!" When he resigned as Georgia's top klansman in April 1968—less than three weeks after Martin Luther King's assassination—even the *Atlanta Constitution* had editorialized:

> Just supposing that we have to have a Ku Klux Klan—which we emphatically and categorically deny, but just suppose—we couldn't have had a much less objectionable Grand Dragon for one than Calvin F. Craig. We always suspected that he had a good streak hidden in him some place, and it showed through when he quit both his grand dragonship and the Klan . . .

In *Atlanta* magazine, James L. Townsend once wrote:

> Calvin Craig is not a killer, and most assuredly he's not a nut. It's just that he's got a few killers and a few nuts in his organization, and he, personally, doesn't have the moral courage to repudiate them. He

doesn't have the courage to give up his place in the sun—the role of Grand Dragon—and risk anonymity. It's too bad. He's a nice guy.

Although Georgia had been the center of Klan affairs since its 1915 revival, the state experienced much less violence during the Civil Rights Movement than the deeper South. Craig had done his share of shouting from the backs of flatbed trucks and encouraging his members to protest sit-ins and demonstrations. An interview in 1970 quoted the former Grand Dragon as saying, "I trained most of my people for some of the most violent ..." He had not completed the sentence but admitted, however, holding two bomb-making training schools for klansmen. The HUAC had also noted that Craig and Robert Shelton had attended special sessions on the manufacture and use of explosives in October 1961. Yet many observers credited Craig with holding down violence, a feat he readily took credit for the night we talked.

"When I seen the men were kind of restless, I would always go out and promote some type of activity to let them get a lot of the steam off," he reminisced. "Demonstrations, counterdemonstrations. I think it helped on both sides because long as you got people organized that feels the same way, you got control of them and you can keep violence down. But if you have maybe fifteen or twenty or thirty different groups, and they are organized together, then that's when you have a problem that might generate into an act of violence you can't pinpoint down to who."

At the time of his resignation, Craig urged "extremists of both the black groups and the white groups to sit down at the conference table and work out the problems so we can have peace in America today." He claimed no change in his attitudes toward integration but insisted, "I want to find out more about the problems of the poor man, black and white, and I want to understand how I could possibly make a contribution to eliminate the poverty and unending futility of poor people." He also had tried and failed to convince President Lyndon Johnson of the value of naming Robert Shelton to the Civil Rights Commission. Three months after he resigned, when he ran unsuccessfully for sheriff of Fulton County, he had promised to hire black deputies and matrons and "not to hesitate one minute to arrest a klansman who's committed a crime."

Initially, at Model Cities meetings, Craig shifted chairs whenever a black sat next to him. But soon he had gained the respect and praise of his black co-workers. Xernona Clayton, a black administrator in the program, admitted to the press, "It's the funniest thing, I'm beginning to like the man as a person."

"The black community cannot speak for the conservative side, and the conservatives can't speak for the liberals," Craig told me. "So if you sit them at the conference table and let them realize the problems, desires, the objections of race, then I think ... It all goes back to one thing—economics. If a black out here is well off, he can go anywhere and buy a Cadillac. He can go anywhere and buy a house. But we're not talkin' about people that's well off. We're talking about the average person out here on the street. And I just feel the Klan-type people represent at least seventy percent of the white people, the way they feel. The liberals and the blacks represent the same things. In other words, the Klan will not accept anybody else speakin' for them. And the blacks has got to the point now where they will not accept a white liberal speakin' for them."

Craig acknowledged that his thinking had changed. "I think our resistance to laws has changed to where we have accepted those laws or decisions. I don't think anybody thinks the way they did eight or ten years ago." Nevertheless, he and most people still wanted to associate with their own race in their schools and neighborhoods, and he conceded that the reaction to a black moving into an all-white neighborhood would depend on the locality.

At the time Craig left the Klan, many outsiders questioned his motives. When he rejoined, their suspicions were reinforced. Although several klansmen had been critical of his reinstatement and Robert Jones had accused him of "selling us down the river" during the HUAC investigations, Shelton had stated that Craig had left the organization in good standing. And it was the Imperial Wizard who had approached Craig about rejoining as his public relations man for Georgia.

Now the topic turned to his friendship with Charles Weltner, with Craig recalling how their mutual respect had grown. They first met in Washington, but their friendship began later when both were candidates for public office, speaking at a shopping center rally. During ensuing campaigns, they helped each other get votes. They had talked an hour by telephone on the night before about Craig's current bid for the Clayton County commission. Weltner, recently appointed a Superior Court judge in adjoining Fulton County, had promised to lend his verbal support.

If Craig and Weltner, the latter from a prominent old Atlanta family, differed in backgrounds and racial views, they shared an enthusiasm for politics. Craig had run unsuccessfully for a half-dozen public offices. For him, the fascination dated back to childhood. "I know a lot of politicians. I can remember a time or two my dad used to take us to political rallies and all that stuff. I was eight, nine years old, somethin' like that."

"What were your thoughts when he took you to the rallies?"

"Well, a man drawin' *all* these people, like at a church. Outside, though. I remember one time they had one over at Grant Park. I remember Roosevelt. When he had them fireside chats, the house was just as quiet as ever'thang so we could hear. The whole family would just sit there and listen to that speaker."

In 1962, his first bid for office—the state senate—never got off the ground because he failed to qualify. After that, he was defeated in races for the state house of representatives, the Fulton County Democratic executive committee, and for sheriff. And at one point, both Democratic and Republican leaders issued statements that the Grand Dragon belonged to the other party. Running for office was not his only political involvement. As Grand Dragon, he had arranged for klanspeople to conduct voter registration drives in local shopping centers.

"Were you disappointed when you lost?" I asked.

"No," he insisted. "I just couldn't overcome that black vote. See, in two races now in Fulton County I've taken almost every white precinct, but I've only taken it by just a *small* vote. But I lose the black precincts by, say, a hundred to one. And you can't take fifty votes in a white precinct and then go into a black community and lose it by, say, four hundred to forty."

His current goal was a seat on the Clayton County commission. Ultimately, he would like to be elected to the state assembly, to give the people a voice. While the modern Klan lacked the political clout of the twenties, Craig nevertheless gave the Hooded Order credit for putting Lester Maddox and George Wallace in office. "I could name a lot of them, but it wouldn't do any good because a lot of them is livin' and still in office today and it might hurt 'em."

"Would you say there are any high up in politics who have been members of the Klan?" I pushed.

"Has been members of the Klan?" he verified. I nodded, and he answered a soft but firm "Yes."

"At a local, state, or national level? I'm not talking just about Georgia," I emphasized.

"Yeah," he repeated.

"What about who are currently members?"

"Well, I don't know. See, there isn't any way in the world I have access to that. Today, of course, they ain't as powerful as they were in the sixties."

"Who are you for in the presidential race?" I asked.

"Jimmy Carter."

"Most Klan people I've talked to don't feel that way," I observed.

"Well, there you go again, see. Jimmy—now, I know Jimmy . . ."

"Do you?"

"Yeah," he confirmed. "I've been knowing Jimmy for, well, . . . you know, there again, he was one of the politicians who was looking for the Klan support when he run for gov . . ."

"Did he ask for it?" I asked.

"Per se, no," he dodged.

"How do you mean, then, that he did it?"

Craig ignored the question and handed me a newspaper clipping with his photograph at a meeting of the Concerned Citizens of Clayton County.

In his own campaign, he speculated his Klan affiliation had helped him in the white communities and harmed him in the black ones. Running as a Democrat, he did not see the Klan as an issue in the upcoming race, but if it did come up, it would be an asset. Seventy-five percent of his area was white.

"Has your speaking at rallies helped you in your campaigns? In other words, has the Klan enabled you to develop speaking skills to get your point across to the people?"

"Oh, yeah," he was positive. "Speaking before a crowd of people, you just gotta use key words, anyway. You can get people emotional by talking about different things. If you go into a Klan rally, you can talk about . . . you can get their emotions so stirred up, you know, that they are ready to fight. Basically, there's three things on people's minds whether you're at a political rally or a Klan rally. Now what are those three things?" he challenged.

I guessed education, and he prompted, "Say, you talk with someone . . . you talk with 'em fifteen minutes. What are the three things they gonna bring up, normally, in just a normal conversation about affairs in the country?"

"Are you talking about things like Watergate?"

"All right, that's political corruption . . ."

"Race relations."

"There you go." He was excited. "Now what's the next one?"

"Taxes."

He nodded. "Taxes and welfare. You can take *those* three things and go anywhere in the country, and you are hitting it on the head."

He handed me a green business card with his photograph and VOTE CALVIN CRAIG on one side; on the other, there was a boxed sentence with instructions to count the Fs aloud.

"So this will cause people to look at this card long enough and they'll remember Calvin Craig?" I responded.

"Don't you feel that way?" he asked.

"Yes, that's clever," I complimented him.

He was pleased. By now he was engrossed in going through clippings of his political and civic activities, including a drive by the Concerned Citizens of Clayton County, an organization he formed to defeat a bond issue to build a civic center that would have raised taxes. The bond issue had lost eleven to one, he announced with pride.

He was active in a nearby Baptist church and enjoyed fishing with his son, but politics had always been his hobby. "To me the Klan and politics was almost the same. I always felt that way."

"Do you think," I speculated, "that was one of the things that attracted you to the Klan?"

"It might be." Craig thought a moment, then reconsidered, "I would think so."

Forty-seven and now a Superior Court judge, Charles Weltner looked back on the HUAC hearings with mixed emotions. After the stepped-up violence in 1964 and the sniper shooting of Viola Liuzzo in March 1965, he had become concerned about a Klan revival. In his second term in Congress, he had asked to be placed on the HUAC from which he called for the investigation. The hearings had been criticized from the time they were announced: Many felt the HUAC was not the proper vehicle for a Klan inquiry, and the Committee itself had a less than desirable reputation because of its Communist witch-hunting. Newspapers and magazines questioned the appropriateness of such an investigation. Many people—including Calvin Craig—had accused Weltner of using it to further his political career. "There was a lot of criticism about that," Weltner remembered now, "and probably justifiable to some extent."

Attempting to settle into his new chambers in between congratulatory calls, Judge Weltner took time out to reflect on the hearings, which he described as "disappointing" and "bad," yet he felt they had curbed Klan growth and violence.

"The result was that although we didn't learn a damn thing about the Klan that everybody didn't know, the Klan went away," he recalled. "It really did, simply because nobody wanted to come to Washington, nobody wanted to be embarrassed, they didn't want to go to jail, and even though the means were somewhat questionable, the results were very good for the time."

The problem, as Weltner saw it, was the lack of direction given by Chairman Edwin Willis and the tedious Fifth Amendment litany. "He left it all to Mister Appell, who is a good investigator, but they were nickel-and-diming these guys. Their checkbooks didn't balance. Well, what the hell, mine don't balance either. And by the time we came along, there was just nothing of substance to go on." Too much time, he complained, had been wasted on "picky" questions.

"Do you feel they didn't zero in on the violence as much as they did the money?" I asked.

"They tried to, but I don't fault them for that," he conceded. "What they did . . . they did an excellent job of finding out the extent and the code names of the present Klan situation, and just the exposure of that to public opinion had a tremendous effect. But nothing came out of that.

I mean, they didn't prove that somebody did something really bad. They proved that they were a bunch of good ol' boys who would get drunk and drive around in cars on dirt roads and raise hell and have a good time and scare hell out of all the black folks. We put a stop to it for a while, was really what it boiled down to. And there's no doubt about the prison sentences having a good effect on cutting down the threats of violence, the fear of violence."

When I asked if his feelings about the Klan were changed by the hearings, Judge Weltner was thoughtful. "I had an entirely different view. What I didn't understand at the time of all that was the sense of frustration and rejection that causes something like this to come into existence. What I didn't understand then was that nothing like that happens unless there is a damn good reason for it. I understand that now. If I had known what I learned from the investigation before the beginning of it, I don't think I would have called for it."

"What would you have done?" I asked.

"Well," he pondered, "if there had been an investigation, it would not have been the kind of accusatory thing that was the HUAC's sole capability. It would have been rather a sense of what is it these folks are trying to say that nobody's paying any attention to. And whether or not that would have been profitable for a congressional investigation, I don't know."

He agreed with Craig's earlier observation to me, that the answer was to give klanspeople a legitimate forum for their opinions. "This is a very broad brush, but the public decision-making machinery—and this isn't just for klanspeople—has got to be altered to give people a voice in deciding what happens with their own lives."

Weltner said he had not felt the country faced "wholesale" violence. Rather, he saw the possibility that isolated communities would be put in fear. "When the sheriff attends a Klan meeting, you know the poor guy in the croppers' shack, he don't have nobody to call. And I felt that was very real. In isolated instances there was fear. I know that's *still* the case. But it wasn't as though we were going to have an armed uprising in the South and law enforcement was going to fall down."

"Do you mean that there are still sheriffs and law enforcement people in the Klan?" I probed.

"No, what I mean is still the case is that the black guy in the croppers' shack doesn't have much confidence in the sheriff seeing that anything is being done about justice."

"Is that fear justified?"

He nodded. "Justified from long and sordid history as well as from present circumstances. But that's a generalization. There are lots of sheriffs. There are a hundred and fifty-nine sheriffs in Georgia. And that's one Southern state."

"But you do think there are isolated instances?"

"Yes, I'm sure that's the case," he answered. "And I'm sure *that* will be the case for a long time."

When I asked about Calvin Craig, Weltner readily considered him a friend and again related their meeting at the shopping-center rally. Even before they became friends, Weltner had suggested to officials that Craig be fined and placed on probation instead of being sent to prison.

Now Weltner offered, "He's a good guy. I like him."

"How would you describe him besides being a good guy?"

"He's a good ol' boy. You know what a good ol' boy is, don't you?" he chuckled. He credited Craig with working long and hard at the Model Cities project and at trying to change the public's preconception of a klansman. Yet the stereotype had prevailed, and most people had continued to think of him as "a Kluxer."

"Were you surprised when he rejoined the Klan?" I asked.

"Sort of," Weltner answered, speculating as to the reasons he had. "I think it was just a matter of frustration. Craig tried to present an aspect to the public and conduct himself in a way that didn't fit the public's view of Ku Kluxers, and they didn't pay any attention to him. They sort of kicked him back in."

22

Maryland: The Struggles Within

Baltimore, Maryland

The bold red letters exploded off the three-by-three inch slip of paper with the kick of a .12 gauge shotgun:

YOU ARE BEING WATCHED
BY THE KNIGHTS OF
THE KU KLUX KLAN

"That," Will Minton announced coolly, "is the first warnin' people receive. A narcotics pusher. A dope addict. A Communist. Black Panthers. Anybody that's antipatriotic, anti-Christian."

"What about ordinary black people?" I asked.

He stopped rummaging through a briefcase filled with Klan literature and looked up. "If they don't bother us, we won't bother them. Now forced integration . . . If we have a black family moves into an all-white area, they *will* receive a warnin'. And this *has* happened. Three months ago, in an all-white section of Baltimore City here, a group of blacks moved in, and they were warned to leave, and *they left."*

"Just from this note?"

"From that note and a couple other warnin's. There was a cross burnt. And after the cross was burnt, they left."

Minton lit a cigarette and settled back into the sofa. Heir apparent to the Grand Dragonship of the Maryland Knights of the Ku Klux Klan, he fit the Clint Eastwood tough-guy role to perfection: the leisure suit, the boots, the height, the build, the hair color and cut, the dialogue, especially his line, "We do not use violence unless we have to, but when we have to, *we will."*

Except for half-hourly reminders from a cuckoo clock, the modest house in north Baltimore was quiet on this morning in March 1977. Two teenaged girls and a small boy leaned against the kitchen door frame, spellbound by their bachelor uncle. Now thirty, Minton had moved from North Carolina to Baltimore in 1950 with his parents and an older brother. He had quit school in tenth grade to join the army and now worked as a chemical technician. Two years ago, he joined the Klan, primarily because it was a way to fight integration.

The "warning" was more polite than some others I had seen that threatened, "You have just been paid a friendly visit by THE KNIGHTS of the KU KLUX KLAN—THE NEXT ONE WILL BE A REAL ONE." Still, the red type was intimidating even if it now was intended to educate, not to eliminate.

"Where do you put these?" I asked.

"On their house. On their cars. On *them,* if necessary," he laughed, not as if he found it funny but to relieve tension. He was serious. Dead serious.

"Do you do this very often?"

Again, Minton produced his serious laugh. "See, you're givin' me a hard question to answer. There's a lot of cross burnings, but the Klan hasn't done 'em all. Now if we deem it necessary, we *will* burn a cross, and we *will* show violence if we have to."

Within the past two years—especially since January 1977—a rash of cross burnings and "warnings" in the Maryland suburbs of Washington had prompted a special meeting of almost two hundred frightened residents and a stern, front-page warning by the archbishop of Washington, D.C., that Catholics were not to join the Klan. Just three weeks before—William Marx Aitcheson—a University of Maryland student who, along with thirty or forty others, had split with Minton's group to form an independent Klan—had been arrested for mailing a threatening letter to Coretta King and plotting to blow up a local NAACP office and the communications facilities and generating plant at Fort Meade, home for the First Army headquarters and the National Security Agency. Aitcheson, Exalted Cyclops of the Robert E. Lee klavern, also had been charged with a half-dozen cross burnings.

I asked Minton if he was referring to the small cross traditionally burned in front yards. "Yeah, it's four by six. That's average. Wood wrapped in burlap." A miniature, he explained, of the thirty- to forty-foot cross used at rallies.

"What happens after the cross in the yard?"

"The next step," he answered without hesitation, "is the house won't be there, one way or 'nother, if they won't take the first two warnin's."

Had he resorted to that?

"No," he said casually, "they usually come around by the second warnin'. You don't have to go too far."

"How easily *would* you do that?" I pressed.

The morning sun bounced off the living room's orange walls, recreating the glow of the fiery cross, yet Minton remained cool, his answers firm but controlled. "That would depend on the circumstances. Like I say, we do not use violence unless we have to. But when we have to, *we will.*"

"Have you had to use *any* kind of violence?"

"Yes," he answered, but balked when I asked him to talk about it. "That would be an admission of guilt on my part."

Minton in person seemed different from the image projected by the gruff voice that intercepted a call I had placed to Tony LaRicci, the Maryland Dragon I had met at a rally in South Carolina. At that time, LaRicci gave me a phone number and agreed to an interview when I returned to the East Coast. When I dialed the number in February 1977, a recording said it had been changed and gave a new number, which, when dialed, was followed by a similar recording and still another number. At that one, an older woman offered to take a message. Days passed. LaRicci never answered. I repeated the process several times with no results. I tried the number of Frances Reed, whom he had introduced as state secretary and his girl friend. It, too, had been disconnected. Finally, armed with addresses, I went to Baltimore and for six hours followed false leads, leaving written notes "to call" along the way. That night, an angry young woman—LaRicci's daughter-in-law, she said—telephoned with still another number. Another woman answered. When I asked for LaRicci, she muffled a side conversation with someone in the background. Then an abrasive male voice informed me, "This is Will Minton. *I'm* head of the Klan now, not LaRicci."

I explained my interest, but he already knew about my book: he had gotten the earlier messages for LaRicci. "That was headquarters, and you were talking to my mother." He agreed to an interview on condition I not mention LaRicci in the book, not even his name. "Or the deal's off, understand? I'm goin' to have a paper here for you to sign."

But now Minton produced no paper, nor did he mention the ban. The green membership cards he pulled from the briefcase bore Tony LaRicci's rubber-stamped signature. And in explaining the significance of the colored robes, he referred to himself as Grand Klaliff.

"You were Grand Klaliff before?"

"I'm Grand Klaliff until May."

"So you're *both* Grand Klaliff and Grand Dragon?"

"No, I'm Grand Dragon as of May first. But I'm in charge of the state *now.*"

Minton identified the Maryland Knights as one of the dozen or so independents loosely affiliated with Robert Scoggin of South Carolina. "We most likely will be having an Imperial Wizard before long, and Bob Scoggin would be the man for the job." When I asked about other Klan groups in Maryland, he was insistent, "We're the onliest one. If you go to the liberry, you'll see one post office box for the Klan in Maryland, and that is ours." UKA had a small group in the Rising Sun area, where it rallied in the early seventies because it was a half mile below the Mason-Dixon line. But Minton never conferred with them; they were "too small."

Will Minton had been reared in a middle-income family and in the Methodist church. Now he considered the racial beliefs and feelings he remembered growing up with. "I don't believe anybody in my family likes niggers, basically likes them," he said bluntly. "But my parents, more or less they could tolerate anybody. 'You leave me alone, an' I'll leave you alone.' But you see, now, that was back in the fifties. That was a good time to live."

Although he lumped his own reasons for joining to "the Klan's good ideas," he admitted, "Segregation is number one. Some other Klan members, they may believe dope peddlers are number one. Or Communist conspiracy's number one. But to my opinion, segregation is."

With his hair carefully teased and sprayed, his coordinated suit and shirt, his swaggering manner, I speculated that machismo might more than outweigh his distaste for blacks; that he was motivated by a desire to impress the ladies with his toughness, his bravery, his power, especially in *the* green robe.

"How do the women you date react when they find out you're a klansman?" I asked.

"Most of 'em have nothing to say about it," he answered nonchalantly. "Ever' once in a while, you'll find one that does, but when you do, then you get rid of that one and find another one. That's all. No problem."

As for the chemical company where he worked, he said he had had no problems except with the union. "In their bylaws, it's against their constitution to belong to the union and the Klan . . ."

"Klan specifically?" I interrupted.

"Yes. *Any* Klan."

"I mean the Klan as opposed to another organization?"

"Ah, well, see now, if you've noticed, the N-double A-C-P and the Black Panthers and your CORE is black, right? Okay, when they're black, they can do it, but the whites can't do it. That's just another point why the white people are getting tired."

"How did you resolve that?"

"I just told 'em, I said, 'Look,' I said, 'you're talking about discrimination.' I said, 'If you say anythang to me about belonging to the Klan, you're discriminating against me because that's *my* right.' And it was already lined up with my lawyer. He said, 'If they do say anything, we'll sue 'em.' Which we would have done, and we would have won."

The clause was still in the bylaws, but, he noted proudly, it wasn't being enforced. "There's no way they can enforce it." A Klan predecessor, however, was not so fortunate. In 1965, Vernon Naimaster, UKA's acting Grand Dragon, was fired from his job as a Baltimore city bus driver after the state NAACP president called for his ouster and the drivers' union—two-thirds of them black—threatened to strike. Naimaster then unsuccessfully sued the NAACP and its Maryland president.

Over the years, the Klan often had posed job problems for its members, sometimes at the instigation of the FBI, which—especially in the sixties—mailed anonymous postcards to employers and/or visited them. To date, no clear-cut precedent had emerged from the decisions handed down in the cases taken to court. Although Naimaster had lost, Harold Murray, fired when he became Grand Dragon of the North Carolina Knights of the Ku Klux Klan, won his legal battle and was reinstated as a clerk in the city of Charlotte's building inspection department in 1971. But three years after Earl Schoonmaker, Jr., was dismissed as a teacher at the Eastern New York Correctional Facility, the Grand Dragon of the Independent Northern Klans was still appealing his case.

Even today, many Maryland klansmen refused to be quoted by more than a first name or initials. Shelton, who had freely given me his leaders' names and numbers, refused to put me in touch with his Maryland representative, explaining, "They don't like to come out in public." There was also speculation that Tony LaRicci was keeping a low profile partly because of his employer, and Minton, too, would not name the company where he had worked five years. Until he was quoted in a newspaper article a few months back, neither his employer nor most of his co-workers were aware of his Klan affiliation.

I started on another topic. "Some people say the Klan today is different. If so, what is new? what is the Klan trying to do? In the sixties, for instance, rightly or wrongly, it had a bad reputation . . ."

Minton agreed. "Sure, they had a bad reputation in the sixties. They had a bad reputation in the thirties. They had a *worse* reputation in eighteen sixty-six, when they originated. The Klan has been around a hundred and eleven years, and there's been a lot of people killed, there's been a lot of places burned, and I'm not going to say there's not going to be some *more* people killed and some *more* places burned because there *are* going to be." Uncharacteristically, his voice rose to a crescendo, then calmed as he added, with a shrug, "I can only do what I think is best at the time."

Still in the kitchen doorway, the nieces and nephew were engrossed even by the way Minton lit another cigarette and coolly blew out the match.

"Now what my members do, I have *no* authority over," he informed me.

"What do you mean?"

"If I'm not there to watch 'em, I can't guarantee what they're gonna do." He exhaled, watching the smoke mingle with the fire-red sunlight.

"I have heard," I began, "that some leaders—not *all* leaders but some leaders—say they would rather not know what's going on. They don't tell their members *not* to do it . . ."

Minton interrupted, "I'll tell you jist like I tell my people: 'Do what you want, but don't tell me what you do.' "

"So, in a way, that's condoning it, isn't it?"

"No, it's not condoning it. It's not doin' anything," he argued. "It's just staying out of it one hundred percent. If a house is burned and they questioned me . . . They'd say, 'Well, did you know about this?' I'd say 'No,' and I'd be honest in saying 'no' because if the members don't tell me they're going to do it, I have no authority, no power to stop 'em. I'm out of it *one hundred percent.*"

The Maryland State Police already had described this procedure among Exalted Cyclops and their Klan higher-ups and the increased formation since the early seventies of small "action groups" that operated independently of the leaders and general membership. The police had described them as "very difficult to penetrate" because the groups were confined to three or four men, specifically to keep out informers. Similar groups—flamboyantly named "Terrors," "Holy Terrors," and "Execution Squad"—had been blamed for much of the violence during the Civil Rights Movement. They, too, had operated under the "Don't tell me" rule.

I asked Minton if such groups, or inner circles, existed in his Klan.

"Every group has 'em," he answered emphatically, reiterating that they acted "on their own."

"That means a group can pretty much go out and do what it wants to do," I summarized.

"Right," Minton agreed, "but if they do something they're *not* supposed to do . . . Now, I'm not sayin' every member I have is perfect. I have some radicals. If they do somethin' they're not supposed to do, eventually I *would* find out which one did it and they *would* be suspended."

In the next room the clock cuckooed twice. Minton continued: "Put it this way, if they have a personal grudge against somebody and they want to burn their house down or tear their car up or jump on them, whatever, now that's wrong, see. *That's* personal. The Klan should not be brought into that, and anytime I find a member that is doing somethin' like this, he *will* be suspended. If one of my members gets in a barroom fight and goes to get more members to help him, I *will* suspend them."

When I asked if he condoned killing, in view of his earlier prediction that more houses would be burned and more people killed in the future, he detoured, "I did not say there *would* be.'I said there's a *possibility* of it."

"But how do you feel about the things the Klan was accused of in the sixties?" I pushed. "For instance, the Philadelphia, Mississippi, incident and the Viola Liuzzo killing—the things that made headlines?"

Minton creased his brow. "You mean like the school-bus bombings and church burnings?"

"Yes, and the shooting of the woman on the highway," I prompted.

"Oh, that was in Louisiana . . . er, Mississippi?"

"Alabama . . . Selma," I offered.

"Yeah, okay, gotcha." He sat back, relieved that he had the facts straight. "Well, first off, she was from New York, right?"

"No, Detroit."

"And what was she, a Puerto Rican, I believe?"

"I don't know."

"Well, she had no business down in the South with the Freedom Riders and her outside agitation when they had enough agitation down there as it was."

"But do you think that's grounds to kill somebody?"

He snickered. "The onliest thang I can tell you, I wouldn't send her any flowers."

"What would you have done if the men had been members of your group?"

"I wouldn't do anything because I wouldn't know anything about it. Like I said, I would only investigate my members if they had done something they shouldn't, a personal grudge or somethin'. Now that there would be fightin' against integration, I believe, so therefore I wouldn't know about it."

Was he for real? Or was this an act? I was baffled by Minton's bizarre openness and his bravado as the conversation unfolded like a movie script designed to create a superjock image for impressionable females. Was he actually trying to persuade me about something he believed in, a belief he both sanctioned and followed?

"What about the student at the University of Maryland?" I asked.

"Bill Aitcheson?" I nodded and asked if he was a member of Minton's group. "He's not now. He's been banished. We had a slight split here a while back . . . November, to be exact . . . and he went with a group led by Vernon Vail, which is just misfits. They were banished from the Maryland Klan, and they are just a group of people running around saying they're klansmen."

"Misfits?"

Nodding, Minton volunteered his definition: "They're not wanted. That's why they was banished. They was not serving the purpose they swore to do."

He was blunt about the charges against Aitcheson. "He was stupid because he was caught. I mean, you do not make a pipe bomb and give it to a fire marshal."

The Maryland police had pieced together what, at first, seemed like isolated incidents during the spring of 1976 to make its case against Bill Aitcheson: a cross burning at the university, the letter to Coretta King's home in Alabama, a bomb threat the night before she spoke on campus, numerous cross burnings in the Washington suburbs. They began to sense that the Klan, dormant in Maryland since the early seventies, was again on the move; real violence, not mere rhetoric, was in the making; random night riding had progressed to "structured" violence. They began to connect the increased rallies with the cross burnings and threats and to take the Klan more seriously, possibly as a force to be reckoned with.

State membership of UKA, the Maryland Knights, and the latest splinter group added up to no more than two to three hundred. While the Klan appeared to lose one member for each new one, it was recruiting "like mad" in schools, nearby military bases, neighborhood bars, and shopping centers. Cases of "symbolic" violence—designed to damage property and intimidate rather than maim—had escalated from cross burnings to bomb plots.

Almost a year before Aitcheson's arrest on March 2, 1977, the press had quoted him anonymously as "a University of Maryland student." A *Baltimore Sun* article on the Klan described him as "coming on like a firebrand" when he spoke at a LaRicci rally, calling the university "the Berkeley of the East" and denouncing Communists, liberals, Common Cause, and food co-ops on campus.

According to the article, Aitcheson had shouted from the platform:

We're going to have a little Bolshevik America unless we keep our powder dry, clean our weapons and get ready to go out into the streets. I tell you something. You got this robe, but it don't mean a thing unless you've got something to back it up. I mean a good weapon, a rifle, a good pistol. And ammunition ... thousands of rounds, not hundreds. The next war is going to be a big one and it's going to last a long time. The only way this country can ever revive its laws, can ever revive the laws of God is going to be through violence.

The morning of his first arrest, at his parents' home, police found nine pounds of black powder and "several" weapons and bomb components in his bedroom and the basement. Less than a month later, he was indicted for warning Martin Luther King, Jr.'s widow to "stay off the University of Maryland campus or you will die," after federal investigators found twenty-five identifiable fingerprints that matched his on the letter.

Aitcheson pleaded guilty to the latter charge and was sent September 7, 1977, to serve ninety days at the Federal Treatment Facility in Springfield, Missouri. In state court, he pleaded guilty to two of the six cross burnings and to the manufacture of explosives without a license. For those, he was sentenced to two years in prison and placed under four years' supervised probation. All but thirty days, to be served concurrently with his federal sentence, were suspended. No charges, however, were brought in the bomb plots for lack of sufficient evidence to prosecute.

Aitcheson's arrest and disclosure by the state police of the Klan's stepped-up covert activity against military installations and government-funded institutions shook the entire Invisible Empire. Vernon Vail, Grand Dragon of the splinter group, told a reporter the incident had "set the Klan back fifty years" and was rumored to have resigned both from his office and the organization. But police speculated that the group—affiliated nationally with Dale Reusch—was merely lying dormant and that Vail was a "silent" Dragon.

Minton, however, declared the prodigal sons "dead," insisting "Vail's out of it, and their group has already split. So from November to February, that's how long they lasted."

"Isn't the splintering and the bickering a problem?" I asked.

"It's, uh, a slight problem." He shrugged. "It's like a headache, it's all. But other than that, it's no problem. You're talking about losing a dozen people each time. As long as I got the rest of 'em, I don't worry about the dozen or two dozen or hundred or two hundred."

The police had estimated that thirty to thirty-five people originally broke away from the Minton-LaRicci group, supposedly because they wanted more action. No more than a dozen were actually involved in the alleged violence, the police figured. Whether they resigned or were banished depended on which group was talking.

Shortly after the split, Vail, a tow-truck operator, circulated a letter to "Members of the Ku Klux Klan" informing them that his followers had resigned from LaRicci, who was neither a true Grand Dragon nor a true klansman:

He is illegally useing [sic] the name of the Ku Klux Klan for his own benefit to profit off the people. Tony has lied, cheated and stolen from the State Board and members of the Klan. This we have proof, and are sending out fliers showing you the proof. He has embezzled Klan money, borrowed money from Klan members and refused to pay back on agreement.

The letter further charged that LaRicci had threatened to notify employers of "silent members" who had left him and that he had reneged on his written resignation as Grand Dragon if "someone would put up the bond for Frances Reid [sic] to get out of jail," holding a "crooked election" as soon as his girl friend was freed.

Like the rest of the Invisible Empire, the Maryland Klan was not unfamiliar with splintering. In the midsixties, a group broke away from the then-dominant UKA and unofficially affiliated with George Lincoln Rockwell's American Nazi Party. Around that time, LaRicci became Grand Dragon of the UKA faction in what has been described as "a palace coup" engineered by him and three other Exalted Cyclops. He and UKA went their separate ways in 1969 when Robert Shelton sided with members who were at odds with LaRicci. The latter and his newly named Maryland Knights associated with Jimmy Venable's National Knights until August 1975 when the aging Imperial Wizard and five of his Grand Dragons feuded. Until the formation in June 1977 of the Confederation of Independent Orders, LaRicci and his Maryland Knights remained on their own, loosely associating with Bob Scoggin of South Carolina.

Even though nearly a thousand klansmen paraded through downtown Annapolis in 1924, the Hooded Order in Maryland never enjoyed the success it had in other states. A talk by one of the Klan's many ex-nuns who traveled around the country lecturing on the evils of the Catholic church caused a near riot in Baltimore; an attempt was made to burn the building where the Thomas Dixon Klan met; and in nearby Havre de Grace, the First Klan Church of Maryland was dedicated under guard, having been burned before its first opening.

Minton had resumed his briefcase inventory, handing me a prayer book, a Kloran, a leaflet from the American Party, and a carbon of the Maryland Knights' bylaws that began, "Any man that says we are not doing anything, is to be told to go out and do what he can for the organization. There is plenty to do and he doesn't have to be told." Last on the list was the rule "No man shall ever be ordered to participate in any violation of local or Federal laws."

Next, he produced a small, silver-covered booklet. "Here's our funeral service," he said.

"Funeral service?"

"Sure, we got a funeral service. Doesn't ever'body have a funeral service?" When I asked to keep it, he shook his head. "No, I might have to bury somebody, but you can comment out of it."

Reshuffling the briefcase's contents, Minton pulled out an application blank and a membership card. The Klan was a lot less violent than it had been a hundred years ago, it included many more women and professional people, and it was striving to shed the nightrider image, he enlightened me. Some of the Klan's present targets were Communism, drug pushers, and forced integration, the latter still holding top priority with him.

"Are there *any* black people you like at all?" I asked.

"No." He cleared his throat. "I can't think of one."

"You've never known *one* in your life that you liked?"

"No, to be honest with you."

"Why do you feel that way?" I probed.

"Because they're inferior. They're very low-class people. I guess I've always felt that way. Matter of fact, I don't even wanta be in the same room with 'em."

Minton then spoke loftily about the Klan's growth, attributing it to unemployment, forced busing, residential and economic problems. "People get fed up and they finally decide they want to do somethin'. And by joining the Klan, that's how they feel they can do the best."

"You think the Klan can solve some of this?"

"Definitely." He was confident. "If I didn't believe it, I wouldn't be in it."

On the lamp table next to the sofa was a pair of ceramic praying hands with the glazed quotation: "God grant me the serenity to accept the things that I cannot change, the courage to change the things I can, and wisdom to know the difference." Minton silently reviewed the Klan's progress and what still lay ahead.

"What would be a utopia for a klansman?"

"A place completely free of blacks," he answered decisively. "I'd like to see an all-white world with no narcotics. That's basically the main ingredients for a good world."

When I asked how he would accomplish that, he paused. "Mmmmm, well, that's goin' to be hard to do, but like I say, we're workin on it. Eventually, *you* know and *I* know there's goin' to be a race war sooner or later. There's no way you're going to get out of it."

"Is the Klan preparing for this?"

"The Klan is *always* prepared for it!"

Whereas he would not discuss the stocking of arms and military training sessions, Minton was confident every Klan member in Maryland had a number of weapons and ammunition. He himself collected high-powered rifles. I had read also about the Klan Beret, a paramilitary unit of select men and women—put together by Tony LaRicci—that met monthly to practice guerrilla warfare.

In spite of the red Cadillac out front, Minton seemed an economically, educationally, and socially deprived man who, like most klanspeople, was disgruntled with everything in the world except, maybe, himself. What would it take to make him happy? How would he react if he *got* his wish for an all-white world?

"What would the Klan do if the things it's fighting for were accomplished?"

"The Klan would still be here," he declared. "It would be here to make sure ever'thang stays the way we put it, see. And then you'd have just about all Klan, wouldn't you?" Even that thought did not brighten his face or his voice. If there were no enemy, no cause to fight, what would be left for him, for the others who looked to the Klan to give meaning to their lives?

The front door opened and slammed shut behind two men: one short, stocky, dressed in black; the other, young and slender in a turtleneck sweater and slacks.

"Helloooooooo!" the black-clad newcomer yodeled, grinning as he draped a plastic laundry bag over a chair. The two joined us, asking that I use only their first names. "My job, you know," John R., the one in black, explained. Thirty-seven and married, he had a round face that smiled like a human gap-toothed jack-o'-lantern. He had joined the Klan a year ago, partly because he felt "somepin's gotta be done" and partly because he *was* a joiner: Loyal Order of Moose and sundry neighborhood clubs.

"This was the only org'nization that's not superradical like the American Nazi Party, which I thought was a little *too,* you know?" he explained. "They're not afraid to go out and do anything. But the Klan, they were trying to get it together right, the way I like to do."

A fat, jovial man, his eyes twinkled like Christmas morning. "They are tryin' to make it like it was in the forties and fifties, when you was able to walk down the streets at night and nobody bothered you. I remember those days when the little man went up and lit the gas lights, put his ladder up against the pole and lit 'em. I remember the streetcars, and, uh, it was nice." He became defensive. "But it's not nice anymore. Somepin's gotta be done. It's gettin' outta hand. My wife, she's afraid to drive the car at night. And the way the country's runnin' now, it's just not right. Or at least the way I see it. I think ever'body else does. The papers prove that."

Al, twenty-seven and single, sat quietly as his companion poured out the feelings he had struggled with for two years before deciding the Klan was the answer. Smiling again, John boasted, "I'm glad I joined. I'm proud of it!" He was also proud that he was already an officer, Night-Hawk, a sort of sergeant-at-arms and custodian of the fiery cross.

I asked the trio if they remembered their first rally. Minton responded with a remote "Yes," but John eagerly exclaimed, "I remember mine!"

and pulled out his wallet, flipping it open to a colored snapshot of a burning cross. "That was my first rally! I was in that picture!" He leaned over, pointing to a speck in the corner. "You can hardly see me, and I didn't have a robe then, but my wife took this picture."

"Do you carry that because it's sentimental?"

Big John R. blushed. "More or less." He looked down, momentarily bashful. "My first rally in the org'nization. The Klan's not the same as it used to be. People still have the same old image, but it's not the same. The Klan has progressed. Like we let Catholics in and all . . . because I'm a Catholic."

"Do you go to church often?"

"Not like I used to," he admitted, embarrassed.

"Were you an altar boy or anything like that when you were growing up?"

"Dominus-vobiscum-et-cum-spiritu-tu-ooo," he chanted lightheartedly. "Ha, ha, ha. No, I wasn't an altar boy, but I would've loved to been. I just never got the opportunity because there was always too many others. Them nuns *were* rough!" He laughed again. "I remember 'em knocking my head against the blackboard because I couldn't figure out a math problem. But I think a Catholic school was better than a public school. You got more discipline and more, uh, education than in public schools."

Why had John quit school in the tenth grade? "That's a good question. Why *did* I stop?" he asked, as if for the first time. "My mother was dead. My father was out of work, so I just quit and went to work."

Like many klanspeople, John was making up for many things he had missed. He had bought himself a big diamond ring for his little finger and a navy-blue Cadillac. He had status in the Klan.

He believed in violence "only when necessary. When they drive you up against the wall. *Any* animal'll fight back when it's cornered. But most of the people in the Klan aren't violent. They're just fed up. Myself, I don't know if I could go out and kill a person. But pushed against the wall, you don't know what you'd do."

Al listened shyly but seemingly in agreement with John. His shaggy, shoulder-length hair and mustache contrasted with his trim white-duck trousers and turtleneck sweater. He wore a red-stoned ring with gold-embossed army insignia from three years in the military, one of them in Vietnam. Now he was working part-time as a security guard and studying prelaw. He had joined the Klan about the same time as John. A bachelor, Al admitted his Klan membership held a certain amount of appeal for some of the women he dates.

"Do they feel like you're more manly?" I asked.

"I wouldn't say manly. I'd say," he hesitated thoughtfully, "it makes 'em think you're the type of person that's concerned about things that's going on at this time."

We moved into the dining room for a picture-taking session with a Washington photographer. John and Al slipped into their white satin robes and matching masks; Minton posed in his leisure suit, apologetic but not visibly upset at having forgotten his regalia. Unlike John, I felt, he harbored no sentimental attachment toward the robes, only a lust for the green one and maybe, someday, the purple.

Minton's nieces and nephew followed us to the dining-room doorway. "Carol teased his hair too much," sixteen-year-old Mary observed. Then pride replaced the aggravation on her face. "I can't explain it, but I jist love to hear about the Klan and the different thangs. I haven't been to a rally, but I asked him today, you know, and he said he might take me to the one that's comin' up." She squinched her shoulders excitedly. "I just think it's important to have an uncle in the Klan!"

Will Minton and I lingered between my car and his late-model red and white Cadillac, a blood-drop emblem decal on the windshield. As we talked, he opened the trunk and tossed his briefcase on top of three yard-size crosses, wrapped in burlap and ready to burn.

The April rally and Minton's installation as Grand Dragon were postponed. In May, his mother called with the message that all rallies were closed to the press until further notice. Summer came and went; each inquiry about the rallies and the installation met with "I'll have to let you know." By early September, the rallies continued to be off limits, and Minton was still without the title and the green robe, although he assured me that LaRicci was "definitely out" and soon to be charged with "embezzlement." He did not specify who would be making the charges—the Klan or the law. Yet, a disgruntled member informed me, "Minton's kicked out. He's not even permitted on the rally grounds." My earlier intercepted calls and the indefinitely postponed installation were, the Klan member concluded, the result of indecision: while the members suspected LaRicci of personally using Klan money, he was powerful nationally and had good connections; Minton was relatively unknown. Even though LaRicci was said to have stepped down willingly until charges against him were cleared up and to avoid problems with his Jewish employer, he and his handpicked stand-in had become embroiled in a power struggle.

Shortly after talking to Minton, I called William M. Chaney of Indianapolis, Imperial Wizard of the new Confederation of Independent Klans, and he informed me of a rally in Gamber, Maryland, on

September 24, suggesting that I contact the Grand Dragon, Tony LaRicci, about interviews. This call made it through to LaRicci, who agreed to an interview and invited me to the rally.

On the rally grounds, LaRicci paced nervously, issuing orders to a half-dozen young men in fatigues or jeans. The ritual small cross was standing; the larger one, rewrapped in burlap since last night's rally, still lay on the ground.

A small wiry man of fifty, LaRicci, freshly dressed in navy slacks and maroon blazer with a blood-drop emblem over the left breast pocket in preparation for Bill Chaney's arrival, grabbed a hefty wooden mallet and strode across the field to oversee the erection of the cross. Four men on a crude platform pushed from behind, helped by two others shoving a large tree fork, as three more—forming points of a triangle—grasped wires attached to the cross and pulled to steady it in an upright position. As it rose, LaRicci moved to the base, shouting directions.

"A little more . . . little more . . . O.K., Fred, ease it up . . . little more . . . ease up slooow." Between instructions he slammed wedges between the tree trunk and the hole in the earth. "Come on, now . . . little more." *Wham!* "All right, youse ready? Ready?" *Wham!* "Just a hair . . . little more." *Wham!* "Little more . . ." *Wham!*

The cross now firm and as straight as a pine, LaRicci and the men stood back to admire it. The stink of kerosene and gas was overpowering. A blond fellow, wiping his sweaty face on the arm of his T-shirt, exulted, "She *will* go up tonight!"

Momentarily pleased, LaRicci returned to the podium area, where he panicked at the first sprinkle from the heavy clouds above. "It *can't* rain! We've got too much invested in this. We've lifted the ban on press coverage—*that's* how important it is!"

"Why has the ban been lifted?" I asked.

"Because *Mister Chaney* is coming." LaRicci blamed the ban on the media's failure to report fairly previous rallies and their attendance. I suspected, however, it had much more to do with the power struggle between him and his second-in-command, Will Minton, and his members' accusations of theft, coupled with the arrest of his former protégé, Bill Aitcheson.

But when I asked if Will Minton had replaced him for a while, LaRicci was undeterred. Minton had *never* been Grand Dragon. "In fact, he today has been put out of this organization. *I* put him out!" he insisted. "What I was really doing, I knew I was working for Jews and I tried to conceal my identity even though it had came out from time to time. But I knew if my name kept coming out too often it could cost me my job. So I tried to stay in the background, in a silent position more or less, and let Mister Minton—as the second highest officer in the state— come out publicly. This is what he wanted to do. So this is why Mister Minton was up in the public's eye for a little while. But that was a mistake on my part, and it sort of went to his head."

"Did you banish him?"

LaRicci hedged, calling it "an indefinite suspension." "But as long as *I* have the say in the organization, he will never be returned back in as a member. Mister Minton is not of the caliber and the character I thought he was. I've had various complaints. In fact, I was even told by Mister Scoggin I'd better get rid of him because of some of his public statements he made."

"So you don't condone the violence Mister Minton talked about?" I asked.

LaRicci shook his head vigorously. "Of course not."

"Did your views on violence have anything to do with the Aitcheson group leaving?"

"None other than when they left, the statement was made that my group wasn't violent enough. That's why they wanted a Klan of their own. And, well, he didn't get very far, but he went for violence."

LaRicci had been described to me as being close to Aitcheson at one time, trying to bring the University of Maryland student into line, but now he kept a verbal distance. "Aitcheson—if it's true whatever he confessed to—if he did it while he belonged to this organization, it was against our bylaws, and *I* had no knowledge of it. Because, even though we do have a training program . . ."

"The Klan Berets?" I interposed.

He nodded. "It did not exist with the knowledge of any explosives of any kind. Simulations, yes. This they were authorized to do. They could do such things as a smoke bomb. Something of this sort that might simulate explosives, but not explosives themselves."

"What were some of the other things the Klan Berets learned to do?"

"Well," he answered secretively, "I'm not at liberty to reveal this here. However, I will assure you that the informer that the FBI and the police had in the Klan that turned Mister Aitcheson in—I'm sure *he* informed them on what activities took place. See, I never attended any of those. So I don't know, but like I said, it was a guerrilla-warfare training program. But no one was authorized at any time not even to use live ammunition."

"Does it still exist?"

He hesitated. "Vaguely. It died down due to all that was going on, but it will rise again, especially with the way we're building today."

LaRicci's eyes matched the color of the robe he has worn a dozen years and the earnestness in his voice. Yet I questioned his sincerity, remembering the "Don't tell me" rule described by both Minton and the state police. Did LaRicci *really* not know? Or did he conveniently not *want* to know?

Born in Norfolk, Virginia, LaRicci lived in New Jersey until he was ten and since then, in Baltimore. He and his wife were separated but not divorced and had five sons and a daughter, their youngest child aged seventeen. He had been laid off two months ago from his job as a maintenance mechanic.

LaRicci had had run-ins with blacks before he joined the United Klans in 1963. He even sold his house—at a loss, he said—when blacks began moving into his all-white neighborhood.

"I've been taken to court a couple times for arguing with Negroes. If it wasn't over a dog, it was over kids or this or that. In fact, I remember one remark a Negro made in court to the judge—I happened to have a corner home, right on the corner—and this Negro said, 'That was LaRicci's corner.' So, I guess they knew my feelings. I was antinigger then."

"When you were growing up, what did your parents teach you, racially?" I asked.

"They didn't teach me anything, racially, because at that time there was really no movement—no Klan movement, no Civil Rights Movement," he replied. "Now I do have respect in a way for some colored people. But we're looking at an overall picture, and we're looking at the movement today and what's behind it and how it's being forced on us. And *these* are the ones—the agitators and the big-mouth niggers."

In the past, LaRicci had expressed pride in being the first American of Italian descent to become a Grand Dragon. When I asked how he felt about being called "wop," he hesitated. "Well, let's put it this way, it's according to how somebody calls me a 'wop.' Friends and all would call you 'wop,' but I don't mean that way. My name has came out many times publicly and in the back of my head I can just picture two niggers talking and saying, 'That goddamn wop.' I know this here is taking place although it's not being done in front of me. So how do I look at it?" He shrugged. "I guess the same way as they would look at it when I speak against them, call 'em 'damn nigger.' So there's a similarity, but, uh, they don't really compare because there's still a lot of difference between a 'wop' and a 'nigger.' "

Over the years, he had controlled the Klan with as firm a grip as he'd had on that corner, keeping members and outsiders alike in line and somehow managing to come out on top of every feud. In 1976, LaRicci told a *Baltimore Sun* reporter: "We will not put up with any insubordination, like somebody getting ambitious all of a sudden. I don't need it." During the Minton struggle, LaRicci had seemed on the verge of toppling, but again, he emerged victorious.

One observer recently likened him to a "little Napoleon" who used the Klan to intimidate outsiders and to gain popularity with his members, dangling or withholding high offices in exchange for favors and attention. The man who engineered the touching presentation of a ring in appreciation for LaRicci's years as Grand Dragon was rewarded by being named Minton's successor.

Soon after joining UKA, LaRicci rose to Exalted Cyclops of his local klavern and, after a year, replaced Vernon Naimaster as Imperial Representative, as the Grand Dragon position was temporarily called. His turbulent tenure was marked by the arrest of himself and four members for conspiracy to kidnap a drug pusher, who turned out to be a police informer, and by numerous inner disputes. His split with Shelton resulted in the formation of the group now centered around Rising Sun and LaRicci's Maryland Knights of the Ku Klux Klan. A year later, at the advice of Robert Scoggin, the Maryland Knights joined with Venable's National Knights. That affiliation lasted until the 1975 squabble between the elderly Imperial Wizard and a half dozen of his Dragons, including LaRicci and Dale Reusch.

"And then you were with Reusch for a while?" I asked.

"No, I never really was with him," he countered. "I had met with him, and I was at one meeting with him in West Virginia, which prompted all this with Mister Venable. Mister Reusch, even at that time in my estimation, I knew was not qualified to be an Imperial Wizard. However, I would have backed him up on a temporary basis, as *acting* Imperial Wizard, till such time that we could band ourselves together.

"Well," LaRicci sneered, "this didn't go over so good with Mister Reusch. Right off the bat, he went out and got himself an Imperial Wizard robe. No election or nuthin'. There was only five of us. So I never attended no more meetings and that prompted the dispute between Mister Reusch and I. And through certain things that happened, *I myself* put banishment papers out on Mister Reusch, even though I was not affiliated with him. I felt that someday we will all band together and these papers would uphold if Mister Reusch at that time still tries to be a member of the Knights of the Ku Klux Klan."

I looked toward the concession stand at Frances Reed, LaRicci's girl friend, and wondered if she, too, might have played a part in the feud. Earlier, she had told me of joining the Klan in her native West Virginia through Reusch, who had trained her "just like the men," and of meeting LaRicci when she went to Stone Mountain with Reusch. Shortly after I met her in South Carolina, in May 1976, she had moved back to West Virginia, not returning to Maryland and LaRicci until this past May. In the interim, Reusch and his wife had been divorced.

LaRicci viewed the handful of followers and the threatening clouds optimistically. "I'm hoping tonight—if my members support me as I asked them to do—that I will *show* the state of Maryland, especially law officials who say we have only twenty-five or thirty people. I think this has been disputed because at every rally we never have *less* than fifty members going around the cross-lighting ceremony. But tonight! I estimate a *lot* more than that. I estimate one of our biggest rallies I've ever held here in Maryland."

He paused, then added forcefully, "Tony LaRicci *is* the Klan!"

As the time for Chaney's plane neared, he could sit still no longer. He paced back and forth and issued orders, checking and rechecking the rally details and giving his security guards and their uniforms a last-minute inspection before they headed for the airport.

"Youse don't have anything on you?" he interrogated one, eyeing the guard's naked belt.

"Everything's locked up," the guard assured LaRicci, slamming the back doors shut. He and two others climbed into the van and drove off, followed by the Grand Dragon and a young man in a mirror-polished car. Left behind, the guys in sweaty T-shirts and Levis watched the departure, envious of their assignment.

23

Bill Chaney:
The Purple Robe

Gamber, Maryland

The beer-bellied men's laughter and horseplay stopped abruptly as the spit-shined car eased up the slope on to the Gamber rally grounds and parked even with the small group that had worked the afternoon assembling the cross.

"That's the Big Man. The Imperial Wizard," a young blond nudged his buddy. The companion, his eyes fixed on the car and its two-abreast passengers, asked, "Which one?"

"The one next to Tony," the blond answered, just loudly enough for people around him to hear but softly enough to reflect reverence and awe.

A lean security guard in full dress ceremoniously opened the rear door. The man next to Tony LaRicci stepped out and gazed around at his audience and the countryside, standing as mute as the people, who had lined up quietly as if along a presidential parade route.

He was a large man, robust in size if not presence. Even his bold-plaid suit and yellow shirt added poundage without power, for he—like the people—seemed awkward and unsure of protocol, looking to LaRicci for directions. The Maryland Dragon lifted his arm in a curt motion to another man in the crowd. Now! The people crept forward to get their first close look at an Imperial Wizard, their new leader, closing in but not crowding him. As the special visitor and his public exchanged shy stares, a short, plump woman edged to the front. Her chin snug against her chest, she looked up at the big man, and he, down at her and an elaborately iced cake with its frosted greeting—"Welcome Imperial Wizard." He smiled broadly, like a small boy glimpsing his birthday cake.

"We wondered . . . ," the woman started nervously, as though remembering the old admonition that children were to be seen and not heard. "We thought—if it's awright with the Imperial Wizard—we thought maybe we could have a cake cutting in his honor." Her eyes were wide with shyness and excitement as Bill Chaney, silently glowing, reread the frosting.

"If it's all right with the Imperial Wizard ...," Tony LaRicci prompted.

"That would be real fine," Chaney spoke at last in a soft nasal drawl that meshed his Southern origins and his midwestern adulthood.

Encouraged, the cake bearer excitedly told how the bakery's saleswoman had been baffled by the inscription until she had explained it was just a joke. She craned her neck up and around as the crowd and Chaney laughed. And she, like the rest, bubbled at the Imperial Wizard's obvious pleasure with his new followers and their reception.

I stepped forward, and LaRicci drew me toward the Imperial Wizard, with the admonition that I could interview Mister Chaney for a half hour, after which he would mingle with his followers. I agreed, having read in their faces their eagerness to shake his hand, just to touch an Imperial Wizard. LaRicci ushered us to a pair of folding chairs behind the speaker's platform. Throughout the interview, the Imperial Wizard's assigned security guard—a slim, mustached young man—stood rigidly behind Chaney, his eyes glancing down but giving no other indication that he was listening to our discussion.

Chaney's appearance and manner lived up to his telephone image. He was dressed with a flair for color, if not taste, teaming the brown-plaid suit and yellow shirt with maroon socks. Instead of a Klan emblem, he wore a Masonic pin in his lapel, a wedding band and two Masonic rings. Close-cut brown hair fringed his balding head, and his mustache, once a waxed handlebar, had grown to an ample bush, perhaps to fit the image of a fifty-five-year-old grandfather and national leader.

The son of a Baptist minister and reared in rural Kentucky until he moved to Indianapolis in 1950, he nevertheless had enjoyed the reputation of a party-er. Even now, he was jovial, open, and by his own description, "pretty much a talker." Over the years, Chaney's assorted careers—with "Grand Dragon of Indiana from January 1, 1967 through May 31, 1976" heading the list—had included farmer, coal miner, outdoor advertising, trucker, deputy sheriff, and constable. Now he ran air freight out of the Indianapolis airport into O'Hare part-time and held another job "too political in nature to discuss."

Unlike most Klan leaders, he seemed to have entered the Invisible Empire for much the same reason he joined the Masons and the American Legion: because he enjoyed getting together with the boys as much as he opposed integration. He seldom—not even from the podium—spouted the Jew-Communist conspiracy rhetoric picked up along the way. And his confessions of sundry arrests for possession of dynamite and concealed weapons came across more as admitted pranks by an overgrown boy than as sinister crimes. Chaney also lacked the usual obsession with Klankraft, eagerly digressing from that topic to boast that he had soldiered with the U.S. Army Infantry in Louisiana and the Asiatic-Pacific theater during the forties, that his name—originally spelled "Cheyne"—had come to England with William the Conqueror, and that, while he only recently had earned a high school diploma, his three children had attended college.

Nevertheless, in the two weeks between our phone conversation and this rally, Chaney had mailed to me several envelopes fattened with the typical assortment of Klan applications, racial "joke" cards, and "hate" literature. A biographical sketch, on UKA letterhead, had been updated to include his current titles: Imperial Wizard of the new Confederation of Independent Orders—Invisible Empire—Knights of the Ku Klux Klan, and National Coordinator of its affiliated Northern and Southern Knights of the Ku Klux Klan.

In the three-way struggle among Bob Scoggin, Bill Wilkinson, and Dale Reusch to control the numerous independent state and local Klans that multiplied and divided like amoeba, Chaney had surfaced as the unexpected victor of the spoils. When a long-planned Unity Conference ended June 5, 1977, it was William Marshall Chaney—long considered a go-between among Klans—who came away with the purple robe. Near the end, Scoggin had led the contestants, yet mysteriously bowed to his old friend Chaney and opted for Imperial Emperor, the same honorary lifetime title bestowed upon Colonel William Joseph Simmons when he was maneuvered into "retirement" in November 1922.

Now, sitting behind the platform out of view of the milling crowd, Chaney vowed, "It was certainly something I wasn't a candidate for, an honor I didn't go out and campaign for."

When I repeated the description by Jan and Earl Schoonmaker of New York that he was "just a wonderful man" and David Duke's words of praise for his effort to unite the Klans, Chaney ducked his head modestly. "Well, I git along with all the Klan leaders, except Mister Shelton. An' I haven't publicly criticized *him*. When we start fightin' among ourselves, it jist gives the enemy a tool to use to divide us, to degrade us. Where we might disagree on certain issues, in gen'ral we're together, and our goals are practically the same."

A jazzed-up version of "Dixie" muffled Chaney's soft drawl, but he seemed oblivious to the music as he proceeded to compliment other Klan leaders—his competitors now. "Far as Dave Duke's concerned, I know Dave reeeal well. An' James Venable, he's a sincere old man. His health's against him. So's his age. But it's jist amazin' the money of his own he pumps into the program. He's a man with a lotta ability, but for some reason or 'nother, he's jist never been able to git his movement off the ground. 'Course, he's mainly built his org'nization from what you might say 'renegades'—people that have broken with other Klan leaders. An' it's rather hard to control that type of people because they really don't believe in discipline.

"Dale's a good speaker. That's about all I can say for Dale." He chuckled. "He's not an org'nizational man, an' he's used the wrong means to git publicity. Runnin' for president. Governor. Sheriff. Well, not so bad runnin' for sheriff, perhaps. You know him?" I nodded, and Chaney laughed again. "I always tell him he has a good German name, but he looks like Mussolini. He doesn't appreciate that. But I know him real well.

"Even Bill Wilkinson. I know Bill reeeal well, an' he's an ex-serviceman. An ol' submariner. I have a lotta respect for a man like that. I think he jist tried to git the bull by the horns an' kinda run with it. He didn't follow the channels of due process, an' that probably hurt him. Otherwise, he might have been in my job, had it not been for that."

Chaney described the new organization as a "loose" confederation of twenty-six state Klans, with Northern and Southern subdivisions. Unlike UKA and most national Klans, each group maintained local control—setting its own dues and rules—with the Imperial Wizard serving somewhat as a roving ambassador. Each, regardless of size, paid an annual assessment of a hundred dollars instead of the traditional Imperial Tax. Elected for one year, the Imperial Wizard was answerable to a council composed of the other Imperial officers and representatives from the member groups. He was paid office and travel expenses but currently not a salary.

"We're not as vulnerable as an org'nization under a more central control," Chaney contended. "We're more flexible, and we feel like we have more harmony within the Confederation due to local control than you do in a more militant-type gover'ment such as the United Klans, where the Imperial Wizard has more direct authority.

"These independent Klans, in recent years they've seen a need to consolidate their efforts at the national level. An' it's been kicked about for quite a while. We really got down to serious business two or three years ago. A lotta people—like myself—hated to part comp'ny with the org'nization they were presently affiliated with because they realized it would split the org'nization they had within their particular states an' that they wouldn't be able to take all the people with 'em. For that reason, they were a little hesitant to move."

His head lowered, he wrinkled his forehead and peered through the top of his eyeglasses. "But after givin' it serious thought, why, they decided it was in the best interest of the movement to take the step." The

officers of the new Confederation—listed on its red and blue letterhead—
included several men I had met during my travels, at other rallies, in
other Klans: Dan Smithers of Texas, Earl Schoonmaker of New York,
W. A. "Smitty" Summer of South Carolina, the Reverend Raymond
Doerfler of Pennsylvania, even Ed Dawson, the North Carolina security
guard who had talked so candidly about his reasons for joining the Klan.

For Chaney, the break with UKA had come May 31, 1976, at the
Pulaski, Tennessee, rally. During our trip from Tuscaloosa to Amite,
Shelton told me he had ousted the Indiana Dragon because "he was
there with a woman in his motel room and drinking." Chaney blamed
the break on several things: money, too much lip service and too little
action, and an "incident" at a national Klonvokation that had "rubbed
him the wrong way."

"After we parted company, I shook hands with Shelton an' told him
he could kiss Indiana good-by an' I think I've made my word good," he
boasted before detailing *his* charges against his former Imperial Wizard.

"It seemed like Mister Shelton an' some of the others were *forever*
interested in increasing the dues. Seem like ever'thang was goin' out and
nuthin' comin' back in," he complained. "And in our legal problems—we
had many through the years—we put a lot more money into the United
Defense Fund than we ever got out of it. Far as the restraining orders on
rallies, to prevent rallies and street walks and what have you, we had to
fight those at a state level."

In the background, the loudspeaker started the standard rally reper-
toire of Amos n' Andy Klan records and patriotic marches, nearly
drowning out Chaney's case against Shelton. Unperturbed, he continued
to detail the elaborate plans made at Klonvokations and never carried
out and complained about having no central source from which to buy
Klan merchandise and literature.

"You mean the robes and things are not-sold through the Imperial
office?" I asked, curious about the allegations of kickbacks to Shelton.

"Well, we had a robe factory . . . ," he started.

"The one in Columbia, South Carolina?"

"Yes, an' it was approved by the Imperial office. Then—well, I'd rather
not go into it—but they circulated the story that the robe factory was
turning in the names and address of the orders that came in to the FBI.
But what *really* happened, Bob Scoggin, he split with the U-nited Klans,
and Heritage continued to sell him robes. An' I think this was why they
stopped us from buying robes. Now they are made at the state level, but
they have regulations that govern the type of robes the people wear.
'Course they did away with the colors an' went to all-white robes with a
military chevron to designate their rank an' grade. Pers'nally, I like the
colors much better."

"Have you got your purple robe yet?"

"Yes, yes I have. Jist got it in!" He grinned.

"Is this your *first* time to wear it, tonight?"

The grin widened. "Yes. I'm a real tenderfoot tonight. I feel a lot more at home in my green robe."

Bill Chaney first donned a Klan robe in 1963, but at heart, he speculated, he had been a klansman all his life. "My grandfather on my mother's side of the family was real active in the Klan in Danville, Illinois, and in Somerset, Kentucky. An' I don't know, he was always kind of a hero to me. I felt like whatever Granddad did was jist *it*. Another thing, I'm a real strong believer in segregation."

When I asked if he had ever thought he would wear a purple robe, he demurred, "I was more or less satisfied jist to be Grand Dragon."

"But you *were* excited when you got to be Imperial Wizard, weren't you?"

His clear blue eyes betrayed him before he verbally conceded, "Right, but I do feel a little bit like Harry Truman did after the sudden departure of FDR. He said he felt like the roof had fell in on him."

"Has it changed your life in any way?"

"No, not really," he answered, thoughtfully adding, "I guess I've changed my life some in recent years. I've got older an' I don't do some of the things I use to do. I don't party as much as I use to."

"You were a party-er before?"

He smirked. "Awwwww, a little bit. For a few years. I always jist turned it off an' on like water. When I went in the service, I did my part of it. Then for a while afterwards, I dropped booze for almost twenty-three years. Didn't even touch it in any way. An' then went back and started drinkin'. I was drinkin' *real* heavy for almost four years. An' now I'm off it again. So, I don't know as it's changed my life in any way. Maybe my thinkin' a little bit."

"Did that have anything to do with what happened at Pulaski?"

He hesitated. "Wellll, perhaps. Mister Shelton might've used that as one of his excuses, but *overall*, I'd say no."

If Shelton's accusations were true, it was not the first time alcohol and women had contributed to the downfall of an Indiana Klan leader. During the twenties, a transplanted Texan named David Clarke Stephenson built the Hoosier State into an empire that controlled both state politics and the law. Known as "The Old Man," although only in his early thirties, Stephenson had been awarded custody of twenty-three Northern and midwestern states by Wizard Hiram Evans in return for helping to overthrow Simmons. Stephenson, both a master salesman and politician, boosted Indiana's Klan membership to five thousand within a few months, continuing to expand it weekly by the thousands.

He was also a man with a flair for dramatics: traveling to an Atlanta Klonvokation by private railway car; installing eight telephones—including a fake "direct line to the White House"—in his Indianapolis suite of offices; arriving at his inauguration as Grand Dragon by plane and attributing his lateness to a command visit to the White House to counsel the president; scheming to purchase Valparaiso University; organizing his own private police force and proclaiming "I am the law."

Although a power struggle brewed between the flamboyant Stephenson and Imperial Wizard Evans—erupting at one point in Stephenson's banishment and, in turn, his libel suit against Evans—the two put aside their differences to work toward gaining political control of the state. One newspaper described the 1924 Republican state convention as a Klan Kloncilium, with Stephenson's choices for major officers—from local school boards up to governor—winning, along with the Hooded Order's favored presidential candidate, Calvin Coolidge. Most had promised their allegiance to "The Old Man" in return for his support, some even agreeing to consult with him on appointments. Stephenson had his own eye on a seat in the U.S. Senate and, possibly, the Republican's 1928 presidential nomination. But he never made it to Congress or the White House. His career was cut short at thirty-six by the excesses of his own vices.

Known for fast living and a fondness for pretty women, he nevertheless took a liking to a somewhat plump, rather unattractive woman employed at the state house. Madge Oberholtzer, twenty-eight and never married, was flattered by his attention. One evening in March 1925, when one of his bodyguards called for her, she went willingly to Stephenson's Irvington home, where the two drank heavily. Later, he forced her aboard his drawing room on a train to Chicago and, en route, attacked her, badly chewing her body. The next morning, they checked into a Hammond, Illinois, hotel to wait for his car to be driven up from Indianapolis. Madge Oberholtzer slipped out and drank poison. In spite of her pain, she repeatedly refused Stephenson's offer to take her to a hospital if she would marry him. She died several weeks later, and Stephenson was charged with her murder. The well-publicized trial ended in a conviction of second-degree murder and a lifetime sentence—also, in the downfall of the Indiana Klan and its hand-picked politicians.

Unable to wangle a pardon by the summer of 1927, Stephenson decided to talk, divulging the contents of his "little black box," crammed with affidavits and photostats of signed agreements by public officials to swap favors for campaign contributions. These disclosures set off a chain of bribery trials, including that of Klan-picked Governor Ed Jackson.

About his own brushes with the law, Chaney freely admitted he had been arrested several times, on bombing charges, for possession of dynamite, and for carrying concealed weapons in a motor vehicle. Most of the charges had been dropped, or else he had been acquitted. His most recent arrest, in May 1976, was for allegedly fire bombing an Indianapolis outdoor advertising company where he once had worked and had been the president of the union. By newspaper accounts, an off-duty deputy, seeing Chaney run from the scene, stopped him and found a pair of gasoline-soaked gloves in the front seat of his car. Chaney, however, told me he had driven past the plant and had been stopped two blocks beyond it by a plainclothesman. Found guilty on three counts, he then took the case to Chicago's Seventh Circuit Court of Appeals, which threw out the decision and ordered a new trial on the grounds that the first judge may have pressured the jury into returning the verdict. In November 1977, Chaney was again found guilty and filed another appeal. In the meantime, one of his attorneys, NSRP head J. B. Stoner, was busy with his own legal battles: fighting extradition from Georgia to Alabama, where he was indicted September 28, 1977, in connection with the 1954 bombing of a Birmingham church.

Lights on the KNIGHTS of the KU KLUX KLAN sign flashed at the entrance as headlights sporadically edged through the darkening haze on to the dirt path that headed up the slope to the rally grounds. Across the road, three state police cars—one unmarked—parked as the crowd slowly grew to a few hundred, mostly young people in their teens and twenties, with a sprinkling of older adults and children.

The increased security guard, riot sticks and mace now attached to their belts, included two females in white blouses and Confederate-blue slacks with matching armbands and sea caps initialed KWP—Klan Women's Patrol.

Nightfall and the brightness of the platform hid the hovering clouds as the tempo picked up, loud marches and drum rolls adding to the excitement. Finally, LaRicci sternly commanded, "Klansmen! put on your robes!"

Satin robes—most of them white, a few green and red, and one black—were slipped from laundry bags and car trunks over the klanspeople's jeans and pant suits. Chaney stepped from behind the platform in a purple robe that had the sheen and smell of just-off-the-bolt satin. Glowing like a youngster in a new Easter outfit, he squinched his shoulders under its newness, appearing comical rather than impressive, his stomach bulging over its sash and the peaked hat rising like a dunce cap. He paced about until the music halted, and Tony LaRicci led off an assortment of speakers as mismatched as the musical selections that had preceded them.

The Maryland Dragon pleaded for God, country, family, and segregation. Three young leaders of a self-identified "Nazi Klan" took turns lashing out at "the devil Jews" and goading the audience: "If you had any guts, next time some white woman gets abused by some nigger, he'd be swinging from the tree, and not by his tail—by his neck!" Pennsylvania Dragon Raymond Doerfler, greeting the people as "fellow terrorists," took potshots at his predecessor, Roy Frankhouser, whose glass eye he had offered for auction at the South Carolina Dragons Conference.

Even in the shimmering purple robe, Chaney proved no match for the Nazi trio, who had drawn shouts of *"White power!"* and *"Yahooooo!"* Shadowed by the sober security guard, he mounted the platform and began reading from a note pad, moving from topic to topic like a Model T Ford that backfired occasionally but chugged uncertainly along. Now and then, his listeners responded with polite applause. Otherwise, he might have been reading aloud to himself, even when vowing he would join the N-double-A-C-P if he was a nigger! and verbalizing his stand on violence. He didn't advocate it, "but sometimes we have to, uh, uh, take some sort of physical action to accomplish our end results."

"We've talked an' we've talked down through the years, but what have we accomplished?" he asked. When there was no response, he peppered the rambling low-key speech with more inflammatory words. "We've lost ground. We see that the niggers have infiltrated our schools, our public entertainment. We see our young white ladies on the streets escorted by black bucks. We don't like it, but what are we doin' about it? Our fathers wouldn't tolerate it. An' we ourselves are goin' to have to redirect our course of action."

Silence.

"Now we must stand for somethin'. I've often heard it said, if you don't stand for somethin', you don't stand for nuthin'. You agree?" The audience returned anemic applause. "I know that's why you're all out here toniiight, because you stand for somepin'. You're opposed to the triplets that are takin' over our land: Jew, Communistic, niggerism."

Now, for the first time, the crowd lauded him with a vigorous chorus of *"Yahooooo! Yeaaaa!"* Chaney glanced up from his notes and smiled, raising his voice to uncharacteristic fieriness as he tackled Jimmy Carter and his family "with its draft evaders and bad-conduct charges."

" 'Course, blood always runs thicker 'an water, and uh, uh, through his efforts he's made it possible for the draft evader and the deserters to return to this land an' be accepted into society. And as a klansman, I say to *you* toniiight, an' as a combat vet'ran of World War Two, that any man that will not fight for that flag—I don't care who he is—doesn't deserve a country! An' I don't give a damn if he's the president's son or whoever he might be!"

The crowd cheered again before Chaney lapsed into a monotonous plea to "speak up in your Sunday schools, lodges, labor unions, and local politics." The listeners shifted impatiently, waiting for the big man they had eagerly come to hear—*their* Imperial Wizard—to end his verbal stumbling so they could light the cross and head for home or nearby taverns.

For the past few years, Scoggin, Wilkinson, and Reusch each had courted the splinter groups, traveling from trouble spot to trouble spot in the quest for followers, indiscriminately picking up the remnants of inner squabbles. Reusch had sought admiration and attention by running for president and then vice-president; Scoggin had portrayed himself as a martyr of both World War II and the HUAC hearings; young Wilkinson had put together an impressive two-color tabloid crammed with Klan news—most cut and pasted directly from legitimate newspapers and wire services without permission.

I looked now at the big man and wondered how he had captured the prize that the other three had fought for long and hard.

Chaney had admitted that Wilkinson might have been in his place had not the ambitious Louisianian—in Tony LaRicci's words—pushed too hard, too fast. Was it because Wilkinson had not followed the proper chain of command? Or was it rather that a strong, dominant man never could head the independent leaders, that the egos of the Grand Dragons, each inwardly coveting the purple robe, would never bow to a forceful man who might usurp their power? Would they concede only to a figurehead, a purple-robed ambassador who cranked out reams of literature and drew people to their rallies but never threatened their own position, their own prestige? Had Chaney been made a mere titular ruler for the self-governing independents?

Reusch's bids for the country's highest offices had gained him a certain amount of admiration, but could the Dragons also have felt threatened by his political ambition and his undue haste in ordering a purple robe after the five-way split with Jimmy Venable? Even though he was not a strong nor charismatic leader, did they view him as such? As a threat? And, finally, after he and some thirty or more followers were clobbered again on Labor Day 1977 on the Columbus, Ohio, State House steps by five hundred club-wielding anti-Klan demonstrators, shouting, "Ku Klux Klan, scum of the land!" did they view him as an embarrassment?

Wilkinson had lost ground for different reasons, perhaps because he *was* strong and aggressive, because he had come across as a hero among klansmen after his Plains, Georgia, rally attracted the president's mother and an avowed Klan hater plowed his Jaguar into the crowd. At the Conference of Eastern Dragons in South Carolina, where I first met him in the spring of 1976, Bill Wilkinson had been the featured speaker, distinguished among the green-satined Dragons by his crisp white cotton robe. From the podium, Scoggin had praised the then Grand Dragon of Louisiana and his tabloid, and the conference had adopted the paper as the independents' "official" publication. By July, when I arrived in Louisiana, Wilkinson had laid claim to the Imperial Wizard title and begun building his own empire, listing his constantly shifting Realms in the *Klansman*. Following the example of his former leader, David Duke, he sought publicity by opening Klan bookstores and headquarters with elaborate ribbon cuttings and taking credit for headline events, like the Klan's infiltration at the Marine Corps' Camp Pendleton. Following the July Fourth rally, the press had annointed him *the* Klan leader of tomorrow, destined to overshadow the more articulate Duke and even Robert Shelton. But by summer's end, Wilkinson was left with little more than his self-imposed title.

In the end, this struggle had been lost to one who seemed an unlikely choice, a jolly, likable man with a reputation for making friends among the many Klans. Perhaps, the Dragons had no fear that he would invade their territory. But could he hold the independents together? Might he, in fact, become the leader of the future? Would he—like Shelton—endure?

During the Civil Rights Movement Shelton gave every appearance of being a tough, even violent leader, but his wrath had been directed toward the government and integration, toward championing his people—a stance that made him a hero in their eyes. In those days, his organization saw little inner turmoil and splintering other than that engineered by the FBI. In the sixties, many of his Dragons had been more dynamic and forceful than Shelton himself, yet never managed to knock him from the throne.

Now, in the seventies, had Shelton truly mellowed? Or had he intentionally replaced his once strong-willed leaders with acquiescent men? Was his low-key behavior—the bland front, the monotone delivery, the seeming inability to be moved to anger—the secret of his ability to survive?

Even Bob Scoggin, the Confederation's first choice, was looked upon by many—including the law—as being more of a joke than a threat. And both Colonel William Joseph Simmons and James Venable were overthrown simply because their ambitious underlings had grown restless waiting for them to retire.

Before the rally, Bill Chaney surveyed the group of followers and considered his new rank. "I stand alone, in a sense. As Grand Dragon, I looked at several people out there in green robes, an' we could go off to one side by ourselves. We might even criticize the Wizard a little bit." Like a school boy telling tales on himself, Chaney sniggered. "But now it's on the other foot."

How, I wondered, could the color of a robe transform a follower into a leader? For all its fearsome reputation, might it be that only the weak could successfully lead the Ku Klux Klan?

Epilogue

Only a week after I mailed in my manuscript to my publisher, David Duke called long-distance to say he was home from London.

"I'm a folk hero over there," he raved. "I'd say I'm probably the best-known American outside of Jimmy Carter."

Out of three immigration officers, Duke had chosen the line of a black officer and passed through undetected, he said, gloating, "It was poetic justice."

The British loved him, he bubbled, and had made no effort to turn him over to Scotland Yard. He gloried in the front-page coverage he received in London and throughout the world, and he again had made a good showing on British television. His month-long stay had been marred only by the less publicized entry and ouster of rival klansman Bill Wilkinson.

I hung up the telephone, frustrated. There was so much more to write about the Klan. During my two years of research and writing, I sometimes felt the book would never end, that the Klan slogan "Yesterday, Today, Tomorrow, Forever" fitted both the Hooded Order and a book about it. There seemed to be no limit to the material.

Friends and acquaintances often asked, "Aren't you tired of the subject?" My answer was always *no*. The events, the interviews, the phone calls, were never the same, even as the klanspeople themselves weren't. Once, in Houston, I dragged myself halfheartedly to an interview with a former Grand Dragon. I inserted a tape cassette, pressed the record button, and sat back anticipating more routine Klankraft. The man started with the familiar blasts, but midway, I was jolted.

"... but he has a family and he has been through hell and back. Believe me, you go through hell and back with the FBI and CIA and the rest of them," Frank Converse charged. "I know they will commit murder. I *know* they will go to any extent because I was involved here with the overthrow of the Panama Canal to see that the presidente was put back in the position and the general that's down there now taken out. My job was to be the executioner, with the CIA operating."

"So you were with the CIA?" I asked.

"The CIA was in the *same* room with me," he answered, explaining that five meetings were held in 1969 in motels with a number of leading Houston businessmen present. Converse said he had been contacted by a "well-known banker" and offered to take a lie-detector test to prove the validity of his claims. "My job and one more—an ex-Gestapo man—was to execute the general. They were going to fly a mercenary army in there. The CIA was in on that."

I looked incredulously at the man sitting opposite me. In his midfifties, he bore a striking resemblance to Archie Bunker, but there was nothing humorous in the story he told.

"Did they offer you money to do this?" I asked.

"Yes, ma'am. Anything I desired."

"Did they name a figure?"

"No figure was made."

The plot—to use a car bomb—was never carried out, he said, because Washington had refused the *presidente* the necessary money.

"Besides you and the leading Houston citizens in the room ...," I started, but Converse interrupted me. "I can't go too far into it, because I want to think about my own life and my grandchildren."

"But there was a member of the CIA there?"

He nodded. "That's right."

"Why do you think they approached you to do this?"

"Maybe," he said thoughtfully, "it's because they know I'm the type of man that would do it."

There was more to that story, just as there were more stories, more leads, more tips, that I longed to follow up.

"The book has to stop somewhere," many counseled me. But if I could only do one more chapter ... There was the Kentucky klansman who gave me my first "calling card" during UKA's bicentennial rally in Pulaski and talked freely about "carding" blacks and the people involved with school busing. His own teenage son told of "carding" a teacher he didn't like. The morning after I arrived in Louisville, the *Courier-Journal* reported that green paint had been splashed on the car of a Jamaican couple who lived in a mostly white neighborhood. Tucked underneath the windshield wipers, a card warned, "You Have Been Paid a Visit by the Ku Klux Klan." Then, in March 1977, eleven Kentucky klansmen—including UKA Grand Dragon Sherman Adams—were indicted for allegedly staging a private drug raid during a teenage party in a trailer. According to news accounts, the trailer door was kicked open and fifteen or twenty men—most of them armed with rifles or pistols—appeared, the leader announcing they were there to conduct a raid. Several wore ski masks; the others made no effort to hide their identities. The guests were herded into a back bedroom and warned, "If somebody comes out, you'll be sorry." The men, who boasted that they were with the Klan, ransacked the living room and sprayed the ceiling and walls with bullets before they vanished into the night.

Just one more chapter, I wished. Especially when a former colleague on the *Philadelphia Inquirer* called in the midst of my deadline panic to ask what I knew about Jimmy Mitchell Rosenberg. One Jimmy Mitchell, introduced as a representative of the New York Klan, had spoken at the Gamber, Maryland, rally I attended. He was memorable because of his announced plans to join the Rhodesian army. My journalist friend told of intriguing charges and countercharges between the young man and the Grand Dragons of New York and Pennsylvania. Mitchell had admitted to the Philadelphia reporter that his name was, indeed, Rosenberg, that he was part Jewish, and that, at the request of Pennsylvania Dragon Ray Doerfler, he had become an "agent" for the ADL in order to spy on that organization. The latter claim was backed up by New York Dragon Earl Schoonmaker. Doerfler, however, told the *Inquirer* that Mitchell was a true ADL agent spying on the Klan.

Even after the book progressed to page proofs, there were the much-publicized marches by the Klan and a black civil rights group in racially tense Tupelo, Mississippi, and the disclosure, during July 1978, that informant Gary Thomas Rowe may have participated in and helped plan Klan terrorism the FBI hired him to monitor. There was also the revelation by a St. Louis man that he was offered fifty thousand dollars to assassinate Martin Luther King at a time when the man's brother-in-law was incarcerated in a Missouri prison with James Earl Ray.

And so the stories continued past deadline, just as the Klan—or a counterpart—will continue, as long as human beings come in assorted colors, races, and economic disparities. For unless society finds a way to treat the causes rather than the symptoms of racism, there will continue to be the need by some to look both up and down, a need now filled for them only by the Klan.

At Christmas time 1977, when I flew to Houston to visit my parents, I looked again at the little black Pandora's box, the one that started me on my search. As I re-examined its contents, my father commented, "Your Great-Grandfather Jake Shanks was a member of the Reconstruction Klan, and he was *proud* of it."

Washington, D.C.
July 29, 1978

Glossary

The language of the Ku Klux Klan is cloaked in as much mystery as the Hooded Order itself. Although some groups have fashioned their own vocabularies, here is a guide to the more commonly used terms:

AKIA a password meaning "A Klansman I am"; often seen on decals and bumper stickers

Alien a person who does not belong to the Klan

AYAK? a password meaning "Are You a Klansman?"

Banish to kick a member out of the Klan for any of a number of reasons, including "pollution of the Caucasian blood through miscegenation," "excessive or habitual drunkenness," and turning informer for a law enforcement agency. The accused is supposed to be given a trial by a tribunal, after which he may be, in Klan lingo, "banished *forever*"

CA BARK a password meaning "Constantly Applied By All Real Klansmen"

CLASP a password meaning "Clannish Loyalty A Sacred Principle"

Exalted Cyclops the top officer, or president, of a klavern, usually referred to as the "E.C."

Furies the Province officers, with the exception of the Great Titan

Genii the collective name for the national officers. Also known as the Kloncilium, or the advisory board to the Imperial Wizard

Ghouls term for rank and file members, though seldom used

Grand the preface for any office title on the state level, such as Grand Kludd

Grand Dragon the top officer of a Realm, or state president

Grand Giant former Grand Dragon

Grand Wizard the title conferred on General Nathan Bedford Forrest, head of the Reconstruction Klan, comparable to Imperial Wizard

Great the preface for any office title on the Province level, such as Great Titan

Great Giant former Great Titan

Great Titan   head of a Province, or congressional district

Hydras   the Realm officers, with the exception of the Grand Dragon

Imperial   the preface for any office title on the national level, such as Imperial Klaliff

Imperial Giant   former Imperial Wizard

Imperial Klonvokation   national convention, usually held biennially

Imperial Representative   an appointed officer in a state with a membership too small to warrant a Grand Dragon. This title usually exists only in the United Klans of America, Inc.

Imperial Tax   a percentage of the dues sent to national headquarters

Imperial Wizard   the overall, or national, head of a Klan, which it sometimes compares to the president of the United States

Inner Circle   small group of four or five members who plan and carry out "action" such as cross burnings, lynchings, bombings, and other harassment. Its members and activities are not disclosed to the general membership

Invisible Empire   a Ku Klux Klan's overall geographical jurisdiction, which it compares to the United States although none exist in every state

Kalendar   klan calendar, which dates events from both the origin and its 1915 rebirth. *Anno Klan* means "in the year of the Klan" and is usually written "AK." The months are called Bloody, Gloomy, Hideous, Fearful, Furious, Alarming, Terrible, Horrible, Mournful, Sorrowful, Frightful, and Appalling. The weeks are Woeful, Weeping, Wailing, Wonderful, and Weird, and the days are Dark, Deadly, Dismal, Doleful, Desolate, Dreadful, and Desperate. Thus, "blue Monday" is "deadly" even on the Klan Kalendar

Kardinal Kullors   white, crimson, gold, and black. Secondary Kullors are gray, green, and blue. The Imperial Wizard's Kullor is "royal" purple

K.B.I.   Klan Bureau of Investigation

KIGY!   a password meaning "Klansman, I Greet You!"

KKKK   Knights of the Ku Klux Klan, the name officially used since the Klan was revived in 1915

Klabee   see Terrors

Kladd   see Terrors

Klaliff   see Terrors

Klan Giant   honorary title bestowed on former Exalted Cyclops in good standing

Klankraft   the practices and beliefs of the Klan

Klanton   the jurisdiction of a klavern

Klarogo   see Terrors

Klavern   a local unit or club; also called "den"

Kleagle   an organizer whose main function is to recruit new members. In some Klans, he gets a percentage of the initiation fees

Klectokon   initiation fee, usually $15. Traditionally, the Klectokon is split among the klavern and state and national offices. Dues vary from Klan to Klan, ranging from $24 to $36 a year

Klepeer   delegate elected to Imperial Klonvokation

Klexter   see Terrors

Kligrapp   see Terrors

Klokan   see Terrors

Klokann   see Klokan

Klokard   see Terrors

Kloncilium   see Genii

Klonkave   secret klavern meeting

Klonverse   Province convention

Klonvokation   see Imperial Klonvokation

Kloran   official book of Klan rituals

Klorero   Realm convention

Kludd   see Terrors

Night-Hawk   see Terrors

Province   a subdivision of a Realm, comparable to—but not necessarily—a congressional district

Realm   a subdivision of the Invisible Empire, usually referring to a state

Realm Tax   a percentage of the dues sent to state headquarters

SAN BOG   a password meaning "Strangers Are Near, Be On Guard."

Splinter groups   a varying number of organizations that go by the name "Knights of the Ku Klux Klan" (KKKK) but are not affiliated. They use prefixes and suffixes to distinguish themselves from each other and are usually formed when disgruntled members of one Klan break away, or "splinter," to form their own group

Terrors   the Exalted Cyclops' officers, which consist of:

      Klaliff—vice-president

      Klokard—lecturer or teacher of Klankraft

          (practices and beliefs of Klan)

    Kludd—chaplain

      Kligrapp—secretary

      Klabee—treasurer

      Kladd—conductor of ceremonies

      Klarogo—inner guard

      Klexter—outer guard

      Klokan—head of the three-man Klokann Board, which investigates prospective members and acts as auditor

Night-Hawk—custodian of the fiery cross and of applicants immediately prior to their initiation, and, in some Klans, responsible for seeking out violence. The office is often designated by a black robe

The above officers or aides also exist on the national, state, and province levels. Their titles are then prefaced by "Imperial" on the national level, "Grand" on the state level, and "Great" on the Province level.

The People of Klan Country

Here is a partial census of the people who inhabit the Invisible Empire or whose lives are touched by it. Since the population is constantly shifting, the members and leaders may be affiliated with Klans other than those listed by the time you read this book.

Appell, Donald chief investigator for the House Un-American Activities Committee probe of the Ku Klux Klan in 1965–66

Alexander, Henry arrested in 1957 for a series of bombings in Montgomery, Alabama, and accused in 1976, along with three others, of forcing a black truck driver to jump to his death into the Alabama River in 1957. The case was dropped because of technicalities

Ainsworth, Kathy a member of several Klans, including the White Knights of Mississippi, killed in a shoot-out with police when she and Thomas A. Tarrants, III attempted to bomb the home of a Jewish business man in Meridian

Aitcheson, William Marx   a University of Maryland student and former member of the Maryland Knights, who was charged in March 1977 with a half-dozen cross burnings, plotting to blow up communications facilities and a generating plant at Fort Meade, and mailing a threatening letter to Coretta King

Bacon, Mary well-known jockey, who spoke at Louisiana rally of Knights of the Ku Klux Klan

Baxley, William J.   attorney general of Alabama

Beam, Louis one of two Grand Titans of Texas, Knights of the Ku Klux Klan

Bergeron, Sandra Giant, or the top officer, for Jefferson Parish (county), Louisiana, for David Duke's Knights of the Ku Klux Klan

Black, Don Alabama organizer and National Information Director, Knights of the Ku Klux Klan; formerly associated with National States Rights Party (NSRP)

Booker, Ray one of the two Grand Titans of Texas for Knights of the Ku Klux Klan; operates Klan book store in Vidor, Texas

Bowers, Sam Holloway, Jr. alleged Imperial Wizard, White Knights of Mississippi

Britt, Raymond C., Jr. former klansman who turned states evidence in the 1976 case in which he and three others were accused of forcing a black truck driver to jump into the Alabama River in 1957; also indicted, but not convicted in a series of Montgomery bombings in the late fifties

Britton, Neuman associated with NSRP and the National Emancipation of Our White Seed (NEWS), an association of right-wing organizations

Broadway, Steve member of United Klans of America's (UKA) South Carolina state board

Bryan, Muddy mother-in-law of J. Robertson Jones, former UKA Grand Dragon of North Carolina

Bryant, Joe acting Grand Dragon of North Carolina for UKA while J. Robertson Jones served a year in prison following the HUAC hearings; later formed the North Carolina Knights

Burros, Daniel UKA Grand Dragon of New York, who committed suicide in 1965 after *The New York Times* disclosed he was Jewish

Campbell, the Reverend Will D. director, Committee of Southern Churchmen

Chambliss, Robert former klansman convicted in 1977 of the 1963 bombing of the Sixteenth Street Baptist Church in Birmingham

Chaney, James one of three civil rights workers murdered in 1964 in Philadelphia, Mississippi

Chaney, William M. Imperial Wizard, Confederation of Independent Klans, and former UKA Grand Dragon of Indiana

Chopper, Phillip one of several Klan leaders who surfaced during the Louisville, Kentucky, school-busing demonstrations; also briefly associated with David Duke's Knights of the Ku Klux Klan

Clark, Obie president, Meridian chapter, NAACP

Clarke, Edward Young contracted, along with Elizabeth "Bessie" Tyler, to promote and recruit for the Knights of the Ku Klux Klan after its 1915 revival

Cole, James ("Catfish") the late Grand Dragon of the Carolina Knights; better known for a raid by the Lumbee Indians of a rally staged by him in 1958 near Maxton, North Carolina

Cox, Judge W. Harold U.S. District Court judge who presided over the federal conspiracy trial in the murders of the three civil rights workers in Philadelphia, Mississippi

Craig, Calvin former UKA Grand Dragon of Georgia; now in charge of UKA's public relations within the state

Crommelin, Admiral John G. retired navy admiral, who ran for the U.S. Senate in Alabama and as the States' Rights Party's vice-presidential candidate in 1960; now associated with Knights of the Ku Klux Klan

Cusimano, Ellen security guard for Knights of the Ku Klux Klan in New Orleans area

Dahmer, Vernon NAACP leader killed in 1966 when the White Knights of Mississippi allegedly fire bombed and shot into his home

Davidson, Robert Lee ("Wild Bill") Imperial Wizard of U.S. Klans after 1960 death of Eldon Edwards

Dawson, Ed colonel in charge of North Carolina Knight's Security Guard and Imperial Kladd, Confederation of Independent Orders; formerly on UKA's North Carolina state board

De la Beckwith, Byron tried twice but never convicted in the slaying of Mississippi civil rights leader Medgar Evers

DeMent, Ira U.S. attorney, Middle District of Alabama

Dennis, the Reverend Delmar Methodist minister who belonged to White Knights of Mississippi and turned paid FBI informer after the murders of the three civil rights workers in Philadelphia

DePugh, Robert former leader of the ultra right-wing Minutemen

Doar, John U.S. assistant attorney who acted as prosecutor during federal conspiracy trial for defendants in the murder of three civil rights workers in Philadelphia, Mississippi

Doerfler, the Reverend Raymond Grand Dragon of Pennsylvania, Invisible Empire, Knights of the Ku Klux Klan, and Imperial Night-Hawk, Confederation of Independent Orders

Dorsett, George UKA's Imperial Kludd as well as its security guard chaplain and Titan for North Carolina until 1967 when he helped form the Confederate Knights; later belonged to North Carolina Knights of the Ku Klux Klan and in 1975 was identified as a paid FBI informer

Duke, Chloe wife of David Duke, National Director of Knights of the Ku Klux Klan

Duke, David National Director (Imperial Wizard) of New Orleans-based Knights of the Ku Klux Klan

Dunaway, Hulon member of the Original Knights of Louisiana during racial turmoil in Bogalusa, Louisiana, in 1965 and now of Bill Wilkinson's Invisible Empire

Dutton, Jerry veteran right-winger who served briefly as Grand Dragon of New Orleans-based Knights of the Ku Klux Klan before affiliating with Bill Wilkinson's Invisible Empire, Knights of the Ku Klux Klan, in Denham Springs, Louisiana

Edwards, Eldon succeeded Dr. Samuel Green as Imperial Wizard in 1949, simultaneously absorbing the Association of Georgia Klans into the U.S. Klans

Evans, Dr. Hiram W. a Texas dentist who succeeded William Joseph Simmons as Imperial Wizard of the Knights of the Ku Klux Klan in 1922

Goodman, Andrew one of three civil rights workers slain in Philadelphia, Mississippi, in June 1964

Green, Dr. Samuel formed the Association of Georgia Klans in 1946 after a $685,000 back federal-tax bill forced James. A Colescott to declare the Knights of the Ku Klux Klan defunct; served as Imperial Wizard until his death in August 1949

Griffin, Virgil Grand Dragon, North Carolina Knights of the Ku Klux Klan

Hall, Eugene S. an associate of Imperial Wizard James R. Venable; arrested in connection with several bombings in Montgomery, Alabama, during racial turmoil in the late fifties

Hanes, Arthur former mayor of Birmingham, who has served as defense attorney for several klansmen. He and his son, Arthur Hanes, Jr., represented Robert Chambliss in his 1977 trial for the Sixteenth Street Baptist Church bombing in Birmingham

Hatcher, Mike Meridian police officer injured during 1968 shoot-out with Thomas Tarrants, III, when the latter attempted to plant a bomb at the home of a Jewish civic leader

Higgins, George, Jr. UKA Grand Dragon of Mississippi

Holden, Pete UKA Grand Dragon of Louisiana

Horn, Alvin former Grand Dragon of Alabama, U.S. Klans

Howard, John Grand Dragon of South Carolina, for Dale Reusch's Invisible Empire, Knights of the Ku Klux Klan

Hudgins, Robert former UKA Imperial Kligrapp; charges of contempt of Congress made, then dropped by HUAC

Jones, Calvin E. a founder of the Reconstruction Klan

Jones, J. Robertson former UKA Grand Dragon of North Carolina

Jordan, James E. defendant in federal conspiracy trial in the murders of three civil rights workers in Philadelphia, Mississippi

Kennedy, John B. a founder of Reconstruction Klan

Kidd, W. J. former UKA Grand Dragon of Louisiana

Killen, Edgar Ray defendant in federal conspiracy trial involving the murders of three civil rights workers in Philadelphia, Mississippi

Kornegay, Marshall former UKA Grand Dragon of Virginia; charges of contempt of Congress made, then dropped by HUAC

LaRicci, Tony Grand Dragon of the Maryland Knights

Lester, John C. a founder of the Reconstruction Klan

Liuzzo, Viola Detroit civil rights worker shot while shuttling partici-
pants in the Alabama Freedom March between Selma and
Montgomery in 1965

Livingston, William Kyle "Sonny," Jr. arrested in a series of bombings
in Montgomery in the late fifties and mistakenly identified as one of
the men who forced a black truck driver to jump to his death into
the Alabama River in 1957. The case, which came to light in 1976,
was dismissed due to technicalities

Lumpkin, Pete Imperial Klaliff and former Grand Dragon of Georgia,
National Knights

Lynch, Charles Conrad "Connie" a minister of the right-wing Church
of Jesus Christ, Christian, and NSRP organizer for California, who,
before his death in 1972, established a reputation as an inflamatory
racial orator at NSRP and Klan rallies

Mars, Grady UKA's Grand Klaliff of North Carolina who committed
suicide shortly after he was questioned by HUAC

McCord, Frank a founder of Reconstruction Klan

McDaniel, E. L. former UKA Grand Dragon of Mississippi; also
helped organize White Knights of Mississippi

McNair, Denise killed in the 1963 bombing of the Sixteenth Street
Baptist Church in Birmingham

Miles, Robert E. former UKA Grand Dragon of Michigan; sentenced
in the 1971 school-bus bombings

Miller, Sergeant Wallace Meridian police officer who joined White
Knights of Mississippi, then turned paid FBI informer

Miller, W. B., II Grand Dragon of West Virginia, for Dale Reusch's
Invisible Empire, Knights of the Ku Klux Klan

Minton, Will former Grand Klaliff, Maryland Knights

Murphy, Matt the late UKA Klonsul, whose Klan defendants included
Collie Leroy Wilkins, tried for the murder of Viola Liuzzo

Nelson, Scott Monroe "White" selected to run for vice-president of the
United States on a Klan ticket with Dale Reusch; former Imperial
Wizard of Texas Fiery Knights

Norton, the Reverend Rick California official with the right-wing New
Christian Crusade Church

Pecoraro, Clara "Bip" security guard chief, southern Province of
Louisiana, Knights of the Ku Klux Klan

Penn, Lemuel black educator from Washington, D.C., killed in 1964 on
a road outside Athens, Georgia, as he and two companions were en
route from reserve military training at Fort Benning

Pierce, Paul, Jr. Grand Titan of Louisiana's Sixth Congressional

District for Bill Wilkinson's Invisible Empire, Knights of the Ku
Klux Klan

Price, Deputy Sheriff Cecil Ray a defendant in the federal conspiracy
trials in the murders of three civil rights workers in Philadelphia,
Mississippi

Prins, Jack Grand Dragon of Canada for Dale Reusch's Invisible
Empire, Knights of the Ku Klux Klan; also active in the Western
Guard, an extreme right-wing group based in Toronto

Ray, Jerry brother of James Earl Ray, accused assassin of Martin
Luther King

Reusch, Dale Imperial Wizard, Invisible Empire, Knights of the Ku
Klux Klan; nominated to head National Knights' 1976 U.S.
presidential ticket; won West Virginia's U.S. vice-presidential
primary

Roberts, Alton Wayne defendant in the federal conspiracy trials that
grew out of the murders of three civil rights workers in Philadelphia; also paid informer who allegedly tipped off Meridian
police about a Klan-planned bombing that lead to the capture of
Thomas A. Tarrants, III

Robert, Raymond paid informer in same case with his brother, Alton
Wayne Roberts

Robertson, Carol killed in 1963 Sixteenth Street Baptist Church
bombing in Birmingham

Rockwell, George Lincoln late head of the American Nazi Party, now
the National Socialist White People's Party

Rogers, John Paul UKA's Grand Dragon of Florida

Rowe, Gary Thomas, Jr. paid FBI informer within UKA's Alabama
Realm; was a passenger in the car driven by klansmen accused of
the sniper shooting of Viola Liuzzo

Schoonmaker, Earl, Jr. Grand Dragon of New York, Independent
Northern Klans, and Imperial Klokard, Confederation of Independent Orders

Schwerner, Michael one of three civil rights workers slain in Philadelphia, Mississippi

Scoggin, Robert E. Grand Dragon of South Carolina, Invisible Empire,
Knights of the Ku Klux Klan; formerly with UKA and served a
year in prison for contempt of Congress

Sexton, Melvin acting UKA Imperial Wizard during Robert Shelton's
year in prison for contempt of Congress after HUAC hearings

Shelton, Robert Imperial Wizard, UKA

Shows, Jack chief investigator for Alabama attorney general

Simmons, Colonel William Joseph resurrected the Ku Klux Klan in
1915

Smithers, Dan Grand Dragon of Texas, Invisible Empire, Knights of the Ku Klux Klan; also Imperial Klaliff, Confederation of Independent Orders

Smithers, Pat wife of Dan Smithers and Queen Kleagle of Texas

Spears, the Reverend James UKA's Imperial Kludd

Stephenson, David Clark Grand Dragon of Indiana in the twenties

Stoner, Jesse B. "J. B." chairman, NSRP

Tarrants, Thomas A, III a former member of the White Knights, captured after a shoot-out with Meridian, Mississippi, police when he attempted to plant a bomb outside the home of a Jewish civic leader

Taylor, John Ross member in the Western Guard, a right-wing group based in Toronto

Tucker, the Reverend Buddy a Knoxville, Tennessee, minister and a leader of the National Emancipation of the White Seed (NEWS), an association of right-wing groups

Tyler, Bessie responsible, along with Edward Young Clarke, for recruiting and promoting the Klan after its 1915 revival

Venable, James R. Imperial Wizard, National Knights; family once owned Stone Mountain, where William Joseph Simmons staged a cross lighting to mark the 1915 Klan revival

Ward, Tom investigator for Alabama attorney general

Warner, James K. head of New Christian Crusade Church; formerly National Information Director and Grand Dragon of Louisiana for David Duke's Knights of the Ku Klux Klan

Weltner, Judge Charles L. called for HUAC hearings when he was a congressman from Georgia

Wesley, Cynthia killed in 1963 bombing of the Sixteenth Street Baptist Church in Birmingham

Wilkinson, Bill Imperial Wizard, Invisible Empire, Knights of the Ku Klux Klan; formerly associated with David Duke's Knights of the Ku Klux Klan

Williams, Dean UKA Grand Dragon for South Carolina

Willis, Edwin E. the late congressman who presided over the HUAC, hearings in 1965–66

York, James arrested in 1957 for several racially triggered bombings in Montgomery and indicted in 1976 for forcing a black truck driver to jump into the Alabama River in 1957. The case was dropped.

Bibliography

BOOKS

Cash, W. J. *The Mind of the South.* New York: Alfred A. Knopf, Inc., 1941.

Chalmers, David M. *Hooded Americanism.* New York: Doubleday, 1965.

Greenhaw, Wayne. *Watch Out for George Wallace.* Englewood Cliffs, N.J.: Prentice-Hall, 1976.

Kearns, Doris. *Lyndon Johnson and the American Dream.* New York: Harper & Row, 1976.

Lester, J. C. and Wilson, D. L. *Ku Klux Klan: Its Origin, Growth and Disbandment.* Nashville: Wheeler, Osborn & Duckworth, 1884.

Randel, William Pierce. *The KKK: A Century of Infamy.* Radnor, Penn.: Chilton Books, 1965.

Rowe, Gary Thomas, Jr. *My Undercover Years With the Ku Klux Klan.* New York: Bantam Books, 1976.

Trelease, Allen W. *White Terror: The KKK Conspiracy and Southern Reconstruction.* New York: Harper & Row, 1971.

Williams, T. Harry. *Huey Long.* New York: Knopf, 1969.

Whitehead, Don. *Attack on Terror: The FBI Against the Ku Klux Klan in Mississippi.* New York: Funk & Wagnalls, 1970.

DOCUMENTS/REPORTS

Epstein, Benjamin R., and Forster, Arnold. *Report on the Ku Klux Klan.* New York: Anti-Defamation League of B'Nai B'rith, 1965.

The Facts. New York: Anti-Defamation League of B'nai B'rith, 1951–71.

Illinois Legislative Investigating Commission. 1976. *Ku Klux Klan: A Report of the Illinois General Assembly.* Printed by the authority of the State of Illinois.

U.S. House of Representatives. 1965-6. *Activities of Ku Klux Klan Organizations in the United States.* A report in Parts I-V of hearings before the Committee on Un-American Activities, Eighty-ninth Congress, First and Second Sessions. Published by the U.S. Government Printing Office.

U.S. House of Representatives. December 11, 1967. *The Present-Day Ku Klux Klan Movement.* A Report by the Committee on Un-American Activities, Ninetieth Congress, First Session. Published by the U.S. Government Printing Office.

U.S. Senate. 1976. *Final Report of the Select Committee to Study Government Operations With Respect to Intelligence Activities. Intelligence Activities and the Rights of Americans.* Book II. Ninety-fourth Congress, Second Session. Published by the U.S. Government Printing Office.

Walls, Dwayne. *The Klan: Collapsed and Dormant.* Nashville: Race Relations Information Center, 1970.

MAGAZINES/BOOKLETS

Alsop, Stewart, "Portrait of a Klansman," *The Saturday Evening Post,* 9 April 1966.

Armbrister, Trevor, "Portrait of an Extremist," *The Saturday Evening Post,* August 22–29, 1964.

Brock, Lynne, "David Duke: Marketing a New Ku Klux Klan," *New Orleans,* August 1977.

Cleghorn, Reese, "Kommemorating an Anniversary (But very Quietly)." Atlanta, November 1965.

Fairly, Kenneth, and Martin, Harold H., "The Ku Klux Klan: 'We Got Nothing to Hide,'" *The Saturday Evening Post,* 30 January 1965.

Frady, Marshall, "Fighter for Forgotten Men," *Life,* 16 June 1972.

Rapoport, Roger, "The Marine Corps Builds Klansmen," *New Times,* 27 May 1977.

Reinhold, Mary, "A Visit to a KKK Koffee Klatch in Upstate New York." *New Dawn,* 1977.

Romine, Mr. and Mrs. W. B., "A Story of the Original Ku Klux Klan," *The Pulaski Citizen,* 1934.

Weltner, Charles L., "My Friend Calvin," *Atlanta,* October 1969.

Young, Pete, "A Few Soft Words for the Ku Klux Klan," *Esquire.* "The Great White Hope," *Newsweek,* 14 November 1977.

"Espionage: Man of the World," *Newsweek,* 25 September, 1967. "God, No, I'll Talk," *Inside Detective,* December 1967.

NEWSPAPERS

The newspapers, which provided a rich and abundant source of material on the Klan, are far too numerous to name. Particularly helpful were *the New York Times* and its computer index and the following series and articles:

Batten, James K. and Walls, Dwayne, Series on the North Carolina Ku Klux Klan, *Charlotte Observer,* August 1964.

Bierman, William, "Straight From the Dragon's Mouth," *Beacon Magazine, Akron Beacon Journal,* 8 December 1974.

Cohen, Richard M., "The Philadelphia Story," *Washington Post,* 20 July 1975.

Colimore, Edward, "The Klan and Maryland," *Baltimore News American,* 5-7 December 1976.

Goulden, Joseph C., "Puzzles Pile Up in Ray Case," *Philadelphia Inquirer,* 23 June 1968.

Nelson, Jack, "Police Arrange Trap: Klan Terror Is Target," *Los Angeles Times,* 13 February 1970.

Nordheimer, Jon, "Kathy," *Tropic Magazine, Miami Herald,* 10 November 1968.

Scarupa, Henry, "The KKK and Maryland," *Sun Magazine, Baltimore Sun,* 20 June 1976.

Index